VISUAL QUICKPRO GUIDE

PHP ADVANCED

FOR THE WORLD WIDE WEB

Larry Ullman

 **Peachpit Press**

Visual QuickPro Guide
PHP Advanced for the World Wide Web
Larry Ullman

Peachpit Press

1249 Eighth Street
Berkeley, CA 94710
510/524-2178
800/283-9444
510/524-2221 (fax)
Find us on the World Wide Web at: http://www.peachpit.com
To report errors, please send a note to errata@peachpit.com

Peachpit Press is a division of Pearson Education.

Editor: Rebecca Gulick
Production Coordinator: Connie Jeung-Mills
Copyeditor: Brenda Benner
Compositor: Maureen Forys
Additional compositing: Owen Wolfson
Indexer: Karin Arrigoni
Technical Reviewers: Andy Jeffries and Henrik Hansen
Cover design:The Visual Group

ISBN 0-201-77597-2

9 8 7 6 5 4 3 2

Printed and bound in the United States of America

Dedication

To my good friend Michael and his family—
especially Buzz, Judy, Liz, Paul, and Linda
(with a special Hey! out to Jude, Kelsey, and
Nick). I cannot thank you all enough for your
continuing friendship, generosity, and kind-
ness over the past 11+ years.

My Utmost Thanks to:

Jessica, the love of my life, for just about everything.

The good people at DMC Insights, Inc., for giving me the best job I've ever had.

Everyone at Peachpit Press for their support and efforts, including Marjorie, Nancy, Connie (who performed miracles), and all of those without whom this book would not exist.

My most excellent editor, Rebecca. You have my undying gratitude for your diligence, patience, and many, many hours of hard work.

Brenda for her brilliant and attentive editing. It's a better book because you caught every little thing I might not have.

Andy and Henrik for their spot-on technical reviews. Thanks for correcting my misunderstandings and my 3 a.m. slipups, and for throwing in your own two cents worth.

The readers of my first book who took the time to let me know how much they appreciated it (even if they followed that up with a support question). Hearing that someone appreciated the book makes all the long days worthwhile.

Finally, thanks to everyone in the PHP community—from Rasmus Lerdorf and the PHP development team to the folks at PHP.net and Zend.com to the denizens of alt.php and the other newsgroups and forums. You've created a great product, supported those using it, and even gave me some suggestions as to what discuss.

CONTENTS AT A GLANCE

TABLE OF CONTENTS

TABLE OF CONTENTS

TABLE OF CONTENTS

INTRODUCTION

The World Wide Web has undergone numerous changes since its creation, and it will certainly continue to do so. First there was just HTML, which let you make simple Web pages. Then along came scripting technologies such as ASP (Active Server Pages, a Microsoft construct) and CGI scripts (Common Gateway Interface, frequently written in Perl or C). Now there are many options in addition to those, including JSP (Java Server Pages), ColdFusion (recently purchased by Macromedia along with Allaire, ColdFusion's creator), and PHP (PHP: Hypertext Preprocessor). What can we make of this? That the age of static Web sites is behind us. Users want exciting and dynamic pages that are updated frequently, cater to the user, and offer e-commerce.

Now that PHP's use is blossoming—currently PHP is running on almost 7 million Web sites (**Figure i.1**)—programmers are more regularly using databases, creating images on the fly, and beginning to incorporate XML into their Web applications. This book is written for the programmer who is taking the technology and the Web to the next level.

Who Is This Book For?

There are three primary types of reader for this book. The first is programmers who already have a fair-to-solid knowledge of PHP but would like to take their abilities to the next level. Such readers may also appreciate this text as a way to get some hands-on examples of PHP's advanced capabilities. The second type of reader is the person with a strong knowledge of similar Web scripting languages (such as ASP, CGI-Bin scripts, Perl, or JSP) who is just coming to PHP. The assumption is that an experienced programmer can pick up the basic syntax of PHP easily enough but would like a guidebook for creating in-depth PHP Web applications immediately. The third sort of reader would be programmers who are familiar with PHP 3 and would like to see what added advantages PHP 4 has to offer or just generally update their knowledge with what is available in the PHP Web development toolbox today.

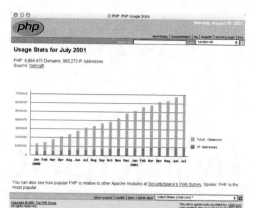

Figure i.1 The PHP usage statistics reveal how PHP's use has been steadily rising since January 2000.

About This Book

As a PHP programmer myself, I know what information is missing in contemporary PHP books; on numerous occasions, I've been unable to find a reference on how to do this or that. As a participant in various PHP newsgroups, I've also been privy to what other programmers would like to understand better. PHP, like all computer technologies, is a rapidly advancing language, which makes it difficult to master. PHP's evolution from version 3 to version 4 has demanded a lot of changes in the way PHP programmers think. Added to that is the burgeoning acceptance of PHP as a viable alternative to ASP and the traditional methods for producing dynamic Web applications.

This book can be divided into three sections, plus the appendices. The first four chapters cover advanced PHP knowledge in general: programming techniques, databases, object-oriented programming, and security. They will relate information that the above-average PHP programmer should be able to comprehend while utilizing practical code examples.

The next four chapters focus on applying these techniques to larger-scale Web applications, still continuing to introduce new information. Here you will develop an advanced Web site, create a solid e-commerce application, use PHP to interact with Internet resources, and see how PHP can work with the server itself.

The remaining four chapters each deal with a specific tie-in to PHP: XML, creating images, creating PDFs, and further PHP developments such as PEAR and PHP-GTK.

This book also contains three appendices that provide the necessary references for programming with PHP (when coupled with the PHP Manual): installation on Linux, Windows, and Macintosh platforms; a MySQL and SQL reference; and a listing of PHP and general Web development resources.

The examples used in this book are intended to be applicable in the real world, omitting the frivolous pieces of code that other books rely upon. Nearly as much focus will be given to the larger-picture philosophy as to the coding itself so that, in the end, you will come away with not just how to do this or that but also how to apply the overarching mentality to your own, individual projects. Finally, I'll add that I'm a strong proponent of not reinventing the wheel. There are already good and freely available PHP-driven applications for managing a forum, so I won't ask you to create another. Conversely, every e-commerce project I've been involved with entails a fair amount of customization, so you'll go through the practice of writing one here.

Conventions

The Visual QuickPro Guide format give you step-by-step instruction rather than lengthy description. I have attempted to create useful examples that you can start using today. Explanatory corresponding text will augment what you are doing within each script.

Because of the constraints of publishing in book form, occasionally one line of code in the text column will be too long to print on a single line and will spill over to the next one. When this occurs, a continuation of the previous line will be indicated by a small gray arrow.

```
<?php

// This line will be too long to print
→ in one column width. Notice the gray
→ arrows and the lack of line numbers.
```

INTRODUCTION

Code text in separate script boxes use line numbers, so the gray arrow isn't necessary.

Some scripts will be built on previously created scripts, in which case the new sections will be highlighted in red (**Script i.1**).

Speaking of line numbers, you should know that these are entered automatically by a text editor and are not something that you should enter into the scripts themselves (which will generate parsing errors immediately upon execution).

Finally, I'll be using XHTML in my scripts instead of HTML. XHTML is like HTML 4.01 and is intended to help move the Web toward a more XML-centric format. The two main distinctions with XHTML are that you should always use lowercase tags and every opening tag must be closed. With tags such as <br>, <hr>, and <p> you can follow them up with </br>, </hr>, and </p> or just write <br />, <hr />, and <p />. More information about XHTML can be found online at www.w3.org/MarkUp.

Compared to the first book

Those readers who have come to this book from my first one may notice a few convention changes in the programming. This is largely because while some techniques (e.g., using the print() statement with both parentheses and quotation marks within the parentheses) will encourage good form for beginners, others (e.g., using echo() instead of print()) have their advantages when programming on a grander scale.

It is not my recommendation to necessarily program exactly as I do but rather to find a system that works best for you and stick to it. Ask 10 programmers how to do something and you'll receive 15 different answers—with little tangible quality difference. Unless you are coding within a team, consistency to yourself is the most important consideration.

Script i.1 Frequently, information learned in a section will be demonstrated by augmenting an existing script. In such cases, the new lines will be highlighted.

```
                    script
1   <?php
2   // This line will be too long to print in
    one column width. Notice the lack of line
    numbers.
3   // This comment is new and will be
    highlighted to indicate such.
4   ?>
```

About PHP 4

Although version 4 of PHP has been out since May 2000 (when the first non-beta version was released), there are still a large number of servers running older versions of PHP, particularly outside of the United States. This book was written with version 4 in mind, but throughout the text I will continue to point out alterations that may need to be made if you are running a machine with an older version.

The majority of differences between versions 4 and 3 of PHP are concerned with how PHP itself operates with the server and will not affect specifically how you program. (In fact, the good people who made version 4 attempted to make it as backward-compatible as possible.) A quick look at these would cover:

◆ Use of the Zend Engine, creating a "compile-then-execute" schematic, which is faster than the previous "execute-while-parsing" one. PHP is still not a compiled language, though it acts more like one now.

◆ Improved PHP architecture for better performance, extensionality, and stability

◆ Ability to run PHP with IIS (Internet Information Server—a popular Windows Web server) as an ISAPI module, rather than the slower binary. PHP already functions with Apache as a module.

◆ Better memory management

Some functions and features are new to PHP 4 and will not work in earlier versions, including:

◆ A number of array-specific functions

◆ Creating and using HTTP sessions

◆ Support for Java, XML, COM/DCOM (Windows platform only), and more

◆ Development and incorporation of PEAR (the PHP Extension and Application Repository)

◆ FTP capability

◆ Expanded object-oriented programming features

Obviously, it would be preferable to work on a server using the latest version of PHP, but since you cannot always control these things, this book will try to write version-indifferent code as much as possible. However, understand that certain chapters (e.g., Chapter 12, Extending PHP, which discusses PEAR) will be less applicable unless you are running version 4 of PHP.

INTRODUCTION

What You'll Need

At the very least, to follow along with this book—and to use PHP—you will need access to a PHP-enabled server, preferably featuring the most recent version of PHP (4.0.6 at the time of this writing).

You can take your own Linux (or Unix or Solaris), Windows, or Macintosh computer and turn it into a Web server for little or no money. Appendix A, Installation, covers a handful of installation techniques on these three platforms. There are also many options on the Internet for free PHP-enabled Web hosting (see the links page at www.DMCinsights.com/phpadv, **Figure i.2**). You can also use PHP.net's host listing—http://hosts.php.net—and its online form (**Figure i.3**) to help define your search. Generally, it will not make a difference whether you are using an online or an offline server, but running your own in-house machine will give you more flexibility in terms of what extensions and version you can install.

As you work with the scripts in this book, keep in mind that while PHP is generally cross-platform compatible, it is not universally so. Thus, while one system (i.e., Linux with Apache) accepts referring to an array's key without single or double quotation marks:

```
$Array[Key]
```

other systems (Windows NT with PWS) may generate odd error messages unless you alter the code to use some form of quotation marks:

```
$Array['Key']
```

```
$Array["Key"]
```

This is but one example meant to indicate that if you follow a script exactly and you still see errors, consider what server-specific alterations you may need to make to the code.

Once you have your PHP-enabled server, you will need to decide on which text editor you will do your PHP programming. Whether you use free software that comes with your operating system (e.g., NotePad or WordPad for Windows, SimpleText for Macintosh) or a commercial application will not make a difference in PHP functionality, only in terms of editor features and ease of programming. It's a grand idea, though, to take the time upfront

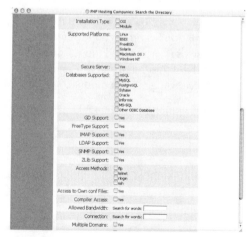

Figure i.2 Among the many things you will find at this book's accompanying Web site is a list of useful links. As of this writing there are about 150 links organized into a dozen categories.

Figure i.3 PHP.net has a detailed search form allowing you to find a good host based on your own criteria.

INTRODUCTION

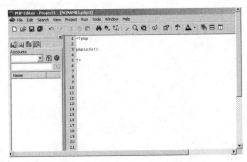

Figure i.4 PHPEd is a popular application for developing PHP on the Windows operating system.

Figure i.5 BBEdit for the Macintosh gets rave reviews as an all-purpose text editor. Version 6 has improved PHP support and runs native on OS X.

to learn all the capabilities and features that your chosen text editor has to offer, be it Vi on Linux, PHPEd on Windows (**Figure i.4**), or BBEdit on Macintosh (**Figure i.5**).

Unless you are coding directly on a Web server (e.g., by telneting into a Linux box and using Emacs), you will need to use an FTP application to transfer the scripts you've written to your Web server. Any application will suffice, although, again, some have better features than others and will make your work easier.

Naturally, you will need to have a Web browser to test and view the scripts you've written. Most Web developers use several versions of the primary browsers—Microsoft's Internet Explorer, Netscape's Navigator, Opera, and Lynx—to be sure that their sites work consistently regardless of the user's software. Because PHP is a server-side technology, most of the work you do based on this book will not behave differently regardless of the browser or the operating system of the end user. Certain aspects of PHP programming—cookies and sessions are just two—will react differently in different browsers, and some chapters will require that you use a browser of a specific version (e.g., 4.x) or higher.

Finally, for the scripts in some of the chapters to work—particularly the last five—your PHP installation will have to include support for the corresponding technology, and that technology's library may need to be installed, too. Fortunately PHP 4 comes with built-in support for XML and MySQL, and the GD library (necessary for generating images) is a common package on most servers. If the scripts in a particular chapter require special extensions, that will be referenced in the chapter's introduction.

INTRODUCTION

PHP Resources

Fortunately, the list of available PHP resources is expanding rapidly, giving you many options for support. Naturally, this book is designed to be one place to turn to, but here are some other likely candidates:

The PHP Manual

The most important PHP resource is the PHP Manual available at PHP.net (**Figure i.6**). The manual comes in many formats—PDF, HTML, Palm—and in several languages—English, Portuguese, German, French, and more. I tend to keep an HTML or PDF version on the computer I'm working on and then check the online version frequently for more updated information (this way, if my Internet connection goes down and I forget the parameters for the `date()` function, I can still find the answer I need). It's important to refer to a copy of the manual that corresponds to the version of PHP you are working with because the functions do go through slight changes on occasion. Sometimes checking the right version of the manual may explain the peculiar results you see here or there.

At PHP.net, you can also view an annotated version of the manual—`www.php.net/manual/en`—where other PHP users add commentary to the descriptions of the various functions (**Figure i.7**).

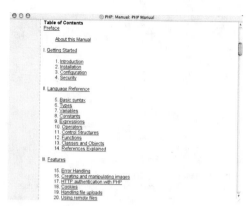

Figure i.6 The online version of the PHP manual is updated frequently and includes user comments (Figure i.7).

Figure i.7 The PHP manual can contain user-submitted comments for each page. Some are merely useful tips, while others may just solve that odd problem you've been experiencing.

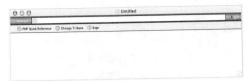

Figure i.8 The tips page at PHP.net (`www.PHP.net/tips.php`) tells how you can bookmark the quick reference tool so you can add it to the toolbar favorites section of your browser.

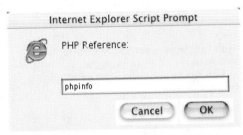

Figure i.9 When you click on the PHP Quick Reference link (Figure i.8), a JavaScript popup window appears. Enter a function name into this box and your browser will take you to the corresponding page in the PHP Manual (Figure i.10).

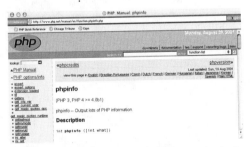

Figure i.10 While you (hopefully) will not need to look up the `phpinfo()` function, this quick reference trick is great when you cannot remember, for example, how to use `imagestring()`.

Another feature I like is the QuickReference link, which you can bookmark. **Figures i.8** through **i.10** demonstrate how I've added this bookmark to my Internet Explorer's Favorites sites menu, allowing me to easily look up any particular function (see `www.php.net/tips.php` for more information about this).

Newsgroups

For specific questions and issues, send an email to one of the existing newsgroups (assuming you have access): alt.php, ba.php, or any of those available in other languages. I, as well as more brilliant minds than my own, frequent these newsgroups and provide timely responses to your queries. For the most part you will not get the RTM ("Read the manual") or stronger RTFM (no explanation necessary) response that other newsgroups frequently offer up. That being said, you should always check the manual before asking any questions for the sake of everyone's time.

INTRODUCTION

PHP Advanced for the World Wide Web: Visual QuickPro Guide Web Site

I have developed a Web site to correspond to this book, available at www.DMCinsights. com/phpadv (**Figure i.11**). This site lists errata and contains downloadable versions of every script found herein, and it will list updates when the technologies change. Note that the examples displayed in this book will not be available for execution online (they have been developed on offline servers).

The downloadable scripts are available online for two purposes: first, as a more up-to-date example of the code (should errors be found in the printed scripts, the online versions will be updated) and, second, as a convenience to you. Especially as some of the scripts get into the hundreds of lines, typing in all that code may seem unduly burden-some. I feel that typing the code in manually is the better way to learn, as monotonous as that may seem, but I leave the final decision up to you.

Appendices

Finally, more in-depth resources have been listed and described in the appendices. While not exhaustive, these pages detail some of the other places you can turn for many different types of questions and they provide a reference to most of the information presented within the book.

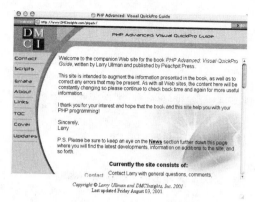

Figure i.11 The corresponding Web site to the book, available at www.DMCinsights.com/phpadv consists of the book's table of contents, errata, updates, links, and more.

INTRODUCTION

Advanced
PHP Programming

At the most basic level good programming is determined by whether or not an application or script works as intended. This is where the beginning programmer will leave things, and there is nothing wrong with that. However, the advanced programmer will work past that point, striving toward improved efficiency, reliability, security, and portability. This book teaches you how to develop the skills of an advanced PHP programmer.

This chapter in particular covers some new functions and features in PHP 4, techniques that will be used throughout the book, and a few tips and tricks of the trade. While you may already know how to use arrays, perhaps you are not familiar with the new `foreach` construct or the older but still very handy `array_walk()` function. You have probably written your own functions by this point but may not understand how to use recursion and static variables. Issues like these will be discussed as well as other fundamentals such as code documentation and structure, constants, and references. Explanation will be given on using `print` versus using `echo` and how to create aliases to your variables—a technique that is also new to PHP 4. Finally, in the process of writing the example scripts, you'll see just one way that you can build a dynamic Web application with a simple, text file database.

In this first chapter, you'll create a handful of scripts for creating and managing an online sports pool where users predict winning teams. The success rate of each user is automatically calculated each week and throughout the season with minimal administration. I picked this example not only because it suits the subjects herein, but also because it harkens back to my early days with PHP; I learned the language (after making the switch from Perl) while creating a similar application. Of course, back then I stopped when the script worked! Needless to say, the scripts demonstrated here are more efficient, reliable, secure, and portable than anything I did back then.

Code Structure and Documentation

Quality code structure and documentation is truly at the core of advanced PHP programming even though it will not affect how well your applications function. Proper structure and documentation is something that should be incorporated into code for your own good, for your client's, for your co-workers' (if applicable), and for the programmer in the future who may have to alter or augment your work.

When I refer to code structure, I mean physically how your PHP is organized within the document itself. (In Chapter 5, *Developing Web Applications*, I'll discuss the larger issue of site structure.) Compare **Scripts 1.1** and **1.2**: Both are valid PHP documents, but which would you rather review and possibly edit?

The fundamentals of code structure refer to how you indent your code, skip blank lines, use braces and parenthesis, and so forth. General rules are:

- Indent blocks of code (e.g., results of conditionals or function content) one tab stop or four spaces. (Formally, one should use spaces in lieu of tabs, but coders use the more convenient tab option regardless.)

- Use blank lines to visually establish related sections of code.

- Put spaces between words, function arguments, operators, and so forth, as allowed (PHP is generally, but not universally, insensitive to white space).

- Place functions at the beginning of a document.

Script 1.1 This script will work just fine but is far more difficult to edit or understand than Script 1.2.

```
1    <!DOCTYPE html PUBLIC "-//W3C//DTD XHTML
     1.0 Transitional//EN"
2    "http://www.w3.org/TR/2000/REC-xhtml1-
     20000126/DTD/xhtml1-transitional.dtd">
3    <html xmlns="http://www.w3.org/1999/xhtml">
4    <head>
5    <title>Football Picks</title>
6    </head>
7    <body>
8    <?php
9    define ("W", $w);
10   function write_data ($v, $k, $fp) {
11   static $fl;
12   if (!$fl) {
13   fputs ($fp, "Dummy Line\n");
14   $fl = TRUE;
15   }
16   fputs ($fp, "$v\n");
17   }
18   $f = '2001/picks_' . W . '_Winners_.txt'; /
19   if ($fp = @fopen ($f, "w")) {
20   array_walk ($w, 'write_data', $fp);
21   fclose ($fp);
22   echo 'The winners have been
     stored!<br></br>';
23   } else {
24   echo "Could not open the file $f! Please
     make sure the W variable has a
     value.<br></br>";
25   }
26   function read_picks ($dp, $d) {
27   global $p;
28   if ($fn = readdir ($dp)) {
29   if (substr($fn, 0, 6) == "picks_") {
30   $pfn = explode ("_", $fn);
31   if (($pfn[1] == W) and ($pfn[2] !=
     "Winners")) { /
32   $un = $pfn[2];
33   $tf = $d . $fn;
34   $up = file ($tf);
35   $p[$un] = $up;
36   }
37   }
38   read_picks ($dp, $d);
```

(script continues on next page)

Script 1.1 *continued*

```
                    script

39   }
40   }
41   $p = array();
42   $d = '2001/';
43   $dp = opendir ($d);
44   read_picks ($dp, $d);
45   closedir ($dp);
46
47   while (list ($k, $v) = each ($p)) {
48   $ws = 0;
49   $ls = 0;
50   while (list ($k2, $v2) = each ($v)) {
51   $v2 = substr ($v2, 0, (strlen($v2) - 1));
52   if (($v2 == $w[$k2]) and ($k2 != 0)) {
53   $ws++;
54   } elseif ($k2 != 0 ) {
55   $ls++;
56   }
57   }
58   $r[$k] = array ('ws' => $ws, 'ls' => $ls);
59   }
60   ksort ($r);
61   function write_results ($v, $k, $fp) {
62   static $fl2;
63   if (!$fl2) {
64   fputs ($fp, "User\tws\tls\n");
65   $fl2 = TRUE;
66   }
67   $d = implode ("\t", $v);
68   fputs ($fp, "$k\t$d\n");
69
70   $f2 = '2001/results_' . W . '_.txt';
71   if ($fp2 = @fopen ($f2, "w")) {
72   array_walk ($r, 'write_results', $fp2); .
73   fclose ($fp2); // Close the file.
74   echo 'The results have been
     stored.<br></br>';
75   } else {
76   echo "Could not open the Wly results file,
     $f2.<br></br>";
77   }
78   ?>
79   </body>
80   </html>
```

After you structure your code, you should make sure it is well-documented. Code documentation is the programmer's equivalent of leaving yourself yellow sticky notes. Arguably, one cannot over-document one's work. Make notes about functions, variables, sections of code, and pages as a whole. **Script 1.3** shows what Script 1.2 looks like with documentation. A few guidelines on documentation:

◆ Note what the purpose of a variable is if it would not be already completely obvious to the most basic programmer.

◆ State the use of a function.

◆ Explain what sequences of code are going to do.

◆ Indicate the purpose of a conditional.

◆ List what files the current file interacts with, requires, etc.

◆ Mark the closing brackets for complex functions and control structures (conditionals, loops, etc.).

Script 1.2 Simply by inserting blank lines and tabs, I've greatly improved the readability of this script.

```
1    <!DOCTYPE html PUBLIC "-//W3C//DTD XHTML
     1.0 Transitional//EN"
2    "http://www.w3.org/TR/2000/
     REC-xhtml1-20000126/DTD/xhtml1-
     transitional.dtd">
3    <html
     xmlns="http://www.w3.org/1999/xhtml">
4    <head>
5        <title>Football Picks</title>
6    </head>
7    <body>
8    <?php
9
10   define ("WEEK", $week);
11
12   function write_data ($value, $key, $fp) {
13
14       static $first_line;
15
16       if (!$first_line) {
17           fputs ($fp, "Dummy Line\n");
18           $first_line = TRUE;
19       }
20
21       fputs ($fp, "$value\n");
22   }
23
24   $file = '2001/picks_' . WEEK .
     '_Winners_.txt'; /
25
26   if ($fp = @fopen ($file, "w")) {
27
28       array_walk ($winners, 'write_data',
         $fp);
29       fclose ($fp);
30
31       echo 'The winners have been
         stored!<br></br>';
32
33   } else {
34       echo "Could not open the file $file!
         Please make sure the week variable
         has a value.<br></br>";
35   }
36
37   function read_picks ($dp, $directory) {
38
39       global $picks;
40
```

Script 1.2 *continued*

```
41       if ($file_name = readdir ($dp)) {
42
43           if (substr($file_name, 0, 6) ==
             "picks_") {
44
45               $parse_file_name = explode
                 ("_", $file_name);
46
47               if (($parse_file_name[1] ==
                 WEEK) and
                 ($parse_file_name[2] !=
                 "Winners")) { /
48
49                   $username =
                     $parse_file_name[2];
50                   $the_file = $directory .
                     $file_name;
51                   $users_picks = file
                     ($the_file);
52                   $picks[$username] =
                     $users_picks;
53               }
54           }
55
56           read_picks ($dp, $directory);
57       }
58   }
59
60   $picks = array();
61
62   $directory = '2001/';
63   $dp = opendir ($directory);
64   read_picks ($dp, $directory);
65   closedir ($dp);
66
67
68   while (list ($key, $value) = each
     ($picks)) {
69
70       $wins = 0;
71       $losses = 0;
72
73       while (list ($key2, $value2) = each
         ($value)) {
74
75           $value2 = substr ($value2, 0,
             (strlen($value2) - 1));
76
77           if (($value2 == $winners[$key2]) and
             ($key2 != 0)) {
```

(script continues on next page)

4

Script 1.2 *continued*

```
script
78            $wins++;
79        } elseif ($key2 != 0 ) {
80            $losses++;
81        }
82    }
83
84    $results[$key] = array ('wins' =>
      $wins, 'losses' => $losses);
85 }
86
87 ksort ($results);
88
89
90 function write_results ($value, $key,
   $fp) {
91
92    static $first_line2;
93
94    if (!$first_line2) {
95        fputs ($fp,
          "User\tWins\tLosses\n");
96        $first_line2 = TRUE;
97    }
98
99    $data = implode ("\t", $value);
100   fputs ($fp, "$key\t$data\n");
101
102
103 $file2 = '2001/results_' . WEEK .
    '_.txt';
104
105 if ($fp2 = @fopen ($file2, "w")) {
106
107   array_walk ($results,
        'write_results', $fp2); .
108   fclose ($fp2); // Close the file.
109   echo 'The results have been
        stored.<br></br>';
110
111 } else {
112
113   echo "Could not open the weekly
        results file, $file2.<br></br>";
114 }
115 ?>
116 </body>
117 </html>
```

Script 1.3 This version of Script 1.2 now has adequate documentation, although there's certainly room to add more.

```
script
1   <?php
2   // *****************************
3   // Online Football Picks System
4
5   // Developed by: Larry E. Ullman
6
7   // Written: August 2001
8   // Modified: August 14, 2001
9
10  // Contact: php@DMCinsights.com
11
12  // The process_winners.php page handles
    the pick_winners.php page. It determines
    how each player did and stores this
    information in a text file.
13
14  // *****************************
15  ?>
16  <!DOCTYPE html PUBLIC "-//W3C//DTD XHTML
    1.0 Transitional//EN"
17  "http://www.w3.org/TR/2000/REC-xhtml1-
    20000126/DTD/xhtml1-transitional.dtd">
18  <html xmlns="http://www.w3.org/
    1999/xhtml">
19  <head>
20      <title>Football Picks</title>
21  </head>
22  <body>
23  <?php
24
25  // Set the week as a constant.
26  define ("WEEK", $week);
27
28  /* -------------------------- */
29  /* Store the winners in a file. */
30  /* -------------------------- */
31
32  function write_data ($value, $key, $fp) {
    // The write_data function stores the
    picks in the file.
33
34      static $first_line;
35
36      if (!$first_line) { // Write a first
        dummy line but only once.
37          fputs ($fp, "Dummy Line\n");
38          $first_line = TRUE;
39      }
```

(script continues on next page)

Script 1.3 *continued*

Script 1.3 *continued*

```
40
41        fputs ($fp, "$value\n"); // Add a
          return to place each item on its own
          line.
42    }
43
44    $file = '2001/picks_' . WEEK .
      '_Winners_.txt'; // Identify the file in
      the format 'picks_1_Winners_.txt'.
45
46    if ($fp = @fopen ($file, "w")) { // Read
      the file into an array.
47
48        array_walk ($winners, 'write_data',
          $fp); // Send the entire array to the
          write_data function.
49        fclose ($fp); // Close the file.
50
51        echo 'The winners have been
          stored!<br></br>';
52
53    } else { // If it couldn't open the file,
      print an error message.
54        echo "Could not open the file $file!
          Please make sure the week variable
          has a value.<br></br>";
55    }
56
57
58    /* --------------------------- */
59    /* Retrieve the players' picks. */
60    /* --------------------------- */
61
62    function read_picks ($dp, $directory) {
      // The read_picks file does just that.
63
64        global $picks;
65
66        if ($file_name = readdir ($dp)) { //
          Check each file in the directory.
67
68            if (substr($file_name, 0, 6) ==
              "picks_") { // If it's a picks
              file continue.
69
70                $parse_file_name = explode
                  ("_", $file_name); // Turn
                  the file name into a usable
                  format.
```

```
71
72                if (($parse_file_name[1] ==
                  WEEK) and ($parse_
                  file_name[2] != "Winners")) {
                  // If the file isn't the
                  winners and it's the right
                  week...
73
74                    $username =
                      $parse_file_name[2];
75                    $the_file = $directory .
                      $file_name;
76                    $users_picks = file
                      ($the_file);
77                    $picks[$username] =
                      $users_picks;
78                }
79            }
80
81            read_picks ($dp, $directory); //
              Loop through the function again.
82        }
83    }
84
85    $picks = array(); // Initialize the main
      variable.
86
87    $directory = '2001/';
88    $dp = opendir ($directory);
89    read_picks ($dp, $directory);
90    closedir ($dp);
91
92
93    /* --------------------------- */
94    /* Calculate the week's results. */
95    /* --------------------------- */
96
97    while (list ($key, $value) = each
      ($picks)) { // Loop through the main
      array.
98
99        $wins = 0; // Set to 0 for each
          array.
100       $losses = 0; // Set to 0 for each
          array.
101
102       while (list ($key2, $value2) = each
          ($value)) { // Loop through each
          user's array.
```

(script continues on next page)

CODE STRUCTURE AND DOCUMENTATION

Script 1.3 *continued*

Script 1.3 *continued*

```
script
103
104         $value2 = substr ($value2, 0,
            (strlen($value2) - 1)); // Remove
            the return character.
105
106         if (($value2 == $winners[$key2])
            and ($key2 != 0)) { // If the
            user's pick matches the winning
            team, give them credit but don't
            count line 1.
107             $wins++;
108         } elseif ($key2 != 0 ) {
109             $losses++;
110         }
111     }
112
113     $results[$key] = array ('wins' =>
        $wins, 'losses' => $losses); // Store
        each user's performance in an array.
114 }
115
116 ksort ($results); // Aphabetize the
    array.
117
118
119 /* ----------------------- */
120 /* Store the week's results. */
121 /* ----------------------- */
122
123 function write_results ($value, $key,
    $fp) { // Writes results data to a file.
124
125     static $first_line2;
126
127     if (!$first_line2) { // Write a first
        dummy line but only once.
128         fputs ($fp, "User\tWins\tLosses\
            n"); // Add a return to place
            each item on its own line.
129         $first_line2 = TRUE;
130     }
131
132     $data = implode ("\t", $value);
133     fputs ($fp, "$key\t$data\n"); // Add
        a return to place each item on its
        own line.
134 }
135
136 $file2 = '2001/results_' . WEEK .
    '_.txt'; // Identify the file in the
    format 'results_1_.txt'.
```

```
script
137
138 if ($fp2 = @fopen ($file2, "w")) { //
    Open the file for writing.
139
140     array_walk ($results,
        'write_results', $fp2); // Send the
        entire array to the write_results
        function.
141     fclose ($fp2); // Close the file.
142     echo 'The results have been
        stored.<br></br>';
143
144 } else { // If it couldn't open the file,
    print an error message.
145
146     echo "Could not open the weekly
        results file, $file2.<br></br>";
147 }
148 ?>
149 </body>
150 </html>
```

A lot of thought has already been put into good code structure and documentation. The consensus document on the subject—the PHP Coding Standard—can be found at www.DMCinsights.com/phpadv/coding_standard.php (**Figures 1.1** and **1.2**). It details the how's and why's of formally writing PHP code. Throughout this book, I'll point out conventions—and where I break from them—but keep in mind three ideas:

First, I cannot stress enough that consistency is the most important consideration, whether or not you follow the PHP Coding Standard or my habits. Not only is inconsistency at odds with any standard, it will lead to unnecessary errors and extra hours of debugging. Further, if you are working on a team, be sure to devise a plan that all team members will follow. If you are programming for a client, leave clear, concise documentation so that they, or another programmer, can easily comprehend your work.

Second, code structure and documentation is something you should implement when you begin coding and continue as you work. Attempting to go in after the fact to make notes will never be as successful and frequently won't happen at all. What seems obvious at the time of creation will be perplexing just three months later. If you haven't experienced this yourself, well, you will one day, guaranteed.

Third, because of the confines of the book format, the scripts developed from here on out will not be as well-documented or organized as I would prefer (or as you should). There's a limit to how much valuable book space should be taken up with lines of `// Developed by: Larry E. Ullman`.

Three conventions I always follow (and will continue to do so in this book) are:

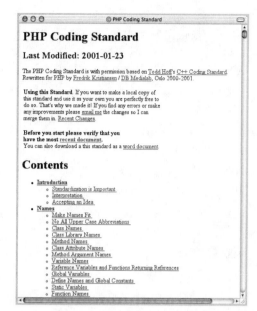

Figure 1.1 The PHP Coding Standard is the "grammar" guide for programming with PHP.

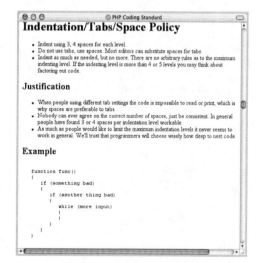

Figure 1.2 The PHP Coding Standard does an excellent job of explaining a rule, justifying it, and demonstrating how to follow the rule in your code.

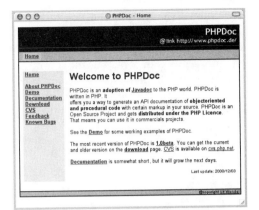

Figure 1.3 PHPDoc is being developed to automate the documentation process. It uses regular expressions to run through your code and make notes along the way.

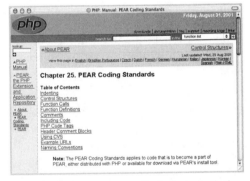

Figure 1.4 If you are programming for inclusion in the PEAR code library, be sure to follow its own specific rules for documentation and structure.

◆ Variable names should be all lowercase, using the underscore as a separator between terms. Some would suggest that global variables should begin with a lowercase g, although I do not do this.

◆ Because XML uses short tags (<? ?>) for its own purpose, you have to use the formal PHP tags (<?php ?>) when using XML, as you'll see in Chapter 9, *XML*. The recommendation is to use the formal tags regardless because that is the best way to insure cross-server compatibility.

◆ It is suggested that .php is always used as the file extension for pages that are to be treated as PHP scripts. (Includes such as classes and configuration pages may use different extensions.) Acceptable file extensions are determined by the Web server's configuration, but within the PHP community the movement is toward making .php the default. (PHP 3's common extension, .php3, will still work on most machines now running PHP 4, but it seems out of place considering the newer version.)

✔ Tips

■ An open source PHP-driven application, PHPDoc, has been written based on the popular JavaDoc (for documenting Java) and is intended to facilitate the code documentation process. For more information, check out the PHPDoc Web site at www.PHPDoc.de (**Figure 1.3**).

■ If you plan to develop code to be incorporated into PEAR (see Chapter 12, Extending PHP), be sure to follow PEAR's own formatting rules (**Figure 1.4**).

CODE STRUCTURE AND DOCUMENTATION

Arrays

An array is a special type of variable that can act like a list or like a table in a spreadsheet program. Because of their power and flexibility, arrays are widely used in advanced PHP programming. I'll run through a couple of the strongest array functions now.

New to PHP 4 is the `foreach` construct, designed to more easily access all of an array's keys and values. Assuming you have an array of name `$array`, you can access every element using the following code:

```
foreach ($array as $key => $value) {
    // Code
}
```

I tend to use `foreach` when dealing with arrays and will do so in this book. If you are running an earlier version of PHP, you'll need to rewrite the above code as:

```
reset ($array);
while (list($key, $value) = each
→ ($array)) {
    // Code
}
```

(One main difference between `foreach` and `while` is that the former loop will automatically reset an array back to the beginning whereas the latter will not.)

Another array function that I incorporate frequently is `array_walk()`, although it is not new to PHP 4. It allows you to run each element of an array through your own defined function.

```
function print_albums ($value, $key) {
    echo $value . " <br />\n";
}
$array = array ("Pablo Honey", "The
→ Bends", "OK Computer", "Kid A",
→ "Amnesiac");
array_walk ($array, 'print_albums');
```

According to the syntax, the `array_walk()` function takes an array as its first parameter and the name of the function—without any parentheses or arguments—as the second. The function will then receive, while `array_walk()` iterates through the array, each respective array key and value. The above would generate:

```
Pablo Honey <br />
The Bends <br />
OK Computer <br />
Kid A <br />
Amnesiac <br />
```

You will see in the following scripts how to pass more arguments to the function when calling it with `array_walk()`.

Note that `array_walk()`works only with user-defined functions and not with PHP's built-in ones. Also, in PHP 4, the array must be reset after using `array_walk()` if you intend to access the array again.

To demonstrate some advanced array techniques, you'll write the first part of the sports pool application. It's intended for professional American football, but you can easily adapt it to any other interest you may have. The first two scripts will dynamically generate a form wherein users can make their selections. Also, since not everyone has access to a database, this application will use a flat text file system for storing information.

Script 1.4 The data for the pool will be stored in tab-delimited text files like this one.

```
                          script
1    Away            Home
2    New Orleans     Buffalo
3    New England     Cincinnati
4    Seattle         Cleveland
5    Tampa Bay       Dallas
6    Detroit         Green Bay
7    Oakland         Kansas City
8    Carolina        Minnesota
9    Indianapolis    NY Jets
10   Pittsburgh      Jacksonville
11   Chicago         Baltimore
12   St. Louis       Philadelphia
13   Washington      San Diego
14   Atlanta         San Francisco
15   Miami           Tennessee
16   NY Giants       Denver
```

To use arrays:

1. Create a new text file in your text editor.

2. Write a caption line (**Script 1.4**).

   Away   Home

   In the text file, the visiting team will be listed first, followed by the home team, with each game using one line. This header line expresses the arrangement and also acts as a work-around for one of the array peculiarities. When this file is read into an array, it will begin—as arrays always do—indexing with 0. Because I would prefer that the array keys match up with the game number and I want the game numbers to be 1 through 15 (or 14 or 16 or whatever), I'm essentially skipping one line so that the first game is listed on line 2, which will be indexed at 1.

3. Add the games:

   New Orleans   Buffalo
   New England   Cincinnati
   Seattle   Cleveland
   Tampa Bay   Dallas
   Detroit   Green Bay
   Oakland   Kansas City
   Carolina   Minnesota
   Indianapolis   NY Jets
   Pittsburgh   Jacksonville
   Chicago   Baltimore
   St. Louis   Philadelphia
   Washington   San Diego
   Atlanta   San Francisco
   Miami   Tennessee
   NY Giants   Denver

   The games are listed in the format of Away Team [TAB] Home Team [RETURN] (without the spaces). The tab will be used to distinguish between the two items on each line.

   continues on next page

ARRAYS

4. Save the file as week1.txt.

5. Continue creating similar documents for the other weeks in the season, called, in this example, week2.txt through week17.txt. If you are following this example as is, you can download all of these scripts from www.DMCinsights.com/phpadv. Do not put any comments within these files because that would mess up how the files are used (and only PHP will be reading them anyway).

6. Establish a directory on your Web server called 2001 or whatever term you will use to refer to the season as a whole.

7. Set the permissions on the directory to 777 (universal read, write, search). For security purposes, you ought to place this directory below the Web document root, if possible. If you do so, make sure you appropriately refer to it in all the subsequent scripts (e.g., using ../2001/ instead of 2001/).

8. Upload all of the weekly files to the 2001 directory.

Now that the raw data containing all of the season's games has been established, it's time to write the script that will turn this data into an HTML form.

9. Create a new HTML document in your text editor (**Script 1.5**).

```
<!DOCTYPE html PUBLIC "-//W3C//DTD
→ XHTML 1.0 Transitional//EN"
"http://www.w3.org/TR/2000/
→ REC-xhtml1-20000126/DTD/xhtml1-
→ transitional.dtd">
<html xmlns="http://www.w3.org/1999/
→ xhtml">
<head>
<title>Football Picks</title>
</head>
```

continues on page 16

ARRAYS

Script 1.5 This script dynamically generates a form based on data stored in a plain text file.

```
                                    script
1    <!DOCTYPE html PUBLIC "-//W3C//DTD XHTML 1.0 Transitional//EN"
2    "http://www.w3.org/TR/2000/REC-xhtml1-20000126/DTD/xhtml1-transitional.dtd">
3    <html xmlns="http://www.w3.org/1999/xhtml">
4    <head>
5        <title>Football Picks</title>
6    </head>
7    <body>
8    <?php
9
10   $file = '2001/week' . $week . '.txt'; // Identify the file based upon which week it is.
11
12   if ($games = @file ($file)) { // Read the file into an array.
13
14       // If it read the file, print the form.
15       echo '<form action="store_picks.php" method="post">
16   <table border="1" width="80%" cellspacing="4" cellpadding="4" align="center">
17       <tr align="center" valign="top">
18           <td colspan="3" width="100%" align="center" valign="top" nowrap="nowrap">Enter Your
             Username:
19           <input type="text" name="username" size="20" maxlength="20"></td>
20       </tr>
21           ';
22
23       foreach ($games as $key => $array) { // Use an array to print out each game.
24
25           if ($key != 0) { // Don't print the Away Home line.
26
27               $second_array = explode ("\t", $array); // Turn each line of the array into its own
                 array.
28               $away = $second_array[0]; // The first item is the Away team.
29               $home = substr ($second_array[1], 0, (strlen($second_array[1]) - 1)); // The second
                 item is the Home team but delete the return character.
30
31               echo "   <tr align=\"center\" valign=\"top\">
32           <td align=\"left\" valign=\"top\" nowrap=\"nowrap\"><input type=\"radio\"
             name=\"picks[$key]\" value=\"$away\">$away</td>
33           <td align=\"center\" valign=\"top\">at</td>
34           <td align=\"right\" valign=\"top\" nowrap=\"nowrap\"><input type=\"radio\"
             name=\"picks[$key]\" value=\"$home\">$home</td>
35       </tr>\n";
36           }
37       }
38
39       // Complete the form and the table.
40       echo "   <tr align=\"center\" valign=\"top\">
41           <td colspan=\"3\" width=\"100%\" align=\"center\" valign=\"top\"><input type=\"submit\"
             name=\"Submit\" value=\"Submit!\">
42       </tr>
43   </table>
44   <input type=\"hidden\" name=\"week\" value=\"$week\">
45   </form>\n";
46
47   } else { // If it couldn't open the file, print an error message.
48       echo "Could not open the file $file! Please make sure the week variable has a
         value.<br></br>";
49   }
50   ?>
51   </body>
52   </html>
```

Echo, Print, and Quotation Marks

There are several ways in PHP to send text to the browser, with echo and print being the most popular. There are only subtle differences in how the two work; which you use when tends to be more of an issue of personal preference than anything.

One distinction is that echo is marginally, perhaps imperceptibly, faster than print. The justification is that while print returns a value upon successful operation (*1* indicates that it worked), echo does not.

A feature of echo that is not found in print is the potential for easily placing a variable's value within HTML. Commonly, part of an HTML form may read (in your script):

```
<input type="text" name="username" value="<?php echo $username; ?>"
```

There are two shortcuts you can use in such an instance. First, you can always omit the final semicolon in a PHP script, although it's normally not good form to do so. Second, with echo, you can abbreviate the code by following the initial PHP tag with the equals sign (but only when using the short form of the tag) so

```
<?php echo $username; ?>
```

becomes

```
<?=$username ?>
```

More important than which function (technically they aren't functions, they are language constructs) you use is whether you use single or double quotation marks.

Both echo and print can use either quotation mark, the difference being how variables are treated and what characters need to be escaped (to escape is to precede a character by a backslash). The single quotation mark prints everything as is and requires only that the single quotation mark itself be escaped in order to print it. Thus,

```
echo '<a href="index.php">Home</a>';
```

works without a problem. The double quotation mark equivalent would have to be:

```
echo "<a href=\"index.php\">Home</a>";
```

To print out the double quotation marks in the HTML source (which is required for it to be valid), they must be escaped. Therefore, I tend to use echo with single quotation marks when sending HTML to the Web browser.

One problem with using single quotation marks is that they treat variables and special characters literally, meaning that

```
$variable = 'value';
echo '$variable \n';
```

continues on next page

ARRAYS

Echo, Print, and Quotation Marks *(continued)*

would print out *$variable \n* and not *value* followed by a new line, which this code would:

```
$variable = 'value';
echo "$variable \n";
```

(The same is true when assigning a value to a variable or referring to array indexes.)

```
$variable = 'value';
echo $array['$variable']; // Refers to the element keyed at "$variable".
echo $array["$variable"]; // Refers to the element keyed at "value".
```

With respect to how you print out variables, I should also clarify how PHP treats multidimensional arrays. Normally you can locate the element found within a multidimensional array (an array that consists of arrays) using

```
$arrayname['inner_array_name']['inner_array_index']
```

But attempts to print that element with

```
echo "The value is $arrayname['inner_array_name']['inner_array_index']";
```

will not work. In this case, you have two options. First, you could use the concatenation operator to exit the quotation marks (although this will not work on some systems, e.g., Mac OS X):

```
echo "The value is " . $arrayname['inner_array_name']['inner_array_index'];
```

Or you could use braces within the quotation marks:

```
echo "The value is {$arrayname['inner_array_name']['inner_array_index']}";
```

This is true for both echo and print.

A nice tutorial discussing strings, quotation marks, and more can be found at www.zend.com/zend/tut/using-strings.php.

10. Start the HTML body and enter the initial PHP tag.

```
<body>
<?php
```

11. Identify which file will be used.

```
$file = '2001/week' . $week . '.txt';
```

This script assumes it receives a variable called $week with a value between (in my case) 1 and 17. Thus, generating each week's form is only a matter of passing the week number to this file.

12. Create a conditional that attempts to read the specific file into an array.

```
if ($games = @file ($file)) {
```

If the script can successfully read the file, it will create an array called $games, containing every game for that week. Use of the @ character suppresses error messages that occur if it cannot read the file (compare **Figure 1.5,** which doesn't use @ with **Figure 1.6,** which does).

13. Begin the HTML form.

```
echo '<form action="store_picks.php"
→ method="post">
<table border="1" width="80%"
→ cellspacing="4" cellpadding="4"
→ align="center">
<tr align="center" valign="top">
<td colspan="3" width="100%"
→ align="center" valign="top"
→ nowrap="nowrap">Enter Your
→ Username:
<input type="text" name="username"
→ size="20" maxlength="20"></td>
</tr>
';
```

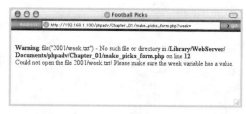

Figure 1.5 Because no week value was entered (see the address bar), this script was unable to read the file. The PHP-generated error message is suppressed by the @ character in Figure 1.6.

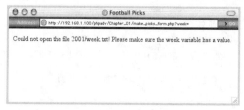

Figure 1.6 The @ symbol helps to keep confusing and ugly technical errors from appearing to the user.

The HTML form is quite simple, taking only the username and the pick for each game. Later on you may want to develop an authentication system before the user gets to this step (which could then automatically enter or store the username).

Note: Concluding the echo with the final quotation mark on a line of its own may seem strange, but the effect is a more legible HTML source. It ensures that the next piece of HTML will begin on its own line instead of butting up against the </tr>.

14. Loop through the array, printing each game to the form.

```
foreach ($games as $key => $array) {
if ($key != 0) {
$second_array = explode ("\t",
 → $array);
$away = $second_array[0];
$home = substr ($second_array[1], 0,
 → (strlen($second_array[1]) - 1));
echo " <tr align=\"center\"
 → valign=\"top\">
<td align=\"left\" valign=\"top\"
 → nowrap=\"nowrap\"><input
 → type=\"radio\" name=\"picks[$key]\"
 → value=\"$away\">$away</td>
<td align=\"center\"
 → valign=\"top\">at</td>
<td align=\"right\" valign=\"top\"
 → nowrap=\"nowrap\"><input
 → type=\"radio\" name=\"picks[$key]\"
 → value=\"$home\">$home</td>
</tr>\n";
}
}
```

The first line here is the new foreach construct, which is an easy, and some argue, faster way to manage arrays.

The second line makes sure that the element being dealt with is not the first one in the file. In the example above (Script 1.4), the value of the array at 0 is Away [TAB] Home, which shouldn't be printed.

If it's not the first element in the array, it will be broken up into its respective parts (away team and home team) using the explode() function. Then each team is formally assigned to its own variable (during which time the return character is chopped off the end of the home team's name).

Finally, a table row is printed using the assembled information.

15. Complete the code for the HTML form and the table.

```
echo " <tr align=\"center\"
 → valign=\"top\">
<td colspan=\"3\" width=\"100%\"
 → align=\"center\" valign=\
 → "top\"><input type=\"submit\"
 → name=\"Submit\" value=\"Submit!\">
</tr>
</table>
<input type=\"hidden\" name=\"week\"
 → value=\"$week\">
</form>\n";
```

Be sure to include the HIDDEN type, which stores the week number so that it is available to the store_picks.php page, which handles this form.

continues on next page

16. Finish the main conditional and close the PHP and HTML.

```
} else {
echo "Could not open the file
→ $file! Please make sure the week
→ variable has a value.<br></br>";
}
?>
</body>
</html>
```

The specific error message generated here is oriented more toward the developer rather than the user (you probably would not want to list a file name in a publicly viewable error message). You could reword this to a more user-friendly message based on how your application is used.

17. Save the file as `make_picks_form.php` and upload it to your server in the same directory as the `2001` directory. Load it in your Web browser, appending the URL with *?week=1* so that it works properly (**Figures 1.7** and **1.8**), although don't submit the form quite yet.

✔ Tips

■ In Chapter 5, Developing Web Applications, I'll discuss the @ character in more detail.

■ In Chapter 4, Security, you'll develop one user registration and authentication system that you could use with these scripts or any other.

Figure 1.7 This is the form created by the `make_picks_form.php` script, allowing a user to pick a winner in all 15 games.

Figure 1.8 Prudent use of the echo statement and white space in the PHP script makes for legible HTML source code.

Constants

Constants are a special type of variable that don't get enough attention, in my humble opinion. Constants, as the name would imply, contain a value that does not, nor cannot, change during the course of a script. Furthermore, constants have the added advantage of being global in scope, meaning they are accessible within your functions automatically.

Constants are case-sensitive, as are all variables in PHP. As a rule, constants are always written in all uppercase letters. When naming constants, use the same rules as you do variables—a letter or underscore followed by letters, numbers, or underscores—but omit the initial dollar sign.

A constant is created by using the `define()` function, like so:

```
define ("CONSTANT_NAME", "value");
```

You can define a constant only as a number (integer or floating-point) or a string. You cannot create an array or object constant, and once a constant has been created, it's value cannot be altered, so you cannot turn a string constant into an integer. You could think of a constant as an invariable variable.

PHP has a number of built-in constants, including `PHP_OS` (the operating system), `PHP_VERSION` (e.g., *4.0.3pl1*), `TRUE`, and `FALSE`. Two built-in constants—`__FILE__` and `__LINE__`, referring to the current file name and line number—do change through the course of a script. They are useful for debugging purposes, as you'll see in Chapter 5, Developing Web Applications.

I like to use constants when I have variables that shouldn't change or when a variable should be accessible throughout my script. As a demonstration of defining and using constants, you'll write the `store_picks.php` script for the online pool application. It will handle the data from the `make_picks_form.php` page previously written.

To use a constant:

1. Create a new HTML document in your text editor (**Script 1.6**).

```
<!DOCTYPE html PUBLIC "-//W3C//DTD
→ XHTML 1.0 Transitional//EN"
"http://www.w3.org/TR/2000/
→ REC-xhtml1-20000126/DTD/xhtml1-
→ transitional.dtd">
<html xmlns="http://www.w3.org/1999
→ /xhtml">
<head>
      <title>Football Picks</title>
</head>
```

2. Start the HTML body and enter the initial PHP tag.

```
<body>
<?php
```

3. Define the WEEK constant.

```
define ("WEEK", $week);
```

Because every page uses the value of the $week variable, you want to ensure that it won't inadvertently change through the course of a script. Thus, turn the variable into a constant.

4. Create a function for storing the user's picks.

```
function write_data ($value, $key,
→ $fp) {
      fputs ($fp, "$value\n");
}
```

The write_data() function will be used in conjunction with the array_walk() function, as described earlier in the chapter. write_data() receives the array's element, its key, and the pointer to the file. The content being written to the file will be the name of the team picked by the user followed by a return. Be sure to use the \n format for creating the return because its alternate, \r, causes problems

Script 1.6 The store_picks.php page defines the week variable as a constant to make sure nothing happens to its value in the course of the script.

```
1   <!DOCTYPE html PUBLIC "-//W3C//DTD XHTML
    1.0 Transitional//EN"
2   "http://www.w3.org/TR/2000/REC-xhtml1-
    20000126/DTD/xhtml1-transitional.dtd">
3   <html xmlns="http://www.w3.org/1999/
    xhtml">
4   <head>
5       <title>Football Picks</title>
6   </head>
7   <body>
8   <?php
9   // This page handles the data from the
    make_picks_form.php script.
10
11  // Set the week as a constant.
12  define ("WEEK", $week);
13
14  // The write_data function stores the
    picks in the file.
15  function write_data ($value, $key, $fp) {
16      fputs ($fp, "$value\n"); // Add a
        return to place each item on its own
        line.
17  }
18
19  $file = '2001/picks_' . WEEK . '_' .
    $username . '_.txt'; // Identify the file
    in the format 'picks_1_Larry_.txt'.
20
21  if ($fp = @fopen ($file, "w")) { // Read
    the file into an array.
22
23      fputs ($fp, "Dummy Line\n"); //
        Create a dummy line.
24      array_walk ($picks, 'write_data',
        $fp); // Send the entire array to the
        write_data function.
25      fclose ($fp); // Close the file.
26      echo 'Your picks have been stored.';
27
28  } else { // If it couldn't open the file,
    print an error message.
29      echo "Could not open the file $file!
        Please make sure the week variable
        has a value.<br></br>";
30  }
31  ?>
32  </body>
33  </html>
```

CONSTANTS

when reading the file on some systems (the former is technically for creating a new line, whereas the later makes a carriage return).

5. Identify the file to be used.

```
$file = '2001/picks_' . WEEK
→ . '_' . $username . '_.txt';
```

The filename is *picks_* followed by which week it is, followed by another underscore, the user's name, and another underscore. It uses a `.txt` extension. You cannot put the constant within either single or double quotation marks because then PHP will interpret it literally as `WEEK` and not as the value the constant represents.

If you placed the 2001 directory outside of the Web document tree, use the appropriate syntax to refer to it here.

6. Attempt to open the file for writing.

```
if ($fp = @fopen ($file, "w")) {
```

If this conditional returns false, double check to make sure you set the permissions on the `2001` directory properly—the most likely cause of a problem since the file itself won't exist yet and thus should be writeable. Another likely cause would be using the wrong parameter, for example, *a* instead of *w*.

7. Write the data to the file.

```
fputs ($fp, "Dummy Line\n");
array_walk ($picks, 'write_data',
→ $fp);
```

A dummy line is first entered into the file, then all of the data is written using a combination of the `array_walk()` function and the already defined `write_data()` function. Theoretically, you could add another function that checks to make sure all the games have been picked before writing the data.

continues on next page

CONSTANTS

8. Close the file and send a message upon completion.

```
fclose ($fp);
echo 'Your picks have been stored.';
```

9. Conclude the conditional, the PHP, and HTML.

```
} else {
echo "Could not open the file $file!
→ Please make sure the week variable
→ has a value.<br></br>";
}
?>
</body>
</html>
```

10. Save the file as store_picks.php and upload it to your server in the same directory as the make_picks_form.php (Script 1.5). Run the latter in your Web browser (Figure 1.7), so that store_picks.php is executed (**Figure 1.9**).

11. Check your 2001 directory to see if the new file was created (**Figure 1.10**). If you want, download the newly created file and examine its contents (**Script 1.7**).

Figure 1.9 If the script worked properly, the user will see this terse message.

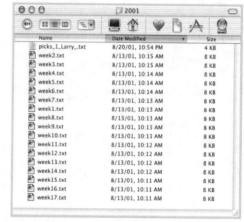

Figure 1.10 The 2001 directory, which is essentially a text file database, stores all of the data, including the newly created picks_1_USERNAME_.txt files.

CONSTANTS

Script 1.7 After running `make_picks_form.php` and `store_picks.php`, this file is created, recording my picks for week 1.

```
                    script
1        Dummy Line
2        Buffalo
3        New England
4        Seattle
5        Tampa Bay
6        Green Bay
7        Kansas City
8        Minnesota
9        Indianapolis
10       Pittsburgh
11       Chicago
12       Philadelphia
13       San Diego
14       San Francisco
15       Miami
16       Denver
```

✔ Tips

■ You can check to see if a constant is defined before using it by running the `defined()` function:

`if (defined(CONSTANT_NAME)) { ...`

Try not to confuse `defined()` with `define()`, which is used to set the constant in the first place.

■ To see a list of all defined constants, use the `get_defined_constants()` function.

■ While it is not secure to have a writeable (permissions set to *777*) directory within the Web documents directory, like the *2001* directory in this example, it is sometimes a necessary evil. There are workarounds and considerations for such instances, which will be discussed in Chapter 4, Securiy. If you can place your writeable directory outside of the Web tree, that would be preferable, although some hosting companies will not give you this option.

CONSTANTS

Function Recursion and Static Variables

In your programming you've most certainly had occasion to define and use your own functions—it's a wonderful tool, helping to organize your code and saving you time. What you may not have experimented with is the capability to use recursion with your functions.

Recursion is the act of a function calling itself.

```
function function_name () {
    // Other code.
    function_name ();
}
```

The end result is that your functions can act both as originally intended and as a loop. The one *huge* warning when using this technique is to make sure your function has an "out" clause. For example, the following code will run ad infinitum.

```
function add_one ($n) {
    $n++;
    add_one ($n);
}
add_one (1);
```

The lack of a condition that determines when to stop execution of the function creates a big programming no-no, the infinite loop. Compare that function to this one:

```
function count_to_100 ($n) {
    if ($n <= 100) {
        echo $n . "<br></br>";
        $n++;
        count_to_100 ($n);
    }
}
count_to_100 (1);
```

This function will continue to call itself until $n is greater than 100, at which point it will stop executing the function.

When working with recursion or, in fact, any script in which the same function may be called multiple times, you might want to consider using the static statement. Static forces the function to remember the value of a variable from function call to function call, without using global variables. The count_to_100() function could be rewritten like so with the same result:

```
function count_to_100 () {
    static $n;
    if ($n <= 100) {
        echo $n . "<br></br>";
        $n++;
        count_to_100 ();
    }
}
count_to_100 ();
```

As the next step in the online picks application, you'll write a script that uses recursion and the static statement. It will allow the administrator to enter the winner of each football game and will then calculate how each player did.

To use recursion and the static statement:

1. Open make_picks_form.php in your text editor (Script 1.5).

   You'll write a slightly different script than this one for the purposes of selecting the winners.

2. Change lines 15-21 of the original document so that the form is handled by a different script and doesn't give a username input option (**Script 1.8**).

```
echo '<form action="process_
→ winners.php" method="post">
<table border="1" width="80%"
→ cellspacing="4" cellpadding="4"
→ align="center">
';
```

Although this form will be very similar to the make_picks_form.php script, it will be handled differently by the process_winners.php page, which you'll write next.

continues on next page

Script 1.8 The pick_winners.php script is only a slight modification of its make_picks_form.php predecessor.

```
1    <!DOCTYPE html PUBLIC "-//W3C//DTD XHTML 1.0 Transitional//EN"
2          "http://www.w3.org/TR/2000/REC-xhtml1-20000126/DTD/xhtml1-transitional.dtd">
3    <html xmlns="http://www.w3.org/1999/xhtml">
4    <head>
5        <title>Football Picks</title>
6    </head>
7    <body>
8    <?php
9
10   $file = '2001/week' . $week . '.txt'; // Identify the file based upon which week it is.
11
12   if ($games = @file ($file)) { // Read the file into an array.
13
14       // If it read the file, print the form.
15       echo '<form action="process_winners.php" method="post">
16   <table border="1" width="80%" cellspacing="4" cellpadding="4" align="center">
17           ';
18
19       foreach ($games as $key => $array) { // Use an array to print out each game.
20
21           if ($key != 0) { // Don't print the Away Home line.
22
23               $second_array = explode ("\t", $array); // Turn each line of the array into its own
                 array.
24               $away = $second_array[0]; // The first item is the Away team.
25               $home = substr ($second_array[1], 0, (strlen($second_array[1]) - 1)); // The second
                 item is the Home team but delete the return character.
26
27               echo "  <tr align=\"center\" valign=\"top\">
28   <td align=\"left\" valign=\"top\" nowrap=\"nowrap\"><input type=\"radio\"
     name=\"winners[$key]\" value=\"$away\">$away</td>
```

(script continues on next page)

3. Change lines 31-35 of the original script so that the generated array is called $winners.

```
echo " <tr align=\"center\"
→ valign=\"top\">
<td align=\"left\" valign=\"top\"
→ nowrap=\"nowrap\"><input
→ type=\"radio\"
→ name=\"winners[$key]\"
→ value=\"$away\">$away</td>
<td align=\"center\"
→ valign=\"top\">at</td>
<td align=\"right\" valign=\"top\"
→ nowrap=\"nowrap\"><input
→ type=\"radio\" name=\
→ "winners[$key]\" value=\
→ "$home\">$home</td>
</tr>\n";
```

This step isn't absolutely necessary except that the process_winners.php page that receives this form should use more appropriate variable names ($winners as opposed to $picks).

4. Save the script as pick_winners.php.

Now you'll write the page that handles the data from the pick_winners.php form.

5. Create a new HTML document in your text editor (**Script 1.9**).

```
<!DOCTYPE html PUBLIC "-//W3C//DTD
→ XHTML 1.0 Transitional//EN"
"http://www.w3.org/TR/2000/
→ REC-xhtml1-20000126/DTD/
→ xhtml1-transitional.dtd">
<html xmlns="http://www.w3.org/1999/
→ xhtml">
<head>
    <title>Football Picks</title>
</head>
```

continues on page 30

Script 1.8 *continued*

```
                                   script
29         <td align=\"center\"
           valign=\"top\">at</td>
30         <td align=\"right\"
           valign=\"top\"
           nowrap=\"nowrap\"><input
           type=\"radio\" name=\
           "winners[$key]\"
           value=\"$home\">$home</td>
31     </tr>\n";
32         }
33     }
34
35     // Complete the form and the table.
36     echo "  <tr align=\"center\"
       valign=\"top\">
37         <td colspan=\"3\" width=\"100%\"
           align=\"center\"
           valign=\"top\"><input
           type=\"submit\" name=\
           "Submit\" value=\"Submit!\">
38     </tr>
39 </table>
40 <input type=\"hidden\" name=\"week\"
   value=\"$week\">
41 </form>\n";
42
43 } else { // If it couldn't open the file,
   print an error message.
44     echo "Could not open the file $file!
       Please make sure the week variable
       has a value.<br></br>";
45 }
46 ?>
47 </body>
48 </html>
```

Script 1.9 This longish script uses static variables and function recursion to write to files, retrieve data from files, and make calculations.

```
1    <!DOCTYPE html PUBLIC "-//W3C//DTD XHTML 1.0 Transitional//EN"
2    "http://www.w3.org/TR/2000/REC-xhtml1-20000126/DTD/xhtml1-transitional.dtd">
3    <html xmlns="http://www.w3.org/1999/xhtml">
4    <head>
5        <title>Football Picks</title>
6    </head>
7    <body>
8    <?php
9
10   // Set the week as a constant.
11   define ("WEEK", $week);
12
13   /* -------------------------- */
14   /* Store the winners in a file. */
15   /* -------------------------- */
16
17   function write_data ($value, $key, $fp) { // The write_data function stores the picks in
     the file.
18
19       static $first_line;
20
21       if (!$first_line) { // Write a first dummy line but only once.
22           fputs ($fp, "Dummy Line\n");
23           $first_line = TRUE;
24       }
25
26       fputs ($fp, "$value\n"); // Add a return to place each item on its own line.
27   }
28
29   $file = '2001/picks_' . WEEK . '_Winners_.txt'; // Identify the file in the format
     'picks_1_Winners_.txt'.
30
31   if ($fp = @fopen ($file, "w")) { // Read the file into an array.
32
33       array_walk ($winners, 'write_data', $fp); // Send the entire array to the write_data
         function.
34       fclose ($fp); // Close the file.
35
36       echo 'The winners have been stored!<br></br>';
37
38   } else { // If it couldn't open the file, print an error message.
39       echo "Could not open the file $file! Please make sure the week variable has a
         value.<br></br>";
40   }
41
42
43   /* -------------------------- */
44   /* Retrieve the players' picks. */
45   /* -------------------------- */
```

(script continues on next page)

FUNCTION RECURSION AND STATIC VARIABLES

6. Start the HTML body and enter the initial PHP tag.

```
<body>
<?php
```

7. Define the WEEK constant.

```
define ("WEEK", $week);
```

Because I don't want this value to change and because it needs to be available to multiple functions, I'm establishing it as a constant up-front.

8. Write the function for storing the list of winners.

```
function write_data ($value, $key,
→ $fp) {
static $first_line;
if (!$first_line) {
fputs ($fp, "Dummy Line\n");
$first_line = TRUE;
}
fputs ($fp, "$value\n");
}
```

The write_data() function basically just puts a line of text into the file. Because I want the first line of the file to be a dummy line, I've created a conditional that will add that to the file but only if the first line hasn't already been written. (I don't want *Dummy Line* written with every call of this function.) Because the $first_line variable, which is set to TRUE once the dummy line has been written, is established as static, its value will be remembered with each iteration of the function. Therefore, on the second call to the function, $first_line is remembered as TRUE, and the conditional is ignored.

9. Select the file to be used.

```
$file = '2001/picks_' . WEEK .
→ '_Winners_.txt';
```

Each week's list of winners will be placed in a file called (e.g., if it's week 1): picks_1_Winners_.txt. The file will be located within the 2001 directory.

10. Write the conditional that opens the file and stores the array of winners therein.

```
if ($fp = @fopen ($file, "w")) {
array_walk ($winners, 'write_data',
→ $fp);
fclose ($fp);
echo 'The winners have been
→ stored!<br></br>';
} else {
echo "Could not open the file $file!
→ Please make sure the week variable
→ has a value.<br></br>";
}
```

This is very similar to the code for the store_picks.php script.

11. Create the function that retrieves all of the existing users' picks.

```
function read_picks ($dp,
→ $directory) {
global $picks;
if ($file_name = readdir ($dp)) {
if (substr($file_name, 0, 6) ==
→ "picks_") {
$parse_file_name = explode ("_",
→ $file_name);
if (($parse_file_name[1] == WEEK)
→ and ($parse_file_name[2] !=
→ "Winners")) {
$username = $parse_file_name[2];
$the_file = $directory . $file_name;
$users_picks = file ($the_file);
$picks[$username] = $users_picks;
}
}
read_picks ($dp, $directory);}
}
```

This function will loop (via the penultimate line that causes recursion) through all of the files in the directory until there are no more to be read. At that time, the conditional will be false and the function will not call itself again.

Should a file match the criteria of being a user's picks file (i.e., `substr($file_name, 0, 6) == "picks_"`), the data will be read and stored into the global `$picks` array, using the username as the key.

12. Create the main array, identify and open the directory, then call the `read_picks()` function.

```
$picks = array();
$directory = '2001/';
$dp = opendir ($directory);
read_picks ($dp, $directory);
closedir ($dp);
```

13. Write a loop that will determine how each player did.

```
while (list ($key, $value) = each
→ ($picks)) {
$wins = 0;
$losses = 0;
while (list ($key2, $value2) = each
→ ($value)) {
$value2 = substr ($value2, 0,
→ (strlen($value2) - 1));
if (($value2 == $winners[$key2])
→ and ($key2 != 0)) {
$wins++;
} elseif ($key2 != 0 ) {
$losses++;
}
}
$results[$key] = array ('wins' =>
→ $wins, 'losses' => $losses);
}
```

There are two loops here. The first runs through the multidimensional `$picks` array, which consists of each user's picks for that week. Then, the second loop runs through each user's array of picks and checks to see if the team the user selected was the winner. If it was, the `$wins` variable is incremented, else the `$losses` variable is incremented. Finally, the tallies are added to the multidimensional `$results` array, which stores each user's wins and losses.

14. Alphabetize the results by username.

```
ksort ($results);
```

The `$results` array in my example now consists of four elements indexed at *Brian, Juan, Larry,* and *Michael* (my four test users). Each element points to another array with keys of *wins* and *losses*. Ksort() will arrange the initial set of indexes—the users' names—in alphabetical order without affecting any of the other data.

15. Create a function that will store the week's results.

```
function write_results ($value,
→ $key, $fp) {
static $first_line2;
if (!$first_line2) {
fputs ($fp, "User\tWins\tLosses\n");
$first_line2 = TRUE;
}
$data = implode ("\t", $value);
fputs ($fp, "$key\t$data\n");
}
```

This function mimics the `write_data()` function, although it uses a different header. Again, a static variable is used so that the header is written only once.

continues on next page

16. Identify the results file and create the conditional that will send all the data to it.

```
$file2 = '2001/results_' . WEEK .
→ '_.txt';
if ($fp2 = @fopen ($file2, "w")) {
array_walk ($results,
→ 'write_results', $fp2);
fclose ($fp2);
echo 'The results have been
→ stored.<br></br>';
} else {
echo "Could not open the weekly
→ results file, $file2.<br></br>";
}
```

This also copies the structure for calling the `write_data()` function earlier in the script. Every user's wins and losses will be stored in a file called (for week 1) `results_1_.txt` when `array_walk()` sends the `$results` array to the `write_results()` function.

Figure 1.11 The `pick_winners.php` page looks like the `make_picks_form.php` one (Figure 1.7), except there's no username option.

Figure 1.12 If all goes well with the `process_winners.php` page, these two messages are what you'll see. You can confirm the script's success by peeking into the 2001 directory (Figure 1.13).

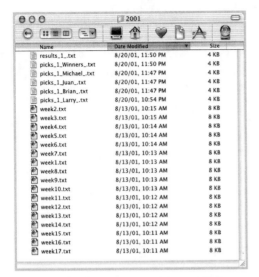

Figure 1.13 The directory now contains a picks_1_ Winners_.txt file that lists the winning teams and a results_1_.txt file that stores how each user did that week.

Script 1.10 The process_winners.php script generates such a results file for each week the pick_winners.php page is run. The results file lists every user and how many wins and losses they had that week.

```
                    script
1    User      Wins     Losses

2    Brian     8        7

3    Juan      11       4

4    Larry     10       5

5    Michael   11       4
```

17. Finish the PHP and the HTML.

```
?>
</body>
</html>
```

18. Save this file as process_winners.php, upload it to the same directory as pick_winners.php (Script 1.8) and run the latter in your Web browser (**Figures 1.11** and **1.12**).

19. If you want, look inside your 2001 directory (**Figure 1.13**) and take a look at the results_1_.txt file (**Script 1.10**).

References and Functions

As a default, functions receive arguments on a call-by-value basis. This means that a function receives the value of a variable, not the actual variable itself. To alter the value of a variable within a function, you need to either use the `global` statement or pass the variable by reference.

Here's an example of how functions normally operate:

```
function change_value ($variable) {
    $variable++;
    echo $variable;
}
$variable = 1;
change_value ($variable);
```

The `echo` statement will print a *2*, but the value of `$variable` is still *1* (remember that `$variable` within the function is not the same as `$variable` outside of it, despite the common name). However, if you were to pass `$variable` to the function as a reference, the value of `$variable` outside of the function would also change.

To pass a variable by reference instead of by value, precede the variable with the ampersand (&). You can do this either on the function call line, in which case that particular variable will be affected, or on the function definition line, in which case every variable sent to the function will be affected.

```
function change_value ($variable) {
    $variable++;
    echo $variable;
}
$variable = 1;
change_value (&$variable);
```

Now the function prints out a *2*, and `$variable` (outside of the function) has a value of *2*. The same result can be achieved using:

```
function change_value (&$variable) {
    $variable++;
    echo $variable;
}
$variable = 1;
change_value ($variable);
```

The difference in this second example is that every variable sent to `change_value()` is automatically sent by reference.

One benefit of using references with functions is that it can save you the hassle of using global variables or returning values from a function. You'll see how when you create one last script in the online sports pool application.

Aliases

New to PHP 4 is the ability to pass values by reference independent of functions. The syntax for doing so is the same:

```
$variable1 = "Chicago Cubs";

$variable2 = $variable1; // $variable2 is a copy of $variable1

$variable3 =& $variable1; // $variable3 is a reference to $variable1

$variable2 = "National League Leaders"; // $variable2 is "National League Leaders";
→ $variable1 is still "Chicago Cubs"

$variable3 .= ", National League Leaders"; // $variable3 and $variable1 are "Chicago
→ Cubs, National League Leaders"
```

When you use references like this, you are creating an *alias*. In the above example, $variable3 is an alias to $variable1 (that particular line establishing the alias could also be written $variable3 = &$variable1;). Any changes made to the one will affect the other.

Using references to your variables in lieu of copies can improve the performance of your applications, especially when dealing with large arrays or objects. While every copy of a variable takes up the same amount of space in memory as the original, an alias uses significantly less.

A good analogy would be when you have a shortcut to a document on your computer. Say you have the document *Venus.txt* in the *Astronomy* folder and you've made an alias, or shortcut, to this document (perhaps residing on your desktop) called *Evening_Star*. Both the shortcut and the document itself refer to the same value (the contents of the document when opened), and any changes to that content will be reflected whether you open the document through the *Evening_Star* shortcut or the *Venus.txt* original. But, while *Venus.txt* may be 40 kb in size, the shortcut could be only 2kb.

REFERENCES AND FUNCTIONS

To make use of references:

1. Create a new HTML document in your text editor (**Script 1.11**).

```
<!DOCTYPE html PUBLIC "-//W3C//DTD
→ XHTML 1.0 Transitional//EN"
"http://www.w3.org/TR/2000/
→ REC-xhtml1-20000126/DTD/xhtml1-
→ transitional.dtd">
<html xmlns="http://www.w3.org/1999/
→ xhtml">
<title>Football Picks</title>
</head>
<body>
```

2. Begin the body and the PHP code.

```
<body>
<?php
```

3. Write a function that will add up wins and losses.

```
function do_the_math ($value, $key,
→ $total) {
if ($key != 0) {
$line = explode ("\t", $value);
$username = $line[0];
$total["$username"]["wins"] +=
→ $line[1];
$total["$username"]["losses"] +=
→ $line[2];
}
}
```

This function receives an array's value, its key, and the $total array. The value, which comes in the form USERNAME [TAB] WINS [TAB] LOSSES [RETURN], will be deconstructed if it is not the first item in the array ($key != 0)—the dummy line. Then the person's wins and losses are added to the ongoing tally.

4. Create a function that reads each week's results from the files.

```
function read_results ($dp,
→ $directory, &$total) {
if ($file_name = readdir ($dp)) {
if (substr($file_name, 0, 8) ==
→ "results_") {
$the_file = $directory . $file_name;
array_walk (file ($the_file),
→ 'do_the_math', &$total);
}
read_results ($dp, $directory,
→ $total);
}
}
```

The read_results() function receives three arguments: the directory pointer (created when the directory was opened), the name of the directory, and the $total array. This last variable is always passed by reference and not by value so that any changes that are made to it within the function will affect the variable outside of the function.

The read_results() function loops through every file in the directory (notice that it uses recursion by calling itself). If it discovers a results file, indicated by a filename of results_WEEK_.txt, it will read the file into an array and pass the array onto the do_the_math() function via array_walk(). Notice again that the $total array is being passed to the do_the_math() function by reference, so any changes made to $total within do_the_math() will be reflected within read_results().

continues on page 38

Script 1.11 The final script in this Web application reads all of the results files and uses references to calculate the season totals to date.

```
                              script
1    <!DOCTYPE html PUBLIC "-//W3C//DTD XHTML 1.0 Transitional//EN"
2           "http://www.w3.org/TR/2000/REC-xhtml1-20000126/DTD/xhtml1-transitional.dtd">
3    <html xmlns="http://www.w3.org/1999/xhtml">
4        <title>Football Picks</title>
5    </head>
6    <body>
7    <?php
8
9    /* ----------------------------- */
10   /* Calculate the season standings. */
11   /* ----------------------------- */
12
13   function do_the_math ($value, $key, $total) { // This function adds up the wins and losses.
14
15       if ($key != 0) { // Ignore the first dummy line.
16
17           $line = explode ("\t", $value); // Separate out the username, wins, and losses.
18           $username = $line[0];
19           $total["$username"]["wins"] += $line[1];
20           $total["$username"]["losses"] += $line[2];
21       }
22   }
23
24   function read_results ($dp, $directory, &$total) {
25
26       if ($file_name = readdir ($dp)) { // Search through the directory.
27           if (substr($file_name, 0, 8) == "results_") { // If it's a results file ...
28               $the_file = $directory . $file_name;
29               array_walk (file ($the_file), 'do_the_math', &$total); // Do the math on all the data.
30           }
31           read_results ($dp, $directory, $total); // Repeat through the directory.
32       }
33   }
34
35   $total = array(); // Initialize the main variable.
36
37   $directory = '2001/';
38   $dp = opendir ($directory);
39   read_results ($dp, $directory, $total); // Start the process.
40   closedir ($dp);
41   echo "<pre>\n";
42   print_r ($total); // Quickly print out the results.
43   echo "</pre>\n";
44   ?>
45   </body>
46   </html>
```

5. Create the main variable, open the directory, and start the calculations process.

```
$total = array();
$directory = '2001/';
$dp = opendir ($directory);
read_results ($dp, $directory,
→ $total);
closedir ($dp);
```

6. Print out the calculations to the Web browser.

```
echo "<pre>\n";
print_r ($total);
echo "</pre>\n";
```

The print_r() function takes a variable as an argument and prints out its content and structure, making it is very useful for quickly analyzing complex variables such as arrays and objects. If you wanted, you could instead take this array and create a formal table for displaying the results. Print_r() is new to PHP 4. If you are using an earlier version, replace it with var_dump().

7. Close the PHP code and the HTML document.

```
?>
</body>
</html>
```

8. Save this file as process_season.php, upload it to your server, and run it in your Web browser (**Figure 1.14**).

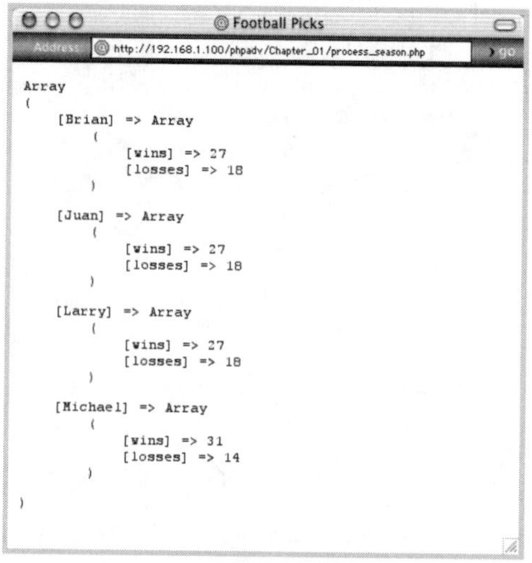

Figure 1.14 As it stands, the process_season.php script simply prints out the results. This information, once determined, could easily be emailed as well.

Figure 1.15 The var_dump() function prints out the same information as print_r() (Figure 1.14), but it adds a little more analysis.

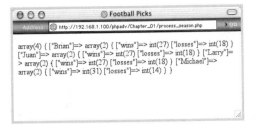

Figure 1.16 Attempting to use either print_r() or var_dump() without the HTML <pre></pre> tags produces ugly, unintelligible results.

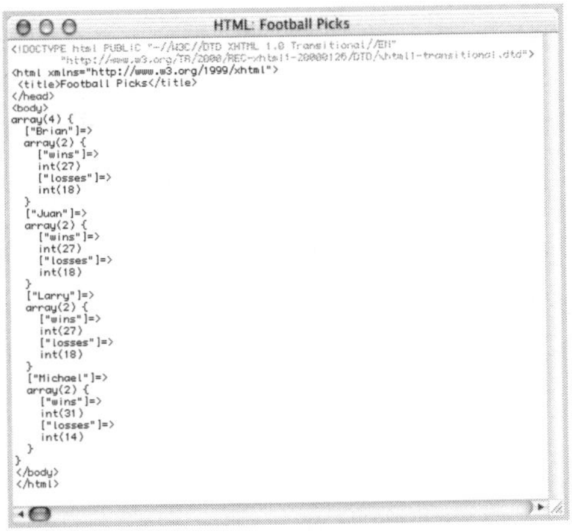

Figure 1.17 Viewing the source of Figure 1.16 improves the display of the array printed with var_dump(), essentially matching Figure 1.15 when <pre></pre> tags were used.

✔ Tips

■ If you would like to compare print_r() to var_dump(), change the last PHP line in the process_season.php page (Script 1.11) to var_dump ($total); then run this in your Web browser (**Figure 1.15**).

■ Use of the <pre></pre> HTML tags forces the display of the arrays in the browser to match that of the source. **Figure 1.16** shows what the result would be without these tags, although the source (**Figure 1.17**) looks legible.

■ For more information about references, see www.php.net/manual/en/language.references.php.

REFERENCES AND FUNCTIONS

OBJECT-ORIENTED PROGRAMMING

Object-oriented programming (commonly abbreviated OOP) is a relative newcomer to the world of programming. Before the advent of OOP, programming languages such as C, Pascal, and BASIC were written on a line-by-line basis. While such linear programming works, over time coders developed this better system that allows the programmer to more rapidly develop and alter sophisticated applications.

Today, Java and C++ are probably the two best-known OOP languages, and OOP is so popular that support for it has been incorporated into PHP even though PHP itself is written in a non-OOP language (namely, C). When working with objects in PHP, keeping in mind that PHP supports objects but is not a true OOP language (and the creators of PHP have no intention to make it so) will save you some confusion. In Java, for example, every script is a matter of creating and using objects. In fact, you cannot write a Java application without using objects. Conversely, PHP programmers can go through their entire careers without ever using objects with no significant limitations on what they can do. Also, PHP objects do not incorporate such common OOP features as the ability to hide data, define public versus private methods and attributes, and use class destructors.

Although PHP is not as strong in its OOP support as it could be, it is still a good idea to understand how to use objects. Any time you modularize your code—be it by creating functions or objects—you've written something that will be easier to modify and faster to reuse in another application. The larger an application gets, the more practical it becomes to use OOP. Using objects also allows you to partition out different processes. This can be handy if you are working with a team of programmers or if you merely want to separate the HTML and graphic design work from the PHP code.

There are two main problems with using objects (besides the issue that PHP is not an object-oriented language) that can confuse those coming to PHP from OOP languages. First, objects' execution can be less efficient than running straight code (just as your own functions can run slower than simple code because of the required function calls). Normally, the time difference between using an object or not is imperceptible to the end user, but you should be aware of this potential side effect. Second, one could argue that creating generalized modules of code that allow you to quickly write new applications is more of a benefit to you than it is to the business client who hired you. Indeed, object-oriented programming could be described as more of a business decision than a programming one. As an example, reusing an existing e-commerce object for a new job will speed up development drastically—saving you time and money—but it also means that someone just purchased a less customized, and perhaps slower, application than they were looking for (whether they know it or not). That being said, business decisions like these are part of programming in the real world, and the increased reliability from reusing objects may outweigh any downsides.

Using OOP with PHP is a relatively simple two-step process: define a class and create an instance of that class (the instance is the object itself). In this chapter you will use objects to separate out your HTML from your PHP code—a very common use for OOP—and in Chapter 3, *Databases*, you'll use objects to create a database abstraction layer. To be able to use objects with PHP requires no special additions to your PHP configuration, but there are some slight differences in how PHP 3 and 4 handle objects, which I will point out.

Defining a Class

To use OOP, you must begin by defining a class. Classes consist of variables and functions, which are also referred to as attributes (or properties) and methods, respectively.

A philosophical example of a class would be Human. A Human class would have characteristics (or attributes) of gender, height, weight, birth date, and so forth. The actions (or methods) of a Human could be eating, sleeping, and more. A class, in short, is a generalized description of a thing.

The syntax of a class, in the simplest form, is:

```
class ClassName {
    var $variable_name;
    function FunctionName () {
        // Function code.
    }
}
```

Notice that within the class you must use the var statement to identify your variables. You may, at this time, give the variables a value—that is to say, *initialize* them—if you want. In PHP 4, you can set this variable to be a scalar value (number, string, array, etc.), but in PHP 3 you could further initialize an attribute as an object or other nonscalar value. Thus, one of the few places where PHP 3 code may cause problems with PHP 4 is within classes.

The PHP Coding Standard argues that class names should begin with a capital letter, use capital letters to separate words (e.g., ClassName), and not use underscores. Furthermore, method (function) names should use the same conventions as attributes (variables), although the latter should begin with a lowercase *m* (e.g., var $mVariableName). Using the same convention for class and method names is quite logical—as you'll see in *Creating Constructors*, later this chapter—but I prefer to use standard variable conventions for my class attributes.

One last oddity with objects is the $this variable. Within each function, you can refer to the instance of a class and its attributes by using the $this->variable_name syntax. Because, as you'll see in the next section, classes will not know the name of the class instance (i.e., the defined class is independent of the individually named objects), the generic $this can refer to the instance in place of a proper name. You'll see how this plays out when defining your first class.

For the first example of using object-oriented programming in PHP, you'll create a series of HTML templates, classes, and instances of these classes to generate Web pages.

To define an HTML class:

1. Begin by creating a new PHP document in your text editor (**Script 2.1**).

   ```
   <?php
   ```

2. Define your class.

   ```
   class HtmlTemplate {
   ```

   This class is named, appropriately enough, HtmlTemplate—not an overly descriptive nomenclature but adequate for your purposes.

3. Establish the class's attributes.

   ```
   var $template;
   var $html;
   var $parameters = array ();
   ```

   The HtmlTemplate class uses three variables. Each of these attributes could change in every instance of the class, so none of them are initially set to a specific value. The $parameters attribute is identified as an array, though.

4. Create the first method.

   ```
   function IdentifyTemplate ($template) {
   $this->template = $template;
   }
   ```

   The class's first method, IdentifyTemplate(), takes a template file name as an argument. It will then assign this file name to the $template attribute within the class. The use of $this->template signifies the class attribute $template, as established on line 7.

5. Write the second method.

   ```
   function SetParameter ($variable,
   → $value) {
   $this->parameters[$variable] =
   → $value;
   }
   ```

Script 2.1 The first class being defined is a very simple one for creating Web pages from templates.

```
1   <?php
2   // This class reads in a template, sets
    the different values, and sends it to the
    browser.
3
4   class HtmlTemplate {
5
6       // Set the attributes.
7       var $template;
8       var $html;
9       var $parameters = array();
10
11      function IdentifyTemplate ($template)
        { // This function sets which
        template will be used.
12          $this->template = $template;
13      }
14
15      function SetParameter ($variable,
        $value) { // This function sets the
        particular values.
16          $this->parameters[$variable] =
            $value;
17      }
18
19      function CreatePage () { // This
        function does the bulk of the work.
20          $this->html = implode ("",
            (file($this->template))); // Read
            the template into an array, then
            create a string.
21
22          foreach ($this->parameters as
            $key => $value) { // Loop through
            all the parameters and set the
            variables to values.
23              $template_name = '{' . $key .
                '}';
24              $this->html = str_replace
                ($template_name, $value,
                $this->html);
25          }
26          echo $this->html;
27      }
28  }
29  ?>
```

The `SetParameter()` function receives two arguments—a variable name and its corresponding value. The method fills the `$parameters` array, identified by `$this->parameters`, with each variable-value pair.

6. Create the third, and most important, method.

```
function CreatePage () {
$this->html = implode ("",
→ (file($this->template)));
foreach ($this->parameters as
→ $key => $value) {
$template_name = '{' . $key . '}';
$this->html = str_replace ($template_
→ name, $value, $this->html);
}
echo $this->html;
}
```

The `CreatePage()` function will do the majority of the work. First, it will read the contents of the template file into an array and then implode this array into one long string that is finally assigned to the `$html` attribute (line 20). The second step will be to loop through every element in the `$parameters` array (lines 22 through 25).

Within this loop, two things are occurring. First, a dummy variable, which does not need to be a class attribute, will be defined as the `$key` value surrounded by braces (for example, in one iteration of the loop, `$template_name` may end up being {PAGE_TITLE}). You will see why you need to do this once you've created your template. Second, every instance of this dummy variable—`$template_name`—will be replaced with the corresponding value

of the key from the `$parameters` array in the existing `$html` string (line 24). Again, this will make more sense once you've seen the entire process in action, but as an example, if `$parameters` contains a key named PAGE_TITLE and its value is *Welcome to my Site!*, then in the `$html` string, every occurrence of {PAGE_TITLE} will be turned into *Welcome to my Site!*.

The final step within the `CreatePage()` method is to send the accumulated code to the Web browser, using the echo statement (line 26).

7. Close the class and the PHP page.

```
}
?>
```

Save your script as `HtmlTemplate.class`. Because your classes will not be executed as PHP pages, you can use any extension you prefer for the file. I think the `.class` extension makes the most sense.

✔ Tips

■ The class `stdClass` is already in use internally by Zend.com and cannot be used in your own code.

■ Two class functions—`__sleep` and `__wakeup`—have special meaning to PHP (they're magical). They'll be discussed later in this chapter. All functions in PHP that begin with two underscores (`__`) are considered magical.

■ True OOP languages have public and private attributes and methods for their classes. There is no distinction between the two in PHP.

Creating an Object

Using OOP is a two-step process. The first—defining a class—you just did when you wrote the `HtmlTemplate` class. The second step is to make use of that class by creating an object (or a class instance).

Going back to my Human class analogy, an instance of this class may be called Jude. Jude's attributes are a gender of male, a height of about 40 inches, a weight of 35 pounds, and a birth date of November 15, 1998. Jude is one instance of the Human class and, as you may have noticed, is also a child. A second instance, Kelsey, has a female gender, a height of nearly 5 feet, a weight of 75 pounds, and a birth date of April 11, 1992. Both Jude and Kelsey are separate objects derived from the same class.

Creating an object is remarkably easy in PHP once you've defined your class.

```
$object = new ClassName();
```

Now the variable `$class` exists and it is of type object (instead of a string or array) as defined by the class `ClassName`. To call the methods of the class, you use this odd syntax:

```
$class->FunctionName();
```

To demonstrate this, you'll create an instance of the `HtmlTemplate` class, defined in Script 2.1. However, this object makes use of an HTML template, so it would be best to write that first.

To make a simple HTML template:

1. Begin by creating a new PHP document in your text editor (**Script 2.2**).

   ```
   <!DOCTYPE html PUBLIC "-//W3C//DTD
   → XHTML 1.0 Transitional//EN"
   "http://www.w3.org/TR/2000/
   → REC-xhtml1-20000126/DTD/
   → xhtml1-transitional.dtd">
   ```

2. Compose the HTML head, inserting the {PAGE_TITLE} code between the `<title>` tags.

   ```
   <html xmlns="http://www.w3.org/1999/
   → xhtml">
   <head>
   <title>{PAGE_TITLE}</title>
   </head>
   ```

   The page title (line 5) is one of the parameters that will be set by the object. Any parameter that you want to be determined on an instance-by-instance basis can be put within braces, preferably in an all-capital letters format.

3. Create the page's body, leaving a space for dynamically added page content.

   ```
   <body>
   <table border="0" width="100%"
   → cellspacing="5" cellpadding="5"
   → align="center">
   <tr align="center" valign="top">
   <td colspan="4" width="100%"
   → align="center" valign="top">
   <!-- Top/Header HTML Code Goes Here -->
   <h3>Header: Graphics, Links, Etc.</h3>
   </td>
   </tr>
   <tr align="center" valign="top">
   <td width="25%" align="left"
   → valign="top">
   <!-- Left Navigation HTML Code Goes
   → Here -->
   ```

continues on page 48

Script 2.2 This simple HTML template allows for two parameters to be set on the fly: the page's title and the content.

```
1   <!DOCTYPE html PUBLIC "-//W3C//DTD XHTML 1.0 Transitional//EN"
2          "http://www.w3.org/TR/2000/REC-xhtml1-20000126/DTD/xhtml1-transitional.dtd">
3   <html xmlns="http://www.w3.org/1999/xhtml">
4   <head>
5       <title>{PAGE_TITLE}</title>
6   </head>
7   <body>
8   <table border="0" width="100%" cellspacing="5" cellpadding="5" align="center">
9       <tr align="center" valign="top">
10          <td colspan="4" width="100%" align="center" valign="top">
11          <!-- Top/Header HTML Code Goes Here -->
12          <h3>Header: Graphics, Links, Etc.</h3>
13          </td>
14      </tr>
15      <tr align="center" valign="top">
16          <td width="25%" align="left" valign="top">
17          <!-- Left Navigation HTML Code Goes Here -->
18          <h4>Navigation:<br></br>
19          Links</h4>
20          </td>
21          <td width="5%" align="center" valign="top">
22          <!-- Spacer --> 
23          </td>
24          <td width="65%" align="left" valign="top">
25          <!-- Page Content Goes here -->
26          <b>{PAGE_CONTENT}</b>
27          </td>
28          <td width="5%" align="right" valign="top">
29          <!-- Spacer --> 
30          </td>
31      </tr>
32      <tr align="center" valign="top">
33          <td colspan="4" width="100%" align="center" valign="top">
34          <!-- Bottom/Footer HTML Code Goes Here -->
35          <small>Footer: Copyright ...</small>
36          </td>
37      </tr>
38  </table>
39  </body>
40  </html>
```

```
<h4>Navigation:<br></br>
Links</h4>
</td>
<td width="5%" align="center"
→ valign="top">
<!-- Spacer --> 
</td>
<td width="65%" align="left"
→ valign="top">
<!-- Page Content Goes here -->
<b>{PAGE_CONTENT}</b>
</td>
<td width="5%" align="right"
→ valign="top">
<!-- Spacer --> 
</td>
</tr>
<tr align="center" valign="top">
<td colspan="4" width="100%"
→ align="center" valign="top">
<!-- Bottom/Footer HTML Code Goes
→ Here -->
<small>Footer: Copyright ...</small>
</td>
</tr>
</table>
</body>
```

Since this is a book on PHP and not on graphic design, I've created a crude example of a Web page. Feel free to design something more appealing if you want. This table creates three rows with a center area for content (**Figures 2.1** and **2.2**).

The important aspect of this part of the script is the {PAGE_CONTENT} code (line 26), which will be replaced, in each individual object, with page-specific data.

4. Finish the HTML page.

```
</html>
```

5. Save the template as `template.inc`.

Once the template has been written, you can create your object.

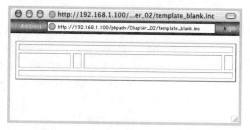

Figure 2.1 The very simple `template.inc` lays out a table with three rows: a header, a footer, and a middle row. The middle section consists of a navigation area on the left and the main content area, surrounded by two spacer columns.

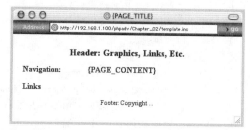

Figure 2.2 If you were to view the template itself in a Web browser, without creating an instance, this is what you would see.

require vs. require_once

New to PHP 4 are the functions `require_once` and `include_once`. While the slight difference between `require` and `include` still remains, there is a significant adjustment between `require` and `require_once`. As their names imply, `require_once` and `include_once` will allow you to include the particular file only once per PHP page. This is a useful debugging feature because you can no longer inadvertently require the same file multiple times, resulting in the *Cannot redeclare class* error message. If you are working with earlier versions of PHP, you will have to continue to use `require` or `include`.

CREATING AN OBJECT

Script 2.3 Once you've defined your class, creating an instance of it is quick and easy. This script uses PHP to generate a Web page without intermixing HTML.

```
script

1    <?php
2    // This is a sample page that uses the
     HtmlTemplate class.
3
4    require_once "HtmlTemplate.class"; //
     Include the class.
5
6    $page = new HtmlTemplate(); // Create an
     instance.
7
8    $page->IdentifyTemplate ("template.inc");
     // Identify the template to use for this
     application.
9
10   $page->SetParameter ("PAGE_TITLE",
     "Welcome to OOP!"); // Set the page
     title.
11   $page->SetParameter ("PAGE_CONTENT",
     "Here is the main part of the page."); //
     Set the main content.
12
13   $page->CreatePage(); // Send the page to
     the browser.
14   ?>
```

To create a object:

1. Begin by creating a new PHP document in your text editor (**Script 2.3**).

   `<?php`

2. Include the file that defines the class.

   `require_once "HtmlTemplate.class";`

   This step is very important. You will not be able to successfully create an instance of a class if the script does not have access to the class definition. Since the class was written in the separate `HtmlTemplate.class` document, this file must be included within the current one.

3. Make an instance of the class.

   `$page = new HtmlTemplate();`

   The **$page** variable is now an object as defined by the `HtmlTemplate` class.

4. Call the `IdentifyTemplate()` method to assign which template will be used.

   `$page->IdentifyTemplate`
   `→ ("template.inc");`

   This aptly named function takes a file name as an argument (refer back to Script 2.1 if necessary). This statement here (line 8) makes use of that method for the **$page** object, associating `template.inc` (Script 2.2) as the template to use.

   continues on next page

5. Set the two applicable values for the template.

```
$page->SetParameter ("PAGE_TITLE",
→ "Welcome to OOP!");

$page->SetParameter ("PAGE_CONTENT",
→ "Here is the main part of the
→ page.");
```

These two values were left open in the template, allowing them to be set by the object. The SetParameter() method assigns key-value pairs to the $parameters array within the function.

These two steps function at the heart of this object system. Because a key named PAGE_TITLE is requested here with the value *Welcome to OOP!*, the HtmlTemplate class will replace the {PAGE_TITLE} string in template.inc with the text *Welcome to OOP!* in Script 2.1, line 24, when the CreatePage() method is called.

6. Create the Web page.

```
$page->CreatePage();
```

This final method does most of the work within the class. Most importantly, it will print the resulting string, full of HTML, to the Web browser.

7. Close the PHP page.

```
?>
```

8. Save the script as instance1.php. Upload it, along with template.inc (Script 2.2) and HtmlTemplate.class (Script 2.1) to the same folder on your Web server, then run instance1.php in your Web browser (**Figures 2.3** and **2.4**).

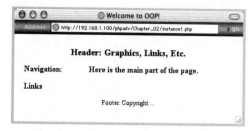

Figure 2.3 The first instance of the HtmlTemplate object renders this Web page.

Figure 2.4 The source of the OOP Web page shows that the {PAGE_TITLE} and {PAGE_CONTENT} parameters have been replaced within the HtmlTemplateclass.

Script 2.4 Changing the two parameters in the script generates a new page (Figure 2.5) based on the same HtmlTemplate class.

```
                    script
1    <?php
2    // This is a sample page that uses the
     HtmlTemplate class.
3
4    require_once "HtmlTemplate.class"; //
     Include the class.
5
6    $page = new HtmlTemplate(); // Create an
     instance.
7
8    $page->IdentifyTemplate ("template.inc");
     // Identify the template to use for this
     application.
9
10   $page->SetParameter ("PAGE_TITLE",
     "Welcome to Another OOP Page!"); // Set
     the page title.
11   $page->SetParameter ("PAGE_CONTENT",
     "Here is the main part of a new page.");
     // Set the main content.
12
13   $page->CreatePage(); // Send the page to
     the browser.
14   ?>
```

✔ Tips

- Because function names in PHP are not case-sensitive, the same is true for method names in classes.

- To test how easy it is to create multiple pages, quickly modify Script 2.3 to make another instance of HtmlTemplate (**Script 2.4**). Call this page instance2. php and test it in your Web browser (**Figure 2.5**).

- Conventionally, when programmers use objects with HTML templates, the braces and all capital letters format is used to indicate a replaceable item (e.g., {SIDEBAR}). This is not required by PHP. You could just as easily use the HTML comment format (<!--SIDEBAR-->), the end result being that unreplaced elements do not display in the Web browser the way {SIDEBAR} would.

Figure 2.5 Minor modifications to your instance1.php script can generate new pages using the same class.

Creating Constructors

A constructor is a function (or method) within a class that has the exact same name as the class itself. The advantage of a constructor is that it will be executed automatically when an instance of the class is created. A constructor could be used to connect to a database, set cookies, or create an HTML header.

The syntax for a constructor is simple:

```
class ClassName {
    function ClassName () {
        // Function code.
    }
}
```

With this format, the following code both creates an instance of the object and then calls the `ClassName()` function, saving a step.

```
$object = new ClassName();
```

Remember that constructors work only if the class contains a method with the same name as the class itself (which is why the protocol is to use the same naming conventions for both).

As a demonstration of using constructors, you'll modify `HtmlTemplate.class` and make a new instance accordingly.

Script 2.5 The HtmlTemplate class (renamed HtmlTemplate2) now contains a constructor that saves you a step when creating an instance (Script 2.6).

```
1    <?php
2    // This class reads in a template, sets
     the different values, and sends it to the
     browser.
3
4    class HtmlTemplate2 {
5
6        // Set the attributes.
7        var $template;
8        var $html;
9        var $parameters = array();
10
11       function HtmlTemplate2 ($template) {
          // This function sets which template
          will be used.
12           $this->template = $template;
13           $this->html = implode ("",
             (file($this->template))); // Read
             the template into an array, then
             create a string.
14       }
15
16       function SetParameter ($variable,
          $value) { // This function sets the
          particular values.
17           $this->parameters[$variable] =
             $value;
18       }
19
20       function CreatePage () { // This
          function does the bulk of the work.
21
22           foreach ($this->parameters as
             $key => $value) { // Loop through
             all the parameters and set the
             variables to values.
23               $template_name = '{' . $key .
                 '}';
24               $this->html = str_replace
                 ($template_name, $value,
                 $this->html);
25           }
26           echo $this->html;
27       }
28   }
29   ?>
```

To create a constructor:

1. Open HtmlTemplate.class in your text editor (Script 2.1).

2. Change the name of the class on line 4 to HtmlTemplate2 to distinguish it from the original (**Script 2.5**).

   class HtmlTemplate2 {

3. Change the IdentifyTemplate() function to make it a constructor.

   function HtmlTemplate2 ($template) {
   $this->template = $template;
   $this->html = implode ("",
   → (file($this->template)));
   }

   There are two changes to this function. First, by changing the name of the function from IdentifyTemplate() to HtmlTemplate2(), this method will be called automatically upon instantiation of the object. Second, the line that reads in the template and turns it into a string has been moved up from the CreatePage() function to this one.

4. Delete line 20—$this->html = implode ("", (file($this->template)));—from Script 2.1.

   Since this line has been added to the HtmlTemplate2() function, it is no longer necessary here.

5. Save the class as HtmlTemplate2.class.

To use a constructor:

1. Open `instance1.php` in your text editor (Script 2.3).

2. Change line 4 to refer to the new class (**Script 2.6**).

   ```
   require_once "HtmlTemplate2.class";
   ```

   Remember to enter in the new class name or else you won't be using the version with the constructor.

3. Alter line 6 so that the object is created properly.

   ```
   $page = new HtmlTemplate2
   → ("template2.inc");
   ```

   Because the constructor method takes an argument—the template name—it must be passed when the object is created.

   For variety sake, I've created a slightly different template, which you can also do (**Script 2.7**). There's no cause to go over it in detail except to note that it includes the {CSS_LINK} parameter allowing you to set this value with your object.

4. Delete line 8, which calls the `IdentifyTemplate()` function.

   Since the `IdentifyTemplate()` method has been renamed and its functionality turned into the `HtmlTemplate2` method, you should no longer call the function.

5. Set the {PAGE_TITLE} and {CSS_LINK} values.

   ```
   $page->SetParameter("PAGE_TITLE",
   → "Another Day, Another Instance!");
   $page->SetParameter("CSS_LINK",
   → "style.css");
   ```

6. Set the {PAGE_CONTENT} parameter.

   ```
   $content = '<form action=
   → "handle_form.php" method="post">
   <table border="0" width="90%"
   → cellspacing="2" cellpadding="2"
   → align="center">
   ```

   ```
   <tr align="center" valign="top">
   <td colspan="2" align="center"
   → valign="top">Login Form</td>
   </tr>
   <tr align="center" valign="top">
   <td width="50%" align="right"
   → valign="top">User Name:</td>
   <td width="50%" align="left"
   → valign="top"><input type=text
   → name="username" size="20"
   → maxsize="20"></td>
   </tr>
   <tr align="center" valign="top">
   <td width="50%" align="right"
   → valign="top">Password:</td>
   <td width="50%" align="left"
   → valign="top"><input type=password
   → name="password" size="20"
   → maxsize="20"></td>
   </tr>
   <tr align="center" valign="top">
   <td colspan="2" align="center"
   → valign="top"><input type=submit
   → name=Submit value="Log in!"></td>
   </tr>
   </table>
   </form>';
   $page->SetParameter("PAGE_CONTENT",
   → $content);
   ```

   I've switched gears slightly here and set a dummy variable, $content, to the value of an HTML form. Then I registered this value as the PAGE_CONTENT variable. (Debatably, this is cheating since I've gone ahead and mixed HTML back in with the PHP, but it's a minor aspect of the script.)

7. Save this modified script as `instance3.php`.

continued on page 57

Script 2.6 Because the class itself has changed, the instantiation of the object also has some modifications, particularly how the class is created when it includes a constructor (line 6).

```
1    <?php
2    // This is a sample page that uses the HtmlTemplate class.
3
4    require_once "HtmlTemplate2.class"; // Include the class.
5
6    $page = new HtmlTemplate2 ("template2.inc"); // Create an instance.
7
8    $page->SetParameter("PAGE_TITLE", "Another Day, Another Instance!");
9    $page->SetParameter("CSS_LINK", "style.css");
10
11   $content = '<form action="handle_form.php" method="post">
12   <table border="0" width="90%" cellspacing="2" cellpadding="2" align="center">
13       <tr align="center" valign="top">
14           <td colspan="2" align="center" valign="top">Login Form</td>
15       </tr>
16       <tr align="center" valign="top">
17           <td width="50%" align="right" valign="top">User Name:</td>
18           <td width="50%" align="left" valign="top"><input type=text name="username" size="20"
             maxsize="20"></td>
19       </tr>
20       <tr align="center" valign="top">
21           <td width="50%" align="right" valign="top">Password:</td>
22           <td width="50%" align="left" valign="top"><input type=password name="password" size="20"
             maxsize="20"></td>
23       </tr>
24       <tr align="center" valign="top">
25           <td colspan="2" align="center" valign="top"><input type=submit name=Submit value="Log
             in!"></td>
26       </tr>
27   </table>
28   </form>';
29
30   $page->SetParameter("PAGE_CONTENT", $content);
31
32   $page->CreatePage(); // Send the page to the browser.
33   ?>
```

Script 2.7 This template has a couple more features than its predecessor (Script 2.2), including the ability to specify its style sheet.

```
script
1    <!DOCTYPE html PUBLIC "-//W3C//DTD XHTML 1.0 Transitional//EN"
2        "http://www.w3.org/TR/2000/REC-xhtml1-20000126/DTD/xhtml1-transitional.dtd">
3    <html xmlns="http://www.w3.org/1999/xhtml">
4    <head>
5        <title>{PAGE_TITLE}</title>
6    <link rel=stylesheet href="{CSS_LINK}" type="text/css">
7    </head>
8    <body bgcolor="gray" "left"margin="0" topmargin="0" marginwidth="0" marginheight="0">
9    <table border="0" width="100%" cellspacing="0" cellpadding="5" align="left">
10       <tr align="left" valign="top">
11           <td colspan="3" width="100%" align="center" valign="top" bgcolor="gray">
12               <!-- Top/Header HTML Code Goes Here -->
13               <br></br><h2>Welcome to this Site!</h2><br></br>
14           </td>
15       </tr>
16       <tr align="left" valign="top">
17           <td width="20%" align="center" valign="top" bgcolor="gray" nowrap="nowrap">
18               <!-- Left Navigation HTML Code Goes Here -->
19               <h5>Navigation: <br></h5>
20               <ul><li>Link 1</li><li>Link 2</li></ul>
21           </td>
22           <td width="60%" align="left" valign="top" bgcolor="white">
23               <!-- Page Content Goes here -->
24               {PAGE_CONTENT}
25           </td>
26           <td width="20%" align="center" valign="top" bgcolor="gray" nowrap="nowrap">
27               <!-- Right Navigation HTML Code Goes Here -->
28               <h5>New Items:<br></br></h5>
29               <ul><li>Item 1</li><li>Item 2</li><li>Item 3</li></ul>
30           </td>
31       </tr>
32       <tr align="left" valign="top">
33           <td colspan="3" width="100%" align="center" valign="top" bgcolor="gray">
34               <!-- Bottom/Footer HTML Code Goes Here -->
35               <small>Copyright 2001 by Larry E. Ullman</small>
36           </td>
37       </tr>
38   </table>
39   </body>
40   </html>
```

Script 2.8 This is a very simple style sheet, but with this system you can create multiple style sheets and change them on an object-by-object basis.

```
                    script
1    body {
2         line-height:150%;
3         font: Verdana, Helvetica, Geneva,
          Arial;
4         font-family:  sans-serif;
5         font-size: 12pt;
6    }
```

8. As a last step, create a simple style sheet, such as **Script 2.8**, called `style.css`. Upload it, along with `instance3.php` (Script 2.6), `template2.inc` (Script 2.7), and `HtmlTemplate2.class` (Script 2.5) to the same folder on your Web server, then run `instance3.php` in your Web browser (**Figures 2.6** and **2.7**).

✔ Tip

- How constructors behave is one of the key differences between PHP 3 and 4. Check the PHP manual for more information on this subject if you are transferring classes from version 3 to version 4.

Figure 2.6 This Web page was designed using a different template, although the class did not significantly change.

Figure 2.7 The source of OOP-generated Web pages in no way reveals to the end user how it was constructed.

Object Inheritance

One of the ways in which objects make programming faster is the ability to use one object to create a second object with expanded variables and functions. This is referred to as object inheritance.

Going back to the Human example, if the Human class has the attributes gender, height, weight, and birth date and it has the methods eating and sleeping, you could create another class called Adult that is an extension of Human. Along with the aforementioned variables and functions, an Adult object might also have the attribute of married and the method of working. As a rule, the child of a parent class inherits all the properties of the parent and then adds some new ones.

To make a child class from a parent, you use the `extends` statement. Assuming you have already defined the `ClassName` object, you can create a child class like so:

```
class ChildClass extends ClassName {
}
```

The class `ChildClass` will possess all the variables (attributes) and functions (methods) as its parent, `ClassName`. Now you can modify this class to adapt it to your specific needs without altering the original class. Ideally, once you've created a solid parent class, you will never need to modify it again and can use child classes to tailor the code to your individual requirements.

To try this, you'll take the `HtmlTemplate2` class and extend it with another method. The added function in the child will dynamically determine the links available by reading through the folders in a directory.

Script 2.9 The HtmlNavTemplate is a child of the HtmlTemplate2 class, inheriting all of the parent's attributes and methods while adding a function of its own.

```
1    <?php
2    // This class is an extension of the
     HtmlTemplate2 class. It adds the
     DetermineLinks() method, which searches a
     directory for subfolders.
3
4    class HtmlNavTemplate extends
     HtmlTemplate2 {
5
6        // No attributes necessary as
         $template, $html, and $parameters and
         automatically included.
7
8        function DetermineLinks () { // This
         function creates a list of links to
         subfolders.
9
10           $open = opendir ("."); // Open
             the current directory.
11           while ($file = readdir ($open)) {
             // Read through all the files.
12               if ((is_dir ($file)) and
                 (substr ($file, 0, 1) !=
                 ".")) { // If it's a
                 directory and it doesn't
                 begin with a decimal, make it
                 a link.
13                   $name = str_replace ("_",
                     " ", $file); // Replace
                     underscores with a space
                     to look nice.
14                   $nav_links .= "<A
                     HREF=\"$file/\">$name</A>
                     <BR>\n"; // Create the
                     list of links.
15               }
16           }
17           closedir ($open); // Close the
             directory.
18           return $nav_links; // Return the
             created list of links.
19       }
20   }
21   ?>
```

To extend a class:

1. Create a new PHP document in your text editor (**Script 2.9**).

   `<?php`

2. Begin by defining the new class.

   `class HtmlNavTemplate extends HtmlTemplate2 {`

   The recent, modified version of the HtmlTemplate2 class (Script 2.5) is what will be used as parent of this new class. The added feature is a navigation links generator so the class name has been slightly altered accordingly.

3. Write the new method for the class.

   ```
   function DetermineLinks () {
   $open = opendir (".");
   while ($file = readdir ($open)) {
   if ((is_dir ($file)) and (substr
   → ($file, 0, 1) != ".")) {
   $name = str_replace ("_", " ",
   → $file);
   $nav_links .= "<A HREF=\"$file/
   → \">$name</A><BR>\n";
   }
   }
   closedir ($open);
   → return $nav_links;
   }
   ```

   The DetermineLinks() function reads through all of the files in the current directory via the while loop. If a file is a directory that doesn't begin with a decimal point (Unix-based servers have directories called . and .., which refer to the current and previous directories, respectively), the file is a subfolder and will be used as a link.

   continues on next page

To turn the file into a link, any underscore is replaced with a space. Then a link to this file is concatenated to a dummy variable called $nav_links. Finally, the directory is closed and the generated $nav_links string will be returned by the function.

The benefit of this system is that your PHP script can dynamically determine the contents of the Web site when each topic is placed within its own folder.

4. Close the class and the PHP page.

```
}
?>
```

5. Save the script as HtmlNavTemplate.class.

Before creating an instance of this class, you'll create a new template that contains a {NAVIGATION_LINKS} parameter.

6. Open template2.inc (Script 2.7) in your text editor.

7. Replace line 20—<UL><LI>Link 1 </LI><LI>Link 2</LI></UL>—with (**Script 2.10**):

{NAVIGATION_LINKS}

8. Save the script as template3.inc.

Now you can create an object based on the HtmlNavTemplate class.

9. Create a new PHP document in your text editor (**Script 2.11**).

```
<?php
```

continues on page 62

Script 2.10 This template has only one alteration that allows for the navigation links section of the page to be settable.

```
script
1   <!DOCTYPE html PUBLIC "-//W3C//DTD XHTML
    1.0 Transitional//EN"
2       "http://www.w3.org/TR/2000/REC-
        xhtml1-20000126/DTD/xhtml1-
        transitional.dtd">
3   <html xmlns="http://www.w3.org/1999/
    xhtml">
4   <head>
5       <title>{PAGE_TITLE}</title>
6   <link rel=stylesheet href="{CSS_LINK}"
    type="text/css">
7   </head>
8   <body bgcolor="gray" leftmargin="0"
    topmargin="0" marginwidth="0"
    marginheight="0">
9   <table border="0" width="100%"
    cellspacing="0" cellpadding=5
    align="left">
10      <tr align="left" valign="top">
11          <td colspan="3" width="100%"
            align="center" valign="top"
            bgcolor="gray">
12              <!-- Top/Header HTML Code
                Goes Here -->
13              <br></br><h2>Welcome to this
                Site!</h2><br></br>
14          </td>
15      </tr>
16      <tr align="left" valign="top">
17          <td width="20%" align="center"
            valign="top" bgcolor="gray"
            nowrap="nowrap">
18              <!-- Left Navigation HTML
                Code Goes Here -->
19              <h5>Navigation:
                <br></br></h5>
20              {NAVIGATION_LINKS}
21          </td>
22          <td width="60%" align="left"
            valign="top" bgcolor=white>
```

(script continues on next page)

Script 2.10 *continued*

```
                        script
23              <!-- Page Content Goes
                here -->
24              {PAGE_CONTENT}
25          </td>
26          <td width="20%" align="center"
            valign="top" bgcolor="gray"
            nowrap="nowrap">
27              <!-- Left Navigation HTML
                Code Goes Here -->
28              <h5>New Items:<br></br></h5>
29              <ul><li>Item 1</li><li>Item
                2</li><li>Item 3</li></ul>
30          </td>
31      </tr>
32      <tr align="left" valign="top">
33          <td colspan="3" width="100%"
            align="center" valign="top"
            bgcolor="gray">
34              <!-- Bottom/Footer HTML Code
                Goes Here -->
35              <small>Copyright 2001 by
                Larry E. Ullman</small>
36          </td>
37      </tr>
38  </table>
39  </body>
40  </html>
```

Script 2.11 This object, based on the HtmlNavTemplate class (itself a child of the HtmlTemplate2 class), uses both classes' functions to generate the Web page (Figure 2.9).

```
                        script
1   <?php
2       // This is a sample page that uses
        the HtmlNavTemplate class.
3
4   require_once "HtmlTemplate2.class";
    // Include the parent class.
5   require_once "HtmlNavTemplate.class";
    // Include the child class.
6
7   $page = new HtmlNavTemplate
    ("template3.inc"); // Create an instance
    and identify the template to use for this
    application.
8
9   $page->SetParameter ("PAGE_TITLE",
    "Another Day, Another Instance!");
    // Set the page title.
10  $page->SetParameter ("CSS_LINK",
    "style.css"); // Set the main content.
11  $page->SetParameter ("PAGE_CONTENT",
    "<B>Please click on the links to the
    left.</B>"); // Set the main content.
12  $page->SetParameter ("NAVIGATION_LINKS",
    $page->DetermineLinks());
13
14  $page->CreatePage(); // Send the page to
    the browser.
15  ?>
```

OBJECT INHERITANCE

10. Include the two class files.

```
require_once "HtmlTemplate2.class";
require_once "HtmlNavTemplate.class";
```

Because `HtmlNavTemplate` is an extension of `HtmlTemplate2`, the file that creates an instance of `HtmlNavTemplate` must have access to both the parent and the child classes. Failure to include both will generate an error message like that in **Figure 2.8**.

11. Create the object.

```
$page = new HtmlNavTemplate
→ ("template3.inc");
```

12. Set the `PAGE_TITLE`, `CSS_LINK`, and `PAGE_CONTENT` values.

```
$page->SetParameter ("PAGE_TITLE",
→ "Another Day, Another Instance!");
$page->SetParameter ("CSS_LINK",
→ "style.css");
$page->SetParameter ("PAGE_CONTENT",
→  "<B>Please click on the links to
→ the left.</B>");
```

13. Set the `NAVIGATION_LINKS` value.

```
$page->SetParameter ("NAVIGATION_
→ LINKS", $page->DetermineLinks());
```

Since the `DetermineLinks()` function will return a string that represents all the appropriate links, a call to this method can be placed as the value argument for the `SetParameter()` function. The `SetParameter()` method, which is written into the parent class, can be used just as readily as the `DetermineLinks()` method from the child class.

14. Create the page and complete the PHP script.

```
$page->CreatePage();
?>
```

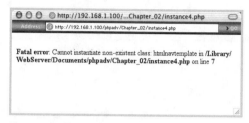

Figure 2.8 Failure to include all the necessary classes will generate error messages such as this one.

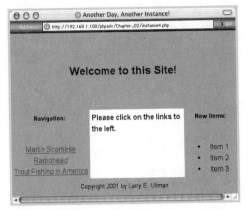

Figure 2.9 The child class used to create this page inherits its parent's properties and has its own ability to dynamically generate links.

Figure 2.10 The source of Figure 2.9 shows how the HTML of the dynamically scripted links is written.

15. Save this script as `instance4.php`. Upload it, along with `style.css` (Script 2.8), `template3.inc` (Script 2.10), `HtmlNavTemplate.class` (Script 2.9), and `HtmlTemplate2.class` (Script 2.5) to the same folder on your Web server, then run `instance4.php` in your Web browser (**Figures 2.9** and **2.10**). (You'll also want to create some folders within the directory for the `DetermineLinks()` function to read.)

✔ Tips

- You cannot create a child class that inherits fewer properties than its parent. In fact, if that was something you were hoping to do, then the design of the child and the parent should be switched. As classes are extended, they should contain more features, never fewer.

- You can create a function within a child that has the same name as a function within the parent. If you create an instance of the child and then call the function, the child's version of the function will be used. In this way, you can override a parent's method for a particular purpose.

- PHP does not support multiple levels of inheritance, so you could not make a Grandchild class that extends a Child class that in itself is an extension of the Parent class. This is one of the key differences between PHP's support for objects and true object-oriented languages, which don't have this limitation.

- You can determine the parent class of an object using the `get_parent_class ()` function, a companion to the `get_class()` function. For the `$page` object in Script 2.11, you could write:

```
echo get_class($page); // Prints
→ "HtmlNavTemplate"
```

```
echo get_parent_class($page); //
→ Prints "HtmlTemplate2"
```

OBJECT INHERITANCE

Using Class Functions Without Instances

There is a way in PHP 4 (not available in version 3) to make use of a class's method without having to create an instance of the class. This can be useful if there is a function you would like to use, but you do not need the whole class that the function is in. The syntax for doing this (assuming a class called ClassName contains a method named Method) is:

```
ClassName::Method();
```

As an example of this, you'll use the DetermineLinks() function to create a site map page, without creating an instance of HtmlNavTemplate—the class that defines the DetermineLinks() method.

To use the :: operator:

1. Create a new PHP document in your text editor (**Script 2.12**).

   ```
   <?php
   ```

2. Include the class pages.

   ```
   require_once "HtmlTemplate2.class";
   require_once "HtmlNavTemplate.class";
   ```

   To create the object or to use a class's method without creating an object, PHP will need access to the class definition.

3. Create an instance of the HtmlTemplate2 class.

   ```
   $page = new HtmlTemplate2
   → ("template2.inc");
   ```

   For this example, I'll use the simpler template2.inc for my HTML layout.

4. Set the PAGE_TITLE and CSS_LINK values.

   ```
   $page->SetParameter ("PAGE_TITLE",
   → "Welcome to My Life");
   $page->SetParameter ("CSS_LINK",
   → "style.css");
   ```

Script 2.12 The sitemap.php script makes use of the DetermineLinks() function, although it does not directly use the HtmlNavTemplate class.

```
1    <?php
2    // This is a sample page that uses the
     HtmlTemplate2 class.
3
4    require_once "HtmlTemplate2.class"; //
     Include the parent class.
5    require_once "HtmlNavTemplate.class"; //
     Include the child class.
6
7    $page = new HtmlTemplate2
     ("template2.inc");; // Create an instance
     and identify the template.
8
9    $page->SetParameter ("PAGE_TITLE",
     "Welcome to My Life"); // Set the page
     title.
10   $page->SetVParameter ("CSS_LINK",
     "style.css"); // Set the style sheet.
11   $page->SetParameter ("PAGE_CONTENT",
     "Site Map:<BR>" . HtmlNavTemplate::
     DetermineLinks() ); // Set the main
     content.
12
13   $page->CreatePage(); // Send the page to
     the browser.
14   ?>
```

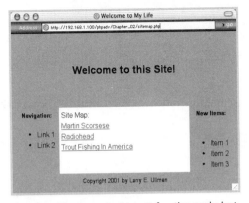

Figure 2.11 The DetermineLinks() function works just the same whether or not the class it's in is used.

Figure 2.12 Again, the source of the page reveals the work that the DetermineLinks() function did.

5. Set the PAGE_CONTENT value.

```
$page->SetParameter ("PAGE_CONTENT",
→ "Site Map:<BR>" . HtmlNavTemplate::
→ DetermineLinks());
```

The content for the site map page will be generated by the HtmlNavTemplate class's DetermineLinks() function. You can do this using :: even though this script does not contain an object based on the HtmlNavTemplate itself but the file which contains the HtmlNavTemplate class must be included into this one.

6. Print the page to your Web browser and close the PHP script.

```
$page->CreatePage();
?>
```

7. Save this script as sitemap.php. Upload it, along with style.css (Script 2.8), template2.inc (Script 2.7), HtmlNavTemplate.class (Script 2.9), and HtmlTemplate2.class (Script 2.5) to the same folder on your Web server, then run sitemap.php in your Web browser (**Figures 2.11** and **2.12**).

✔ Tip

- As an added level of debugging in your script, before using the ClassName::Method() code, you could check to make sure the specific function exists with method_exists().

```
if (method_exists (ClassName::
→ Method())) {…

if (method_exists (HtmlNavTemplate::
→ DetermineLinks())) {…
```

Serializing Objects

Because of the unique nature of objects, they cannot be as easily managed as strings or numbers. This makes them more difficult to store in a database, pass along to a second PHP script, or set as a cookie. To handle such issues, PHP has the `serialize()` function, which takes a variable and turns it into a more manageable version of itself. It works like so:

```
$variable = serialize ($object);
```

To return the serialized variable back into its standard form, use the `unserialize()` function.

```
$object = unserialize ($variable);
```

The only caveat to using these two functions with objects is that the page that unserializes the variable must have access to the class definitions.

As a crude analogy, say you had created a really cool toy with your childhood Erector set, built according to plans. Now you want to show this toy to your friend Scott, but you can't carry it as is on your bicycle. If you dismantle the toy, you can carry it more easily, and as long as you bring along the plans to Scott's house, you'll be able to reconstruct it once you are there. It's a trite analogy but I hope you get the drift of what the serialization process is all about.

I'll incorporate the concept of serialization into the existing OOP information to make a quick and dirty application wherein users can set their HTML layout preferences. This information will be stored as a cookie in their browser so that every page they visit within the domain will follow their preferences. This process will require a new template and a more complicated instance but will still use the `HtmlNavTemplate` class.

__sleep and __wakeup

Two of the magic functions—`__sleep` and `__wakeup`—come into play when serializing objects. When `serialize()` is applied to an object, PHP will look for a `__sleep` function in your class. If present, that function will be executed prior to serialization.

Conversely, when an object is unserialized, PHP looks for a `__wakeup` function. Such a function in your class could help reconstruct the object or reconnect to the database.

To create a template:

1. Create a new HTML document in your text editor (**Script 2.13**).

```
<!DOCTYPE html PUBLIC "-//W3C//DTD
→ XHTML 1.0 Transitional//EN"
"http://www.w3.org/TR/2000/
→ REC-xhtml1-20000126/DTD/xhtml1-
→ transitional.dtd">
```

2. Code for the standard HTML head.

```
<html xmlns="http://www.w3.org/
→ 1999/xhtml">
<head>
<title>{PAGE_TITLE}</title>
<link rel=stylesheet href=
→ "{CSS_LINK}" type="text/css">
</head>
```

The template is still using only the PAGE_TITLE and CSS_LINK in the head, but it could also have JavaScript, META tags, and more.

3. Code for the body, with flexible background and text colors.

```
<body bgcolor="{BG_COLOR}"
→ text="{TEXT_COLOR}" leftmargin="0"
→ topmargin="0" marginwidth="0"
→ marginheight="0">
```

Since you'll want users to be able to set their preferred background color and text color, these two values will be represented by {BG_COLOR} and {TEXT_COLOR}. Practically every parameter in a Web page could be determined by the user, if you want.

4. Code a table with a flexible table width, table background colors, navigation links, and page content.

```
<table border="0" width="
→ {TABLE_WIDTH}%" cellspacing="0"
→ cellpadding="5" align="left">
<tr align="left" valign="top">
<td colspan="3" width="100%"
→ align="center" valign="top"
→ bgcolor="{BG_COLOR}">
```

```
<!-- Top/Header HTML Code Goes
→ Here -->
<br></br><h2>Welcome to Your
→ Personalized Home Page!</h2>
→ <br></br>
</td>
</tr>
<tr align="left" valign="top">
<td width="20%" align="center"
→ valign="top" bgcolor="{BG_COLOR}"
→ nowrap="nowrap">
<!-- Left Navigation HTML Code Goes
→ Here -->
<h5>Navigation:<br></br></h5>
{NAVIGATION_LINKS}
</td>
<td width="60%" align="left"
→ valign="top" bgcolor=white>
<!-- Page Content Goes here -->
{PAGE_CONTENT}
</td>
<td width="20%" align="center"
→ valign="top" bgcolor="{BG_COLOR}"
→ nowrap="nowrap">
<!-- Left Navigation HTML Code Goes
→ Here -->
<h5>New Items:<br></br></h5>
<ul><li>Item 1</li><li>Item
→ 2</li><li>Item 3</li></ul>
</td>
</tr>
<tr align="left" valign="top">
<td colspan="3" width="100%"
→ align="center" valign="top"
→ bgcolor="{BG_COLOR}">
<!-- Bottom/Footer HTML Code Goes
→ Here -->
<small>Copyright 2001 by Larry E.
→ Ullman</small>
</td>
</tr>
</table>
```

continues on page 69

Script 2.13 This template includes several parameters that can be set by an object, based on user preferences.

```
1    <!DOCTYPE html PUBLIC "-//W3C//DTD XHTML 1.0 Transitional//EN"
2        "http://www.w3.org/TR/2000/
         REC-xhtml1-20000126/DTD/xhtml1-transitional.dtd">
3    <html xmlns="http://www.w3.org/1999/
     xhtml">
4    <head>
5        <title>{PAGE_TITLE}</title>
6    <link rel=stylesheet href="{CSS_LINK}" type="text/css">
7    </head>
8    <body bgcolor="{BG_COLOR}" text="{TEXT_COLOR}" leftmargin="0" topmargin="0" marginwidth="0"
     marginheight="0">
9    <table border="0" width="{TABLE_WIDTH}%" cellspacing="0" cellpadding="5" align="left">
10       <tr align="left" valign="top">
11       <td colspan="3" width="100%" align="center" valign="top" bgcolor="{BG_COLOR}">
12           <!-- Top/Header HTML Code Goes Here -->
13           <br></br><h2>Welcome to Your Personalized Home Page!</h2><br></br>
14       </td>
15       </tr>
16       <tr align="left" valign="top">
17       <td width="20%" align="center" valign="top" bgcolor="{BG_COLOR}" nowrap="nowrap">
18       <!-- Left Navigation HTML Code Goes Here -->
19           <h5>Navigation:<br></br></h5>
20           {NAVIGATION_LINKS}
21       </td>
22       <td width="60%" align="left" valign="top" bgcolor=white>
23           <!-- Page Content Goes here -->
24           {PAGE_CONTENT}
25       </td>
26       <td width="20%" align="center" valign="top" bgcolor="{BG_COLOR}" nowrap="nowrap">
27           <!-- Left Navigation HTML Code Goes Here -->
28           <h5>New Items:<br></br></h5>
29           <ul><li>Item 1</li><li>Item 2</li><li>Item 3</li></ul>
30       </td>
31       </tr>
32       <tr align="left" valign="top">
33       <td colspan="3" width="100%" align="center" valign="top" bgcolor="{BG_COLOR}">
34           <!-- Bottom/Footer HTML Code Goes Here -->
35           <small>Copyright 2001 by Larry E. Ullman</small>
36       </td>
37       </tr>
38   </table>
39   </body>
40   </html>
```

Not to belabor the point, but considering the flexibility of this system, it is up to you to determine which HTML parameters the user can set.

5. Close the HTML page.

```
</body>
</html>
```

6. Save the page as `template4.inc`.

Now you'll write the instance that uses this template. This instance will be more complicated than its predecessors because it will do three things:

◆ Upon first coming to the page, it will make a form where the users can set their parameters.

◆ Upon submission of the form, it will set the cookie that stores the parameters.

◆ If, when coming to the page, the cookie exists, it will automatically display the page.

7. Start a new PHP document in your text editor (**Script 2.14**).

```
<?php
```

8. Include the two required class pages.

```
require_once "HtmlTemplate2.class";
require_once "HtmlNavTemplate.class";
```

9. Begin the main conditional.

```
if ($HTTP_COOKIE_VARS['html_object']) {
```

The first condition is to check for the existence of a cookie called `$html_object`. If this cookie exists already, there's no need to either set the cookie or display the form.

10. Unserialize the cookie to re-create the object, then print the Web page.

```
$page = unserialize
→ ($HTTP_COOKIE_VARS['html_object']);
$page->CreatePage();
```

The `$page variable`, heretofore created in a script as a new instance of an object, will be derived by unserializing the serialized, cookie-stored version of the object. Once this object has been remade, simply call the `CreatePage()` method to generate the Web page.

11. Create the second part of the main conditional.

```
} elseif ($HTTP_POST_VARS['submit']) {
```

If the page has been submitted, process the form.

12. Create a new instance of the object and assign the values based on the form submission.

```
$page = new HtmlNavTemplate
→ ("template4.inc");
$page->SetParameter
→ ("PAGE_TITLE", $page_title);
$page->SetParameter
→ ("CSS_LINK", "style.css");
$page->SetParameter
→ ("BG_COLOR", $bg_color);
$page->SetParameter
→ ("TEXT_COLOR", $text_color);
$page->SetParameter ("TABLE_WIDTH",
→ $table_width);
$page->SetParameter
→ ("NAVIGATION_LINKS",
→ $page->DetermineLinks());
$page->SetParameter
→ ("PAGE_CONTENT", "Here is your
→ custom page.");
```

continues on page 72

Script 2.14 Although this is the most complicated script in this chapter because of its three-part behavior, each individual creation of an object is straightforward.

```
                                      script
1    <?php
2    // This is a page that uses object serialization.
3
4    require_once "HtmlTemplate2.class"; // Include the class.
5    require_once "HtmlNavTemplate.class"; // Include the class.
6
7    if ($HTTP_COOKIE_VARS['html_object']) {
8
9        $page = unserialize ($HTTP_COOKIE_VARS['html_object']);
10
11       $page->CreatePage();
12
13   } elseif ($HTTP_POST_VARS['submit']) {
14
15       $page = new HtmlNavTemplate ("template4.inc"); // Create an instance and identify the
         template to use for this application.
16
17       $page->SetParameter ("PAGE_TITLE", $page_title); // Set the page title.
18       $page->SetParameter ("CSS_LINK", "style.css"); // Set the style sheet.
19       $page->SetParameter ("BG_COLOR", $bg_color); // Set the background color.
20       $page->SetParameter ("TEXT_COLOR", $text_color); // Set the text color.
21       $page->SetParameter ("TABLE_WIDTH", $table_width); // Set the table width.
22       $page->SetParameter ("NAVIGATION_LINKS", $page->DetermineLinks());
23       $page->SetParameter ("PAGE_CONTENT", "Here is your custom page."); // Set the main content.
24
25       setcookie ("html_object", serialize ($page), time() + 100000, "", "", 0);
26
27       $page->CreatePage();
28
29   } else {
30
31       $page = new HtmlNavTemplate ("template4.inc"); // Create an instance and identify the
         template to use for this application.
32
33       $page->SetParameter ("PAGE_TITLE", "Set Your Preferences!"); // Set the page title.
34       $page->SetParameter ("CSS_LINK", "style.css"); // Set the style sheet.
35       $page->SetParameter ("BG_COLOR", "WHITE"); // Set the background color.
36       $page->SetParameter ("TEXT_COLOR", "BLACK"); // Set the text color.
37       $page->SetParameter ("TABLE_WIDTH", "100"); // Set the table width.
38       $page->SetParameter ("NAVIGATION_LINKS", $page->DetermineLinks());
39
40       $content = '<form action="instance5.php" method=post>
41   <table border=0 width="90%" cellspacing="2" cellpadding="2" align="center">
42       <tr align="center" valign="top">
```

(script continues on next page)

Script 2.14 *continued*

```
         script
43              <td colspan="2" align="center" valign="top">Set Your HTML Layout Preferences</td>
44          </tr>
45          <tr align="center" valign="top">
46              <td width="50%" align="right" valign="top">Page Title:</td>
47              <td width="50%" align="left" valign="top"><input type="text" name="page_title"
                size="20" maxsize="50"></td>
48          </tr>
49          <tr align="center" valign="top">
50              <td width="50%" align="right" valign="top">Background Color:</td>
51              <td width="50%" align="left" valign="top">
52                  <select name="bg_color">
53                  <option value="white">WHITE</option>
54                  <option value="black">BLACK</option>
55                  <option value="blue">BLUE</option>
56                  <option value="red">RED</option>
57                  <option value="green">GREEN</option>
58                  </select></td>
59          </tr>
60          <tr align="center" valign="top">
61              <td width="50%" align="right" valign="top">Text Color:</td>
62              <td width="50%" align="left" valign="top">
63                  <select name="text_color">
64                  <option value="white">WHITE</option>
65                  <option value="black">BLACK</option>
66                  <option value="blue">BLUE</option>
67                  <option value="red">RED</option>
68                  <option value="green">GREEN</option>
69                  </select></td>
70          </tr>
71          <tr align="center" valign="top">
72              <td width="50%" align="right" valign="top">Table Width (0-100):</td>
73              <td width="50%" align="left" valign="top"><input type="text" name="table_width"
                size="3" maxsize="3"></td>
74          </tr>
75          <tr align="center" valign="top">
76              <td colspan="2" align="center" valign="top"><input type="submit" name="submit"
                value="Set My Preferences"></td>
77          </tr>
78      </table>
79      </form>';
80
81      $page->SetParameter ("PAGE_CONTENT", $content); // Set the main content.
82
83      $page->CreatePage(); // Send the page to the browser.
84  }
85  ?>
```

SERIALIZING OBJECTS

The various parameters in the template—{BG_COLOR}, {TEXT_COLOR}, etc.—will be assigned to the values coming in from the HTML form.

13. Store the serialized object in a cookie, then create the Web page.

```
setcookie ("html_object",
→ serialize ($page), time() +
→ 100000, "", "", 0);
$page->CreatePage();
```

The $html_object cookie will have a value equal to the serialized version of the $page object. The $page object has already been completely defined except for creating the page itself, the last step. Thus, when subsequent pages access this cookie, all they need to do is unserialize the cookie and run the CreatePage() function (as you see in the first part of this conditional).

14. Conclude the conditional by starting a default object.

```
} else {
$page = new HtmlNavTemplate
→ ("template4.inc");
$page->SetParameter
→ ("PAGE_TITLE", "Set Your
→ Preferences!");
$page->SetParameter ("CSS_LINK",
→ "style.css");
$page->SetParameter ("BG_COLOR",
→ "WHITE");
$page->SetParameter
→ ("TEXT_COLOR", "BLACK");
$page->SetParameter
→ ("TABLE_WIDTH", "100");
$page->SetParameter
→ ("NAVIGATION_LINKS", $page->
→ DetermineLinks());
```

If the user has not submitted the form nor do they already have the $html_object cookie set, a generic $page object will be created with default values. The content of this page will be the HTML form.

15. Create the HTML form.

```
$content = '<form
→ action="instance5.php" method=post>
<table border=0 width="90%"
→ cellspacing="2" cellpadding="2"
→ align="center">
<tr align="center" valign="top">
<td colspan="2" align="center"
→ valign="top">Set Your HTML Layout
→ Preferences</td>
</tr>
<tr align="center" valign="top">
<td width="50%" align="right"
→ valign="top">Page Title:</td>
<td width="50%" align="left"
→ valign="top"><input type="text"
→ name="page_title" size="20"
→ maxsize="50"></td>
</tr>
<tr align="center" valign="top">
<td width="50%" align="right"
→ valign="top">Background
→ Color:</td>
<td width="50%" align="left"
→ valign="top">
<select name="bg_color">
<option value="white">WHITE</option>
<option value="black">BLACK</option>
<option value="blue">BLUE</option>
<option value="red">RED</option>
<option value="green">GREEN</option>
</select></td>
</tr>
```

```
<tr align="center" valign="top">
<td width="50%" align="right"
→ valign="top">Text Color:</td>
<td width="50%" align="left"
→ valign="top">
<select name="text_color">
<option value="white">WHITE</option>
<option value="black">BLACK</option>
<option value="blue">BLUE</option>
<option value="red">RED</option>
<option value="green">GREEN</option>
</select></td>
</tr>
<tr align="center" valign="top">
<td width="50%" align="right"
→ valign="top">Table Width
→ (0-100):</td>
<td width="50%" align="left"
→ valign="top"><input type="text"
→ name="table_width" size="3"
→ maxsize="3"></td>
</tr>
<tr align="center" valign="top">
<td colspan="2" align="center"
→ valign="top"><input type="submit"
→ name="submit" value="Set My
→ Preferences"></td>
</tr>
</table>
</form>';
```

```
$page->SetParameter
→ ("PAGE_CONTENT", $content);
```

The HTML form should match up so
that it allows the user to set all the flexible parameters you have established in
your template.

16. Send the default page to the Web browser, complete the conditional, and finish the PHP page.

```
    $page->CreatePage();
}
?>
```

17. Save this script as instance5.php. Upload it, along with style.css (Script 2.8), template4.inc (Script 2.13), HtmlNavTemplate.class (Script 2.9), and HtmlTemplate2.class (Script 2.5) to the same folder on your Web server, then run instance5.php in your Web browser (**Figures 2.13**, **2.14**, **2.15** and **2.16**).

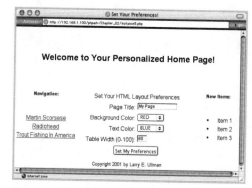

Figure 2.13 The object, upon first arriving at the Web page, will display a form for the user to fill out.

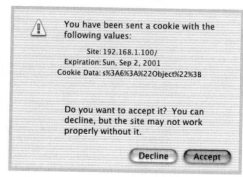

Figure 2.14 The cookie, which gets sent to the user's browser, contains the serialized version of the object. The *Cookie Data* field shows exactly what the serialized object looks like.

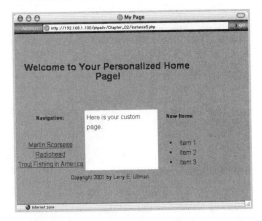

Figure 2.15 Once the form has been filled out, or when the user comes back to the page, the Web page will be generated from an unserialized version of the cookie that stored their preferences.

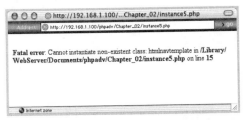

Figure 2.16 If the PHP script does not have access to the original class definition when it attempts to unserialize the object, it will throw out this error message.

✔ Tips

■ One of the benefits of using sessions, which are new to PHP 4 and will be discussed in Chapter 5, *Developing Web Applications*, is that they automatically serialize and unserialize objects.

■ Because PHP requires access to the class definition when unserializing an object, you will be better off if you make your class files available to every PHP page within a Web application to avoid potential complications.

■ Yet another difference between PHP 3 and PHP 4 and how they treat objects arises with serialization. While you can serialize an object with either version of PHP, PHP 3 will lose all of the object's functions in the translation.

■ Depending upon the operating system you are using and how PHP is configured, you may need to use the `urlencode` and `urldecode` functions before and after serialization in order for the object to be successfully passed.

Destroying Objects

True object-oriented programming languages include the ability to destroy an instance of an object using destructors, the opposite of a constructor. Whereas a constructor is immediately called upon creation of an object, a destructor would be automatically called when an object is destroyed. PHP does not have this capability built-in, but you can replicate it to a degree.

Should you want to free up the resources used by an object that's no longer necessary, start by deleting the value of the instance using the unset() function.

```
$object = new ClassName;
unset ($object);
```

As a simple example of destroying an object, I'll modify the instance5.php script.

To destroy an object:

1. Open instance5.php (Script 2.14) in your text editor.

2. Add a line before the closing PHP tag that deletes the created object (**Script 2.15**, line 85).

   ```
   unset ($page);
   ```

   Make sure you place this code after the entire conditional so it will delete the $page variable regardless of where it was originally created.

3. Save this script and upload it, along with style.css (Script 2.8), template4.inc (Script 2.13), HtmlNavTemplate.class (Script 2.9), and HtmlTemplate2.class (Script 2.5) to the same folder on your Web server, then run instance5.php in your Web browser again (**Figure 2.17**).

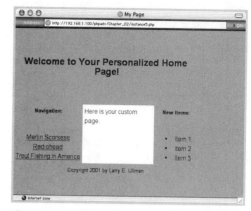

Figure 2.17 While it won't make any difference as to what your user sees, deleting your objects frees up resources on the server.

✔ Tips

■ You also create a destructor-like method with register_shutdown_function(). This function takes a function as an argument and executes that function when a script is finished processing.

■ If you wanted, you could add a link to this page that deletes the object and the cookie, allowing users to reset their preferences.

Script 2.15 The one-line addition to the script now deletes the existing object, thus clearing up the resources it uses, once the Web page has been created.

```
script

1    <?php
2    // This is a page that uses object serialization.
3
4    require_once "HtmlTemplate2.class"; // Include the class.
5    require_once "HtmlNavTemplate.class"; // Include the class.
6
7    if ($HTTP_COOKIE_VARS['html_object']) {
8
9        $page = unserialize ($HTTP_COOKIE_VARS['html_object']);
10
11       $page->CreatePage();
12
13   } elseif ($HTTP_POST_VARS['submit']) {
14
15       $page = new HtmlNavTemplate ("template4.inc"); // Create an instance and identify the
         template to use for this application.
16
17       $page->SetParameter ("PAGE_TITLE", $page_title); // Set the page title.
18       $page->SetParameter ("CSS_LINK", "style.css"); // Set the style sheet.
19       $page->SetParameter ("BG_COLOR", $bg_color); // Set the background color.
20       $page->SetParameter ("TEXT_COLOR", $text_color); // Set the text color.
21       $page->SetParameter ("TABLE_WIDTH", $table_width); // Set the table width.
22       $page->SetParameter ("NAVIGATION_LINKS", $page->DetermineLinks());
23       $page->SetParameter ("PAGE_CONTENT", "Here is your custom page."); // Set the main content.
24
25       setcookie ("html_object", serialize ($page), time() + 100000, "", "", 0);
26
27       $page->CreatePage();
28
29   } else {
30
31       $page = new HtmlNavTemplate ("template4.inc"); // Create an instance and identify the
         template to use for this application.
32
33       $page->SetParameter ("PAGE_TITLE", "Set Your Preferences!"); // Set the page title.
34       $page->SetParameter ("CSS_LINK", "style.css"); // Set the style sheet.
35       $page->SetParameter ("BG_COLOR", "WHITE"); // Set the background color.
36       $page->SetParameter ("TEXT_COLOR", "BLACK"); // Set the text color.
37       $page->SetParameter ("TABLE_WIDTH", "100"); // Set the table width.
38       $page->SetParameter ("NAVIGATION_LINKS", $page->DetermineLinks());
39
40       $content = '<form action="instance5.php" method=post>
41       <table border=0 width="90%" cellspacing="2" cellpadding="2" align="center">
42           <tr align="center" valign="top">
43               <td colspan="2" align="center" valign="top">Set Your HTML Layout Preferences</td>
44           </tr>
```

(script continues on next page)

Script 2.15 *continued*

```
script
45            <tr align="center" valign="top">
46                <td width="50%" align="right" valign="top">Page Title:</td>
47                <td width="50%" align="left" valign="top"><input type="text" name="page_title"
                  size="20" maxsize="50"></td>
48            </tr>
49            <tr align="center" valign="top">
50                <td width="50%" align="right" valign="top">Background Color:</td>
51                <td width="50%" align="left" valign="top">
52                    <select name="bg_color">
53                    <option value="white">WHITE</option>
54                    <option value="black">BLACK</option>
55                    <option value="blue">BLUE</option>
56                    <option value="red">RED</option>
57                    <option value="green">GREEN</option>
58                    </select></td>
59            </tr>
60            <tr align="center" valign="top">
61                <td width="50%" align="right" valign="top">Text Color:</td>
62                <td width="50%" align="left" valign="top">
63                    <select name="text_color">
64                    <option value="white">WHITE</option>
65                    <option value="black">BLACK</option>
66                    <option value="blue">BLUE</option>
67                    <option value="red">RED</option>
68                    <option value="green">GREEN</option>
69                    </select></td>
70            </tr>
71            <tr align="center" valign="top">
72                <td width="50%" align="right" valign="top">Table Width (0-100):</td>
73                <td width="50%" align="left" valign="top"><input type="text" name="table_width"
                  size="3" maxsize="3"></td>
74            </tr>
75            <tr align="center" valign="top">
76                <td colspan="2" align="center" valign="top"><input type="submit" name="submit"
                  value="Set My Preferences"></td>
77            </tr>
78        </table>
79        </form>';
80
81        $page->SetParameter ("PAGE_CONTENT", $content); // Set the main content.
82
83        $page->CreatePage(); // Send the page to the browser.
84    }
85    unset ($page);
86    ?>
```

DESTROYING OBJECTS

DATABASES

The need for databases is increasing as programmers, clients, and users in general demand more and more from Web sites. Most of the really interesting things you'll want to do online will involve a database, even if it is just a flat-file database like the one used in the online sports pool application in Chapter 1. Databases range from the free or inexpensive mSQL, MySQL, and PostgreSQL to the very costly Oracle, although these applications may not be as different in terms of capability, performance, and durability as they are in price. Normally, the decision as to what database application you use is not made by the programmer but rather by the budget, the Web hosting company, the operating system, or the client. Fortunately, PHP can directly interface with every widely available database.

Creating and managing databases used to be a specialized field, mostly because of the complex nature of database structures and how databases are used. But today, with the easy use and widespread availability of, in particular, MySQL and PostgreSQL, Web developers will frequently create and maintain the database. The downside of this trend is that a programmer's knowledge base and inclinations will normally be toward the API (application program interface) to the database and not to the database construction itself. Consequently, a lot of Web applications are misusing a database, or just not using it to its full potential. This chapter will take a two-pronged approach to databases: discussion of some database theories you may not be familiar with (such as normalization) and demonstration of how PHP interacts with a database, with the focus being on SQL and MySQL's abilities.

Before I begin, a few words about the terminology involved. Technically, what is normally called a database is an application that manages structures of documents that are in fact the databases. The application is a DBMS, or Database Management System, or, more popularly today, an RDBMS, a Relational Database Management System. (There are also OODBMS, Object-Oriented Database Management Systems, which will not be covered here.) People commonly refer to the application itself as a database, which is akin to calling Microsoft Excel a spreadsheet, when in fact Excel is an application with which you can manipulate spreadsheets. In the same way, PostgreSQL is an application, namely an RDBMS, with which you can manipulate databases. For the sake of clarity in this chapter I will use DBMS, RDBMS, MySQL, PostgreSQL, or database application to refer to the program itself and the term database to refer to the primary document.

What DBMS you end up using can vary to some degree. MySQL is gaining in popularity to almost the same level as (and possibly because of) PHP, and it has won numerous awards. It's generally free (not necessarily, so be sure to check the MySQL license), well developed and maintained, reliable, and fairly full-featured. Mini SQL (aka, mSQL), lacks some of the features of MySQL and is less involved in Web applications anymore, although it is still being improved upon and promoted. (It is not unusual for a Web host to offer both mSQL and MySQL, and it's only fair to point out that MySQL was essentially created because of mSQL). The third common DBMS for the Unix family of servers is PostgreSQL, which does not get quite the attention that MySQL does but is as solid of a product.

If your Web server is running a Microsoft operating system (preferably Windows 2000 rather or XP than 98 or Me), you will normally come across either Microsoft Access or SQL Server. On the Macintosh platform, FileMaker Pro is considered to be a popular and robust choice. If you are running Mac OS X, you can now use any of the Unix-based databases application. In reality, you will not tend to use either FileMaker Pro or Access as the back-end for a Web application because their design and features (both include a graphical user interface, or GUI, for directly working with them) are more inclined toward desktop rather than server use. This is not to say that it doesn't happen, but it is not ideal.

In this chapter, the primary example for working with databases will be a book collection, but you could easily modify it for music or whatever. I'll start with a discussion of how to create the database on paper using normalization techniques. Then, you'll learn a few useful database techniques such as generating query results pages. Summarizing the information herein, Appendix B, Databases, constitutes a solid compendium for most of your database questions. The treatment of the chapter's subject assumes that you have at least a cursory knowledge of databases (you should already understand how to log in at a bare minimum), as well as access to one.

Database Design and Normalization

Database design and use should—although it frequently does not—begin with a pad of paper and a writing implement. The computer and the DBMS itself shouldn't be involved until a couple of steps into the whole process. (The same is also true for programming—sketching out how a site interacts before you type your first `<?php` can save you hours of alteration time later.) With databases, planning ahead may be the difference between whether it works reliably or not and, at the very least, affects the usability, performance, and scalability of the end product.

To begin the process of creating a database you need to sit down with the people involved—the client perhaps—and determine all the needs of the database, both in terms of data to be stored and how that data is to be accessed. When working with databases, data integrity is key, and the fewer alterations you have to make later, the better off you'll be.

For the purposes of the example here, I'll be creating a database that stores information about the books I own. You could turn this into an inventory system or use it as the foundation for a Web application. The primary thing I'll be documenting are the books themselves (one entry for every copy of every book), taking note of the following information:

- Title

- Author

- Format (e.g., hardcover or paperback)

- Call number (call me crazy but I organize my nonfiction books by LCCN, Library of Congress Call Number)

- Whether the book is signed or not

Pronunciation

Every book has a discussion of how to correctly pronounce these terms, and I would be remiss if I did not do the same. It may seem like a trite point how these terms are pronounced, but PostgreSQL Inc. has even gone so far as to include an audio file with the proper pronunciation. The primary mispronunciation is that many folks will say *sequel* for SQL, which is technically wrong. For the record, here is how you should say the following:

SQL *Ess Que Ell*

MySQL *My Ess Que Ell*

mSQL *Mini Ess Que Ell*

PostgreSQL *Post Gres Que Ell*

Finally, I think I ought to have a generic text field to store other information such as what the inscription is, if applicable. If I wanted to be really formal, I could include the ISBN (International Standardized Book Number), publisher, publication date, edition, genre, and much, much more. With this information, I could create a spreadsheet-like layout similar to **Table 3.1**.

Database normalization was developed in 1970 by an IBM researcher named E.F. Codd. He created this series of steps to optimize a database by ridding it of redundant data and ensuring that the information is presented in the best possible manner. To normalize this database, I'll run it through three normal forms. Each normal form spells out rules to help you structure your database. But first, two database concepts—unique identifiers and table relationships—need to be explained.

Table 3.1 The linear table layout works just fine for a spreadsheet but is restrictive and problematic as a database.

Larry's Books

TITLE	AUTHOR	FORMAT	CALL NUMBER	SIGNED?	NOTES
About a Boy	Nick Hornby	Hardcover	n/a	no	
Crime and Punishment	Fyodor Dostovsky	Mass Market	n/a	no	
High Fidelity	Nick Hornby	Quality Paperback	n/a	no	
Naked Pictures of Famous People	Jon Stewart	Quality Paperback	PN6162 .S845 1998	no	
Notes from Underground	Fyodor Dostovsky	Mass Market	n/a	no	
Song of Solomon	Toni Morrison	Hardcover	n/a	yes	Inscribed 'To Graham, Love Toni'
Tibetan Book of Living and Dying	Sogyal Rinpoche	Quality Paperback	BQ7640 .S64 1992	no	
Winesburg, Ohio	Sherwood Anderson	Quality Paperback	n/a	no	Norton Critical Edition

Unique identifier

Unique identifiers are at the very heart of database normalization. Each table in a database should have one column that acts as an identifier for that table. The requisites for a unique identifier are:

◆ Unique value for each row in the table

◆ Must always have a value (it can never be *NULL*)

◆ The value of the key will never change

Creating a unique identifier with those three attributes gives the database a frame of reference for accessing and modifying the data therein. One common real-world example of a unique identifier is Social Security numbers. Every U.S. citizen is assigned a unique Social Security number that will not change throughout his or her life. The person can age, change hair color, get married, change his or her name, or move and this number will always accurately refer to that person. Before I go any further, I'll add a unique identifier to my table (**Table 3.2**).

Table 3.2 The *Book ID* field will act as a key for the table. Each book entered will get its own unique ID as a reference point.

Larry's Books

Book ID	Title	Author	Format	Call Number	Signed?	Notes
1	About a Boy	Nick Hornby	Hardcover	n/a	no	
2	Crime and Punishment	Fyodor Dostovsky	Mass Market	n/a	no	
3	High Fidelity	Nick Hornby	Quality Paperback	n/a	no	
4	Naked Pictures of Famous People	Jon Stewart	Quality Paperback	PN6162 .S845 1998	no	
5	Notes from Underground	Fyodor Dostovsky	Mass Market	n/a	no	
6	Song of Solomon	Toni Morrison	Hardcover	n/a	yes	Inscribed 'To Graham, Love Toni'
7	Tibetan Book of Living and Dying	Sogyal Rinpoche	Quality Paperback	BQ7640 .S64 1992	no	
8	Winesburg, Ohio	Sherwood Anderson	Quality Paperback	n/a	no	Norton Critical Edition

Notice that the Book ID is irrelevant to the book itself except that it will act as a way for the database to refer to that particular book. In fact, looking at the guidelines for an identifier, you'll see that creating a dummy column is almost always the way to go.

Database designers frequently get tripped up by using an identifier that is not in fact unique. For example, although books the world over already use a unique identifier—their ISBN, I cannot use that as my identifier here. Why? Because I am tracking the copies of books I physically have and I possess multiple copies of some of the books. If I used the ISBN as the unique identifier, then I would not be able to reflect the fact that I own two copies of Zora Neale Hurston's *Their Eyes Were Watching God*—same publisher, same format, same ISBN. Therefore, I manufacture my own identification number and I can—should I choose to do so—use the ISBN as one of the attributes of that Book ID.

Stemming from unique identifiers are *keys*. There are different types of keys in a table that serve different purposes. The unique identifier, which will be the main key—like Book ID—is called the *primary key*. A primary key in one table that relates to a column in another table, which you'll see soon, creates a foreign key.

Relationships between tables

Relational databases work because multiple tables are created that relate to each other in specific ways (although to be precise, the *Relational* in RDBMS refers to the tables themselves, which are technically called *relations*). This is true for MySQL, Oracle, Access, and PostgreSQL. A relationship between two tables can be either *one-to-one*, *one-to-many*, or *many-to-many*.

The relationship is one-to-one if one and only one item in Table A applies to one and only one item in Table B (e.g., each U.S. citizen has only one Social Security number and each Social Security number applies to only one U.S. citizen; no citizen can have two Social Security numbers and no Social Security number can refer to two citizens).

A relationship is one-to-many if one item in Table A can apply to multiple items in Table B. The terms *female* and *male* will apply to many people, but each person can be only one or the other. A one-to-many relationship is the most common one between tables in databases.

Finally, a relationship is many-to-many if multiple items in Table A can apply to multiple items in Table B. For example, a car can have multiple tires and multiple cars can have the same (brand) of tires.

Relationships, unique identifiers, and keys work together in that a key in one table will normally relate to a field in another. Once you grasp the basics of unique identifiers and relationships, you can begin to normalize your database.

First Normal Form

For a database to be in First Normal Form (1NF), each column must contain only one value. A table containing one field for an address would not be in 1NF because it stores the street address, city, state, ZIP code, and possibly country—five different bits of information in one field. In Table 3.2, *Author* is the only problematic field because it records both the author's first and last names. To turn Larry's Books into a 1NF-compliant database, I'll separate the *Author* field into two: *First Name* and *Last Name* (I could also make a middle name field if I wanted). **Table 3.3** shows the new layout.

DATABASE DESIGN AND NORMALIZATION

Second Normal Form

In simplest terms, for a database to be in 2NF, the database must already be in 1NF (you must normalize in order), and every column in a table that is not a key has to relate only to the primary key. This is a complicated rule to explain so it's best to practice with the working example.

Looking at Larry's Books, two rows have the same author of *Nick Hornby* and another two have the same author of *Fyodor Doestoyevsky* (misspelled in the table). Multiple rows have a *Signed* value of *no* and a *Call Number* value of *n/a*. In short, the table as it is contains at least three columns whose value does not directly define that particular row.

To put this database into Second Normal Form, I'll need to separate out these columns into their own tables, where each value will be represented only once (remember that redundancy is the hobgoblin of poor database design). You can help yourself in the normalization process by looking at each column and seeing how it relates to the whole. For example, the *Book ID* refers to an individual copy of a book. The book's *Title* should be particular to each book, as should the book's *Call Number* and definitely the *Notes*. These three columns can stay together as part of what defines a book; i.e., they all relate only to the individual Book ID. (Actually, as stated above, I do own multiple copies of some books and therefore the titles and call numbers will not be unique. I'm turning a blind eye to these instances rather than creating separate *Titles* and *Call Number* tables. See *Overruling Normalization* later in this section.)

Table 3.3 Ensuring that no field contains multiple pieces of data is the first step in normalizing a database. The *Author* field has been divided into its two logical parts.

Larry's Books

Book ID	Title	Author First Name	Author Last Name	Format	Call Number	Signed?	Notes
1	About a Boy	Nick	Hornby	Hardcover	n/a	no	
2	Crime and Punishment	Fyodor	Dostovsky	Mass Market	n/a	no	
3	High Fidelity	Nick	Hornby	Quality Paperback	n/a	no	
4	Naked Pictures of Famous People	Jon	Stewart	Quality Paperback	PN6162 .S845 1998	no	
5	Notes from Underground	Fyodor	Dostovsky	Mass Market	n/a	no	
6	Song of Solomon	Toni	Morrison	Hardcover	n/a	yes	Inscribed 'To Graham, Love Toni
7	Tibetan Book of Living and Dying	Sogyal	Rinpoche	Quality Paperback	BQ7640 .S64 1992	no	
8	Winesburg, Ohio	Sherwood	Anderson	Quality Paperback	n/a	no	Norton Critical Edition

An author will have written multiple books, so each use of the author will not necessarily be unique to a particular book, hence the authors should get their own table. The same applies to the format and signed columns, which, obviously, are not book-specific. Thus, I'll make these tables: *Authors*, *Books*, *Formats*, and *Signed?* (**Figure 3.1**). The *Books* table will be left containing the *Book ID*, *Title*, *Call Number* and *Notes*. The *Authors* table will break down the author's name into the first and last (you could easily add biographical information here, too). The *Formats* table contains only the various book formats. The *Signed?* table will list those possibilities (namely, "Yes, it is signed." or "No, it is not.").

Now, before I continue normalizing the database, there's a problem that needs to be addressed. Although I've separated out redundant data, as it stands I have no way of linking the information together (i.e., I cannot relate the tables). To solve this dilemma, I add a uniquely identifying field to each table as I previously did to the original, when I created the *Book ID* attribute. **Figure 3.2** shows how IDs have be added to the new tables.

Another way to work with the Second Normal Form concept is to hearken back to the relationships discussion. The goal in 2NF is to arrive at preferably one-to-many relationships from the main table to the supporting ones (or from any table to any other table it is related to—not all tables will be related, like *Formats* and *Authors* here). If you have either one-to-one or many-to-many relationships, you may need to rethink the layout. The former could indicate that the two items are the same and the latter may need an intermediary table to turn one many-to-many relationship into two one-to-many relationships.

Books	Authors
Book ID	Author First Name
Title	Author Last Name
Call Number	
Notes	

Formats	Signed?
Format	Yes/No

Figure 3.1 After bringing the database to the Second Normal Form, it contains four tables instead of the original one (Table 3.3).

Books	Authors
Book ID	Author ID
Title	Author First Name
Author ID	Author Last Name
Format ID	
Call Number	
Signed ID	
Notes	

Formats	Signed?
Format ID	Signed ID
Format	Yes/No

Figure 3.2 Part of normalizing your database is assigning foreign keys to help establish the relationships between tables.

In the Larry's Books example, every table is related to the *Books* table. Table *Signed?* has a one-to-many relationship because while many books can be unsigned and many books can be signed, each particular book can only be either signed or unsigned. The same applies to format: A book is going to be in hardcover, quality paperback, or mass market format (although you could have multiple copies in different formats, each individual copy will be only in one format).

The *Authors* table has a many-to-many relationship with *Books*, which is problematic. One author can write multiple books and one book can be written by multiple authors (a many-to-many relationship is like a one-to-many in both directions). If I designed this database for a client or for other nonpersonal uses (where I would want a more precise listing of the authors and books), I would need to solve the Authors-Books dilemma by making a table such as *Author Combinations*. The table would have a one-to-many relationship to both the *Books* and *Authors* tables. The structure of the table would allow for different author combinations (just Nick Hornby; Nick Hornby, Melissa Bank, and Roddy Doyle; etc.). Then each combination, which is assigned a unique identifier, would be linked to each book. As I stated, I could do this, but because it's only for personal use, I choose not to.

Figure 3.3 shows the existing layout using database characters to mark the relationships.

Third Normal Form

A database is in Third Normal Form if it is in 2NF and every nonkey column is independent of every other nonkey column. In other words, the fields of a table other than the keys should be mutually independent. Looking at the database now, one quickly sees that it is in 3NF. The *Books* table contains *Book ID*, *Title*, *Author ID*, *Format ID*, *Call Number*, *Signed*, and *Notes* fields. Each of these relates only to the *Book ID* and do not reflect each other. If the table contained an author's birthday field, it would need to be removed (and placed in the *Authors* table). This normalization rule may seem obvious, but sometimes errant data can slip through the cracks.

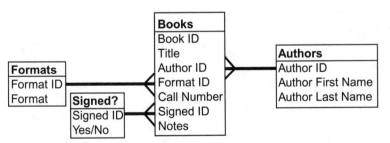

Figure 3.3 A one-to-many relationship is indicated by a line with crow's feet at the many end. This image indicates that, for example, each book will be in only one format but the same format will apply to multiple books.

DATABASE DESIGN AND NORMALIZATION

Now that the database has been normalized, I'll give it one more review before creating it on the RDBMS. This would be a good time to double-check that all the required information is stored. Also, look at the database in terms of what questions will be asked of it; for example:

♦ What books do I own written by J.D. Salinger?

♦ How many books do I have signed copies of?

♦ Who wrote *One Hundred Years of Solitude*?

♦ When was a particular book acquired?

Will the information that is stored as it is organized be able to provide answers to every potential question? If yes, then you are ready to proceed. In my case, I cannot answer the last question, so I'll add a *Date Entered* field to the *Books* table.

Finally, I'll see if there are any rules I want to break. Start by normalizing your database, then work backward. Understand that any

compromise you make will limit the capabilities of the database. The only change I'll make is to reincorporate the *Signed?* table into *Books*. There will only ever be the option of *Yes* or *No* (a book is either signed or not; I don't see this changing) and it can safely be brought in. **Figure 3.4** shows the final database design.

✔ Tips

■ Once you've sketched out a database on paper, you could create a series of spreadsheets that reflect the design (or use an application specifically tailored to this end). This file can act both as a good reference to the Web developers working on the database as well as a nice thing to give over to the client when the project is done.

■ Another benefit to creating keys for a table that are integers is that a database application can search through numbers faster than strings. So the query `SELECT * FROM users WHERE user_id='1'` will run faster than `SELECT * FROM users WHERE username='trout'`.

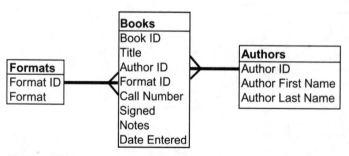

Figure 3.4 The Larry's Books database is now in its final form (as far as the draft process goes) and is just about ready to be created in the RDBMS.

Overruling Normalization

As much as ensuring that a database is in 3NF will help guarantee stability and endurance, you won't necessarily normalize every database you ever work with. Before undermining the proper methods, understand that it may have long-term implications.

The two primary reasons to overrule the layout that normalization would imply are convenience and performance. Fewer tables are easier to manipulate and comprehend than more. Some programmers would rather deal with a minimal number of quick and easy tables than a larger, more complex design. Further, because of its more intricate nature, normalized databases will most likely be slower for updating, retrieving data from, and modifying. So normalization is a trade-off between data integrity-scalability and simplicity-speed.

In the Larry's Books example, I did ignore a few normalization rules but without adversely affecting the intended use of the database. One example is that I do not have a separate *Signed?* table, but I know for a fact that those values won't change, so this will not hurt me. Another example is the inability to associate multiple authors to a book. I'm OK with that, since the database is for my own purposes, but it may be an unacceptable limitation in other conditions.

Creating the Database

Once you have finished laying out the database on paper, you can start creating it with the RDBMS application itself. For the purposes of this example, I'll be using MySQL, although because of the homogenous nature of SQL, you should be able to re-create this database on any system with only minor modifications.

Before I fire up MySQL, I need to finalize all of my table and column names as well as identify what field types to use. Here are some basic rules for naming conventions:

- Table names should be plural, indicating they contain multiple items.

- Column names should be singular, indicating they contain a single value.

- Use underscores for spaces.

- List the primary key first.

- Place other keys and indexes second.

- Every field name should be unique across every table, except for the foreign keys, which should be the same to indicate their lineage.

- Use lowercase names (this is not required, but if you stick to something consistent you will not get tripped up later).

SQL

SQL (Structured Query Language) was, like the relational database design scheme, developed in the 1970s as a way to easily communicate with a database application. Regardless of what RDMS you use, you'll need to understand SQL (Microsoft Access, which has a graphical interface, uses SQL behind the scenes, but it uses it nonetheless.) SQL works a lot like spoken languages and its minimal commands make it fairly easy to learn.

I normally capitalize my SQL commands from my table names and qualifiers to distinguish the two, but this is not required. Here is a short list of the standard commands that every DBMS should accept:

Alter	Change the format of a table
Create	Create a table or database
Delete	Delete rows from a table
Drop	Delete table columns, entire tables, or databases
Insert	Add a row to a table
Select	Retrieve information from a database
Update	Modify a database entry

Again, Appendix B, Database Resources, will cover SQL in greater detail.

Figure 3.5 shows the tables and columns as they are going to be named and ordered. The overall database will be called *larrys_books*.

Next, I'll need to predefine all the field types I want to use. In general, databases use three different field types: numbers, strings, and date/time. Each of these can be further broken up into sub-parts based upon how much information needs to be stored and in what format. **Table 3.4** lists the common MySQL-supported field types and how much space each will take up (Appendix B, Database Resources, contains a more detailed listing).

When choosing a column type keep in mind that larger fields take up more space and are therefore slower to use and the data entered into the table will be constricted to the column type. For example, putting a string into an integer field will result in either a *0* or *NULL* value (but the opposite will work) or placing a 100-character string into a field limited to 50 characters will cut off the second half of the data.

With an understanding of how my database is to be structured, named, and defined, I can now go into my RDBMS and make it happen.

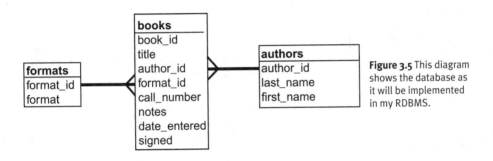

Figure 3.5 This diagram shows the database as it will be implemented in my RDBMS.

Table 3.4 Check with the manual of your DBMS to see what field types are supported. Here are the basic column options for a MySQL database.

MySQL Field Types			
NAME	**REFERS TO**	**EXAMPLE**	**LENGTH**
INT	Integer	8	4 bytes
DECIMAL (Max, Decimal)	A floating-point number of Max length with up to Decimal numbers to the right of the decimal	10.29	Max + 2 bytes
VARCHAR	A string of variable length	Underworld	Length plus 1 bytes
TEXT	A text string	Text is normally used for much longer strings...	Length + 2 bytes
ENUM	A list of options, of which one may be selected	Left	1 or 2 bytes
SET	A list of options, of which many may be selected	Jessica, Karen, Liz, Rebecca	1-4 or 8 bytes
DATE	Date in the format YY-MM-DD	96-04-20	3 bytes
TIME	Time in the format HH:MM:SS	10:23:01	3 bytes
DATETIME	Date and time in the format YY-MM-DD HH:MM:SS	96-04-20 10:23:01	8 bytes

CREATING THE DATABASE

To create the database:

1. Access MySQL via the command-line interface (**Figure 3.6**).

   ```
   mysql -p
   ```

   If you are using a GUI DBMS, you just need to bring up the application. If you need to specify a username, use `mysql -u username -p`. If you need to specify the host (e.g., *localhost*), use `mysql -u username -p -h hostname`.

2. Create the new database (**Figure 3.7**).

   ```
   CREATE DATABASE larrys_books;
   ```

   Remember that you must conclude every MySQL command with a semicolon. In fact, MySQL will not treat what you entered as a command until you've balanced every quotation mark and ended with a semi-colon.

3. Tell MySQL to use this new database (**Figure 3.8**).

   ```
   USE larrys_books;
   ```

   You have the option, with MySQL, of choosing the database at login, too.

Figure 3.6 To work with MySQL, you access the server application through the mysql client.

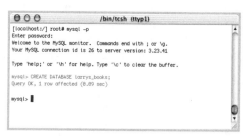

Figure 3.7 Creating a database requires just a three-word command.

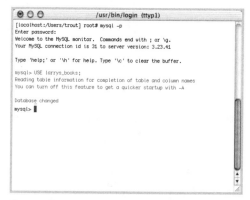

Figure 3.8 Every time you use MySQL you must either tell the application which database you will be using or change every statement to refer to the database (e.g., `SELECT * FROM database.table`).

Figure 3.9 MySQL is somewhat space-insensitive, meaning that you can write your query over several lines to improve readability.

Figure 3.10 The *Query OK* statement that MySQL returns after a query is entered indicates there was no problem (even if 0 rows were affected as is the case when creating tables).

4. Make the books table (**Figure 3.9**).

```
CREATE TABLE books (
book_id INT UNSIGNED NOT NULL
→ AUTO_INCREMENT,
title VARCHAR(100),
author_id INT UNSIGNED,
format_id INT UNSIGNED,
call_number VARCHAR(40),
notes TEXT,
date_entered DATE,
signed ENUM ('Y','N'),
PRIMARY KEY (book_id),
INDEX (title)
);
```

The *books* table, as it is defined here, uses mostly integers for the primary and foreign keys. Two columns—*title* and *call_number*—will be variable-length strings, while the *notes* field allows for longer text. The *signed* column is established as an enumerated list with *Y* and *N* being the options. The *book_id* will act as the primary key and the *title* will also be indexed, for faster searches.

5. Create the authors table (**Figure 3.10**).

```
CREATE TABLE authors (
author_id INT UNSIGNED NOT NULL
→ AUTO_INCREMENT,
last_name VARCHAR(50),
first_name VARCHAR(30),
PRIMARY KEY (author_id),
INDEX (last_name)
);
```

I've indexed only the author's last name in the *authors* table, but I could also index the author's first name, too. MySQL allows up to 16 indexes per table (keep in mind that the PRIMARY KEY is automatically an index).

continues on next page

CREATING THE DATABASE

6. Create the formats table (**Figure 3.11**).

```
CREATE TABLE formats (
format_id INT UNSIGNED NOT NULL
→ AUTO_INCREMENT,
format VARCHAR(15),
PRIMARY KEY (format_id),
INDEX (format)
);
```

✔ Tips

■ As a rule of thumb, you can determine what fields should be indexed by seeing what columns are frequently used in the WHERE parts of queries.

■ Column names can be up to 64 characters long, containing alphanumeric characters (plus the dollar sign and underscore) but cannot be entirely numbers.

■ If you make a mistake when creating tables, such as omitting a column or index, use the ALTER syntax to modify the table (**Figure 3.12**).

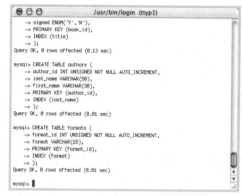

Figure 3.11 The *formats* table—one of the tables created during the normalization process—should be very efficient since one column is the primary key and the other is also indexed.

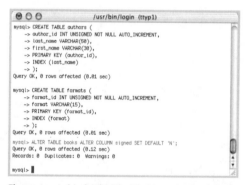

Figure 3.12 In hindsight I decided to make the default value of the *signed* field to be *N*, so I used the ALTER TABLE query to make the change.

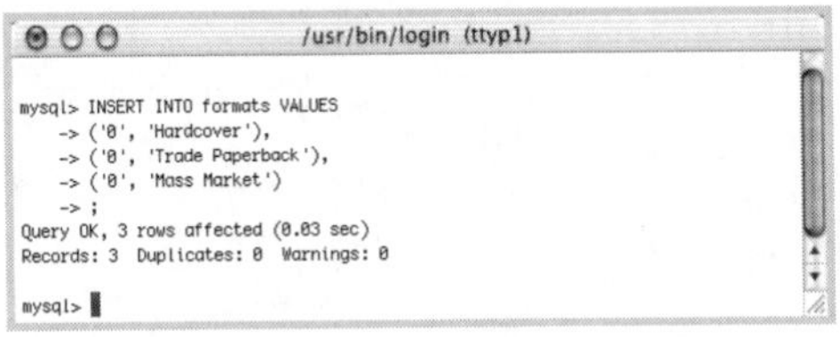

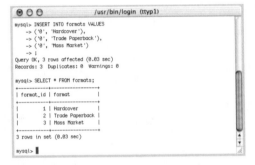

Figure 3.13 I can add values to the *formats* table using the INSERT command. Since the first column is an auto-incremented integer, a value of *0* or *NULL* will automatically set the value as the next integer in the table.

Figure 3.14 By running a SELECT * FROM tablename query on your database, you can view its current structure and values.

Generating Query Results

Now that the database has been created in MySQL, I can write the PHP scripts that will interface with it. First, I'll identify my particular needs here, then explain four database concepts—join, alias, order by, and limit—with which you may or may not be familiar. Most PHP programmers understand the basics of accessing a database but less about the particulars of the database itself. I'm focusing in this section on the capabilities of SQL and the DBMS because using the built-in power of your DBMS can improve the performance and overall quality of your Web application.

My needs for accessing this database are simple: I would like to be able to enter new books and browse through the books that have already been entered. Because I will be the only one using this database, there's no cause for advanced administration or excessive HTML design. In fact, because I've created a rock-solid database using normalization techniques, I know that I can always add features to my RDBMS interface at a later date (e.g., I can add a search engine).

Expanding upon these minimal requirements, I'll need a way to add an author, since they are stored in a different table, and I'd like to be able to browse by author as well. This leaves me with seven pages: add_author.php, add_book.php, index.php, browse_author.php, browse_book.php, view_author.php, and view_book.php (these last two will allow me to look at the particulars of an author or title). Since the *formats* table will not change frequently, I'll plan to manage it via the command-line mysql interface (**Figures 3.13** and **3.14**).

Until I decide to make some pages for updating or deleting the data in the tables, my queries will come down to either an `INSERT INTO` or `SELECT FROM`. You are probably very familiar with the former and conversant with the latter. There are, however, some great ways you can expand upon the `SELECT` query that are worth discussing.

When you create a relational database, as I've done here, using it requires special techniques. How, for example, do you determine who is the author of a book identified as 237 when the *author_id* field merely says 42? The slow way to go about it would be to run one query fetching all the book information, then another fetching the author information that correlates to that *author_id*. The faster way to accomplish this same process would be to use a *join*. A join occurs when you use the information from multiple tables to determine the information for which you are looking. In this example, my query with a join would be

```
SELECT authors.first_name,
→ authors.last_name FROM books, authors
→ WHERE books.book_id = '237' AND
→ books.author_id = authors.author_id;
```

Figure 3.15 shows the result of this query. The join in this example is made by the `books.author_id = authors.author_id`. Rewritten in English, the query says "Tell me the author's first and last name (from the *authors* table) who wrote the book with the ID of 237 (from the *books* table) knowing that the *author_id* in the *books* table is the same thing as the *author_id* in the *authors* table."

Three quick notes about queries like this: First, when doing a join it's best to use the

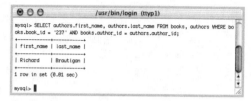

Figure 3.15 This query makes use of a join, displaying the text name of the author who correlates to the *author_id* of the book with an ID of 237.

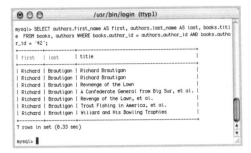

```
● ● ●              /usr/bin/login (ttyp1)
mysql> SELECT authors.first_name AS first, authors.last_name AS last, books.titl
e  FROM books, authors WHERE books.author_id = authors.author_id AND books.autho
r_id = '42';
+-------+----------+--------------------------------------------------+
| first | last     | title                                            |
+-------+----------+--------------------------------------------------+
| Richard | Brautigan | Richard Brautigan                              |
| Richard | Brautigan | Richard Brautigan                              |
| Richard | Brautigan | Revnenge of the Lawn                           |
| Richard | Brautigan | A Confederate General from Big Sur, et al.    |
| Richard | Brautigan | Revenge of the Lawn, et al.                   |
| Richard | Brautigan | Trout Fishing in America, et al.              |
| Richard | Brautigan | Willard and His Bowling Trophies              |
+-------+----------+--------------------------------------------------+
7 rows in set (0.33 sec)

mysql> █
```

Figure 3.16 Aliases allow me to give more specific or useful names to my returned results. Here the simpler *first* and *last* are used in lieu of the formal *first_name* and *last_name*.

dot-syntax to refer to each field (*table.column*) to minimize confusion and problems. Second, contrary to what you might think, you need to select only the fields that you want returned; you do not need to select other fields even if a join is being made upon them (here I have not selected the *author_id* column). Third, it is imperative that you refer to every table involved after FROM in your query because you cannot select from a table not listed.

Sometimes when writing complex queries, when using joins, or when you have excessively long field names, it simplifies matters to make an *alias*. After you refer to the column name you want selected, add AS alias, where *alias* refers to its new label.

```
SELECT authors.first_name AS first,
→ authors.last_name AS last, books.title
→ FROM books, authors WHERE
→ books.author_id = authors.author_id
→ AND books.author_id = '42';
```

Figure 3.16 shows the result of this query. Notice that the generated result will display using these new labels, which means that you must refer to them accordingly in your PHP. You'll see more on this in the scripts that follow.

Two more parameters that you can (and frequently should) add to your queries are ORDER BY and LIMIT (although LIMIT is not supported by every database application). The former is used to determine which of the fields you selected will be the sorting criteria when displaying the query results. To use it, specify the field, then set the order to be either ascending (*ASC*) or descending (*DESC*).

```
SELECT * FROM formats ORDER BY
→ format ASC;
```

Figure 3.17 shows how this query—and its DESC counterpart—affect the returned result. Note that you must apply the ORDER BY to a column that is selected (the database cannot order a list by an unused column).

Finally, the LIMIT argument dictates how many rows are returned and, optionally, where the query should start.

SELECT * FROM authors LIMIT 5;

This query requests every value from the *author* table starting with the first entry, limited to a total of five returned rows (**Figure 3.18**). When using LIMIT, if you do not specify an ORDER BY, the list will be ordered as it was created, which normally, but not necessarily, corresponds to the primary key.

SELECT * FROM authors LIMIT 100, 5;

When you pass two numbers to the LIMIT, the first dictates what row to begin with and the second how many rows to return from that point forward (**Figure 3.19**). Tables, like arrays, begin with the first item at *0*, so LIMIT 100, 5 will return the 101st item through the 105th. You'll use LIMIT this way later in the chapter for generating ordered query results pages like a search engine creates.

On top of all of these different ways to modify your query, your DBMS includes many different functions for manipulating the data returned. With MySQL there are functions for formatting dates, adding up numbers, and more. I'll demonstrate two in the scripts below and others will be listed in Appendix B, Database Resources.

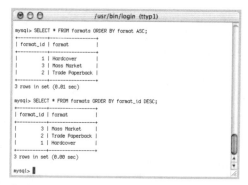

Figure 3.17 The two ORDER BY options—ASC and DESC—dictate how the returned results are sorted.

Figure 3.18 Limiting the number of returned rows allows you to better focus your queries.

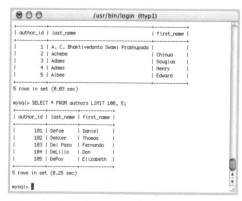

Figure 3.19 Not only can you specify how many rows are returned, but you can also choose the starting point using LIMIT.

To make the PHP interface:

1. Create a new HTML document in your text editor (**Script 3.1**).

   This is going to be my index page, which lists the four options: add an author, add a book, browse the authors, or browse the books. I also print out each letter of the alphabet, which will allow me to browse one letter at a time.

2. Save this file as `index.php` (or `index.html` since it uses no PHP).

The next file I'll write will be for adding an author to the database.

continues on page 101

Script 3.1 The index page for my database administration scripts will list the available options, both administrative and standard.

```
1   <!DOCTYPE html PUBLIC "-//W3C//DTD XHTML 1.0 Transitional//EN"
2   "http://www.w3.org/TR/2000/REC-xhtml1-20000126/DTD/xhtml1-transitional.dtd">
3   <html xmlns="http://www.w3.org/1999/xhtml">
4   <head>
5       <title>Larry's Books Administration</title>
6   </head>
7   <body>
8   Options:
9   <ul>
10      <li><a href="add_author.php">Add An Author</a></li>
11      <li><a href="add_book.php">Add A Book</a></li>
12      <li><a href="browse_book.php">Browse The Books</a> (or browse by letter below):<br />
13  <a href="browse_book.php?letter=A">A</a>
14  <a href="browse_book.php?letter=B">B</a>
15  <a href="browse_book.php?letter=C">C</a>
16  <a href="browse_book.php?letter=D">D</a>
17  <a href="browse_book.php?letter=E">E</a>
18  <a href="browse_book.php?letter=F">F</a>
19  <a href="browse_book.php?letter=G">G</a>
20  <a href="browse_book.php?letter=H">H</a>
21  <a href="browse_book.php?letter=I">I</a>
22  <a href="browse_book.php?letter=J">J</a>
23  <a href="browse_book.php?letter=K">K</a>
24  <a href="browse_book.php?letter=L">L</a>
```

(script continues on next page)

Script 3.1 *continued*

```
                                          script
25   <a href="browse_book.php?letter=M">M</a>
26   <a href="browse_book.php?letter=N">N</a>
27   <a href="browse_book.php?letter=O">O</a>
28   <a href="browse_book.php?letter=P">P</a>
29   <a href="browse_book.php?letter=Q">Q</a>
30   <a href="browse_book.php?letter=R">R</a>
31   <a href="browse_book.php?letter=S">S</a>
32   <a href="browse_book.php?letter=T">T</a>
33   <a href="browse_book.php?letter=U">U</a>
34   <a href="browse_book.php?letter=V">V</a>
35   <a href="browse_book.php?letter=W">W</a>
36   <a href="browse_book.php?letter=X">X</a>
37   <a href="browse_book.php?letter=Y">Y</a>
38   <a href="browse_book.php?letter=Z">Z</a></li>
39       <li><a href="browse_author.php">Browse The Authors</a> (or browse by letter below):<br />
40   <a href="browse_author.php?letter=A">A</a>
41   <a href="browse_author.php?letter=B">B</a>
42   <a href="browse_author.php?letter=C">C</a>
43   <a href="browse_author.php?letter=D">D</a>
44   <a href="browse_author.php?letter=E">E</a>
45   <a href="browse_author.php?letter=F">F</a>
46   <a href="browse_author.php?letter=G">G</a>
47   <a href="browse_author.php?letter=H">H</a>
48   <a href="browse_author.php?letter=I">I</a>
49   <a href="browse_author.php?letter=J">J</a>
50   <a href="browse_author.php?letter=K">K</a>
51   <a href="browse_author.php?letter=L">L</a>
52   <a href="browse_author.php?letter=M">M</a>
53   <a href="browse_author.php?letter=N">N</a>
54   <a href="browse_author.php?letter=O">O</a>
55   <a href="browse_author.php?letter=P">P</a>
56   <a href="browse_author.php?letter=Q">Q</a>
57   <a href="browse_author.php?letter=R">R</a>
58   <a href="browse_author.php?letter=S">S</a>
59   <a href="browse_author.php?letter=T">T</a>
60   <a href="browse_author.php?letter=U">U</a>
61   <a href="browse_author.php?letter=V">V</a>
62   <a href="browse_author.php?letter=W">W</a>
63   <a href="browse_author.php?letter=X">X</a>
64   <a href="browse_author.php?letter=Y">Y</a>
65   <a href="browse_author.php?letter=Z">Z</a></li>
66   </ul>
67   </body>
68   </html>
```

Script 3.2 The add_author.php script is a standard application of using an HTML form to enter data into a table. Script 3.3 is a more complex example.

```
                    script
1    <!DOCTYPE html PUBLIC "-//W3C//DTD
     XHTML 1.0 Transitional//EN"
2    "http://www.w3.org/TR/2000/REC-xhtml1-
     20000126/DTD/xhtml1-transitional.dtd">
3    <html xmlns="http://www.w3.org/1999/
     xhtml">
4    <head>
5        <title>Add An Author</title>
6    </head>
7    <body>
8    <?php
9
10   // Connect to the database.
11   $db_connection = mysql_connect
     ('localhost', 'username', 'password') or
     die (mysql_error());
12   $db_select = mysql_select_db
     ('larrys_books') or die (mysql_error());
13
14   // If the form was submitted, process it.
15   if (isset($submit)) {
16       $query = "insert into authors values
         ('0', '$last_name', '$first_name')";
17       if (@mysql_query ($query)) {
18           echo 'The author has been
             added.';
19       } else {
20           echo 'The author could not be
             added.'. mysql_error();
21       }
22   }
23   ?>
24   <form action="<?=$PHP_SELF ?>"
     method="post">
25   Last Name: <input type="text"
     name="last_name" size="50"
     maxlength="50" /><br />
26   First Name: <input type="text"
     name="first_name" size="30"
     maxlength="30" /><br />
27   <input type="submit" name="submit"
     value="Submit" />
28   </form>
29   </body>
30   </html>
```

3. Begin a new HTML document
   (**Script 3.2**).

```
<!DOCTYPE html PUBLIC "-//W3C//DTD
→ XHTML 1.0 Transitional//EN"
"http://www.w3.org/TR/
→ 2000/REC-xhtml1-20000126/DTD/
→ xhtml1-transitional.dtd">
<html xmlns="http://www.w3.org/1999/
→ xhtml">
<head>
<title>Add An Author</title>
</head>
<body>
```

4. Create a PHP section beginning with the
   database information.

```
<?php
$db_connection = mysql_connect
→ ('localhost', 'username',
→ 'password') or die (mysql_error());
$db_select = mysql_select_db
→ ('larrys_books') or die
→ (mysql_error());
```

Each script, except for the index page, will need to access the database (obviously). As a habit, I assign the result of the mysql_connect() and mysql_select_db() functions to a variable, although this is not required (when using mysql_query() you can use the $db_connection variable as an optional parameter). The or die (mysql_error()) will stop the script should it be unable to connect to or select the database. Since there's no point in continuing if I cannot do these two things, killing the script is appropriate.

continues on next page

GENERATING QUERY RESULTS

5. Process the form.

```
if (isset($submit)) {
$query = "insert into authors
→ values ('0', '$last_name',
→ '$first_name')";
if (@mysql_query ($query)) {
echo 'The author has been added.';
} else {
echo 'The author could not be
→ added.'. mysql_error();
}
}
```

Since this page will both display and handle the HTML form, I add a conditional to check if the form has been submitted. The query itself is simple, inserting the three values into the *authors* table.

Using *0* or *NULL* as the value for the first column—*author_id*, which is an auto-incremented integer—will tell the database to use the next logical number for that column. You do not want to specify a value for your auto-incremented primary key fields.

If the query went through OK, a message is displayed. If not, another message is displayed along with the error that MySQL reported. Using the @ symbol in the query suppresses any unsightly error messages that mysql_query() may generate.

6. Close the PHP and make the HTML form.

```
?>
<form action="<?=$PHP_SELF ?>"
→ method="post">
Last Name: <input type="text"
→ name="last_name" size="50"
→ maxlength="50" /><br />
First Name: <input type="text"
→ name="first_name" size="30"
→ maxlength="30" /><br />
<input type="submit" name="submit"
→ value="Submit" />
</form>
```

```
</body>
</html>
```

As a rule of thumb, using form input names that match up with the names of the columns in your table will lead to less confusion. I don't know how many times in the past I have had database problems because I refer to the wrong variable in the wrong place. Using, for example, *last_name* here will result in a variable of `$last_name`, which will be placed in the *last_name* column of the table.

7. Save the file as `add_author.php`.

Next I'll write the script for adding a book. The way these pages are designed, the plan is to add a new author before adding his or her book. Future books by the same author can be added with just the one step.

8. Start a new HTML document in your text editor (**Script 3.3**).

```
<!DOCTYPE html PUBLIC "-//W3C//DTD
→ XHTML 1.0 Transitional//EN"
"http://www.w3.org/TR/2000/
→ REC-xhtml1-20000126/DTD/
→ xhtml1-transitional.dtd">
<html xmlns="http://www.w3.org/1999/
→ xhtml">
<head>
<title>Add A Book</title>
</head>
<body>
```

9. Create a PHP section beginning with the database information.

```
<?php
$db_connection = mysql_connect
→ ('localhost', 'username',
→ 'password') or die (mysql_error());
$db_select = mysql_select_db
→ ('larrys_books') or die
→ (mysql_error());
```

continues on page 104

Script 3.3 When working with relational databases, you normally need to use queries to create pull-down menus to make the required associations between tables.

```
script

1    <!DOCTYPE html PUBLIC "-//W3C//DTD XHTML 1.0 Transitional//EN"
2        "http://www.w3.org/TR/2000/REC-xhtml1-20000126/DTD/xhtml1-transitional.dtd">
3    <html xmlns="http://www.w3.org/1999/xhtml">
4    <head>
5        <title>Add A Book</title>
6    </head>
7    <body>
8    <?php
9
10   // Connect to the database.
11
12   $db_connection = mysql_connect ('localhost', 'username', 'password') or die (mysql_error());
13   $db_select = mysql_select_db('larrys_books')  or die (mysql_error());
14
15   // If the form was submitted, process it.
16   if (isset($submit)) {
17       $query = "insert into books values ('0', '$title', '$author_id', '$format_id',
         '$call_number', '$notes', NOW(), '$signed')";
18       if (@mysql_query ($query)) {
19           echo 'The title has been added.';
20       } else {
21           echo 'The title could not be added.' . mysql_error();
22       }
23   }
24   ?>
25   <form action="<?=$PHP_SELF ?>" method="post">
26   Title: <input type="text" name="title" size="50" maxlength="100" /><br />
27   Author: <select name="author_id"><option>Select The Author</option>
28   <?php
29
30   // Print all the authors.
31   $query1 = "SELECT author_id, CONCAT(last_name, ', ', first_name) AS name FROM authors ORDER BY
         last_name ASC";
32   $query_result1 = @mysql_query ($query1);
33   while ($row1 = @mysql_fetch_array ($query_result1)) {
34       echo "<option value=\"$row1[author_id]\">$row1[name]</option>\n";
35   }
36   ?>
37   </select><br />
38   Format: <select name="format_id"><option>Select The Format</option>
39   <?php
40
41   // Print all the formats.
42   $query2 = "SELECT format_id, format FROM formats";
43   $query_result2 = @mysql_query ($query2);
44   while ($row2 = @mysql_fetch_array ($query_result2)) {
45       echo "<option value=\"$row2[format_id]\">$row2[format]</option>\n";
46   }
47   ?>
48   </select><br />
49   Call Number: <input type="text" name="call_number" size="40" maxlength="40" /><br />
50   Notes: <textarea name="notes" rows="5" cols="40">
51   </textarea><br />
52   Signed: <select name="signed"><option>Is the book signed?</option>
53   <option value="N">No</option>
54   <option value="Y">Yes</option>
55   </select><br />
56   <input type="submit" name="submit" value="Submit" />
57   </form>
58   </body>
59   </html>
```

10. Process the form.

```
if (isset($submit)) {
$query = "insert into books values
→ ('0', '$title', '$author_id',
→ '$format_id', '$call_number',
→ '$notes', NOW(), '$signed')";
if (@mysql_query ($query)) {
echo 'The title has been added.';
} else {
echo 'The title could not be added.'
→ . mysql_error();
}
}
```

This query is similar to the one in the add_author.php script. Notice that I use MySQL's NOW() function to set the *date_entered* field in the table. NOW() returns the current date and time in the format *YYYY-MM-DD HH:MM:SS*. Because the *date_entered* field is defined as a DATE, the string will be cut down to *YYYY-MM-DD*.

11. Finish the PHP and display the HTML form.

```
?>
<form action="<?=$PHP_SELF ?>"
→ method="post">
Title: <input type="text"
→ name="title" size="50"
→ maxlength="100" /><br />
```

12. Create a pull-down list of authors.

```
Author: <select
→ name="author_id"><option>Select
→ The Author</option>
<?php
$query1 = "SELECT author_id,
→ CONCAT(last_name, ', ',
→ first_name)
→ AS name FROM authors ORDER BY
→ last_name ASC";
$query_result1 = @mysql_query
→ ($query1);
while ($row1 = @mysql_fetch_array
→ ($query_result1)) {
echo "<option value=\"$row1[author_
→ id]\">$row1[name]</option>\n";
}
?>
</select><br />
```

To enter the *author_id* into the *books* table, I need to be able to find the ID that corresponds to a particular author. Thus I want to create a pull-down menu listing the authors but using their IDs as the value for each. In my query, I utilize the CONCAT() function, built into MySQL, to turn the author's first and last names into a format like *Bank, Melissa*. CONCAT(), like PHP's concatenation, combines the fields fed to it into one string. To get the desired result here, I use the two columns and a comma with a space to format the final string. Because I'm essentially creating a new entity, I make this string an alias called *name*.

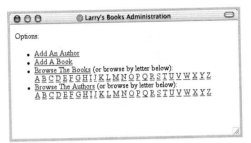

Figure 3.20 The index page allows the user (me) to enter authors and books or browse by either.

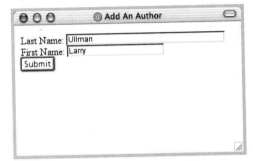

Figure 3.21 Adding an author to the database requires using a two-field HTML form (although I could add the ability to enter in other author data here if I wanted).

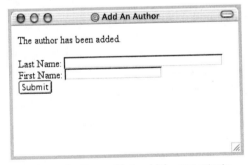

Figure 3.22 If PHP was able to add the new entry to the *authors* table, it prints a message and then redisplays the form.

13. Repeat the authors code to list the available formats.

```
Format: <select name="format_id">
→ <option>Select The Format</option>
<?php
$query2 = "SELECT format_id, format
→ FROM formats";
$query_result2 = @mysql_query
→ ($query2);
while ($row2 = @mysql_fetch_array
→ ($query_result2)) {
echo "<option value=\"$row2[format_
→ id]\">$row2[format]</option>\n";
}
?>
</select><br />
```

14. Complete the form.

```
Call Number: <input type="text"
→ name="call_number" size="40"
→ maxlength="40" /><br />
Notes: <textarea name="notes"
→ rows="5" cols="40">
</textarea><br />
Signed: <select name=
→ "signed"><option>Is the book
→ signed?</option>
<option value="N">No</option>
<option value="Y">Yes</option>
</select><br />
<input type="submit" name="submit"
→ value="Submit" />
</form>
</body>
</html>
```

15. Save this script as add_book.php.

16. Upload these three files to your server and test in your Web browser (**Figures 3.20**, **3.21**, **3.22**, **3.23**, and **3.24**).

continues on next page

Now that the back-end PHP scripts have been written, I'll compose the front-end pages for browsing the database.

17. Create a new HTML document in your text editor (**Script 3.4**).

```
<!DOCTYPE html PUBLIC "-//W3C//DTD
→ XHTML 1.0 Transitional//EN"
"http://www.w3.org/TR/2000/
→ REC-xhtml1-20000126/DTD/
→ xhtml1-transitional.dtd">
<html xmlns="http://www.w3.org/1999/
→ xhtml">
<head>
<title>Browse The Books</title>
</head>
<body>
```

18. Start the PHP section and define how many items will be displayed per page.

```
<?php
$display_number = 20;
```

Since I'm going to browse through the database, I want to limit how many items are displayed per page.

19. Connect to the database.

```
$db_connection = mysql_connect
→ ('localhost', 'username',
→ 'password') or die
→ (mysql_error());
$db_select = mysql_select_db
→ ('larrys_books') or die
→ (mysql_error());
```

20. Write a conditional that will determine how many results pages will be required.

```
if (!isset($num_pages)) {
```

If the $num_pages variable is not set, then the user is coming to this page for the first time and the script needs to see how many results there will be.

continues on page 110

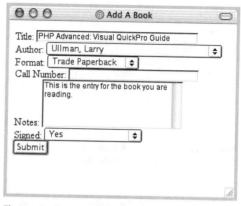

Figure 3.23 The add_book.php page is more complex than its author counterpart, using two pull-down menus dynamically generated from the database.

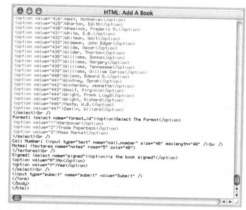

Figure 3.24 Viewing part of the source of add_book.php, you can see how the author's names and IDs have been used to make my pull-down menu. The same is true for the book formats.

Script 3.4 The `browse_book.php` script, along with the `browse_author.php` file (Script 3.5), determine how many rows are in the query result and then generate 20 item result pages.

```
1    <!DOCTYPE html PUBLIC "-//W3C//DTD XHTML 1.0 Transitional//EN"
2    "http://www.w3.org/TR/2000/REC-xhtml1-20000126/DTD/xhtml1-transitional.dtd">
3    <html xmlns="http://www.w3.org/1999/xhtml">
4    <head>
5        <title>Browse The Books</title>
6    </head>
7    <body>
8    <?php
9
10   // How many should be displayed per page.
11   $display_number = 20;
12
13   // Connect to the database.
14   $db_connection = mysql_connect ('localhost', 'username', 'password') or die (mysql_error());
15   $db_select = mysql_select_db('larrys_books') or die (mysql_error());
16
17   // If we don't know how many pages there are, make that calculation.
18   if (!isset($num_pages)) {
19
20       // Determine the query.
21       if (isset($letter)) { // Browsing a particular letter or the whole shebang?
22           $query1 = "SELECT books.title, books.author_id, CONCAT(authors.first_name, ' ',
             authors.last_name) AS author, formats.format FROM books, authors, formats WHERE
             authors.author_id = books.author_id AND formats.format_id = books.format_id AND title
             LIKE '$letter%' ORDER BY title ASC";
23       } else {
24           $query1 = "SELECT books.title, books.author_id, CONCAT(authors.first_name, ' ',
             authors.last_name) AS author, formats.format FROM books, authors, formats WHERE
             authors.author_id = books.author_id AND formats.format_id = books.format_id ORDER BY
             title ASC";
25       }
26
27       // Query the database.
28       $query_result1 = @mysql_query ($query1) or die (mysql_error());
29
30       // Calculate the number of pages required.
31       $num_results = @mysql_num_rows ($query_result1);
32       if ($num_results > $display_number) {
33           $num_pages = ceil ($num_results/$display_number);
```

(script continues on next page)

Script 3.4 *continued*

```
34          } elseif ($num_results > 0) {
35              $num_pages = 1;
36          } else {
37              echo 'There are no books in this category.';
38          }
39
40          $start = 0; // Currently at item 0.
41      }
42
43      // Make the new, limited query.
44      if (isset($letter)) {
45          $query = "SELECT books.book_id, books.title, books.author_id, CONCAT(authors.first_name, ' ',
                authors.last_name) AS author FROM books, authors WHERE authors.author_id = books.author_id
                AND title LIKE '$letter%' ORDER BY title ASC LIMIT $start, $display_number";
46      } else {
47          $query = "SELECT books.book_id, books.title, books.author_id, CONCAT(authors.first_name, ' ',
                authors.last_name) AS author FROM books, authors WHERE authors.author_id = books.author_id
                ORDER BY title ASC LIMIT $start, $display_number";
48      }
49
50      // Print a table.
51      echo '<table align="center" cellpadding="2" cellspacing="2" border="1">
52          <tr align="center">
53              <td align="center"><b>Title</b></td>
54              <td align="center"><b>Author</b></td>
55          </tr>';
56
57      // Print each item.
58      $query_result = @mysql_query ($query);
59      while ($row = @mysql_fetch_array ($query_result)) {
60          echo "  <tr align=\"center\">
61              <td align=\"left\"><i><a href=\"view_book.php?bid=$row[book_id]\">
                $row[title]</a></i></td>
62              <td align=\"left\"><a href=\"view_author.php?aid=$row[author_id]\">$row[author]</a></td>
63          </tr>";
64      }
65
66      // Make the links to other pages, if necessary.
67      if ($num_pages > 1) {
68
```

(script continues on next page)

GENERATING QUERY RESULTS

Script 3.4 *continued*

```
69    echo '  <tr align="center">
70          <td align="center" colspan="2">';
71
72    // Determine what page the script is on.
73    if ($start == 0) {
74        $current_page = 1;
75    } else {
76        $current_page = ($start/$display_number) + 1;
77    }
78
79    // If it's not the first page, make a Previous button.
80    if ($start != 0) {
81        echo '<a href="browse_book.php?start=' . ($start - $display_number) . '&num_pages=' .
             $num_pages . '&letter=' . $letter . '">Previous</a> ';
82    }
83
84    // Make all the numbered pages.
85    for ($i = 1; $i <= $num_pages; $i++) {
86        $next_start = $start + $display_number;
87        if ($i != $current_page) { // Don't link the current page.
88            echo '<a href="browse_book.php?start=' . (($display_number * ($i - 1))) .
                 '&num_pages=' . $num_pages . '&letter=' . $letter . '">' . $i . '</a> ';
89        } else {
90            echo $i . ' ';
91        }
92    }
93
94    // If it's not the last page, make a Next button.
95    if ($current_page != $num_pages) {
96        echo '<a href="browse_book.php?start=' . ($start + $display_number) . '&num_pages=' .
             $num_pages . '&letter=' . $letter . '">Next</a> ';
97    }
98
99    echo '</td>
100       </tr>';
101   }
102   ?>
103   </table>
104   </body>
105   </html>
```

21. Write the query to see how many items will be returned.

```
if (isset($letter)) {
$query1 = "SELECT books.title,
→ books.author_id, CONCAT(authors.
→ first_name, ' ', authors.last_
→ name) AS author FROM books,
→ authors WHERE authors.author_id =
→ books.author_id AND title LIKE
→ '$letter%' ORDER BY title ASC";
} else {
$query1 = "SELECT books.title,
→ books.author_id, CONCAT(authors.
→ first_name, ' ', authors.last_
→ name) AS author FROM books,
→ authors WHERE authors.author_id =
→ books.author_id ORDER BY title
→ ASC";
}
```

The query will differ slightly if the user is browsing by letter or through the entire database. The modification for the former is to add `AND title LIKE '$letter%'` to the `WHERE` part of the query. The `LIKE` keyword allows for things to be similar but not exact. The similarity in this case should be to the specific letter followed by anything (the percent sign being a wildcard).

The query is selecting the book's title and author, ordering the entire list by title. A join is used to find the author's actual name, which will be aliased to *author*.

22. Query the database.

```
$query_result1 = mysql_query
→ ($query1) or die (mysql_error());
```

23. Determine how many pages will be required to display every matching item.

```
$num_results = @mysql_num_rows
→ ($query_result1);
if ($num_results > $display_number)
→ {
$num_pages = ceil ($num_results/
→ $display_number);
} elseif ($num_results > 0) {
$num_pages = 1;
} else {
echo 'There are no books in this
→ category.';
}
```

The `mysql_num_rows()` function will tell me how many items were returned. If there are more items then I want to display per page, I need to divide the one by the other to see how many pages are required. Since any remaining items will need their own page, I take the upper limit, using `ceil()`, of the division as my number of pages. For example, if there are 40 returned rows, I can display 20 each on two pages; if there are 30 returned rows, 30 divided by 20 is equal to 1.5, which gets rounded up to 2, and I still need two pages. The rest of the conditional states that if there are some rows returned (and I already know that number is not greater than the number to display per page), then one page is sufficient. Otherwise, there will be nothing to display.

24. Set the start of the query to 0.

```
$start = 0;
}
```

If the user is here for the first time, I'll want to begin displaying the first item returned, which is indexed at 0.

25. Reapply the query.

```
if (isset($letter)) {
$query = "SELECT books.book_id,
→ books.title, books.author_id,
→ CONCAT(authors.first_name, ' ',
→ authors.last_name) AS author FROM
→ books, authors WHERE authors.
→ author_id = books.author_id AND
→ title LIKE '$letter%' ORDER BY
→ title ASC LIMIT $start, $display_
→ number";
} else {
$query = "SELECT books.book_id,
→ books.title, books.author_id,
→ CONCAT(authors.first_name, ' ',
→ authors.last_name) AS author FROM
→ books, authors WHERE authors.
→ author_id = books.author_id ORDER
→ BY title ASC LIMIT $start,
→ $display_number";
}
```

Here the query has been appended with the LIMIT $start, $display_number code. Even though I may be displaying results over multiple pages, the query will always be the same except for where I start taking rows out of the database. Using 20 as the number of items to display, if I have a query that returns 48 items, page one should display 0 through 19 (LIMIT 0, 20), page two should display 20 through 39 (LIMIT 20, 20), and page three should display 40 through 48 (LIMIT 40, 20). I can use the same query over and over by just changing the $start value on each page.

26. Make a table and print the results.

```
echo '<table align="center"
→ cellpadding="2" cellspacing="2"
→ border="1">
<tr align="center">
<td align="center"><b>Title</b></td>
<td align="center"><b>Author
→ </b></td>
</tr>';
$query_result = @mysql_query
→ ($query);
while ($row = @mysql_fetch_array
→ ($query_result)) {
echo " <tr align=\"center\">
<td align=\"left\"><i><a → href=
→ \"view_book.php?bid=$row[book_id]
→ \">$row[title]</a></i></td>
<td align=\"left\"><a href=
→ \"view_author.php?aid=$row[author_
→ id]\">$row[author]</a></td>
</tr>";
}
```

For the books, I'm going to print out every title along with the author of that book. Clicking on the title will bring up more information on the specific copy I own, and clicking on the author will bring up other works I own by him or her.

27. Print links to the other result pages.

```
if ($num_pages > 1) {
echo ' <tr align="center">
<td align="center" colspan="2">';
if ($start == 0) {
$current_page = 1;
} else {
$current_page = ($start/$display_
→ number) + 1;
}
if ($start != 0) {
echo '<a href="browse_book.php?
→ start=' . ($start - $display_
→ number) . '&num_pages=' .
→ $num_pages . '&letter=' . $letter
→ . '">Previous</a> ';
}
```

continues on next page

```
for ($i = 1; $i <= $num_pages;
→ $i++) {
$next_start = $start + $display_
→ number;
if ($i != $current_page) {
echo '<a href="browse_book.php?
→ start=' . (($display_number *
→ ($i - 1))) . '&num_pages=' .
→ $num_pages . '&letter=' .
→ $letter . '">' . $i . '</a> ';
} else {
echo $i . ' ';
}
}
if ($current_page != $num_pages) {
echo '<a href="browse_book
→ .php?start=' . ($start +
→ $display_number) . '&num_pages='
→ . $num_pages . '&letter='
→ . $letter . '">Next</a> ';
}
echo '</td>
</tr>';
}
```

This section of code will be applied only if there are multiple pages to be displayed. It will create a list of options like *Previous 1 2 3 Next*, all linked to results pages. The first step is to determine what page is currently being valued, calculated based upon the value of **$start**. If it's not the first page, a *Previous* link is made. Then numbers are printed from 1 to the number of necessary pages (they are all linked except for the current page). Finally, a *Next* link is made unless it is currently on the last page. You'll understand better how this works when you see the script in action.

Every link made in this section also received three variables: what number the query should start with (**$start**), the total number of pages this query requires (**$num_pages**, which could be recalculated each time, if you wanted), and what letter is being viewed, if a specific one (**$letter**).

28. Conclude the PHP and the HTML.

```
?>
</table>
</body>
</html>
```

29. Save the file as browse_book.php.

The browse_author.php script, which you are about to write, is a modification of browse_book.php. I'll write it out while only discussing its minor differences.

30. Create a new HTML document in your text editor. (**Script 3.5**).

```
<!DOCTYPE html PUBLIC "-//W3C//
→ DTD XHTML 1.0 Transitional//EN"
"http://www.w3.org/TR/2000/
→ REC-xhtml1-20000126/DTD/xhtml1-
→ transitional.dtd">
<html xmlns="http://www.w3.org/
→ 1999/xhtml">
<head>
<title>Browse The Authors</title>
</head>
<body>
```

continues on page 115

Script 3.5 This script works exactly like its book counterpart (Script 3.4), although with author last names as opposed to book titles.

```
                                    script
1   <!DOCTYPE html PUBLIC "-//W3C//DTD XHTML 1.0 Transitional//EN"
2       "http://www.w3.org/TR/2000/REC-xhtml1-20000126/DTD/xhtml1-transitional.dtd">
3   <html xmlns="http://www.w3.org/1999/xhtml">
4   <head>
5       <title>Browse The Authors</title>
6   </head>
7   <body>
8   <?php
9
10  // How many should be displayed per page.
11  $display_number = 20;
12
13  // Connect to the database.
14  $db_connection = mysql_connect ('localhost', 'username', 'password') or die (mysql_error());
15  $db_select = mysql_select_db('larrys_books');
16
17  // If we don't know how many pages there are, make that calculation.
18  if (!isset($num_pages)) {
19
20      // Determine the query.
21      if (isset($letter)) { // Browsing a particular letter or the whole shebang?
22          $query1 = "SELECT author_id, CONCAT(first_name, ' ', last_name) AS author FROM authors
                WHERE last_name LIKE '$letter%' ORDER BY last_name ASC";
23      } else {
24          $query1 = "SELECT author_id, CONCAT(first_name, ' ', last_name) AS author FROM authors
                ORDER BY last_name ASC";
25      }
26
27      // Query the database.
28      $query_result1 = mysql_query ($query1) or die (mysql_error());
29
30      // Calculate the number of pages required.
31      $num_results = @mysql_num_rows ($query_result1);
32      if ($num_results > $display_number) {
33          $num_pages = ceil ($num_results/$display_number);
34      } elseif ($num_results > 0) {
35          $num_pages = 1;
36      } else {
37          echo 'There are no authors in this category.';
38      }
39
40      $start = 0; // Currently at item 0.
41  }
42
43  // Make the new, limited query.
44  if (isset($letter)) {
45          $query = "SELECT author_id, CONCAT(first_name, ' ', last_name) AS author FROM authors
                WHERE last_name LIKE '$letter%' ORDER BY last_name ASC LIMIT $start, $display_number";
46      } else {
```

(script continues on next page)

Script 3.5 *continued*

```
script

47          $query = "SELECT author_id, CONCAT(first_name, ' ', last_name) AS author FROM authors
            ORDER BY last_name ASC LIMIT $start, $display_number";
48      }
49
50      // Print each item.
51      $query_result = @mysql_query ($query);
52      while ($row = @mysql_fetch_array ($query_result)) {
53          echo "<a href=\"view_author.php?aid=$row[author_id]\">$row[author]</a><br />\n";
54      }
55
56      // Make the links to other pages, if necessary.
57      if ($num_pages > 1) {
58
59          echo '<hr width="50%" align="left" />';
60
61          // Determine what page the script is on.
62          if ($start == 0) {
63              $current_page = 1;
64          } else {
65              $current_page = ($start/$display_number) + 1;
66          }
67
68          // If it's not the first page, make a Previous button.
69          if ($start != 0) {
70              echo '<a href="browse_author.php?start=' . ($start - $display_number) . '&num_pages=' .
                  $num_pages . '&letter=' . $letter . '">Previous</a> ';
71          }
72
73          // Make all the numbered pages.
74          for ($i = 1; $i <= $num_pages; $i++) {
75              $next_start = $start + $display_number;
76              if ($i != $current_page) {
77                  echo '<a href="browse_author.php?start=' . (($display_number * ($i - 1))) .
                      '&num_pages=' . $num_pages . '&letter=' . $letter . '">' . $i . '</a> ';
78              } else {
79                  echo $i . ' ';
80              }
81          }
82
83          // If it's not the last page, make a Next button.
84          if ($current_page != $num_pages) {
85              echo '<a href="browse_author.php?start=' . ($start + $display_number) . '&num_pages=' .
                  $num_pages . '&letter=' . $letter . '">Next</a> ';
86          }
87
88      }
89      ?>
90      </body>
91      </html>
```

31. Duplicate the `browse_book.php` PHP, altering the query and HTML accordingly.

```php
<?php
$display_number = 20;
$db_connection = mysql_connect
→ ('localhost', 'username',
→ 'password') or die (mysql_error());
$db_select = mysql_select_db
→ ('larrys_books');
if (!isset($num_pages)) {
if (isset($letter)) {
$query1 = "SELECT author_id,
→ CONCAT(first_name, ' ', last_name)
→ AS author FROM authors WHERE
→ last_name LIKE '$letter%' ORDER BY
→ last_name ASC";
} else {
$query1 = "SELECT author_id,
→ CONCAT(first_name, ' ', last_name)
→ AS author FROM authors ORDER BY
→ last_name ASC";
}
$query_result1 = @mysql_query
→ ($query1);
$num_results = @mysql_num_rows
→ ($query_result1);
if ($num_results > $display_number) {
$num_pages = ceil ($num_results/
→ $display_number);
} elseif ($num_results > 0) {
$num_pages = 1;
} else {
echo 'There are no authors in this
→ category.';
}
$start = 0;
}
if (isset($letter)) {
```

```php
$query = "SELECT author_id,
→ CONCAT(first_name, ' ', last_name)
→ AS author FROM authors WHERE
→ last_name LIKE '$letter%' ORDER BY
→ last_name ASC LIMIT $start,
→ $display_number";
} else {
$query = "SELECT author_id,
→ CONCAT(first_name, ' ', last_name)
→ AS author FROM authors ORDER BY
→ last_name ASC LIMIT $start,
→ $display_number";
}
$query_result = @mysql_query
→ ($query);
while ($row = @mysql_fetch_array
→ ($query_result)) {
echo "<a href=\"view_author.php?
→ aid=$row[author_id]\">$row[author]
→ </a><br />\n";
}
if ($num_pages > 1) {
echo '<hr width="50%" align=
→ "left" />';
if ($start == 0) {
$current_page = 1;
} else {
$current_page = ($start/
→ $display_number) + 1;
}
if ($start != 0) {
echo '<a href="browse_author.php?
→ start=' . ($start - $display_
→ number) . '&num_pages=' .
→ $num_pages . '&letter=' .
→ $letter . '">Previous</a> ';
}
for ($i = 1; $i <= $num_pages;
→ $i++) {
```

continues on next page

```
$next_start = $start +
→ $display_number;
if ($i != $current_page) {
echo '<a href="browse_author.php?
→ start=' . (($display_number *
→ ($i - 1))) . '&num_pages=' .
→ $num_pages . '&letter=' .
→ $letter . '">' . $i . '</a> ';
} else {
echo $i . ' ';
}
}
if ($current_page != $num_pages) {
echo '<a href="browse_author.php?
→ start=' . ($start + $display_
→ number) . '&num_pages=' .
→ $num_pages . '&letter=' .
→ $letter . '">Next</a> ';
}
}
?>
</body>
</html>
```

The only significant change here is in the query itself, where it's grabbing just the author names from the one table. Because the information being presented is more basic, I'm not using a table here either. The structure and most of the code is duplicated from browse_book.php.

32. Save the file as browse_author.php.

I'm now left with the two remaining scripts, view_book.php and view_author.php. Each will show only one book or author but in greater detail.

Script 3.6 The file for viewing a particular title in detail, `view_book.php`, makes use of MySQL's `DATE_FORMAT()` function to alter the structure of the *date_entered* field.

```
1    <!DOCTYPE html PUBLIC "-//W3C//DTD XHTML
     1.0 Transitional//EN"
2        "http://www.w3.org/TR/2000/
         REC-xhtml1-20000126/DTD/
         xhtml1-transitional.dtd">
3    <html xmlns="http://www.w3.org/
     1999/xhtml">
4    <head>
5        <title>View A Book</title>
6    </head>
7    <body>
8    <?php
9
10   // Connect to the database.
11   $db_connection = mysql_connect
     ('localhost', 'username', 'password') or
     die (mysql_error());
12   $db_select = mysql_select_db
     ('larrys_books') or die (mysql_error());
13
14   // Query the database.
15   $query = "SELECT books.title,
     books.author_id, formats.format,
     books.call_number, books.signed,
     books.notes, DATE_FORMAT(books.date_
     entered, '%M %e, %Y') AS de, CONCAT
     (authors.first_name, ' ', authors.last_
     name) AS author FROM books, authors,
     formats WHERE books.book_id = '$bid' AND
     authors.author_id = books.author_id AND
     formats.format_id = books.format_id";
16   $query_result = @mysql_query ($query));
17   $row = @mysql_fetch_array
     ($query_result);
18   echo "<i><b>$row[title]</b></i><br />
19       <b>Author:</b><a href=\"view_author.
         php?aid=$row[author_id]\">$row
         [author]<a><br />
20       <b>Format:</b> $row[format]<br />
21       <b>Date Entered:</b> $row[de]<br />
22       <b>LCCN:</b> $row[call_number]<br />
23       <b>Signed?</b> $row[signed]<br />
24       <b>Notes:</b> $row[notes]\n";
25   ?>
26   </body>
27   </html>
```

33. Create a new HTML document in your text editor (**Script 3.6**).

```
<!DOCTYPE html PUBLIC "-//W3C//DTD
→ XHTML 1.0 Transitional//EN"
"http://www.w3.org/TR/2000/
→ REC-xhtml1-20000126/DTD/
→ xhtml1-transitional.dtd">
<html xmlns="http://www.w3.org/1999/
→ xhtml">
<head>
<title>View A Book</title>
</head>
<body>
```

34. Start a section of PHP code and connect to the database.

```
<?php
$db_connection = mysql_connect
→ ('localhost', 'username',
→ 'password') or die (mysql_error());
$db_select = mysql_select_db
→ ('larrys_books') or die
→ (mysql_error());
```

35. Query the database.

```
$query = "SELECT books.title,
→ books.author_id, formats.format,
→ books.call_number, books.signed,
→ books.notes, DATE_FORMAT
→ (books.date_entered, '%M %e, %Y')
→ AS de, CONCAT(authors.first_name,
→ ' ', authors.last_name) AS author
→ FROM books, authors, formats WHERE
→ books.book_id = '$bid' AND
→ authors.author_id = books.author_
→ id AND formats.format_id =
→ books.format_id";
$query_result = @mysql_query
→ ($query);
```

continues on next page

The query for the `view_book.php` script will retrieve all of the particulars for a specific book, using the *book_id* as the reference point. I'm making a join with both the *author* and *format* tables to retrieve language descriptions of those two categories (and aliasing the format as *author* as you've already witnessed). Also, I use the **DATE_FORMAT()** function to turn the date stored in the table into a prettier version. Remember that *date_ entered* in the table will be like *2001-01-26*. Feeding **DATE_FORMAT()** the parameter *%M %e, %Y* will turn this into *January 26, 2001*, much like PHP's **strftime()** function behaves. **Table 3.5** lists some of the available formatting parameters. Converting the date with MySQL instead of PHP helps balance the load on the server and improves performance.

36. Print out the result.

```
$row = @mysql_fetch_array
→ ($query_result);
echo "<i><b>$row[title]</b></i><br />
<b>Author:</b><a href=\"view_
→ author.php?aid=$row[author_id]
→ \">$row[author]<a><br />
<b>Format:</b> $row[format]<br />
<b>Date Entered:</b> $row[de]<br />
<b>LCCN:</b> $row[call_number]<br />
<b>Signed?</b> $row[signed]<br />
<b>Notes:</b> $row[notes]\n";
```

If you want to improve upon the format of the information printed here, run the *notes* data through nl2br(), which will convert every return entered by the user in to a <br />.

Table 3.5 Here are some of the more common parameters for the DATE_FORMAT() function.

DATE_FORMAT() Parameters	
TERM	**RESULT**
%a	Weekday as three-letter abbreviation (Sun, Mon...)
%e	Day of the month (1-31)
%h	Hour as two digits (01, 02...)
%i	Minute as two digits (01, 02...)
%l	House as one or two digits (1, 2...)
%M	Month (January, February...)
%p	A.M. or P.M.
%r	Time as HH:MM:SS a.m. (p.m.)
%T	Time as HH:MM:SS
%W	Weekday (Sunday, Monday...)
%y	Year as two digits
%Y	Year as four digits

Script 3.7 The final script in the application uses two queries to print the author's name then all of his or her books (although I could have combined these into one query).

```
1    <!DOCTYPE html PUBLIC "-//W3C//DTD XHTML
     1.0 Transitional//EN"
2        "http://www.w3.org/TR/2000/
         REC-xhtml1-20000126/DTD/
         xhtml1-transitional.dtd">
3    <html xmlns="http://www.w3.org/1999/
     xhtml">
4    <head>
5        <title>View An Author</title>
6    </head>
7    <body>
8    <?php
9
10   // Connection to the database.
11   $db_connection = mysql_connect
     ('localhost', 'username', 'password') or
     die (mysql_error());
12   $db_select = mysql_select_db
     ('larrys_books') or die (mysql_error());
13
14   // Query the database.
15   $query = "SELECT CONCAT(authors.
     first_name, ' ', authors.last_name)
     AS author FROM authors WHERE author_
     id = '$aid'";
16   $query_result = @mysql_query ($query);
17   $row = @mysql_fetch_array
     ($query_result);
18   echo "<b>$row[author]</b><br />\n";
19
20   // Print each title.
21   $query1 = "SELECT book_id, title FROM
     books WHERE author_id = '$aid' ORDER BY
     title ASC";
22   $query_result1 = @mysql_query ($query1);
23   while ($row1 = @mysql_fetch_array
     ($query_result1)) {
24       echo "<i><a href=\"view_book.php?
         bid=$row1[book_id]\">$row1[title]</a>
         </i><br />\n";
25   }
26   ?>
27   </body>
28   </html>
```

37. Close the PHP and the HTML page.

```
?>
</body>
</html>
```

38. Save this script as `view_book.php`.

The last step is to write `view_author.php`, a parallel to `view_book.php`.

39. Start with a new HTML document in your text editor (**Script 3.7**).

```
<!DOCTYPE html PUBLIC "-//W3C//DTD
→ XHTML 1.0 Transitional//EN"
"http://www.w3.org/TR/2000/
→ REC-xhtml1-20000126/DTD/xhtml1-
→ transitional.dtd">
<html xmlns="http://www.w3.org/1999/
→ xhtml">
<head>
<title>View An Author</title>
</head>
<body>
```

40. Connect to, select, and query the database.

```
<?php
$db_connection = mysql_connect
→ ('localhost', 'username',
→ 'password') or die (mysql_error());
$db_select = mysql_select_db
→ ('larrys_books') or die
→ (mysql_error());
$query = "SELECT CONCAT(authors.
→ first_name, ' ', authors.last_
→ name) AS author FROM authors WHERE
→ author_id = '$aid'";
$query_result = @mysql_query
→ ($query);
$row = @mysql_fetch_array
→ ($query_result);
echo "<b>$row[author]</b><br />\n";
```

continues on next page

119

The first query on the `view_author.php` page will just retrieve the author's full name from the table.

41. Retrieve all of that author's books.

```
$query1 = "SELECT book_id, title
→ FROM books WHERE author_id =
→ '$aid' ORDER BY title ASC";

$query_result1 = mysql_query
→ ($query1) or die (mysql_error());

while ($row1 = mysql_fetch_array
→ ($query_result1)) {

echo "<i><a href=\"view_book.php?
→ bid=$row1[book_id]\">$row1[title]
→ </a></i><br />\n";

}
```

42. Conclude the PHP and the HTML.

```
?>
</body>
</html>
```

43. Save this file as `view_author.php`, upload it to your server along with `browse_book.php`, `browse_author.php`, and `view_book.php`, then test all four in your Web browser (**Figures 3.25**, **3.26**, **3.27**, **3.28**, and **3.29**).

Title	Author
Caleb Williams	William Godwin
Caretaker & the Dumb Waiter	Harold Pinter
Catch-22	Joseph Heller
Cecilia	Fanny Burney
Celestine Prophecy	James Redfield
Certain Things Last	Sherwood Anderson
Challenge of Effective Speaking	Editor
Chaos	James Gleick
Children of a Lesser God	Mark Medoff
Cicero Pro Archia	Marcus Tullius Cicero
Cicero's Oration for Archias the Poet	Marcus Tullius Cicero
Circle of Stones, Volume 1	Judith Duerk
Civilization and its Discontents	Sigmund Freud
Civilization and Transcendence	A. C. Bhaktivedanta Swami Prabhupada
Clasic Vegetarian Cuisine	Rosemary Moon
Class American Short Stories	Editor
Classes, Power, and Conflict	Editor
Clinical manual for laryngectomy and head/neck cancer rehabilitation	Janina Casper
Coleridge's Poems	Samuel Taylor Coleridge
Collected Shorter Works	Samuel Beckett
1 2 3 Next	

Figure 3.25 Browsing by books (here I'm looking at titles that begin with the letter *C*) displays a list of titles with the option to view a particular book (Figure 3.26) or author (Figure 3.27) in more detail.

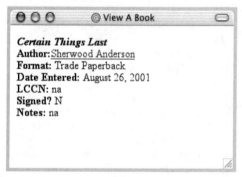

Figure 3.26 Clicking on a title brings up the `browse_book.php` page, showing all the details for that copy.

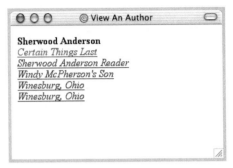

Figure 3.27 Viewing a specific author lists every title in the database by him or her. Multiple copies of the same book are reflected.

Figure 3.28 The site automatically generates all the necessary links (at the bottom) for quickly scrolling through the list.

Figure 3.29 The user can jump to any page with the numbers at the bottom or go forward or backward one page at a time.

✔ Tips

- Functions are space-sensitive in MySQL, meaning that COUNT(column) is OK but COUNT (column) is not (the parentheses must immediately follow the function name).

- You must conclude every MySQL statement with a semicolon when working from a command-line interface. However, in your PHP code, semicolons are not required.

- MySQL treats column names as case-insensitive but may or may not treat database and table names that way, depending upon the version of MySQL being used. This is why I always use lowercase names.

- Ascending (ASC) is the default when using ORDER BY in queries; descending is indicated by DESC.

- Another way you can modify your queries is to use GROUP BY to organize the data by a particular column. See the MySQL manual for more information.

SECURITY

With more and more personal information being stored on the Web—credit card data, social security numbers, maiden names—today's PHP developer cannot afford to be ignorant about security.

Security is a battle, not between programmers and hackers (or crackers), but between what you would like your site to do and what is safe for it to do. The most secure Web site would not use PHP or CGI or have HTML forms. But then it wouldn't be very interesting, either. It's my contention that the responsibility of the Web developer is to stay informed and understand when compromises are being made and what the possible ramifications of those compromises are, not necessarily to strive in vain for the unattainable, perfectly secure application. For every smart programmer, there's someone even more clever who could abuse a minor loophole. With this in mind, a security plan entails three steps:

◆ Identify the needs up front and the potential weaknesses

◆ Try to minimize those necessary holes when programming

◆ Have a backup plan available for when things do go wrong

When programming, you need to think about security from the very outset of planning to the final point of live operation. Think of security first. Think about it last. And don't let it slip in between.

This chapter will begin by demonstrating some PHP code-specific security issues: how to check incoming data from HTML forms and how to use JavaScript on the client side to do the same, use of the Mcrypt library for securely storing data, and how to use HTTP authentication. Then I'll generally discuss the Web server itself and how PHP is installed and configured. These concerns are all related to the back end, so you may or may not have control over them but should comprehend the issues regardless.

One of the examples in this chapter requires installation of special software, Mcrypt, which means that the libmcrypt must be installed (see Appendix A, Installation, for more information). For the most part, when discussing server security, the focus in this chapter will be on using the Apache Web server since it is the most popular—especially on Unix systems—but concerns for other systems will be addressed.

Validating Forms

Security begins with the server's operating system and ends with the user interface. One very common and slippery issue is HTML forms. HTML forms are ubiquitous on the Web, particularly in more advanced Web applications. The security concern lies in the fact that the PHP page handling the form will do something with the information the user enters: store it in a database, pass it along to another page, or send an email. If the information the user enters is tainted, you could have a major problem on your hands. As a rule, do not trust the user! Mistakes can happen, either on purpose or by accident, that could reveal flaws in your code, cause the loss of data, or bring your entire system to a crashing halt.

This first code example is a security two-parter. On the one hand, it will function as a registration page. This naturally leads to a user log-in system you can use to add an accessibility feature to your site, as you will in Chapter 5, Developing Web Applications. At the same time, you'll see how to securely handle data returned from an HTML form.

But first, here are a few suggestions for handling HTML forms:

◆ If possible, use the POST method in your form. POST has a limitation in that the resulting page cannot be bookmarked, but it is far more secure and does not have the limit on transmittable data size that GET does. If a user is entering passwords, you really must use the POST method lest the password be visible.

◆ Refer to the proper and specific incoming variables in your PHP handling page (see Web Server Security, Variable Order, later in this chapter).

◆ Use regular expressions and PHP's built-in functions to validate all the data received.

Although it may seem easier as a programmer to code separate pages—the HTML form and the script that processes it—frequently you will find that having the same page display and handle the form is the best way to go. It saves users from having to go back with their Web browser if problems are found and allows you to retain the information, error messages, and the form in one place.

Just as I did in Chapter 1, Advanced PHP Programming, I'll be using a simple text file system to store information here. Although this is not as efficient as using databases, it's valuable to understand how to use a text file like this because you will not always have access to a database. In Chapter 5, Developing Web Applications, I'll create a similar system with MySQL instead.

To validate a form:

1. Create a new PHP document in your text editor (**Script 4.1**):

```
<?php
```

2. Create the section of the script that handles the submitted form.

```
if (isset($HTTP_POST_VARS[Submit])) {
```

Your script should always handle the form before it could possibly redisplay it (on errors found). This is because if the form is filled out completely and the data passes every test, the page will redirect the user, and you do not want any HTML or white space sent to the browser beforehand.

If the form was submitted, the $Submit variable will be TRUE and this conditional will be entered. I use the isset() function and refer to the $HTTP_POST_VARS array for extra security. On some systems or if PHP is set to report every problem, you may need to use single-quotation marks when using associative arrays like so:

```
$HTTP_POST_VARS['Submit']
```

3. Check the username to see if it's valid.

```
if (eregi ("^[[:alnum:]]+$",
→ $HTTP_POST_VARS[username])) {
$a = TRUE;
} else {
$a = FALSE;
$message[] = "Please enter a username
→ that consists only of letters and
→ numbers.";
}
```

Using regular expressions, I'm going to run each piece of user-submitted data through a conditional to see if it is of the format I'm expecting. If it is, a dummy

variable will be set to TRUE. If it is not, the dummy variable is set to FALSE and an error message is added to the array that stores them all. At the end of this section, if all of the dummy variables are TRUE, the data passed; if any of them is FALSE, every error message will be printed and the user will see the form again.

The regular expression in this case, ^[[:alnum:]]+$, is case-insensitive but ensures that what is entered begins (^) and ends ($) with only alphanumeric characters and that something (+) is entered. Because the string must begin and end with alphanumeric characters and because there are no other allowed characters, this pattern dictates that the whole string must be of the alnum class.

4. Validate the submitted password.

```
if (eregi ("^[[:alnum:]]{8,16}$",
→ $HTTP_POST_VARS[pass1])) {
$b = TRUE;
} else {
$b = FALSE;
$message[] = "Please enter a password
→ that consists only of letters and
→ numbers, between 8 and 16
→ characters long.";
}
```

The regular expression for a password mandates that it must consist only of alphanumeric characters and that it must be between 8 and 16 characters long ({8,16}).

The *username* variable did not have a length requirement, but you could add one by replacing the plus sign on line 6 with something like {4,10} or {6,} (the latter meaning it must be at least six characters long).

continues on page 131

Script 4.1 This page displays a registration form and processes it all in one. It validates the submitted data and reports on errors found.

```
1    <?php
2
3    if (isset($HTTP_POST_VARS[Submit])) { // If the form was submitted, process it.
4
5        // Check the username.
6        if (eregi ("^[[:alnum:]]+$", $HTTP_POST_VARS[username])) {
7            $a = TRUE;
8        } else {
9            $a = FALSE;
10           $message[] = "Please enter a username that consists only of letters and numbers.";
11       }
12
13       // Check to make sure the password is long enough and of the right format.
14       if (eregi ("^[[:alnum:]]{8,16}$", $HTTP_POST_VARS[pass1])) {
15           $b = TRUE;
16       } else {
17           $b = FALSE;
18           $message[] = "Please enter a password that consists only of letters and numbers,
                  between 8 and 16 characters long.";
19       }
20
21       // Check to make sure the password matches the confirmed password.
22       if ($HTTP_POST_VARS[pass1] == $HTTP_POST_VARS[pass2]) {
23           $c = TRUE;
24           $password = crypt ($HTTP_POST_VARS[pass1]); // Encrypt the password.
25       } else {
26           $c = FALSE;
27           $message[] = "The password you entered did not match the confirmed password.";
28       }
29
30       // Check to make sure they entered their first name and it's of the right format.
31       if (eregi ("^([[:alpha:]]|-|')+$", $HTTP_POST_VARS[first_name])) {
32           $d = TRUE;
33       } else {
34           $d = FALSE;
35           $message[] = "Please enter a valid first name.";
36       }
37
38       // Check to make sure they entered their last name and it's of the right format.
39       if (eregi ("^([[:alpha:]]|-|')+$", $HTTP_POST_VARS[last_name])) {
40           $e = TRUE;
41       } else {
42           $e = FALSE;
43           $message[] = "Please enter a valid last name.";
44       }
45
46       // Check to make sure they entered a valid email address.
47       if (eregi("^([[:alnum:]]|_|\.|-)+@([[:alnum:]]|\.|-)+(\.)([a-z]{2,4})$",
             $HTTP_POST_VARS[email])) {
48           $f = TRUE;
49       } else {
50           $f = FALSE;
```

(script continues on next page)

Script 4.1 *continued*

```
script

51              $message[] = "Please enter a valid email address.";
52          }
53
54          // Check to make sure they entered a valid birth date.
55          if (checkdate ($HTTP_POST_VARS[birth_month], $HTTP_POST_VARS[birth_day],
            $HTTP_POST_VARS[birth_year])) {
56                  $g = TRUE;
57          } else {
58                  $g = FALSE;
59              $message[] = "Please enter a valid birth date.";
60          }
61
62          //  If the data passes all the tests, check to ensure a unique member name, then register
            them.
63          if ($a AND $b AND $c AND $d AND $e AND $f AND $g) {
64
65              if ($fp = @fopen ("../users.txt", "r")) { // Open the file for reading.
66
67                  while ( !feof($fp) AND !$user_found ) { // Loop through each line, checking each
                    username.
68                      $read_data = fgetcsv ($fp, 1000, "\t"); // Read the line into an array.
69                      if ($read_data[0] == $HTTP_POST_VARS[username]) {
70                          $user_found = TRUE;
71                      }
72                  }
73                  fclose ($fp); // Close the file.
74
75                  if (!$user_found) { // If the username is OK, register them.
76
77                      if ($fp2 = @fopen ("../users.txt", "a")) { // Open the file for writing.
78                          $write_data = $HTTP_POST_VARS[username] . "\t" . $password . "\t" .
                            $HTTP_POST_VARS[first_name] . "\t" . $HTTP_POST_VARS[last_name] . "\t" .
                            $HTTP_POST_VARS[email] . "\t" . $HTTP_POST_VARS[birth_month] . "-" .
                            $HTTP_POST_VARS[birth_day] . "-" . $HTTP_POST_VARS[birth_year] . "\n";
79                          fwrite ($fp2, $write_data);
80                          fclose ($fp2);
81                          $message = urlencode ("You have been successfully registered.");
82                          header ("Location: homepage.php?message=$message"); // Send them on
                            their way.
83                          exit;
84                      } else {
85                          $message[] = "Could not register to the user's file! Please contact the
                            Webmaster for more information.<br />";
86                      }
87                  } else {
88                      $message[] = "That username is already taken. Please select another.";
89                  }
90
91              } else { // If it couldn't open the file, print an error message.
92                  $message[] = "Could not read the user's file! Please contact the Webmaster for more
                    information.<br />";
93              }
```

(script continues on next page)

Script 4.1 *continued*

```
                                              script
94        }
95
96
97    } // End of Submit if.
98    ?>
99    <!DOCTYPE html PUBLIC "-//W3C//DTD XHTML 1.0 Strict//EN"
100   "http://www.w3.org/TR/2000/REC-xhtml1-20000126/DTD/xhtml1-strict.dtd">
101   <html xmlns="http://www.w3.org/1999/xhtml">
102   <head>
103       <title>Register</title>
104   </head>
105   <body>
106   <?php
107   // Print out any error messages.
108   if ($message) {
109       echo "<div align=\"left\"><font color=red><b>The following problems occurred:</b><br />\n";
110       foreach ($message as $key => $value) {
111           echo "$value <br />\n";
112       }
113       echo "<p></p><b>Be sure to re-enter your passwords and your birth date!</b></font></div><br
              />\n";
114   }
115   ?>
116   <form action="register.php" method="post">
117   <table border="0" width="90%" cellspacing="2" cellpadding="2" align="center">
118       <tr>
119           <td align="right">Username</td>
120           <td align="left"><input type="text" name="username" size="25" maxsize="16"
              value="<?=$HTTP_POST_VARS[username] ?>"></td>
121           <td align="left"><small>Maximum of 16 characters, stick to letters and numbers, no
              spaces, underscores, hyphens, etc.</small></td>
122       </tr>
123       <tr>
124           <td align="right">Password</td>
125           <td align="left"><input type="password" name="pass1" size="25"></td>
126           <td align="left"><small>Minimum of 8 characters, maximum of 16, stick to letters and
              numbers, no spaces, underscores, hyphens, etc.</small></td>
127       </tr>
128       <tr>
129           <td align="right">Confirm Password</td>
130           <td align="left"><input type="password" name="pass2" size="25"></td>
131           <td align="left"><small>Should be the same as the password.</small></td>
132       </tr>
133       <tr>
134           <td align="right">First Name</td>
135           <td align="left"><input type="text" name="first_name" size="25" maxsize="20"
              value="<?=$HTTP_POST_VARS[first_name] ?>"></td>
136           <td align="left"> </td>
137       </tr>
138       <tr>
139           <td align="right">Last Name</td>
```

(script continues on next page)

VALIDATING FORMS

Script 4.1 *continued*

```
                                          script
140            <td align="left"><input type="text" name="last_name" size="25" maxsize="20"
               value="<?=$HTTP_POST_VARS[last_name] ?>"></td>
141            <td align="left"> </td>
142        </tr>
143        <tr>
144            <td align="right">Email Address</td>
145            <td align="left"><input type="text" name="email" size="25" maxsize="60"
               value="<?=$HTTP_POST_VARS[email] ?>"></td>
146            <td align="left"><small>Use whichever email address you want to receive notices
               at.</small></td>
147        </tr>
148        <tr>
149            <td align="right">Birth date</td>
150            <td align="left" colspan="2">
151    <?php
152    echo '<select name="birth_month">
153    <option value="">Month</option>
154    ';
155    for ($n = 1; $n <= 12; $n++) {
156        echo "<option value=\"$n\">$n</option>\n";
157    }
158    echo '</select>
159    <select name="birth_day">
160    <option value="">Day</option>
161    ';
162    for ($n = 1; $n <= 31; $n++) {
163        echo "<option value=\"$n\">$n</option>\n";
164    }
165    echo '</select>
166    <select name="birth_year">
167    <option value="">Year</option>
168    ';
169    for ($n = 1900; $n <= 2001; $n++) {
170        echo "<option value=\"$n\">$n</option>\n";
171    }
172    ?>
173            </select></td>
174        </tr>
175        <tr>
176            <td align="center" colspan="3"><input type="submit" name="Submit" value="Register!">
                     <input type="reset" name="Reset" value="Reset"></td>
177        </tr>
178    </table>
179    </form>
180    </body>
181    </html>
```

5. Check that the entered password matches the confirmed password.

```
if ($HTTP_POST_VARS[pass1] ==
→ $HTTP_POST_VARS[pass2]) {

$c = TRUE;

$password = crypt ($HTTP_POST_
→ VARS[pass1]);

} else {

$c = FALSE;

$message[] = "The password you
→ entered did not match the confirmed
→ password.";

}
```

This is always a good thing to add in a registration page because it is very easy for users to misspell or enter their passwords incorrectly and then not be able to log in. If the passwords do match, a new variable, $password, will be created that is an encrypted version of the submitted passwords.

6. Validate the user's first and last names.

```
if (eregi ("^([[:alpha:]]|-|')+$",
→ $HTTP_POST_VARS[first_name])) {

$d = TRUE;

} else {

$d = FALSE;

$message[] = "Please enter a valid
→ first name.";

}

if (eregi ("^([[:alpha:]]|-|')+$",
→ $HTTP_POST_VARS[last_name])) {

$e = TRUE;

} else {

$e = FALSE;

$message[] = "Please enter a valid
→ last name.";

}
```

The pattern for checking the users' first and last names is similar to the one used to check their passwords and usernames. The primary difference is that a name may contain the apostrophe or a hyphen, so these have been added to the mix. I use the pipe symbol (|) to say that the characters can be either alphanumeric, a hyphen or an apostrophe.

7. Validate the user's submitted email address.

```
if (eregi("^([[:alnum:]]|_|\.|-
→ )+@([[:alnum:]]|\.|-)+(\.)([a-z]
→ {2,4})$", $HTTP_POST_VARS[email]))
→ {

$f = TRUE;

} else {

$f = FALSE;

$message[] = "Please enter a valid
→ email address.";

}
```

There are any number of patterns you can use to validate an email address, depending on how strict or liberal you want to be. This one, `^([[:alnum:]]|_|\.|-)+@([[:alnum:]]|\.|-)+(\.)([a-z]{2,4})$`, seems to work pretty well for me. Breaking it down, it states that the submitted information must begin with one or more alphanumeric characters, underscores, periods, or hyphens (`^([[:alnum:]]|_|\.|-)+`). That is followed by the required at symbol (@) and the domain name (`[[:alnum:]]|\.|-`). The email address must end with a period followed by two to four letters (`(\.)([a-z]{2,4})$`). Certainly some invalid email addresses could slip through this expression, but it does add a sufficient level of security for my needs. Feel free to use a different pattern if you have one to your liking. Keep in mind that a user could enter a valid e-mail address that does not actually exist.

continues on next page

VALIDATING FORMS

8. Check to see if the user entered a valid birthday.

```
if (checkdate ($HTTP_POST_VARS
→ [birth_month], $HTTP_POST_VARS
→ [birth_day], $HTTP_POST_VARS
→ [birth_year])) {
$g = TRUE;
} else {
$g = FALSE;
$message[] = "Please enter a valid
→ birth date.";
}
```

There is really no way of knowing if the information users enter is in fact their birthday, but PHP's built-in `checkdate()` function can confirm whether or not that date existed. If the user implied there were 31 days in a September or a February 29 in a nonleap year, this test would catch it. Sometimes security is a matter of taking away the easy routes people can use to trick a system.

9. Check to see if the data passed every test.

```
if ($a AND $b AND $c AND $d AND $e
→ AND $f AND $g) {
```

If every one of the dummy variables is TRUE, it's safe to register the user. If any one is FALSE, the error message(s) will be printed and the user will be given the chance to try again. Because the dummy variables are being used only here, I never bothered to use more elaborate names, although you may want to (like $username_okay, $password_okay, etc.).

10. Open the file that stores the usernames.

```
if ($fp = @fopen ("../users.txt",
→ "r")) {
```

Because this file is being read from and written to, it should be located outside of the Web document structure.

11. Check to see if that username is already taken.

```
while ( !feof($fp) AND !$user_found
→ ) {
$read_data = fgetcsv ($fp, 1000,
→ "\t");
if ($read_data[0] == $HTTP_POST_VARS
→ [username]) {
$user_found = TRUE;
}
}
fclose ($fp);
```

This loop will continue to read each line from the file until it comes to the end of the file (`!feof($fp)`) or the particular username is discovered (`!$user_found`). On each iteration of the loop, it reads in a line of data with the `fgetcsv()` function. This function takes three arguments—the file pointer, the length to read, and the delimiting character—and turns each read line into an array.

In this case, the data is stored as a tab-delimited row with the username first. If the username read from the file (`$read_data[0]`) matches the submitted username, then the `$user_found` variable will be TRUE and the loop will end. If not, the loop will continue.

12. If the username is not already taken, write the user's information to the file.

```
if (!$user_found) {
if ($fp2 = @fopen ("../users.txt",
→ "a")) {
$write_data = $HTTP_POST_VARS[user-
→ name] . "\t" . $password . "\t" .
→ $HTTP_POST_VARS[first_name] . "\t" .
→ $HTTP_POST_VARS[last_name] . "\t" .
→ $HTTP_POST_VARS[email] . "\t" .
→ $HTTP_POST_VARS[birth_month] . "-" .
→ $HTTP_POST_VARS[birth_day] . "-" .
→ $HTTP_POST_VARS[birth_year] . "\n";
```

```
fwrite ($fp2, $write_data);

fclose ($fp2);
```

All of the submitted data will be appended to the user's file with tabs separating each piece of information. The birth month, day, and year are complied together in the form *1-1-1900* and the stored password is the encrypted version, *not* the submitted one. Ideally, you should never store passwords on your system in an unencrypted form. Web application security involves protecting both yourself (and your system) and the site's other visitors.

13. Create a message to indicate successful registration and forward the user to the next page.

```
$message = urlencode ("You have been
→ successfully registered.");

header ("Location: homepage.php?
→ message=$message");

exit;
```

You must use the `urlencode()` function to pass along the message successfully to the next page, since it will be appended to the URL. If you don't, the received message will be cut off at the first blank space or special character.

Also, be sure to use the `exit` statement (in either this form or the more formal `exit()`) so that the page does not continue to be processed.

14. Finish the necessary conditionals.

```
} else {

$message[] = "Could not register to
→ the users file! Please contact the
→ webmaster for more information.
→ <br />";

}

} else {

$message[] = "That username is
→ already taken. Please select
→ another.";
```

```
}

} else {

$message[] = "Could not read the
→ user's file! Please contact the
→ Webmaster for more information.
→ <br />";

}

}
```

These three `else` statements add to the `$message` array for any problem encountered: not being able to write to the user's file, a particular username already being taken, or if the script could not read the user's file.

15. Close the primary conditional and the PHP section.

```
}

?>
```

16. Create the HTML head and body.

```
<!DOCTYPE html PUBLIC "-//W3C//DTD
→ XHTML 1.0 Strict//EN"

"http://www.w3.org/TR/2000/
→ REC-xhtml1-20000126/DTD/
→ xhtml1-strict.dtd">

<html xmlns="http://www.w3.org/1999/
→ xhtml">

<head>

<title>Register</title>

</head>

<body>
```

17. Open another PHP section and print out any error messages.

```
<?php

if ($message) {

echo "<div align=\"left\"><font
→ color=red><b>The following
→ problems occurred:</b><br />\n";

foreach ($message as $key => $value)
→ {
```

continues on next page

```
echo "$value <br /><br />\n";
}
echo "<p></p><b>Be sure to re-enter
→ your passwords and your birth
→ date!</b></font></div><br />
→ <br />\n";
}
?>
```

This section of PHP must come after the HTML head and will be used only once the form has been submitted and errors were found. Because the messages were stored in an array in case there were multiple problems, you'll loop through and print each individual message, along with a caption.

18. Begin the HTML registration form.

```
<form action="register.php"
→ method="post">
<table border="0" width="90%"
→ cellspacing="2" cellpadding="2"
→ align="center">
<tr>
<td align="right">Username</td>
<td align="left"><input type="text"
→ name="username" size="25"
→ maxsize="16"
value="<?=$HTTP_POST_VARS[username]
→ ?>"></td>
```

It's always a good idea to use the `maxsize` attribute for your inputs. Although it's possible for a user to circumvent this, it's a good way to limit the amount of data entered, particularly if that data is going to be stored in a database with a fixed-length column (e.g., a *username* column of type `VARCHAR(16)`).

Notice also that I print out the existing value of each element, if it already exists, using PHP's `<?=$variable` shortcut, as introduced in Chapter 1, Advanced PHP Programming. Thanks to this, if users make a mistake and have to reprocess the form, they will not have to re-enter every piece of information. The form has two exceptions to this: the passwords, which in HTML will not display an explicitly stated value regardless, and the three birthday fields, for which I did not think it worth the extra processing time to have PHP automatically reselect each element for the user.

The form should be referred back to the same page it is on by using either `action="register.php"` (as I did here) or `action="<?=$PHP_SELF ?>"`. Technically, if you do not put in an action attribute, the page will automatically submit to itself, but it is bad form (pun intended) to do so.

19. Complete the HTML form.

```
<td align="left"><small>Maximum of
→ 16 characters, stick to letters
→ and numbers, no spaces, under
→ scores, hyphens, etc.</small></td>
</tr>
<tr>
<td align="right">Password</td>
<td align="left"><input type=
→ "password" name="pass1"
→ size="25"></td>
<td align="left"><small>Minimum of 8
→ characters, maximum of 16, stick
→ to letters and numbers, no spaces,
→ underscores, hyphens, etc.</small>
→ </td>
</tr>
<tr>
<td align="right">Confirm
→ Password</td>
<td align="left"><input type=
→ "password" name="pass2"
→ size="25"></td>
```

```
<td align="left"><small>Should be
→ the same as the password.</small>
→ </td>
</tr>
<tr>
<td align="right">First Name</td>
<td align="left"><input type="text"
→ name="first_name" size="25"
→ maxsize="20" value="<?=$HTTP_POST_
→ VARS[first_name] ?>"></td>
<td align="left"> </td>
</tr>
<tr>
<td align="right">Last Name</td>
<td align="left"><input type="text"
→ name="last_name" size="25" m
→ axsize="20"
value="<?=$HTTP_POST_VARS[last_name]
→ ?>"></td>
<td align="left"> </td>
</tr>
<tr>
<td align="right">Email Address</td>
<td align="left"><input type="text"
→ name="email" size="25" maxsize=
→ "60" value="<?=$HTTP_POST_VARS
→ [email] ?>"></td>
<td align="left"><small>Use
→ whichever email address you want
→ to receive notices at.</small>
→ </td>
</tr>
<tr>
<td align="right">Birth date</td>
<td align="left" colspan="2">
<?php
echo '<select name="birth_month">
<option value="">Month</option>
';
for ($n = 1; $n <= 12; $n++) {
```

```
echo "<option value=\"$n\">$n
→ </option>\n";
}
echo '</select>
<select name="birth_day">
<option value="">Day</option>
';
for ($n = 1; $n <= 31; $n++) {
echo "<option value=\"$n\">$n
→ </option>\n";
}
echo '</select>
<select name="birth_year">
<option value="">Year</option>
';
for ($n = 1900; $n <= 2001; $n++) {
echo "<option value=\"$n\">$n
→ </option>\n";
}
?>
</select></td>
</tr>
<tr>
<td align="center" colspan="3">
→ <input type="submit" name="Submit"
→ value="Register!">    
→   <input type="reset"
→ name="Reset" value="Reset"></td>
</tr>
</table>
</form>
```

The form is very straightforward, so I will not go over it in detail. I did save myself some HTML coding by using PHP loops to generate the three birthday pull-down menus, but that was not necessary. You could, if you wanted to take the script a step further, have the year loop go until date("Y")—the current year in four-digit form—instead of hard-coding 2001.

continues on next page

20. Finish the HTML page.

```
</body>
</html>
```

21. Save the file as `register.php` and upload it to your server.

22. Create a blank text file called `users.txt` and save it on your server in the directory above `register.php`. Make all attempts to place the file outside of the Web document root, then refer back to the proper location in this script (e.g., use `../users.txt` instead of merely `users.txt`).

23. Set the permissions on `users.txt` to 666 (universal read-write).

Any time you state universal read-write permissions on a file or directory, it is a security risk, which is why you ought to place these files outside of the Web document root. I'll explain further:

If I have a file, `users.txt`, set to 666 and stored in the main Web directory (frequently `html` or `www`), a script on another server could just as easily read from and write to it as my own PHP scripts, potentially placing malicious code or data there, let alone reading everything stored. (This is assuming that a hacker is aware your file exists, of course.) If it is not possible for you to place such a file below the Web document tree, you should take precautions such as using Apache's `.htaccess` files to limit accessibility, as I'll discuss later in this chapter.

24. Make a simple `homepage.php` that displays the registration message to the user (**Script 4.2**).

```
<!DOCTYPE html PUBLIC "-//W3C//DTD
→ XHTML 1.0 Strict//EN"
"http://www.w3.org/TR/2000/
→ REC-xhtml1-20000126/DTD
→ /xhtml1-strict.dtd">
```

Script 4.2 This is a very, very simple page that the user is redirected to upon successful registration. It will report to the user any messages received.

```
1   <!DOCTYPE html PUBLIC "-//W3C//DTD XHTML
    1.0 Strict//EN"
2   "http://www.w3.org/TR/2000/
    REC-xhtml1-20000126/DTD/xhtml1-
    strict.dtd">
3   <html xmlns="http://www.w3.org/1999/
    xhtml">
4   <head>
5       <title>Home Page</title>
6   </head>
7   <body>
8   <?php
9   if ($message) {
10      $message = urldecode($message);
11      echo "<div align=\"left\"><font
        color=blue><b>$message</b></font>
        </div><br />\n";
12  }
13  ?>
14  </body>
15  </html>
```

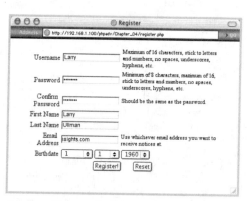

Figure 4.1 When users first come to `register.php`, this is the form they will see.

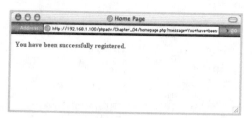

Figure 4.2 If all of the data passed through the various checks, the user's information will be recorded in `users.txt` and the user will be redirected to `index.php` where the message is displayed.

Script 4.3 After registering, users.txt now stores the user's information, including an encrypted version of their passwords.

```
1.    Larry    secGBN1BHq1FA    Larry    Ullman
      php@DMCinsights.com 1-1-1960
```

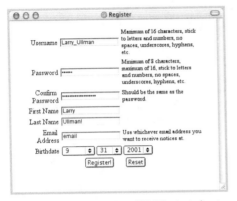

Figure 4.3 This registration will fail for just about every reason because most of the data is invalid. Figure 4.4 shows the result.

Figure 4.4 A lot of mistakes were made in this registration attempt and they were each reported back to the user. Notice how most of the form data is retained, a convenience to the user.

```
<html xmlns="http://www.w3.org/
→ 1999/xhtml">
<head>
<title>Home Page</title>
</head>
<body>
<?php
if ($message) {
$message = urldecode($message);
→ echo "<div align=\"left\"><font
→ color=blue><b>$message</b></font>
→ </div><br />\n";
}
?>
</body>
</html>
```

One thing to note here is that the PHP uses the urldecode() function to turn the passed message back into a readable form. Presumably, your home page will do a lot more than this one.

25. Run and test register.php in your Web browser (**Figures 4.1**, **4.2**, **4.3**, **4.4**, and **4.5**).

26. Open users.txt in your text editor to confirm the results (**Script 4.3**).

Figure 4.5 If someone has already registered with the particular username, an error is reported and the user can try registering with a different name.

✔ Tips

■ Placing HIDDEN values in HTML forms can be a great way to pass information from page to page without using cookies or sessions. But be careful what you hide in your HTML code, because those HIDDEN values can be seen by viewing a page's source. This technique is a convenience, not a security measure.

■ Similarly, you should not be too obvious or reliant upon information PHP passes via the URL. For example, if the home-page.php page requires receipt of a user ID—and that is the only mandatory information for access to the account—someone else could easily break in. (e.g., *www.dmcinsights.com/phpadv/userhome.php?user=2* could quickly be turned into *www.dmcinsights.com/phpadv/userhome.php?user=3*, granting access to someone else's information).

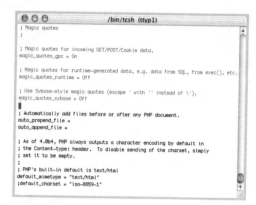

Figure 4.6 The invaluable php.ini file allows you to set any number of parameters for how PHP operates, including turning Magic Quotes on and off.

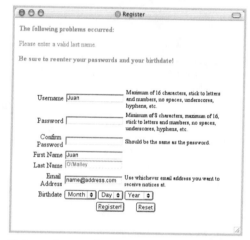

Figure 4.7 Because Magic Quotes are turned on and the script does not use stripslashes() before testing the data, the user's last name was rejected when it is perfectly valid.

Magic Quotes

Built into PHP is a feature referred to as Magic Quotes. Magic Quotes take single and double quotation marks and escape them, turning each into \' and \". This renders them safe to print to the browser and safe to store in databases. Magic Quotes can be turned on or off either during PHP installation or by manually editing the `php.ini` file (**Figure 4.6**) and restarting your Web server.

There are two types of Magic Quotes: *gpc* and *runtime*. The former stands for "GET, POST, COOKIES" and applies to data received by PHP from one of those sources. The second affects data retrieved from databases or files.

I mention magic quotes here because if `magic_quotes_gpc` are turned on in your server, then the data from the form in this example may be rejected by the regular expressions. For example, the last name *O'Malley* will be turned into *O\'Malley*, and the backslash is not allowed by the last name pattern. Further, when the error message is returned and the form is redisplayed with the existing values, the last name will appear as *O\'Malley* (**Figure 4.7**).

If Magic Quotes are enabled on your server, you can undo its impact before running through the regular expressions by using the `stripslashes()` function:

```
$variable = stripslashes($variable);
```

Conversely, if Magic Quotes are not enabled, use `addslashes()` to create the same effect before storing the data (if necessary).

If you do not have the authority to see and modify the `php.ini` file, you can quickly determine if the two different Magic Quotes settings are on or off by calling the `get_magic_quotes_gpc()` and `get_magic_quotes_runtime()` functions, which return *1* if the Magic Quote is set to *On* or *0* if it is set to *Off*.

You can also use the `set_magic_quotes_runtime()` function to change the value for a particular script, although this will affect only *runtime* and not *gpc*:

```
set_magic_quotes _runtime (0);
```

Validating Forms with JavaScript

JavaScript is not a true security measure in itself, but rather an added level of security and a convenience to your users. Because JavaScript is a client-side technology (whereas PHP is server-side), incorporating it into your pages can save users the hassle of having to submit a form to the Web server, have it checked by PHP, and have the data sent back upon errors. Instead, you can use JavaScript to immediately run through some tests and then, if the data passes, send the form information along to PHP. However, JavaScript does this at the cost of a larger file size for the user to initially download.

I say that JavaScript in itself is not a security measure because it can be easily turned off in a user's browser setting (**Figure 4.8**), rendering it completely useless. It is critical that you view JavaScript in this light and continue to use PHP as your primary security measure.

As a convenience to the site's users and to demonstrate that security measures are in place (kind of like having a *This house is protected by...* sticker on your site's window), I'll add JavaScript checking to the registration page. The checks will be comparable to the existing PHP ones although not as detailed and precise.

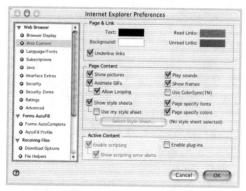

Figure 4.8 Really old browsers won't run JavaScript and users can turn scripting off in their preferences panel—just two reasons why you cannot rely upon JavaScript as your only security measure.

Figure 4.9 Because the user submitted the form before entering a username, JavaScript creates an alert box that the user must approve before continuing.

Figure 4.10 After the alert window is OK'd, the username field is highlighted and set to *** *Username* to get the user's attention.

To validate a form with JavaScript:

1. Open `register.php` in your text editor (Script 4.1).

2. Within the head section of the HTML, add the following JavaScript (**Script 4.4**):

```
<script type="text/javascript"
→ language="Javascript">
<!--
function CheckData() {
if (document.form.username.
→ value.length <= 0) {
alert ("Enter a username.");
document.form.username.value = "***
→ Username";
document.form.username.focus();
var problem = true;
}
```

This JavaScript function, `CheckData()`, will make sure that the user entered some value for each of the fields in the form. The construct `document.form.username.value.length` refers to the length of the value entered into the *username* input for the form in this document. If the user entered something, the length will be greater than 0. If the user didn't, the length will be less than or equal to 0. If the user did not enter a username, then an alert pop-up window will be created (**Figure 4.9**) and the user's attention will be directed to the field in the Web browser (**Figure 4.10**) via JavaScript's `focus()` method.

If there was a problem, the `problem` variable is set to `true`. (JavaScript does not use a dollar sign or other initial character to indicate a variable.) Notice also that JavaScript uses the format `true`, whereas PHP uses `TRUE` (in fact, if you were to write `TRUE` in your JavaScript, you'll encounter

continues on page 146

Script 4.4 While register.php is only marginally more secure now, it is better for your users and, therefore, the whole site.

```php
1    <?php
2
3    if (isset($HTTP_POST_VARS[Submit])) { // If the form was submitted, process it.
4
5        // Check the username.
6        if (eregi ("^[[:alnum:]]+$", $HTTP_POST_VARS[username])) {
7            $a = TRUE;
8        } else {
9            $a = FALSE;
10           $message[] = "Please enter a username that consists only of letters and numbers.";
11       }
12
13       // Check to make sure the password is long enough and of the right format.
14       if (eregi ("^[[:alnum:]]{8,16}$", $HTTP_POST_VARS[pass1])) {
15           $b = TRUE;
16       } else {
17           $b = FALSE;
18           $message[] = "Please enter a password that consists only of letters and numbers,
                 between 8 and 16 characters long.";
19       }
20
21       // Check to make sure the password matches the confirmed password.
22       if ($HTTP_POST_VARS[pass1] == $HTTP_POST_VARS[pass2]) {
23           $c = TRUE;
24           $password = crypt ($HTTP_POST_VARS[pass1]); // Encrypt the password.
25       } else {
26           $c = FALSE;
27           $message[] = "The password you entered did not match the confirmed password.";
28       }
29
30       // Check to make sure they entered their first name and it's of the right format.
31       if (eregi ("^([[:alpha:]]|-|')+$", $HTTP_POST_VARS[first_name])) {
32           $d = TRUE;
33       } else {
34           $d = FALSE;
35           $message[] = "Please enter a valid first name.";
36       }
37
38       // Check to make sure they entered their last name and it's of the right format.
39       if (eregi ("^([[:alpha:]]|-|')+$", $HTTP_POST_VARS[last_name])) {
40           $e = TRUE;
41       } else {
42           $e = FALSE;
43           $message[] = "Please enter a valid last name.";
44       }
45
46       // Check to make sure they entered a valid email address.
47       if (eregi("^([[:alnum:]]|_|\.|-)+@([[:alnum:]]|\.|-)+(\.)([a-z]{2,4})$",
             $HTTP_POST_VARS[email])) {
48           $f = TRUE;
49       } else {
50           $f = FALSE;
51           $message[] = "Please enter a valid email address.";
52       }
53
54       // Check to make sure they entered a valid birth date.
55       if (checkdate ($HTTP_POST_VARS[birth_month], $HTTP_POST_VARS[birth_day],
             $HTTP_POST_VARS[birth_year])) {
56           $g = TRUE;
57       } else {
58           $g = FALSE;
59           $message[] = "Please enter a valid birth date.";
```

(script continues on next page)

VALIDATING FORMS WITH JAVASCRIPT

Script 4.4 *continued*

```
                                            script
60        }
61
62        //  If the data passes all the tests, check to ensure a unique member name, then register them.
63        if ($a AND $b AND $c AND $d AND $e AND $f AND $g) {
64
65            if ($fp = @fopen ("../users.txt", "r")) { // Open the file for reading.
66
67                while ( !feof($fp) AND !$user_found ) { // Loop through each line, checking each
                  username.
68                    $read_data = fgetcsv ($fp, 1000, "\t"); // Read the line into an array.
69                    if ($read_data[0] == $HTTP_POST_VARS[username]) {
70                        $user_found = TRUE;
71                    }
72                }
73                fclose ($fp);
74
75                if (!$user_found) { // If the username is OK, register them.
76
77                    if ($fp2 = @fopen ("../users.txt", "a")) { // Open the file for writing.
78                        $write_data = $HTTP_POST_VARS[username] . "\t" . $password . "\t" .
                          $HTTP_POST_VARS[first_name] . "\t" . $HTTP_POST_VARS[last_name] . "\t" .
                          $HTTP_POST_VARS[email] . "\t" . $HTTP_POST_VARS[birth_month] . "-" .
                          $HTTP_POST_VARS[birth_day] . "-" . $HTTP_POST_VARS[birth_year] . "\n";
79                        fwrite ($fp2, $write_data);
80                        fclose ($fp2);
81                        $message = urlencode ("You have been successfully registered.");
82                        header ("Location: homepage.php?message=$message"); // Send them on their way.
83                        exit;
84                    } else {
85                        $message[] = "Could not register to the user's file! Please contact the
                          Webmaster for more information.<br />";
86                    }
87                } else {
88                    $message[] = "That username is already taken. Please select another.";
89                }
90
91            } else { // If it couldn't open the file, print an error message.
92                $message[] = "Could not read the user's file! Please contact the Webmaster for more
                  information.<br />";
93            }
94        }
95
96
97    } // End of Submit if.
98    ?>
99    <!DOCTYPE html PUBLIC "-//W3C//DTD XHTML 1.0 Strict//EN"
100          "http://www.w3.org/TR/2000/REC-xhtml1-20000126/DTD/xhtml1-strict.dtd">
101   <html xmlns="http://www.w3.org/1999/xhtml">
102   <head>
103       <title>Register</title>
104   <script type="text/javascript" language="Javascript">
105   <!-- // Begin to hide script contents from old browsers.
106   function CheckData() {
107       if (document.form.username.value.length <= 0) {
108           alert ("Enter a username.");
109           document.form.username.value = "*** Username";
110           document.form.username.focus();
111           var problem = true;
112       }
113       if (document.form.first_name.value.length <= 0) {
114           alert ("Enter your first name.");
115           document.form.first_name.value = "*** First Name";
116           document.form.first_name.focus();
```

(script continues on next page)

Script 4.4 *continued*

```
         script

117            var problem = true;
118        }
119        if (document.form.last_name.value.length <= 0) {
120            alert ("Enter your last name.");
121            document.form.last_name.value = "*** Last Name";
122            document.form.last_name.focus();
123            var problem = true;
124        }
125        if (document.form.email.value.length <= 0) {
126            alert ("Enter your email address.");
127            document.form.email.value = "*** Email Address";
128            document.form.email.focus();
129            var problem = true;
130        }
131        if (document.form.pass1.value.length < 8) {
132            alert ("Enter a password at least 8 characters long.");
133            var problem = true;
134        }
135        if (document.form.pass1.value != document.form.pass2.value) {
136            alert ("Your confirmed password does not match the entered password.");
137            var problem = true;
138        }
139        if ((document.form.birth_month.value == 0) || (document.form.birth_month.selectedIndex == 0)) {
140            alert ("Please select your month of birth.");
141            var problem = true;
142        }
143        if ((document.form.birth_day.value == 0) || (document.form.birth_day.selectedIndex == 0)) {
144            alert ("Please select your day of birth.");
145            var problem = true;
146        }
147        if ((document.form.birth_year.value == 0) || (document.form.birth_year.selectedIndex == 0)) {
148            alert ("Please select your year of birth.");
149            var problem = true;
150        }
151
152        if (problem == true) {
153            return false;
154        } else {
155            return true;
156        }
157    }
158    //-->
159    </script>
160    </head>
161    <body>
162    <?php
163    // Print out any error messages.
164    if ($message) {
165        echo "<div align=\"left\"><font color=red><b>The following problems occurred:</b><br />\n";
166        foreach ($message as $key => $value) {
167            echo "$value <br />\n";
168        }
169        echo "<p></p><b>Be sure to re-enter your passwords and your birth date!</b></font></div><br
           />\n";
170    }
171    ?>
172    <form name="form" action="register.php" method="post" onsubmit="return CheckData()">
173    <table border="0" width="90%" cellspacing="2" cellpadding="2" align="center">
174        <tr>
175            <td align="right">Username</td>
176            <td align="left"><input type="text" name="username" size="25" maxsize="16"
               value="<?=$HTTP_POST_VARS[username] ?>"></td>
177            <td align="left"><small>Maximum of 16 characters, stick to letters and numbers, no spaces,
               underscores, hyphens, etc.</small></td>
```

(script continues on next page)

Script 4.4 *continued*

```
                                          script

178        </tr>
179        <tr>
180            <td align="right">Password</td>
181            <td align="left"><input type="password" name="pass1" size="25"></td>
182            <td align="left"><small>Minimum of 8 characters, maximum of 16, stick to letters and
               numbers, no spaces, underscores, hyphens, etc.</small></td>
183        </tr>
184        <tr>
185            <td align="right">Confirm Password</td>
186            <td align="left"><input type="password" name="pass2" size="25"></td>
187            <td align="left"><small>Should be the same as the password.</small></td>
188        </tr>
189        <tr>
190            <td align="right">First Name</td>
191            <td align="left"><input type="text" name="first_name" size="25" maxsize="20"
               value="<?=$HTTP_POST_VARS[first_name] ?>"></td>
192            <td align="left"> </td>
193        </tr>
194        <tr>
195            <td align="right">Last Name</td>
196            <td align="left"><input type="text" name="last_name" size="25" maxsize="20"
               value="<?=$HTTP_POST_VARS[last_name] ?>"></td>
197            <td align="left"> </td>
198        </tr>
199        <tr>
200            <td align="right">Email Address</td>
201            <td align="left"><input type="text" name="email" size="25" maxsize="60"
               value="<?=$HTTP_POST_VARS[email] ?>"></td>
202            <td align="left"><small>Use whichever email address you want to receive notices
               at.</small></td>
203        </tr>
204        <tr>
205            <td align="right">Birthdate</td>
206            <td align="left" colspan="2">
207    <?php
208    echo '<select name="birth_month">
209    <option value="">Month</option>
210    ';
211    for ($n = 1; $n <= 12; $n++) {
212        echo "<option value=\"$n\">$n</option>\n";
213    }
214    echo '</select>
215    <select name="birth_day">
216    <option value="">Day</option>
217    ';
218    for ($n = 1; $n <= 31; $n++) {
219        echo "<option value=\"$n\">$n</option>\n";
220    }
221    echo '</select>
222    <select name="birth_year">
223    <option value="">Year</option>
224    ';
225    for ($n = 1900; $n <= 2001; $n++) {
226        echo "<option value=\"$n\">$n</option>\n";
227    }
228    ?>
229            </select></td>
230        </tr>
231        <tr>
232            <td align="center" colspan="3"><input type="submit" name="Submit" value="Register!">
                     <input type="reset" name="Reset" value="Reset"></td>
233        </tr>
234    </table>
235    </form>
236    </body>
237    </html>
```

VALIDATING FORMS WITH JAVASCRIPT

script errors on some platforms). After running all the checks, if `problem` is `true`, which means that it failed at least one test, the form will not be submitted.

3. Repeat the length test for the user's first and last names, email address, and password.

```
if (document.form.first_name.value.
→ length <= 0) {
alert ("Enter your first name.");
document.form.first_name.value = "***
→ First Name";
document.form.first_name.focus();
var problem = true;
}
if (document.form.last_name.value.
→ length <= 0) {
alert ("Enter your last name.");
document.form.last_name.value = "***
→ Last Name";
document.form.last_name.focus();
var problem = true;
}
if (document.form.email.value.length
→ <= 0) {
alert ("Enter your email address.");
document.form.email.value = "***
→ Email Address";
document.form.email.focus();
var problem = true;
}
if (document.form.pass1.value.length
→ < 8) {
alert ("Enter a password at least 8
→ characters long.");
var problem = true;
}
```

Because the `password` input type will not allow a value to be set, the two middle lines (`document.form.pass1.value…` and `document.form.pass1.focus()`) of each conditional can be skipped for the password.

4. Check to see that the passwords match.

```
if (document.form.pass1.value !=
→ document.form.pass2.value) {
alert ("Your confirmed password does
→ not match the entered password.");
var problem = true;
}
```

5. Make sure the user selected a value for birth month, day, and year.

```
if ((document.form.birth_month.value
→ == 0) ||
(document.form.birth_month.
→ selectedIndex == 0)) {
alert ("Please select your month of
→ birth.");
var problem = true;
}
if ((document.form.birth_day.value ==
→ 0) || (document.form.birth_day.
→ selectedIndex == 0)) {
alert ("Please select your day of
→ birth.");
var problem = true;
}
if ((document.form.birth_year.
→ value == 0) || (document.form.
→ birth_year.selectedIndex == 0)) {
alert ("Please select your year of
→ birth.");
var problem = true;
}
```

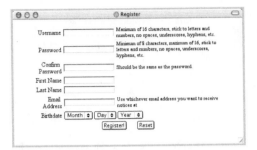

Figure 4.11 The registration form looks the same, but the file size is a little bigger and the overall page is much improved, thanks to the JavaScript addition (Figure 4.12).

```
⬤⬤⬤              HTML: Register
```

Figure 4.12 Viewing the source reveals all of the newly entered code.

Using JavaScript on pull-down menus is one of the many ways in which Netscape Navigator and Microsoft Internet Explorer, the two primary Web browsers, differ. The `…birth_month.value == 0` code will work for IE, but you have to use `…birth_month` `.selectedIndex == 0` for Netscape to function properly. I've included both as my condition with an *OR* (the double pipe) linking them. As long as one of those is `true`, it will pass the test.

6. Complete the `CheckData()` function.

```
if (problem == true) {
return false;
} else {
return true;
}
}
```

If the `problem` variable is `true`, which means that any one of the above tests failed, this function will return the value of `false`. Otherwise, it will return `true`. You'll see how this is affects the page shortly.

7. Complete the JavaScript.

```
//-->
</script>
```

8. Alter line 116 of the original code (Script 4.1) so that the `CheckData()` function is called (Script 4.4, line 172).

```
<form name="form" action="register.
→ php" method="post" onsubmit="return
→ CheckData()">
```

Two changes have been made. First, the form is given a name, albeit a very generic one, so that the `document.form` part of the JavaScript refers to the right object. In other words, you could name your form *Registration* or *Karen* as long as you change the JavaScript to `document.Registration` or `document.Karen`.

continues on next page

VALIDATING FORMS WITH JAVASCRIPT

The second change is the addition of `onsubmit="return CheckData()"`. This tells the page that as soon as the *Submit* button is clicked, the `CheckData()` function should be called. If `CheckData()` returns a `false` value, the form will not actually be submitted, meaning the user stays put. If `CheckData()` returns a `true` value, the form will be submitted and then processed by PHP.

9. Save your file and test in your Web browser (**Figures 4.11**, **4.12**, **4.13**, **4.14**, and **4.15**).

✔ Tips

■ Unlike PHP, which is roughly 99 percent browser-independent, JavaScript operates differently on the various Web browsers and platforms. Be sure to write JavaScript code for the lowest common denominator.

■ JavaScript does support regular expressions, although only in more recent versions of the language. For the code to be more backward-compatible, I avoided using JavaScript regular expressions here.

■ For more information about JavaScript, see Appendix C, General Resources.

Figure 4.13 Because the user didn't enter anything in the email address field, JavaScript alerts the user to the omission.

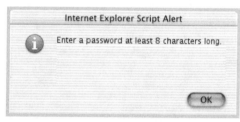

Figure 4.14 The JavaScript ensures that passwords are at least eight characters long and checks that they match each other.

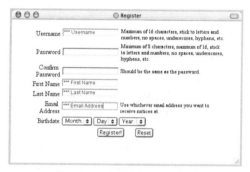

Figure 4.15 After I submitted the form, my Web browser never left this page because I failed the JavaScript tests.

Figure 4.16 This is the home page of Mcrypt, where you can download both the library and the stand-alone software.

Mcrypt

There are security problems with almost any Web application you develop and the simple registration form created so far is no exception. It does use HTML, JavaScript, and PHP to check the user-submitted data and it protects the user's password by encrypting it, but there is still one major concern: the user's personal data—first and last names, email address, and birthday—are stored unencrypted in a readable text file.

One solution might be to use the `crypt()` function to encrypt this information before storing it. However, the `crypt()` function has no `decrypt()` counterpart you could use to turn the encoded data back into readable form. Storing an encrypted email address that you could not decrypt serves no purpose at all.

It would be preferable to encrypt the data, store it, then decrypt it when you would like to read the information again. For this, you will need to use Mcrypt, available at http://mcrypt.hellug.gr (**Figure 4.16**). Mcrypt is a security application and its corresponding library, libmcrypt, can enable you to use PHP's built-in Mcrypt functions to encode and decode data.

To use Mcrypt, you begin by defining your key, which should be a string of a particular length depending upon the cipher you use (more on this shortly).

```
$mcrypt_key = "string";
```

continues on next page

MCRYPT

Then, with libraries 2.4.x and higher, you start by identifying which algorithm and module to use (see the PHP manual for the less involved way to use libmcrypt with earlier versions of the library or earlier versions of PHP). Mcrypt comes with dozens of different algorithms, or ciphers, each of which encrypts data differently. If you are truly interested in how each works, see Appendix C, General Resources, for where to look. For most purposes, you'll find that TripleDES is sufficient.

```
$mcrypt_module = mcrypt_module_open
→ (MCRYPT_TripleDES, "",
→ MCRYPT_MODE_CBC, "");
```

Here I've stated to use the TripleDES module in the CBC (Cipher Block Chaining) mode. CBC will suit most of your needs, especially when encrypting blocks of text. More information about the various algorithms and modes can be found in the Mcrypt documentation and within the Mcrypt section of the PHP manual.

The second and fourth arguments fed to the mcrypt_module_open() function are for explicitly stating where PHP can find the algorithm and mode files. These are not required unless PHP is unable to find a cipher and you know for certain it is installed.

Once the module is open, you create an IV (Initialization Vector), which is somewhat akin to another key. This is required,

optional, or unnecessary depending upon the mode being used. I'll use it with CBC.

Basically, the IV tells the module how to begin. It's like a key in that the same IV must be used to encrypt and decrypt a piece of data, just as the same key must be used. Here's how the PHP manual recommends to do it (although you must call the srand() function before this line to ensure the random generation):

```
$mcrypt_iv = mcrypt_create_iv
→ (mcrypt_enc_get_iv_size
→ ($mcrypt_module), MCRYPT_RAND);
```

The final step before you are ready to encrypt data is to create the buffers that Mcrypt needs to perform encryption.

```
mcrypt_generic_init ($mcrypt_module,
→ $mcrypt_key, $mcrypt_iv);
```

Once you have gone through these steps, you are ready to encrypt data.

```
$encrypted_data = mcrypt_generic
→ ($mcrypt_module, $data);
```

Finally, after you have finished encrypting everything, you should close all the buffers and modules.

```
mcrypt_generic_end ($mcrypt_module);
```

Assuming you have access to a server with Mcrypt enabled, update the register.php script to secure the user's data.

Script 4.5 Now this script is almost as safe as it can be, since Mcrypt is used to protect the users' data.

```
                    script
1    <?php
2
3    if (isset($HTTP_POST_VARS[Submit])) { //
     If the form was submitted, process it.
4
5          // Check the username.
6          if (eregi ("^[[:alnum:]]+$",
           $HTTP_POST_VARS[username])) {
7               $a = TRUE;
8          } else {
9               $a = FALSE;
10              $message[] = "Please enter a
                username that consists only of
                letters and numbers.";
11         }
12
13         // Check to make sure the password is
           long enough and of the right format.
14         if (eregi ("^[[:alnum:]]{8,16}$",
           $HTTP_POST_VARS[pass1])) {
15              $b = TRUE;
16         } else {
17              $b = FALSE;
18              $message[] = "Please enter a
                password that consists only of
                letters and numbers, between 8
                and 16 characters long.";
19         }
20
21         // Check to make sure the password
           matches the confirmed password.
22         if ($HTTP_POST_VARS[pass1] ==
           $HTTP_POST_VARS[pass2]) {
23              $c = TRUE;
24              $password = crypt
                ($HTTP_POST_VARS[pass1]); //
                Encrypt the password.
25         } else {
26              $c = FALSE;
27              $message[] = "The password you
                entered did not match the
                confirmed password.";
28         }
29
30         // Check to make sure they entered
              their first name and it's of the
              right format.
31         if (eregi ("^([[:alpha:]]|-|')+$",
           $HTTP_POST_VARS[first_name])) {
32              $d = TRUE;
33         } else {
34              $d = FALSE;
35              $message[] = "Please enter a
                valid first name.";
36         }
37
38         // Check to make sure they entered
              their last name and it's of the right
              format.
```

(script continues on next page)

To use Mcrypt:

1. Open register.php in your text editor (Script 4.4).

2. Delete line 78 of the original script and begin the Mcrypt process (**Script 4.5**):

   $mcrypt_key = "Hey! Here's the
   → KEY.1776";

   The first step is to define your key. Ideally, the key should be stored in a safe place, such as a configuration file located outside of the Web document root. Furthermore, you could make the key a constant in the configuration file.

   Each cipher has a maximum key length. For TripleDES, the maximum is 24 characters, which this key happens to be. Naturally, the longer and more random your key is, the better.

3. Open and prepare Mcrypt.

   $mcrypt_module = mcrypt_module_open
   → (MCRYPT_TripleDES, "",
   → MCRYPT_MODE_CBC, "");

   srand ((float) microtime() * 1000000);

   $mcrypt_iv = mcrypt_create_iv
   → (mcrypt_enc_get_iv_size
   → ($mcrypt_module), MCRYPT_RAND);

   mcrypt_generic_init ($mcrypt_module,
   → $mcrypt_key, $mcrypt_iv);

   Nothing has changed here from the explanation of using Mcrypt except that the required srand() function is called here with the preferred (float) microtime() * 1000000 argument.

4. Encrypt the user-submitted data.

   $data = "$HTTP_POST_VARS[first_name]
   → \t$HTTP_POST_VARS[last_name]\t$HTTP
   → _POST_VARS[email]\t$HTTP_POST_VARS[
   → birth_month]-$HTTP_POST_VARS[birth_
   → day]-$HTTP_POST_VARS[birth_year]";

   $encrypted = mcrypt_generic
   → ($mcrypt_module, $data);

continues on page 156

Script 4.5 *continued*

```
┌────────────────────────────────────────────────────────────────────────────────────┐
│ ▣                                     script                                      ▣ │
├────────────────────────────────────────────────────────────────────────────────────┤
 39        if (eregi ("^([[:alpha:]]|-|')+$", $HTTP_POST_VARS[last_name])) {
 40              $e = TRUE;
 41        } else {
 42              $e = FALSE;
 43              $message[] = "Please enter a valid last name.";
 44        }
 45
 46        // Check to make sure they entered a valid email address.
 47        if (eregi("^([[:alnum:]]|_|\.|-)+@([[:alnum:]]|\.|-)+(\.)([a-z]{2,4})$",
           $HTTP_POST_VARS[email])) {
 48              $f = TRUE;
 49        } else {
 50              $f = FALSE;
 51              $message[] = "Please enter a valid email address.";
 52        }
 53
 54        // Check to make sure they entered a valid birth date.
 55        if (checkdate ($HTTP_POST_VARS[birth_month], $HTTP_POST_VARS[birth_day],
           $HTTP_POST_VARS[birth_year])) {
 56              $g = TRUE;
 57        } else {
 58              $g = FALSE;
 59              $message[] = "Please enter a valid birth  date.";
 60        }
 61
 62        //  If the data passes all the tests, check to ensure a unique member name, then register them.
 63        if ($a AND $b AND $c AND $d AND $e AND $f AND $g) {
 64
 65           if ($fp = @fopen ("../users.txt", "r")) { // Open the file for reading.
 66
 67              while ( !feof($fp) AND !$user_found ) { // Loop through each line, checking each
                 username.
 68                 $read_data = fgetcsv ($fp, 1000, "\t"); // Read the line into an array.
 69                 if ($read_data[0] == $HTTP_POST_VARS[username]) {
 70                    $user_found = TRUE;
 71                 }
 72              }
 73              fclose ($fp);
 74
 75              if (!$user_found) { // If the username is OK, register them.
 76
 77                 if ($fp2 = @fopen ("../users.txt", "a")) { // Open the file for writing.
 78
 79                    // **** Mcrypt *****
 80
 81                    // Create a key.
 82                    $mcrypt_key = "Hey! Here's the KEY.1776";
 83
 84                    // Open and initialize Mcrypt.
 85                    $mcrypt_module = mcrypt_module_open (MCRYPT_TripleDES, "", MCRYPT_MODE_CBC,
                       "");
 86                    srand ((float) microtime() * 1000000);
 87                    $mcrypt_iv = mcrypt_create_iv (mcrypt_enc_get_iv_size ($mcrypt_module),
                       MCRYPT_RAND);
 88                    mcrypt_generic_init ($mcrypt_module, $mcrypt_key, $mcrypt_iv);
 89
 90                    // Encrypt the data.
 91                    $data = "$HTTP_POST_VARS[first_name]\t$HTTP_POST_VARS[last_name]\
                       t$HTTP_POST_VARS[email]\t$HTTP_POST_VARS[birth_month]-
                       $HTTP_POST_VARS[birth_day]-$HTTP_POST_VARS[birth_year]";
```

(script continues on next page)

MCRYPT

Script 4.5 *continued*

```
 92                         $encrypted = mcrypt_generic ($mcrypt_module, $data);
 93                         $encrypted = base64_encode ($encrypted);
 94                         $mcrypt_iv = base64_encode ($mcrypt_iv);
 95
 96                         // Close mcrypt.
 97                         mcrypt_generic_end ($mcrypt_module);
 98
 99                         $write_data = "$HTTP_POST_VARS[username]\t$password\t$encrypted\
                            t$mcrypt_iv\n";
100                         fwrite ($fp2, $write_data);
101                         fclose ($fp2);
102                         $message = urlencode ("You have been successfully registered.");
103                         header ("Location: homepage.php?message=$message"); // Send them on their way.
104                         exit;
105                     } else {
106                         $message[] = "Could not register to the user's file! Please contact the
                            Webmaster for more information.<br />";
107                     }
108                 } else {
109                     $message[] = "That username is already taken. Please select another.";
110                 }
111
112             } else { // If it couldn't open the file, print an error message.
113                 $message[] = "Could not read the user's file! Please contact the Webmaster for more
                    information.<br />";
114             }
115         }
116
117
118     } // End of Submit if.
119     ?>
120     <!DOCTYPE html PUBLIC "-//W3C//DTD XHTML 1.0 Strict//EN"
121             "http://www.w3.org/TR/2000/REC-xhtml1-20000126/DTD/xhtml1-strict.dtd">
122     <html xmlns="http://www.w3.org/1999/xhtml">
123     <head>
124         <title>Register</title>
125     <script type="text/javascript" language="Javascript">
126     <!-- // Begin to hide script contents from old browsers.
127     function CheckData() {
128         if (document.form.username.value.length <= 0) {
129             alert ("Enter a username.");
130             document.form.username.value = "*** Username";
131             document.form.username.focus();
132             var problem = true;
133         }
134         if (document.form.first_name.value.length <= 0) {
135             alert ("Enter your first name.");
136             document.form.first_name.value = "*** First Name";
137             document.form.first_name.focus();
138             var problem = true;
139         }
140         if (document.form.last_name.value.length <= 0) {
141             alert ("Enter your last name.");
142             document.form.last_name.value = "*** Last Name";
143             document.form.last_name.focus();
144             var problem = true;
145         }
146         if (document.form.email.value.length <= 0) {
147             alert ("Enter your email address.");
```

(script continues on next page)

MCRYPT

153

Script 4.5 *continued*

```
148            document.form.email.value = "*** Email Address";
149            document.form.email.focus();
150            var problem = true;
151        }
152        if (document.form.pass1.value.length < 8) {
153            alert ("Enter a password at least 8 characters long.");
154            var problem = true;
155        }
156        if (document.form.pass1.value != document.form.pass2.value) {
157            alert ("Your confirmed password does not match the entered password.");
158            var problem = true;
159        }
160        if ((document.form.birth_month.value == 0) || (document.form.birth_month.selectedIndex == 0)) {
161            alert ("Please select your month of birth.");
162            var problem = true;
163        }
164        if ((document.form.birth_day.value == 0) || (document.form.birth_day.selectedIndex == 0)) {
165            alert ("Please select your day of birth.");
166            var problem = true;
167        }
168        if ((document.form.birth_year.value == 0) || (document.form.birth_year.selectedIndex == 0)) {
169            alert ("Please select your year of birth.");
170            var problem = true;
171        }
172
173        if (problem == true) {
174            return false;
175        } else {
176            return true;
177        }
178    }
179    //-->
180    </script>
181    </head>
182    <body>
183    <?php
184    // Print out any error messages.
185    if ($message) {
186        echo "<div align=\"left\"><font color=red><b>The following problems occurred:</b><br />\n";
187        foreach ($message as $key => $value) {
188            echo "$value <br />\n";
189        }
190        echo "<p></p><b>Be sure to re-enter your passwords and your birth date!</b></font></div><br
                   />\n";
191    }
192    ?>
193    <form name="form" action="register3.php" method="post" onsubmit="return CheckData()">
194    <table border="0" width="90%" cellspacing="2" cellpadding="2" align="center">
195        <tr>
196            <td align="right">Username</td>
197            <td align="left"><input type="text" name="username" size="25" maxsize="16"
                   value="<?=$HTTP_POST_VARS[username] ?>"></td>
198            <td align="left"><small>Maximum of 16 characters, stick to letters and numbers, no spaces,
                   underscores, hyphens, etc.</small></td>
199        </tr>
200        <tr>
201            <td align="right">Password</td>
202            <td align="left"><input type="password" name="pass1" size="25"></td>
203            <td align="left"><small>Minimum of 8 characters, maximum of 16, stick to letters and
                   numbers, no spaces, underscores, hyphens, etc.</small></td>
```

(script continues on next page)

154

MCRYPT

Script 4.5 *continued*

```
                                    script

204      </tr>
205      <tr>
206          <td align="right">Confirm Password</td>
207          <td align="left"><input type="password" name="pass2" size="25"></td>
208          <td align="left"><small>Should be the same as the password.</small></td>
209      </tr>
210      <tr>
211          <td align="right">First Name</td>
212          <td align="left"><input type="text" name="first_name" size="25" maxsize="20"
         value="<?=$HTTP_POST_VARS[first_name] ?>"></td>
213          <td align="left"> </td>
214      </tr>
215      <tr>
216          <td align="right">Last Name</td>
217          <td align="left"><input type="text" name="last_name" size="25" maxsize="20"
         value="<?=$HTTP_POST_VARS[last_name] ?>"></td>
218          <td align="left"> </td>
219      </tr>
220      <tr>
221          <td align="right">Email Address</td>
222          <td align="left"><input type="text" name="email" size="25" maxsize="60"
         value="<?=$HTTP_POST_VARS[email] ?>"></td>
223          <td align="left"><small>Use whichever email address you want to receive notices
         at.</small></td>
224      </tr>
225      <tr>
226          <td align="right">Birthdate</td>
227          <td align="left" colspan="2">
228  <?php
229  echo '<select name="birth_month">
230  <option value="">Month</option>
231  ';
232  for ($n = 1; $n <= 12; $n++) {
233      echo "<option value=\"$n\">$n</option>\n";
234  }
235  echo '</select>
236  <select name="birth_day">
237  <option value="">Day</option>
238  ';
239  for ($n = 1; $n <= 31; $n++) {
240      echo "<option value=\"$n\">$n</option>\n";
241  }
242  echo '</select>
243  <select name="birth_year">
244  <option value="">Year</option>
245  ';
246  for ($n = 1900; $n <= 2001; $n++) {
247      echo "<option value=\"$n\">$n</option>\n";
248  }
249  ?>
250          </select></td>
251      </tr>
252      <tr>
253          <td align="center" colspan="3"><input type="submit" name="Submit" value="Register!">
               <input type="reset" name="Reset" value="Reset"></td>
254      </tr>
255  </table>
256  </form>
257  </body>
258  </html>
```

In this case, you'll encrypt all of the data except for the username and password. These two elements need to be in unencrypted form for the user to log in without PHP having to decrypt everything. While it would be more secure to store this information encrypted, you'll be giving up some performance by doing so. Security is frequently a trade-off between safety and convenience. Besides, the password is already encrypted once.

5. Transform the encrypted data into a more storable format.

```
$encrypted = base64_encode
→ ($encrypted);

$mcrypt_iv = base64_encode
→ ($mcrypt_iv);
```

The encrypted information is currently in a binary format. If this were being stored in a database set up to hold binary data, that would be fine, but since it is going into a text file, it needs to be altered. The base64_encode() function turns data into a MIME-safe format, such as a string, for example. Because the IV also needs to be stored (so that the data can be accurately decrypted), this too needs to be transformed with base64_encode().

6. Close Mcrypt and write the data to the file.

```
mcrypt_generic_end ($mcrypt_module);

$write_data = "$HTTP_POST_VARS
→ [username]\t$password\t$encrypted\
→ t$mcrypt_iv\n";
```

The data being written are the username followed by a tab, followed by the password and another tab, followed by the encrypted data, and concluding with the Initialization Vector used and a new line. Because you must use the same IV to encrypt and decrypt data, each line's IV—which will be different and random with each use—is written to the file as well. Because IV's do not need to be secret, while keys do, this is not an unsecure thing to do.

7. Save the file as `register.php` and upload it to your server.

For the sake of seeing the results, I'll write a very quick administration form that decrypts all the user information and displays it.

8. Create a new HTML document in your text editor (**Script 4.6**).

```
<!DOCTYPE html PUBLIC "-//W3C//DTD
→ XHTML 1.0 Strict//EN"
"http://www.w3.org/TR/2000/
→ REC-xhtml1-20000126/DTD/
→ xhtml1-strict.dtd">
<html xmlns="http://www.w3.org/
→ 1999/xhtml">
<head>
<title>Current Users</title>
</head>
<body>
```

9. Create the PHP section of the page.

```
<?php
```

Script 4.6 This administration page decrypts and reveals all the stored user information.

```
                    script
1    <!DOCTYPE html PUBLIC "-//W3C//DTD XHTML
     1.0 Strict//EN"
2    "http://www.w3.org/TR/2000/REC-xhtml1-
     20000126/DTD/xhtml1-strict.dtd">
3    <html xmlns="http://www.w3.org/1999/
     xhtml">
4    <head>
5        <title>Current Users</title>
6    </head>
7    <body>
8    <?php
9
10   if ($file_array = @file
     ("../../users.txt")) { // Read
     the file into an array.
11
12       // **** Mcrypt *****
13
14       // Create a key.
15       $mcrypt_key = "Hey! Here's the
     KEY.1776";
16
17       // Open and initialize Mcrypt.
18       $mcrypt_module = mcrypt_module_open
     (MCRYPT_TripleDES, "",
     MCRYPT_MODE_CBC, "");
19
20       foreach ($file_array as $key =>
     $value) { // Loop through each line.
21
22           $line = explode ("\t", $value);
23           // Decrypt the data.
24           $mcrypt_iv = base64_decode
     (trim($line[3]));
25           mcrypt_generic_init ($mcrypt_
     module, $mcrypt_key, $mcrypt_iv);
26           $data = mdecrypt_generic
     ($mcrypt_module,
     base64_decode($line[2]));
27
28           echo "<pre>$line[0] $line[1]
     $data</pre><p></p>\n"; // Print
     the data.
29
30       }
31
32       // Close Mcrypt.
33       mcrypt_generic_end ($mcrypt_module);
34
35   } else { // If it couldn't read the file,
     print an error message.
36       echo "Could not read the user's
     file!<br />";
37   }
38   ?>
39   </body>
40   </html>
```

10. Read the users.txt file into an array.

```
if ($file_array = @file
("../../users.txt")) {
```

Since this script will be for administration purposes only, it will be stored in its own folder two directories above the users.txt file.

11. Identify your key and open Mcrypt as you had before.

```
$mcrypt_key = "Hey! Here's the
→ KEY.1776";
$mcrypt_module = mcrypt_module_open
→ (MCRYPT_TripleDES, "",
→ MCRYPT_MODE_ECB, "");
```

12. Loop through each element in the users.txt file, decrypting and printing the data as you go.

```
foreach ($file_array as $key =>
→ $value) {
$line = explode ("\t", $value);
$mcrypt_iv = base64_decode
→ (trim($line[3]));
mcrypt_generic_init ($mcrypt_module,
→ $mcrypt_key, $mcrypt_iv);
$data = mdecrypt_generic
→ ($mcrypt_module,
→ base64_decode($line[2]));
echo "<pre>$line[0] $line[1]
→ $data</pre><p></p>\n";
}
```

This loop reads through each line of the $file_array one at a time. First it will break up this line into its own array. Second, it will determine the IV used to encrypt the data by trimming the element and then applying base64_decode().

continues on next page

MCRYPT

The IV will be fed into the `mcrypt_generic_init()` function and finally the data can be decrypted using `mdecrypt_generic()`. Again, the `base64_decode()` function is used before decryption.

13. Close the Mcrypt module and conclude the conditional.

```
. mcrypt_generic_end ($mcrypt_module);
} else {
echo "Could not read the user's
→ file!<br />";
}
```

14. Close the PHP section and the HTML page.

```
?>
</body>
</html>
```

15. Save this file as `see_users.php`.

16. Create a new directory for administration pages in the same directory as `register.php`. Give your directory an uncommon name (anything but *admin*) such as *dadm1n* or *Orange_gRov3* to marginally increase the security (if a user doesn't know where the administration files are, they'll be more difficult to hack). Store `see_users.php` in the newly created directory and run it in your Web browser (**Figures 4.17** and **4.18**).

17. Open up `users.txt` in your text editor to see what the base64-encoded, Mcrypt-encrypted data looks like (**Script 4.7**).

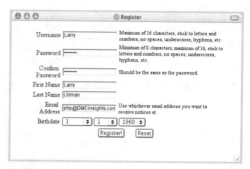

Figure 4.17 The form itself has not changed, although it's infinitely more secure, which your users will appreciate, whether they know it or not.

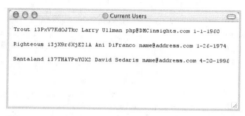

Figure 4.18 The see_users.php page decrypts the stored information and displays it in the browser for an administrator to see. Obviously this page ought to be kept secure.

Script 4.7 The users.txt file now stores the data in this format: unencrypted username, encrypted (using crypt(), not Mcrypt) password, the remaining data encrypted with Mcrypt, and the IV used.

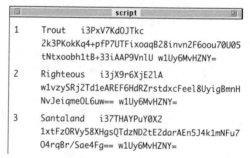

```
1   Trout    i3PxV7KdOJTkc
    2k3PKokKq4+pfP7UTFixoaqB28invn2F6oou70U05
    tNtxoobh1tB+33iAAP9VnlU  w1Uy6MvHZNY=

2   Righteous   i3jX9r6XjE21A
    w1vzySRj2Td1eAREF6HdRZrstdxcFeel8UyigBmnH
    NvJeiqmeOL6uw==  w1Uy6MvHZNY=

3   Santaland   i37THAYPuY0X2
    1xtFzORVy58XHgsQTdzND2tE2darAEn5J4k1mNFu7
    04rqBr/Sae4Fg==  w1Uy6MvHZNY=
```

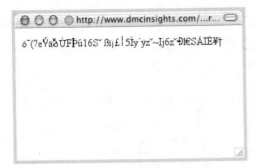

Figure 4.19 The data after being encrypted looks like this which will be problematic. The base64_encode() function is applied after using Mcrypt to transform the data into a more reliable format.

✔ Tips

■ Any information encrypted with Mcrypt that you wish to store in a cookie or append to a URL needs to be run through the base64_encode() function as you did here. **Figure 4.19** shows what data looks like before base64_encode() is applied.

■ If you do not use the exact same key, IV, algorithm (e.g., TripleDES) and mode (CBC) for encryption and decryption, you will not get the same data that you put in. For example, omitting the IV during decryption will normally decrypt part of your string, but not the whole thing.

■ Although the PHP manual and most explanations of Mcrypt use a plaintext key (as I have also done), to get the maximum security with encryption, you should use a hash version of a string as your key. You can use PHP's md5() function to accomplish this.

MCRYPT

HTTP Authentication

HTTP authentication, currently available only in the module (as opposed to the CGI) version running with the Apache Web server is a way to protect a file by requiring users to enter a username and password in a pop-up window to gain access. It's similar to a log-in/registration system but easier to establish and more strict.

The benefits of HTTP authentication are:

◆ Very little PHP code required

◆ Entered username and password remembered without needing to use PHP to send cookies or establish sessions

◆ A clean interface that will not interfere with your page design

The downsides are:

◆ Limited usability (PHP 4 module with Apache only, although Apache is the most popular Web server and PHP its most popular module)

◆ Not able to establish user groups or specify access levels

◆ Inability to set an expiration time

With this in mind, I'll put together three quick scripts that demonstrate how you can use HTTP authentication in your Web application.

Script 4.8 You can authenticate users in PHP 4 on Apache with these lines of code.

```
1   <?php
2
3   // Check to see if they have tried
    logging in.
4   if ( (!isset($PHP_AUTH_USER)) OR
    ($login_page AND
    !strcmp($existing_username,
    $PHP_AUTH_USER)) ) {
5   Header("WWW-Authenticate: Basic
    realm=\"My Web Site\"");
6   Header("HTTP/1.0 401 Unauthorized");
7   echo "Please enter a valid username and
    password!<P>Reload the page to try
    again!\n"; // They hit Cancel.
8   exit;
9   } else {
10  if (($PHP_AUTH_USER == "cozumel") and
    ($PHP_AUTH_PW == "mexico")) { // Proper
    access info.
11      (strstr($PHP_SELF, "login.php")) { //
        If they were on the log-in page, take
        them to the index page.
12          header ("Location:
            index.php");
13          exit;
14      }
15  } else {
16      if (!strstr($PHP_SELF,
        "login.php")) { // If they
        weren't on the log-in page, take
        them there.
17          header ("Location:
            login.php");
18          exit;
19      }
20  }
21  }
22  ?>
23
```

HTTP AUTHENTICATION

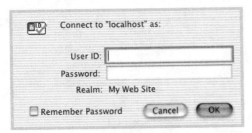

Figure 4.20 HTTP authentication results in a simple pop-up window requesting a username and password while indicating the applicable domain (here, *localhost*) and realm (*My Web Site*).

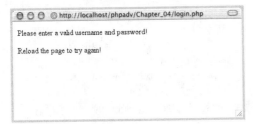

Figure 4.21 If users try to circumvent the authentication by clicking *Cancel*, they'll see this message.

To use HTTP authentication:

1. Create a new PHP document in your text editor (**Script 4.8**).

   ```
   <?php
   ```

2. Check to see if the user has logged in or is coming from the log-in page.

   ```
   if ( (!isset($PHP_AUTH_USER)) OR
   → ($login_page AND !strcmp
   → ($existing_username,
   → $PHP_AUTH_USER)) ) {
   ```

   If $PHP_AUTH_USER does not have a value or if the user is not coming from the log-in page (the second part of the condition), you want PHP to display the authentication window.

3. Write the HTTP code.

   ```
   Header("WWW-Authenticate: Basic
   → realm=\"My Web Site\"");
   Header("HTTP/1.0 401 Unauthorized");
   echo "Please enter a valid username
   → and password!<P>Reload the page to
   → try again!\n";
   exit;
   ```

   The first header line creates the pop-up window with the realm set to *My Web Site* (see **Figure 4.20** for how this appears). The second header line and the echo statement take effect if the user hits the *Cancel* button in the pop-up window (**Figure 4.21**).

4. Create the second part of the conditional.

   ```
   } else {
   ```

   The script starts with two scenarios: the user has not entered a username or the user is coming from the log-in page. In either case, the authentication window appears. If neither is the case, then the authentication needs to be handled.

continues on next page

HTTP AUTHENTICATION

5. Check to see if the user got it right.

```
if (($PHP_AUTH_USER == "cozumel")
→ and ($PHP_AUTH_PW == "mexico")) {
```

Here is where you would enter the proper username and password for access. This page will be stored outside of the Web directory so there's less of a security issue in writing these values in a text file.

6. Send the user to the home page if the user got it right.

```
if (strstr($PHP_SELF, "login.php")) {
header ("Location: index.php");
exit;
}
```

If the user was coming from the log-in page when he was authenticated, this script sends him to the index.php page. Otherwise, they'll be allowed to continue viewing the page they wanted to go directly to. For example, if authentication was required for a standings.php page, upon successful authentication, the user would continue to that page.

7. Complete the conditionals and the PHP.

```
} else {
if (!strstr($PHP_SELF, "login.php"))
{
header ("Location: login.php");
exit;
}
}
}
?>
```

If the user was not authenticated, he will be sent to the log-in page. If the user was already coming from the log-in page, you don't want to send him back there (which would create an endless loop) but rather let him stay there.

8. Save the script as authentication.php and upload it to your server, preferably outside of the Web document tree.

Now you'll need to create a log-in page that gives the user the option to try again.

9. Create a new PHP document in your Web browser (**Script 4.9**).

```
<?php
```

10. Include the authentication page.

```
require_once
("../authentication.php");
```

The authentication page will be stored in the directory below the current one for security purposes (assuming this is outside of the Web documents structure). Every page that begins with this require_once() line will automatically authenticate the user before allowing access.

11. Complete the PHP code and start the HTML.

```
?>
<!DOCTYPE html PUBLIC "-//W3C//DTD
→ XHTML 1.0 Transitional//EN"
"http://www.w3.org/TR/2000/
→ REC-xhtml1-20000126/DTD/xhtml1-
→ transitional.dtd">
<html xmlns="http://www.w3.org/
→ 1999/xhtml">
<head>
<title>Login</title>
</head>
<body>
```

12. Let the user know that authentication failed.

```
<b><big><font color="#CC0000">
→ Authentication Failed!<br />You
→ must have a valid username and
→ password to access this site!
→ </font></big></b><br />Click on
→ 'Try Again' to log in.
```

Script 4.9 The login.php page is needed only to get users to try authentication again without having to restart their Web browser.

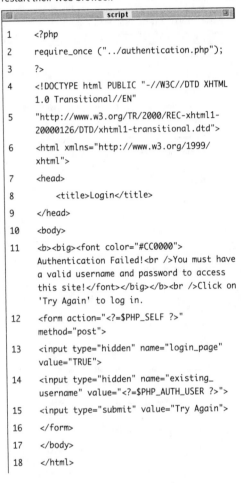

```
1    <?php
2    require_once ("../authentication.php");
3    ?>
4    <!DOCTYPE html PUBLIC "-//W3C//DTD XHTML
     1.0 Transitional//EN"
5    "http://www.w3.org/TR/2000/REC-xhtml1-
     20000126/DTD/xhtml1-transitional.dtd">
6    <html xmlns="http://www.w3.org/1999/
     xhtml">
7    <head>
8        <title>Login</title>
9    </head>
10   <body>
11   <b><big><font color="#CC0000">
     Authentication Failed!<br />You must have
     a valid username and password to access
     this site!</font></big></b><br />Click on
     'Try Again' to log in.
12   <form action="<?=$PHP_SELF ?>"
     method="post">
13   <input type="hidden" name="login_page"
     value="TRUE">
14   <input type="hidden" name="existing_
     username" value="<?=$PHP_AUTH_USER ?>">
15   <input type="submit" value="Try Again">
16   </form>
17   </body>
18   </html>
```

13. Create a form allowing users to reauthenticate themselves.

```
<form action="<?=$PHP_SELF ?>"
→ method="post">
<input type="hidden"
→ name="login_page" value="TRUE">
<input type="hidden" name=
→ "existing_username"
→ value="<?=$PHP_AUTH_USER ?>">
<input type="submit" value="Try
→ Again">
</form>
```

One of the problems with HTTP authentication is that once a username is in memory (so to speak), it stays there. This means that if the user got the username wrong, he would need to completely restart the browser to try again, which is not practical.

The work-around for this is to create a form that stores two values: one that indicates that the user is on the log-in page (i.e., the user has already tried authentication and failed) and the first username he entered. When the user clicks on *Try Again*, he will be returned to this page and the authentication script will be called again. Because the main conditional of the authentication script states that the pop-up window should be created if the user is coming from the log-in page and has entered an incorrect username, the user will be given another opportunity.

14. Complete the HTML.

```
</body>
</html>
```

15. Save the script as login.php and upload it to your server, in the directory above authentication.php.

continues on next page

Finally, you should make a simple index page to receive users once they get everything right.

16. Create a new PHP document in your text editor (**Script 4.10**).

```
<?php
```

17. Include the authentication page.

```
require_once
→ ("../authentication.php");
?>
```

18. Create the HTML.

```
<!DOCTYPE html PUBLIC "-//W3C//DTD
→ XHTML 1.0 Transitional//EN"
"http://www.w3.org/TR/2000/
→ REC-xhtml1-20000126/DTD/
→ xhtml1-transitional.dtd">
<html xmlns="http://www.w3.org/
→ 1999/xhtml">
<head>
<title>Welcome!</title>
</head>
<body>
Welcome to the site!
</body>
</html>
```

19. Save the script as index.php, upload it to your server in the same directory as login.php, and test in your Web browser (**Figures 4.22, 4.23** and **4.24**).

Script 4.10 While the page itself is simple, the important thing to realize is that once your authentication script is written (Script 4.8), one line of code—require_once ("../authentication.php");—adds security to any existing script.

```
1    <?php
2    require_once ("../authentication.php");
3    ?>
4    <!DOCTYPE html PUBLIC "-//W3C//DTD XHTML
     1.0 Transitional//EN"
5    "http://www.w3.org/TR/2000/REC-xhtml1-
     20000126/DTD/xhtml1-transitional.dtd">
6    <html xmlns="http://www.w3.org/
     1999/xhtml">
7    <head>
8        <title>Welcome!</title>
9    </head>
10   <body>
11   Welcome to the site!
12   </body>
13   </html>
```

Figure 4.22 Once users enter the information that corresponds to the authentication.php file, they'll be sent to the index.php page (Figure 4.23).

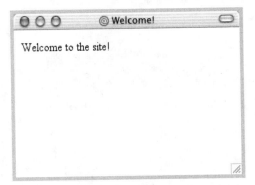

Figure 4.23 The index.php page is where the user ends up after being authenticated, if the user was not trying to get to a specific address (e.g., standings.php).

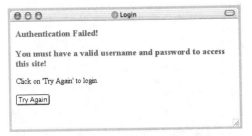

Figure 4.24 If authentication fails, the user will be redirected to login.php, which allows the user to make another attempt.

✔ Tips

- If you are actively using the see_users.php script from the previous section of this chapter, now would be a good time to secure it by adding an HTTP authentication requirement.

- In the Web Server Security section, you'll see how you can do a similar thing using Apache's .htaccess files.

- If you want to improve the security of the above scripts, store the proper username and password in their encrypted forms (using crypt()), then compare them against encrypted forms of the user-submitted values.

HTTP AUTHENTICATION

Web Server Security

Beyond the issue of secure PHP code there are three other primary Internet security considerations: the operating system (Windows, Unix, Mac, etc.), the Web server (Apache, Xitami, IIS, etc.), and how PHP is installed and configured. While these three factors may be beyond your control, it would behoove you as a Web developer to have at least a cursory understanding of the issues. I'll introduce the major players here, and the appendices, particularly Appendix A, Installation, and Appendix C, General Resources, will steer you toward more information for the OS and Web server you are using.

The security of your Web server's operating system is well beyond the scope of a book on PHP, and I would hope that you would never rely on a secondary resource such as this for such an important topic. How much you know and how much time you put into securing your operating system depends upon the use of your Web server—be it an offline computer or an active, online one. Windows NT out of the box is highly unsecure, while Unix is far less so. Macintosh has its own concerns, but now that the new operating system, OS X, is based on FreeBSD Unix, there is less to worry about. Although your operating system is probably a decision that was made for you some time ago, you should investigate some of the security-related Web sites and books listed in Appendix C, General Resource, which will tell you what to be aware of as well as what patches are available to correct the problem.

The Web server application you use is often dictated by the operating system you are running. For Unix, Apache (**Figure 4.25**) is the most common, but there are viable alternatives such as Xitami (**Figure 4.26**). Mac OS X comes with Apache built-in, while Windows users tend to install either PWS

Figure 4.25 The Open-Source Apache server, available at http://httpd.apache.org is the most popular and some would argue the flat-out best Web server available.

Figure 4.26 Xitami, found at www.imatix.com/html/xitami/index.htm, is an inexpensive and reliable alternative to IIS for the Windows platform (and it works on several others as well).

(Personal Web Server) or IIS (Internet Information Server), depending on their needs and budget. Each has its own strengths and weaknesses. My recommendation is to pay attention to the Web sites and user groups for the Web server you are using to stay on top of the relevant security issues. Naturally, you should also read the documentation that comes with each product. One of the benefits of the Open Source Apache is that an entire community of developers is working hard to make sure that it is as efficient and secure as possible. Appendix A, Installation, will show you how to install Apache, IIS, and Xitami on Linux, Windows, and Mac OS X platforms.

One Apache-specific feature you ought to be aware of is .htaccess files. Apache uses files, literally named .htaccess, to define who has access to what. Apache's main configuration file, httpd.conf, dictates the overall server accessibility options, but by placing an .htaccess file in a directory, you can protect that particular folder and all its sub-directories.

An .htaccess file is a simple text document consisting of lines like these:

```
<Directory /Library/WebServer/Documents/
→ includes>

Deny from all

AllowOverride None

</Directory>
```

Those four lines will deny everyone access to the files found in the includes folder. Further, the AllowOverride None statement means that an .htaccess file in a subdirectory cannot alter the permissions set here. This may seem excessive, but it works very well for

securing HTTP access to your files and directories. The Apache manual and Web site goes into more detail regarding .htaccess files, should you be so inclined.

Configuring and installing PHP is the third way you can affect the overall security of your PHP applications. Assuming you have the authority to either install PHP or modify the php.ini file, you can adjust any of the following settings (the PHP manual contains sufficient information on each of these three settings):

◆ **Safe Mode**

Running PHP in Safe Mode is obviously, well, safer. In short, Safe Mode restricts the use of certain functions and improves the security of a multiuser environment, such as an ISP may run.

◆ **open_basedir**

The open_basedir directive tells PHP where it can open files and, therefore, where it cannot. Setting this parameter to a directory (logically the Web document root as defined by your Web server) will improve your server security by keeping PHP's hands off other files.

◆ **Register Globals**

When a form is submitted with an input called *username*, the handling PHP page receives a variable called $username, as you well know. This is a problem in that a user can take advantage of this by passing along malicious code as the value of $username. Turning off Register Globals prevents this possible violation. See *Variable Order* for more information about this topic.

continues on next page

Finally, if given the choice, it is safer to run PHP as a server module rather than a CGI binary. Apache comes with PHP installed as a module, but up until version 4, you had to install the CGI version for Windows (version 4 now works as an IIS module). Also, if you plan to use extra modules with PHP, such as Mcrypt, be sure to retrieve these from reliable sources—such as the module's home page—and keep an eye on how they function. Anything you add to PHP affects its overall security, too.

✔ Tips

- As a side note, you might also want to remove any phpinfo() scripts from your server because they can display more information to the user than would be prudent.

- You can also use .htaccess files in conjunction with .htpasswd files to add HTTP authentication to a directory. On top of that, .htaccess files can redirect users, set error messages, and more. See Apache's documentation for more information.

Table 4.1

PHP Track Variables

Associate Array Name	Refers To
$HTTP_POST_VARS	Every variable sent to the page via the POST method
$HTTP_GET_VARS	Every variable sent to the page via the GET method
$HTTP_COOKIE_VARS	Every variable stored in a cookie which the page can access
$HTTP_SERVER_VARS	Variables that the server sends to PHP
$HTTP_ENV_VAR	Environmental variables
$HTTP_SESSION_VARS	Every variable stored in a session to which the page has access
$HTTP_POST_FILES	Files that are uploaded to the server and handled by PHP

Variable Order

Variables in PHP can come from many, many sources: written in the scripts, environmental, received from HTML forms, etc. What you may not know is that there is a hierarchy to the order in which these are accessed. Why is this relevant? Because if a newer variable has the same name as an older variable, the value of the older variable will be overridden, causing errors in your script and possible security holes.

PHP processes variables in this order (from first to last):

- Built-in

- Cookies

- Post

- Get

- Environment

This means that if you have a defined variable in your script called $db_name and the user passes a value along via the GET method also assigned to $db_name, your original database value will not be replaced. To avoid problems with variables, use the track variables instead—arrays that contain corresponding values—as I have through this chapter and much of the book. **Table 4.1** lists all the track variables.

For extra security, assuming you have access to the php.ini file, turn register globals (**Figure 4.27**) to *Off*, although this may force you to rewrite some of your code and PHP must be configured with --enable-track-vars for this to work..

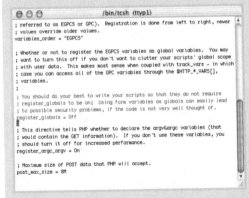

Figure 4.27 Among the many settings you can change in the php.ini file is register globals. You will need to restart your Web server for any changes to take effect.

DEVELOPING
WEB APPLICATIONS

Once you have been programming for a while it becomes rare that you work on anything that consists of only one or two simple scripts. PHP is best used for dynamic Web applications, which means dozens of pages, security, user registration, administration, sending emails, and more. In the past four chapters you have learned about a number of issues at the heart of advanced PHP programming, including object-oriented programming, databases, and security. In this chapter, you will put all of that information together, as well as learn a few new things.

The Web application that will be developed here will be a generic community-sharing type of place, similar to America Online's *Groups* pages. Users will be able to register, log in, look at a calendar of events, and leave each other messages. Security will be kept in mind, and the project will use an object-oriented approach to segregate the HTML from the PHP. The specific technologies discussed here will include sessions (new to PHP 4), establishing your site's structure, debugging, and error control. Since the calendar aspect of the application contains no new information, it will not be described in detail here. However, you will set up the database for it and the corresponding PHP code can be downloaded from www.DMCinsights.com/phpadv. Also, because I would prefer not to reinvent the wheel, I will also use a third-party application written in PHP—phpBB, a popular message forum, for the forum part of this application. The focus in this chapter will be on laying out your site, using objects to separate HTML from PHP on a larger scale and using sessions to track your users.

Database Design

To begin developing the application, you must first design and create the necessary databases. This application is going to do a lot of things, but primarily it will register users and allow them to log in. For this end, you'll need a database that stores the users' registration information.

For the sake of convenience, and because I know it works well, I'll incorporate the `register.php` script developed in Chapter 4, Security, as the registration page. The required information was and will be: a username, first name, last name, password, email address, and birthday. You can run through the normalization techniques as established in Chapter 3, Databases, and what you'll get is a table like **Table 5.1**. On top of the elements listed above, I am also creating a *user_id* field that is a unique integer and will act as the primary key. I'm doing this even though the username will have to be unique since databases can search through number fields faster than text ones.

The *users* table will provide all the information necessary for registration and logging in, but the site will also have a forum and a calendar to it. For the forum, I'll be using phpBB. The calendar is going to store events consisting of a textual description, the date, the start time, the end time, and the user who posted the event. **Table 5.2** shows what the *events* table will look like. A unique *events_id* will be the primary key for the table.

Table 5.1 The *users* table, for the *community* database, is straightforward in its design and will act as the main repository of information.

Table Users	
COLUMN	DATA TYPE
user_id	number
username	text
password	text
first_name	text
last_name	text
email	text
birthday	date

Table 5.2 The *events* table will record information related to specific days, including the start and end times, a title and description, and who submitted the event.

Table Events	
COLUMN	DATA TYPE
event_id	number
event_date	date
start_time	time
end_time	time
description	text
title	text
submitted_by	number (*FOREIGN KEY*)

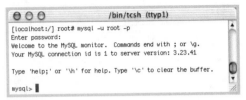

Figure 5.1 If you are accessing your RDMS via Telnet, log in first using your username (e.g., *root*) and password.

```
000                /bin/tcsh (ttyp1)
Your MySQL connection id is 2 to server version: 3.23.41

Type 'help;' or '\h' for help. Type '\c' to clear the buffer.

mysql> CREATE DATABASE community;
Query OK, 1 row affected (0.01 sec)

mysql>
```

Figure 5.2 Creating databases in MySQL is remarkably straightforward (even the capitalization is optional).

```
000                /bin/tcsh (ttyp1)
Type 'help;' or '\h' for help. Type '\c' to clear the buffer.

mysql> CREATE DATABASE community;
Query OK, 1 row affected (0.01 sec)

mysql> USE community;
Database changed
mysql>
```

Figure 5.3 If you don't tell MySQL which database you'll be using up front, you'll need to modify each of your queries to include the database name (e.g., *community.users* and *community.events*).

```
000                /bin/tcsh (ttyp1)
mysql> CREATE TABLE users (
    -> user_id INT UNSIGNED NOT NULL AUTO_INCREMENT,
    -> username VARCHAR(16) NOT NULL,
    -> password VARCHAR(13) NOT NULL,
    -> first_name VARCHAR(20),
    -> last_name VARCHAR(40),
    -> email VARCHAR(60),
    -> birthday DATE,
    -> PRIMARY KEY (user_id),
    -> INDEX (username),
    -> UNIQUE (username)
    -> );
Query OK, 0 rows affected (0.02 sec)

mysql>
```

Figure 5.4 To neatly see what I'm doing, I space out my long queries—such as this one creating the *users* table—over several lines.

To create the database:

1. Connect to your server via Telnet or SSH.

2. Log in to MySQL or PostgreSQL or whichever RDMS you are using (**Figure 5.1**).

   `mysql -u username -p`

   If you are using a different RDMS, you'll need to change some of the following code accordingly to create the same database structure.

3. Create the new database (**Figure 5.2**).

   `CREATE DATABASE community;`

4. Tell the RDMS to use the new database (**Figure 5.3**).

   `USE community;`

   This is a step that is easily skipped, resulting in RDMS errors.

5. Create the *users* table (**Figure 5.4**).

   ```
   CREATE TABLE users (
   user_id INT UNSIGNED NOT NULL
   → AUTO_INCREMENT,
   username VARCHAR(16) NOT NULL,
   password VARCHAR(13) NOT NULL,
   first_name VARCHAR(20),
   last_name VARCHAR(40),
   email VARCHAR(60),
   birthday DATE,
   PRIMARY KEY (user_id),
   INDEX (username),
   UNIQUE (username)
   );
   ```

   When creating the *users* table, a number of restrictions have been placed. The *user_id*, *username*, and *password* columns are set to NOT NULL, meaning they require some data, because they are the three most important columns.

   continues on next page

To save on database size and to improve operation, all of the text files are set as limited VARCHAR columns. The *user_id* field will be the primary key, but *username* is also indexed (and unique) for better performance.

6. Create the events table (**Figure 5.5**).

```
CREATE TABLE events (
event_id INT UNSIGNED NOT NULL
→ AUTO_INCREMENT,
event_date DATE NOT NULL,
start_time TIME NOT NULL,
end_time TIME,
description VARCHAR(255),
title VARCHAR(60) NOT NULL,
submitted_by INT UNSIGNED NOT NULL,
PRIMARY KEY (event_id),
INDEX (event_date)
);
```

The *events* table is organized similar to the *users* table. The *event_id*, *event_date*, *start_time*, *title*, and *submitted_by* fields are all required (NOT NULL), but the *description* and *end_time* are not. The *event_id* is logically the primary key. The *event_date* will be a secondary index, because it will be a frequently referenced field.

7. Check to see that the databases were properly created and defined (**Figure 5.6**).

```
SHOW TABLES;
SHOW COLUMNS FROM users;
SHOW COLUMNS FROM events;
```

I always like to do this to ensure that each table was properly established before I get too far into the programming aspect of the application. It is better to discover a problem now than halfway into your PHP code.

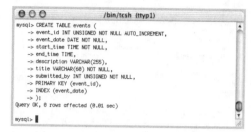

Figure 5.5 The *Query OK* statement returned by the RDMS indicates that the *events* table was successfully created, although it doesn't hurt to confirm this (Figure 5.6).

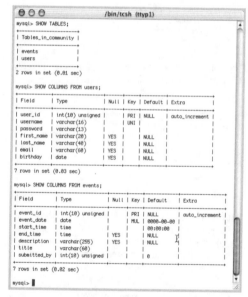

Figure 5.6 Using the SHOW TABLES and SHOW COLUMNS FROM tablename queries reveal the structure of my database.

Table 5.3 If you want to add a groups feature to the Web site, make a table correlating to this one, then add a *group_id* field to the *users* table (Table 5.1).

Table Groups

COLUMN	DATA TYPE
group_id	number
group_name	text
administrator_id	number (*FOREIGN KEY*)

✔ Tips

- For security purposes, you really should create a new RDMS user with access only to the *community* database.

- If you wanted to make a more elaborate application that allowed for different groups of users, create a *groups* table, too (**Table 5.3**).

```
CREATE TABLE groups (
group_id INT UNSIGNED NOT NULL
→ AUTO_INCREMENT,
group_name VARCHAR(20) NOT NULL,
administrator_id INT UNSIGNED NOT
→ NULL,
PRIMARY KEY (group_id),
INDEX (group_name),
);
```

Once you've made the table, add a *group_id* field (of type `INT UNSIGNED NOT NULL`) to the *users* table. That will allow you to identify which group each user is a member of.

DATABASE DESIGN

Site Structure

Much like your code structure and documentation (covered in Chapter 1, *Advanced PHP Programming*), another overarching issue when developing larger Web applications is that of site structure: how the files are organized and stored on the server. Proper site structure is intended to improve security and administration of a site, as well as promote scalability, portability, and ease of modifications.

While site structure does not qualify as a mission-critical issue, I've seen "professional" Web developers throw everything into one folder—HTML, images, and all—resulting in a directory that contained more than 600 items! I can't imagine how frustrating it would be to manage such a project. Developing and following an organization scheme when working

will save you hours of work over the long run of your programming career.

The key to site structure is to break up your code and applications into different modules according to use, purpose, and function. Within the primary Web documents folder, which I'll call *html*, you would have one directory for images (most everyone does do this at least), another for classes, another for functions, and so forth. **Figure 5.7** is a picture of how I lay out my sites. But this is only a recommendation. It can certainly be altered and probably improved upon. Further, I would suggest that you use your own personalized folder names for security purposes. Anytime that a malicious user is blind to the names of folders and documents, the better.

The lynchpin of the system is a configuration file that stores important information such as the database access, necessary constants, and more. Normally I call this file config.inc and

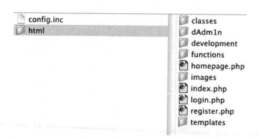

Figure 5.7 This pictorial view of a server is just one way to organize your files. The key is to start planning early and remain consistent.

Script 5.1 This is a simple configuration file that should provide a basis for beginning your Web applications.

```
script
1    <?php
2
3    // ***** config.inc *****
4    // Developed by Larry E. Ullman
5    // Contact: php@DMCinsights.com
6    // Created  September 8, 2001
7    // Last modified September 8, 2001
8    // This is the configuration file for the
9    // Community
10   // Web site.
11   // Base url = http://www.community.com
12
13   // Database-specific information:
14   $db_info[username] = "username";
15   $db_info[password] = "password";
16   $db_info[host] = "localhost";
17   $db_info[dbname] = "community";
18   $db_connection = mysql_connect
        ($db_info[host], $db_info[username],
        $db_info[password]) or die
        (mysql_error());
19   mysql_select_db ($db_info[dbname],
        $db_connection) or die (mysql_error());
20   ?>
```

place it in the level below the Web document root (in other words, in the same directory as the html directory; see Figure 5.7). Thanks to the configuration file, you can make global changes to the site by modifying only one page. For example, if you need to switch databases or servers, updating config.inc should handle most of the required alterations. Also, once you've established a working configuration file, modifications to it can generate the configuration file for new sites.

To write a configuration file:

1. Create a new PHP document in your text editor (**Script 5.1**).

   ```
   <?php
   ```

2. Add all the comments you can think of that would be appropriate to the site.

   ```
   // ***** config.inc *****
   // Developed by Larry E. Ullman
   // Contact: php@DMCinsights.com
   // Created  September 8, 2001
   // Last modified September 8, 2001
   // This is the configuration file for
   // the Community
   // Web site.
   // Base url = http://www.community.
   → com
   ```

   This is just a rough idea of what you might want to say. More documentation and comments are better than less, so do not be afraid to be verbose here. Needless to say, the example URL here— www.community.com—should not be confused with the real www.community. com, which does exist already (I'm developing the site offline where domain names do not matter).

   continues on next page

3. Set the database values.

```
$db_info[username] = "username";
$db_info[password] = "password";
$db_info[host] = "localhost";
$db_info[dbname] = "community";
$db_connection = mysql_connect
→ ($db_info[host], $db_info
→ [username], $db_info[password])
→ or die (mysql_error());
mysql_select_db ($db_info[dbname],
→ $db_connection) or die
→ (mysql_error());
```

4. Close the PHP and save the file as config.inc.

```
?>
```

Now I'll create the site's first page, index.php, which will use OOP to separate out the HTML from the PHP. To do this, I'll code the HTML template first, then the class, followed by the actual index.php instance.

5. Create a new HTML document in your text editor (**Script 5.2**).

```
<!DOCTYPE html PUBLIC "-//W3C//DTD
→ XHTML 1.0 Transitional//EN"
"http://www.w3.org/TR/2000/
→ REC-xhtml1-20000126/DTD/
→ xhtml1-transitional.dtd">
<html xmlns="http://www.w3.org/1999/
→ xhtml">
<head>
<title><!--{PAGE_TITLE}--></title>
<!--{JAVASCRIPT}-->
</head>
```

For this template, I'll be using the HTML comment syntax, as introduced in one of the tips in Chapter 2, Object-Oriented Programming, for the replaceable elements (e.g. <!--{JAVASCRIPT}-->) because some of the elements, like the JavaScript, will be optional. If a page does not use this element, a hidden HTML

comment will be sent to the browser rather than an ugly {JAVASCRIPT}.

6. Continue on with the body of the template.

```
<body background="images/bg1.jpg"
→ link="#0033FF" alink="#0033FF"
→ vlink="#0033FF">
<table border="0" width="600"
→ height="320" cellpadding="0"
→ cellspacing="0">
<tr>
<td width="50%">
<img border="0" src="images/dot.jpg"
→ width="36" height="36" /><img
→ border="0" src="images/dot.jpg"
→ hspace="10" width="36" height="36
→ /><img border="0" src="images/
→ dot.jpg" width="36" height="36" />
→ <img border="0" src="images/
→ dot.jpg" hspace="10" width="36"
→ height="36" /><img border="0"
→ src="images/dot.jpg" width="36"
→ height="36" /><img border="0"
→ src="images/dot.jpg" hspace="10"
→ width="36" height="36" />
</td>
<td width="50%"
→ align="right"><big><b><font
→ color="#0033FF">Community
→ Pages</font></b></big></td>
</tr>
<tr>
<td width="600" colspan="2"
→ height="2"><img src="images/
→ line.gif" width="600" /></td>
</tr>
<tr>
<td width="600" colspan="2"
→ height="2" align="right">
→ <!--{PAGE_HEADER}--></td>
</tr>
```

continues on page 180

Script 5.2 This Web page template makes use of several different replaceable elements, including the title, a JavaScript option, a header, the content (obviously), and the footer.

```
1    <!DOCTYPE html PUBLIC "-//W3C//DTD XHTML 1.0 Transitional//EN"
2        "http://www.w3.org/TR/2000/REC-xhtml1-20000126/DTD/xhtml1-transitional.dtd">
3    <html xmlns="http://www.w3.org/1999/xhtml">
4    <head>
5        <title><!--{PAGE_TITLE}--></title>
6    <!--{JAVASCRIPT}-->
7    </head>
8    <body background="images/bg1.jpg" link="#0033FF" alink="#0033FF" vlink="#0033FF">
9    <table border="0" width="600" height="320" cellpadding="0" cellspacing="0">
10       <tr>
11           <td width="50%">
12               <img border="0" src="images/dot.jpg" width="36" height="36" /><img border="0" src=
                 "images/dot.jpg" hspace="10" width="36" height="36" /><img border="0" src="images/
                 dot.jpg" width="36" height="36" /><img border="0" src="images/dot.jpg" hspace="10"
                 width="36" height="36" /><img border="0" src="images/dot.jpg" width="36" height="36"
                 /><img border="0" src="images/dot.jpg" hspace="10" width="36" height="36" />
13   </td>
14           <td width="50%" align="right"><big><b><font color="#0033FF">Community
             Pages</font></b></big></td>
15       </tr>
16       <tr>
17           <td width="600" colspan="2" height="2"><img src="images/line.gif" width="600" /></td>
18       </tr>
19       <tr>
20           <td width="600" colspan="2" height="2" align="right"><!--{PAGE_HEADER}--></td>
21       </tr>
22       <tr>
23           <td width="600" colspan="2" height="2"><img src="images/line.gif" width="600" /></td>
24       </tr>
25       <tr>
26           <td width="600" colspan="2">
27               <table border="0" cellspacing="0" cellpadding="0">
28                   <tr>
29                       <td width="200" valign="top"><a href="index.php"> <img name="img1"
                         src="images/image1.gif" vspace="3" border="0" align="absmiddle" width="30"
                         height="30" /><b> <i><big>home</big></i></b></a><br></br>
30                       <a href="register.php"> <img name="img2" src="images/image10.gif" vspace="3"
                         border="0" align="absmiddle" width="30" height="30" /><b> <i><big>register
                         </big></i></b></a><br></br>
31                       <a href="calendar.php"> <img name="img3" src="images/image4.gif" vspace="3"
                         border="0" align="absmiddle" width="30" height="30" /><b> <i><big>calendar
                         </big></i></b></a><br></br>
32                       <a href="forum/index.php"><img name="img4" src="images/image7.gif" vspace="3"
                         border="0" align="absmiddle" width="30" height="30" /><b>
                         <i><big>forums</big></i></b></a><br></br></td>
33                       <td width="610" valign="top"><br></br><!--{PAGE_CONTENT}--></td>
34                   </tr>
35               </table>
36       </tr>
37   </table>
38   <table border="0" cellspacing="0" cellpadding="0" width="600">
39       <tr>
40           <td align="center">Copyright &copy; 2001. All rights reserved.<br></br>
             <!--{PAGE_FOOTER}--><br></br></td>
41       </tr>
42   </table>
43   </body>
44   </html>
```

The template being created here will reveal to the user either a log-in form or a personalized greeting based upon whether or not the user is logged in. The `<!--{PAGE_HEADER}-->` slot will be used for one or the other, depending.

7. Write the rest of the template.

```
<tr>
<td width="600" colspan="2"
→ height="2"><img src="images/
→ line.gif" width="600" /></td>
</tr>
<tr>
<td width="600" colspan="2">
<table border="0" cellspacing="0"
→ cellpadding="0">
<tr>
<td width="200" valign="top"><a
→ href="index.php"> <img name="img1"
→ src="images/image1.gif" vspace="3"
→ border="0" align="absmiddle"
→ width="30" height="30" /><b> <i>
→ <big>home</big></i></b></a><br></br>
<a href="register.php"> <img
→ name="img2" src="images/
→ image10.gif" vspace="3" border="0"
→ align="absmiddle" width="30"
→ height="30" /><b> <i><big>register
→ </big></i></b></a><br></br>
<a href="calendar.php"> <img
→ name="img3" src="images/image4.gif"
→ vspace="3" border="0" align=
→ "absmiddle" width="30" height="30"
→ /><b> <i><big>calendar</big></i>
→ </b></a><br></br>
```

```
<a href="forum/index.php"><img
→ name="img4" src="images/image7.gif"
→ vspace="3" border="0" align=
→ "absmiddle" width="30" height="30"
→ /><b> <i><big>forums</big></i></b>
→ </a><br></br></td>
<td width="610" valign="top"><br>
→ </br><!--{PAGE_CONTENT}--></td>
</tr>
</table>
</tr>
</table>
<table border="0" cellspacing="0"
→ cellpadding="0" width="600">
<tr>
<td align="center">Copyright &copy;
→ 2001. All rights reserved.<br>
→ </br><!--{PAGE_FOOTER}--><br></br>
→ </td>
</tr>
</table>
</body>
</html>
```

The template also has replaceable elements called *PAGE_CONTENT* and *PAGE_FOOTER*. The footer will be a combination copyright and *Last modified...* message. The latter part of the footer will be created by PHP on the fly, which is why I designate it as replaceable.

Script 5.3 The HtmlTemplate2 class from Chapter 2, Object-Oriented Programming, while sufficient, will get a minor overhaul for use in this chapter.

```
1    <?php
2    // This class reads in a template, sets
     the different values, and sends it to the
     browser.
3
4    class HtmlTemplate2 {
5
6        // Set the attributes.
7        var $template;
8        var $html;
9        var $parameters = array();
10
11       function HtmlTemplate2 ($template) {
         // This function sets which template
         will be used.
12           $this->template = $template;
13           $this->html = implode ("", (file
             ($this->template))); // Read the
             template into an array, then
             create a string.
14       }
15
16       function SetParameter ($variable,
         $value) { // This function sets the
         particular values.
17           $this->parameters[$variable] =
             $value;
18       }
19
20       function CreatePage () { // This
         function does the bulk of the work.
21
22           foreach ($this->parameters as
             $key => $value) { // Loop through
             all the parameters and set the
             variables to values.
23               $template_name =
                 '{' . $key . '}';
24               $this->html = str_replace
                 ($template_name, $value,
                 $this->html);
25           }
26           echo $this->html;
27       }
28   }
29   ?>
```

8. Save the script as `main_template.inc`.

This is the HTML template for the community site being developed. **Figure 5.8** gives a rough idea of what it will look like. (This template was downloaded with permission from http://freesitetemplates. com. You can grab this or others from that site or download the applicable images from www.DMCinsights.com/ phpadv.)

The class for this site will be based upon *HtmlTemplate2* class (Script 2.5) from Chapter 2, Object-Oriented Programming. I'll make some minor modifications to it here.

9. Open `HtmlTemplate2.class` in your text editor (**Script 5.3**).

continues on next page

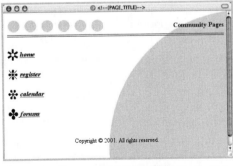

Figure 5.8 The blank template being used in the Web application looks like this, before being objectified. Notice that, except for the page title, all of the replaceable elements are comments that do not appear in the browser.

10. Add another attribute (variable) to the class (**Script 5.4**).

```
var $message;
```

Because this site will entail registration and logging in, I want to add the capacity for reporting errors and messages. The $message variable will be used for this purpose.

11. Alter line 23 of the original script to acknowledge the new replaceable element format.

```
$template_name =
→ '<!--{' . $key . '}-->';
```

Because the elements in the template are in the form <!--{ELEMENT}-->, you also need to change this line or else the elements will not be replaced with their appropriate values.

Script 5.4 The HtmlTemplate2 class has been modified to handle messages and deal with the <!--{ELEMENT}--> format (not the simpler {ELEMENT} format that the original, Script 5.3, used).

```
1    <?php
2    // This class reads in a template, sets the different values, and sends it to the browser.
3
4    class HtmlTemplate2 {
5
6        // Set the attributes.
7        var $template;
8        var $html;
9        var $parameters = array();
10       var $message;
11
12       function HtmlTemplate2 ($template) { // This function sets which template will be used.
13           $this->template = $template;
14           $this->html = implode ("", (file($this->template))); // Read the template into an array,
             then create a string.
15       }
16
17       function SetParameter ($variable, $value) { // This function sets the particular values.
18           $this->parameters[$variable] = $value;
19       }
20
21       function CreatePage () { // This function does the bulk of the work.
22
23           foreach ($this->parameters as $key => $value) { // Loop through all the parameters and
             set the variables to values.
24               $template_name = '<!--{' . $key . '}-->';
25               $this->html = str_replace ($template_name, $value, $this->html);
26           }
27           echo $this->html;
28       }
29
30       function CreateErrorMessages ($the_message) { // This function is for error reporting to the
          user.
31           $the_message = urldecode ($the_message);
32           $this->$message = "<div align=\"left\"><font color=red><b>The following problem(s)
             occurred:</b><br></br>$the_message <br></br><p></p></font></div><br></br>\n";
33           return $this->$message;
34       }
35   }
36   ?>
37
```

Script 5.5 Each page in the Web application will be an object like this one, with the content, page title, and more being assigned on the fly.

```
                    script
1    <?php
2
3    // This is the index page that uses the
     HtmlTemplate2 class.
4    require_once ("../config.inc"); //
     Include the configuration file.
5    require_once ("classes/HtmlTemplate2.
     class"); // Include the class.
6
7    $page = new HtmlTemplate2
     ("templates/main_template.inc"); //
     Create an instance.
8
9    $page->SetParameter("PAGE_TITLE",
     "Welcome to our Community!");
10
11   if ($error_message) {
12       $content = $page->CreateError
         Messages($error_message);
13   } elseif ($good_message) {
14   $content = '<div align="left"><font
     color="blue"><b>' . urldecode ($good_
     message) . '</b></font></div><br></br>';
15
16   }
17
18   $content .= "Hey there!";
19   $page->SetParameter("PAGE_CONTENT",
     $content);
20
21   $footer = "Last modified " . (date("l, F
     j, Y", filemtime("modified.txt")));
22   $page->SetParameter("PAGE_FOOTER",
     $footer);
23
24   $page->CreatePage(); // Send the page to
     the browser.
25   unset ($page);
26   ?>
```

12. Add another function.

```
function CreateErrorMessages
→ ($the_message) {
$the_message = urldecode
→ ($the_message);
$this->$message = "<div align=\
→ "left\"><font color=red><b>The
→ following problem(s) occurred:</b>
→ <br></br>$the_message <br></br><p>
→ </p></font></div><br></br>\n";
return $this->$message;
}
```

While the other functions built into the class will remain the same, this one needs to be added. The `CreateErrorMessages()` function takes a variable that is presumably a urlencoded string sent to the page. It will turn this variable into a properly formatted message.

Considering the level of changes, if you prefer, you could make this a new class that is an extension of the original rather than just modifying it.

13. Save the class as `HtmlTemplate2.class`.

Now that the template and class have been written, you can create the first instance, `index.php`.

14. Create a new PHP document in your text editor and include the configuration file (**Script 5.5**).

```
<?php
require_once ("../config.inc");
```

Although this page may or may not need the database information stored in the configuration file, it's best to include it regardless. In fact, since the whole point of a configuration file is to set universal parameters, it ought to be included in every nontemplate or nonclass file.

continues on next page

15. Include the class file.

```
require_once "classes/HtmlTemplate2.
→ class";
```

16. Create an object of the class and set the different parameters.

```
$page = new HtmlTemplate2
→ ("templates/main_template.inc");
$page->SetParameter("PAGE_TITLE",
→ "Welcome to our Community!");
```

17. Make use of the `CreateErrorMessage()` function to add any message as part of the page's content.

```
if ($error_message) {
$content = $page->CreateError
→ Messages($error_message);
} elseif ($good_message) {
$content = '<div align="left">
→ <font color="blue"><b>' .
→ urldecode ($good_message) .
→ '</b></font></div><br></br>';}
$content .= "Hey there!";
$page->SetParameter("PAGE_CONTENT",
→ $content);
```

The thinking here is that if an error message is received, it will be formatted according to the `HtmlTemplate2`'s guidelines. If a message is received that is not an error message (upon successful registration, for example), it will be more directly formatted within the script itself. In either case, the resulting text marks the beginning of the page content, which is then appended with the actual page-specific content.

Absolute Versus Relative Paths

With Web pages, whether you are dealing with HTML or PHP, you have the option of referring to other files using either absolute or relative paths. An absolute path is a definitive point, accessible from anywhere (e.g., *1600 Pennsylvania Avenue* or */home/users/web*). A relative path is how to get to that point from where you currently are (e.g., *go West 2 miles* or *../images/footer.gif*).

The benefit to using an absolute path is that it will always be accurate as long as the referenced file exists in that particular directory. In other words, if you move every file that refers to, say, `config.inc`, but use an absolute path, those other files will always find it.

The benefit to using a relative path is that you can move everything from server to server or directory to directory, and as long as they keep the same organizational structure in relation to each other, the site will still work.

Another option is to refer to the `$DOCUMENT_ROOT` variable (although it may not work on some servers). The `$DOCUMENT_ROOT` variable refers to the directory leading up to the file it is used in and will therefore always be accurate, despite how the file is moved around. If you intend to use relative paths, then incorporating `$DOCUMENT_ROOT` into the equation is a smart way to program.

SITE STRUCTURE

Figure 5.9 You can see the beginning of the site structure between this figure and Figure 5.10.

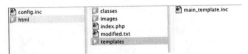

Figure 5.10 As the site develops, containing dozens of individual pages as well as different templates and classes, separating out the files becomes more and more necessary.

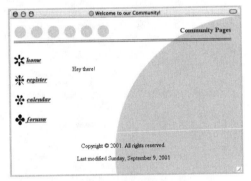

Figure 5.11 This is the home page of the site, which uses the main_template.inc and HtmlTemplate2.class files to generate a Web page object.

18. Use PHP to write a footer.

```
$footer = "Last modified " .
→ (date("l, F j, Y", filemtime
→ ("modified.txt")));
$page->SetParameter("PAGE_FOOTER",
→ $footer);
```

My little trick for writing footers is to place a dummy file on the server called modified.txt. Every time I make alterations to the site, I upload a new copy of this blank file. The PHP code here will determine the last day that modified.txt was modified (i.e., uploaded) using the filemtime() function and will return a formatted date. The resulting footer text is something like *Last modified Tuesday, October 23, 2001.*

19. Send the data to the browser, delete the object, and close the PHP.

```
$page->CreatePage();
unset ($page);
?>
```

20. Save the page as index.php. Upload it, along with config.inc (Script 5.1), main_template.inc (Script 5.2), HtmlTemplate2.class (Script 5.4), and a blank modified.txt file, to your server. Keep these documents organized as indicated in the scripts (**Figures 5.9** and **5.10**). Run index.php in your Web browser (**Figure 5.11**).

SITE STRUCTURE

185

Filename Extensions

For PHP pages, I have been using .php as my file extension, which corresponds to my Web server's settings for processing .php pages with PHP. For including files such as the configuration file and my OOP classes, I use the .inc and .class extensions instead, which the Web server is not set to handle. My thinking is that it helps me to know the purpose of each file both from the filename and its extension.

The result of this schema is that if you went to HtmlTemplate2.class directly, you would be given the opportunity to download the page, or, if it were called HtmlTemplate2.inc, the contents would be displayed in your Web browser as a straight text file (**Figure 5.12**). Conversely, if I named it HtmlTemplate2.php and a user were to go directly there, it would display a blank page (**Figure 5.13**).

The decision as to which extension you use mostly depends on what your options are and what security concerns you have. Very important documents that should never be readable, such as config.inc, ought to be placed outside of the Web document root. If this is not an option, then use a .php extension instead. Understand, though, that a PHP file may still be displayed in a Web browser as text if a server goes down or is improperly configured.

Other files where security is less of an issue can continue using .class or .inc extensions. Or, if you have permission, you can set your Web server to treat these as they would the .php extension. Finally, you could use filename.inc.php or filename.class.php, which will indicate to you it is an included file or class but still be treated by the server as PHP.

Figure 5.12 The downside to using an unconventional extension such as .class or .inc is that the source code will be displayed in the browser if accessed directly.

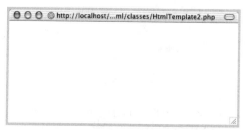

Figure 5.13 Unlike the .class or .inc files (Figure 5.12), .php files, if accessed directly in the browser, will display a blank page, assuming it has no echo or print statements and the server is working properly.

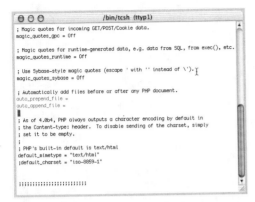

Figure 5.14 The `auto_prepend_file` and `auto_append_file` settings are best used on servers where every file requires the same includes. It's a convenient but heavy-handed alternative to using `include()` or `require()`.

✔ Tips

■ Some programmers use `require()` and some use `include()`. Generally, it doesn't make any difference one way or the other except for the fact that `require()` will always be called, even if it is within a conditional. Also, it is conceivable that `require()` is faster than `include()` but not noticeably so. If you are using PHP 4, use the new `require_once()` and `include_once()` instead.

■ If you can modify the `php.ini` file, you have the option to set the `auto_prepend_file` and `auto_append_file` parameters (**Figure 5.14**). These two lines allow you to set files to be automatically included at the beginning (*prepend*) and end (*append*) of every file in the Web document directory. You would want to do this only if every page on the server would make use of the same included files.

■ With an Apache server, you also have the option of using the ubiquitous `.htaccess` file to specify included files for a particular directory. Check Apache's documentation for the specifics.

PHP and OOP Templates

While using objects can greatly simplify your code and expedite development of a site, it has a number of limitations, as mentioned in Chapter 2, Object-Oriented Programming. One of the big problems you may encounter is how best to interlace PHP and HTML while promoting separation.

For example, I want every page of the site to use a dynamically created footer such as *Last modified Saturday, May 25, 2001*. However, the template for the page itself contains only HTML, and if I were to place PHP within it to generate the footer, it would not be executed because the object process merely reads in the HTML template, replaces certain values, and prints it all out to the browser. No PHP execution takes place.

In the `index.php` object (Script 5.5), I worked around this by executing the PHP within the instance, then passing along the resulting value to the HTML using

```
$page->SetParameter("PAGE_FOOTER",
→ $footer);
```

This site will require registration, which means I'll want to use the well-conceived `register.php` page from Chapter 4, Security. As it stands, `register.php` will not work with the OOP template system being used because, among other things, it uses PHP to enter existing values in the form. In this section, I'll show you how to get PHP and HTML in objects to play along by turning `register.php` into a function OOP version. For it to work properly, I'll need to completely separate the PHP from the HTML, and while I'm at it, I'll make it function with a database instead of a text file.

To incorporate PHP and HTML:

1. Open register.php—the non-Mcrypt version from Chapter 4 in your text editor (**Script 5.6**).

continues on page 194

Script 5.6 The original register.php worked just fine but could not be integrated into an OOP environment as is.

```
1    <?php
2
3    if (isset($HTTP_POST_VARS[Submit])) { // If the form was submitted, process it.
4
5        // Check the username.
6        if (eregi ("^[[:alnum:]]+$", $HTTP_POST_VARS[username])) {
7            $a = TRUE;
8        } else {
9            $a = FALSE;
10           $message[] = "Please enter a username that consists only of letters and numbers.";
11       }
12
13       // Check to make sure the password is long enough and of the right format.
14       if (eregi ("^[[:alnum:]]{8,16}$", $HTTP_POST_VARS[pass1])) {
15               $b = TRUE;
16       } else {
17               $b = FALSE;
18               $message[] = "Please enter a password that consists only of letters and numbers,
                 between 8 and 16 characters long.";
19       }
20
21       // Check to make sure the password matches the confirmed password.
22       if ($HTTP_POST_VARS[pass1] == $HTTP_POST_VARS[pass2]) {
23               $c = TRUE;
24               $password = crypt ($HTTP_POST_VARS[pass1]); // Encrypt the password.
25       } else {
26               $c = FALSE;
27               $message[] = "The password you entered did not match the confirmed password.";
28       }
29
30       // Check to make sure they entered their first name and it's of the right format.
31       if (eregi ("^([[:alpha:]]|-|')+$", $HTTP_POST_VARS[first_name])) {
32               $d = TRUE;
33       } else {
34               $d = FALSE;
35               $message[] = "Please enter a valid first name.";
36       }
37
38       // Check to make sure they entered their last name and it's of the right format.
39       if (eregi ("^([[:alpha:]]|-|')+$", $HTTP_POST_VARS[last_name])) {
40               $e = TRUE;
41       } else {
42               $e = FALSE;
43               $message[] = "Please enter a valid last name.";
44       }
```

(script continues on next page)

Script 5.6 *continued*

```
                                                    script

45
46          // Check to make sure they entered a valid email address.
47          if (eregi("^([[:alnum:]]|_|\.|-)+@([[:alnum:]]|\.|-)+(\.)([a-z]{2,4})$",
            $HTTP_POST_VARS[email])) {
48              $f = TRUE;
49          } else {
50              $f = FALSE;
51              $message[] = "Please enter a valid email address.";
52          }
53
54          // Check to make sure they entered a valid birth date.
55          if (checkdate ($HTTP_POST_VARS[birth_month], $HTTP_POST_VARS[birth_day],
            $HTTP_POST_VARS[birth_year])) {
56              $g = TRUE;
57          } else {
58              $g = FALSE;
59              $message[] = "Please enter a valid birth  date.";
60          }
61
62          //  If the data passes all the tests, check to ensure a unique member name, then register
            them.
63          if ($a AND $b AND $c AND $d AND $e AND $f AND $g) {
64
65              if ($fp = @fopen ("../users.txt", "r")) { // Open the file for reading.
66
67                  while ( !feof($fp) AND !$user_found ) { // Loop through each line, checking each
                    username.
68                      $read_data = fgetcsv ($fp, 1000, "\t"); // Read the line into an array.
69                      if ($read_data[0] == $HTTP_POST_VARS[username]) {
70                          $user_found = TRUE;
71                      }
72                  }
73                  fclose ($fp);
74
75                  if (!$user_found) { // If the username is OK, register them.
76
77                      if ($fp2 = @fopen ("../users.txt", "a")) { // Open the file for writing.
78                          $write_data = $HTTP_POST_VARS[username] . "\t" . $password . "\t" .
                            $HTTP_POST_VARS[first_name] . "\t" . $HTTP_POST_VARS[last_name] . "\t" .
                            $HTTP_POST_VARS[email] . "\t" . $HTTP_POST_VARS[birth_month] . "-" .
                            $HTTP_POST_VARS[birth_day] . "-" . $HTTP_POST_VARS[birth_year] . "\n";
79                          fwrite ($fp2, $write_data);
80                          fclose ($fp2);
81                          $message = urlencode ("You have been successfully registered.");
82                          header ("Location: homepage.php?message=$message"); // Send them on their
                            way.
83                          exit;
84                      } else {
85                          $message[] = "Could not register to the user's file! Please contact the
                            Webmaster for more information.<br></br>";
86                      }
87                  } else {
88                      $message[] = "That username is already taken. Please select another.";
89                  }
```

(script continues on next page)

Script 5.6 *continued*

```
 90                   } else { // If it couldn't open the file, print an error message.
 91                       $message[] = "Could not read the user's file! Please contact the Webmaster for more
 92                       information.<br></br>";
 93                   }
 94           }
 95
 96
 97      } // End of Submit if.
 98      ?>
 99      <!DOCTYPE html PUBLIC "-//W3C//DTD XHTML 1.0 Strict//EN"
100      "http://www.w3.org/TR/2000/REC-xhtml1-20000126/DTD/xhtml1-strict.dtd">
101      <html xmlns="http://www.w3.org/1999/xhtml">
102      <head>
103          <title>Register</title>
104      <script type="text/javascript" language="Javascript">
105      <!-- // Begin to hide script contents from old browsers.
106      function CheckData() {
107          if (document.form.username.value.length <= 0) {
108              alert ("Enter a username.");
109              document.form.username.value = "*** Username";
110              document.form.username.focus();
111              var problem = true;
112          }
113          if (document.form.first_name.value.length <= 0) {
114              alert ("Enter your first name.");
115              document.form.first_name.value = "*** First Name";
116              document.form.first_name.focus();
117              var problem = true;
118          }
119          if (document.form.last_name.value.length <= 0) {
120              alert ("Enter your last name.");
121              document.form.last_name.value = "*** Last Name";
122              document.form.last_name.focus();
123              var problem = true;
124          }
125          if (document.form.email.value.length <= 0) {
126              alert ("Enter your email address.");
127              document.form.email.value = "*** Email Address";
128              document.form.email.focus();
129              var problem = true;
130          }
131          if (document.form.pass1.value.length < 8) {
132              alert ("Enter a password at least 8 characters long.");
133              var problem = true;
134          }
135          if (document.form.pass1.value != document.form.pass2.value) {
136              alert ("Your confirmed password does not match the entered password.");
137              var problem = true;
138          }
139          if ((document.form.birth_month.value == 0) || (document.form.birth_month.selectedIndex == 0)) {
140              alert ("Please select your month of birth.");
141              var problem = true;
142          }
143          if ((document.form.birth_day.value == 0) || (document.form.birth_day.selectedIndex == 0)) {
```

(script continues on next page)

Script 5.6 *continued*

```
                                        script
144            alert ("Please select your day of birth.");
145            var problem = true;
146        }
147        if ((document.form.birth_year.value == 0) || (document.form.birth_year.selectedIndex == 0)) {
148            alert ("Please select your year of birth.");
149            var problem = true;
150        }
151
152        if (problem == true) {
153            return false;
154        } else {
155            return true;
156        }
157    }
158    //-->
159    </script>
160    </head>
161    <body>
162    <?php
163    // Print out any error messages.
164    if ($message) {
165        echo "<div align=\"left\"><font color=red><b>The following problems
           occurred:</b><br></br>\n";
166        foreach ($message as $key => $value) {
167            echo "$value <br></br>\n";
168        }
169        echo "<p></p><b>Be sure to re-enter your passwords and your birth
           date!</b></font></div><br></br>\n";
170    }
171    ?>
172    <form name="form" action="register.php" method="post" onsubmit="return CheckData()">
173    <table border="0" width="90%" cellspacing="2" cellpadding="2" align="center">
174        <tr>
175            <td align="right">Username</td>
176            <td align="left"><input type="text" name="username" size="25" maxsize="16"
               value="<?=$HTTP_POST_VARS[username] ?>"></td>
177            <td align="left"><small>Maximum of 16 characters, stick to letters and numbers, no
               spaces, underscores, hyphens, etc.</small></td>
178        </tr>
179        <tr>
180            <td align="right">Password</td>
181            <td align="left"><input type="password" name="pass1" size="25"></td>
182            <td align="left"><small>Minimum of 8 characters, maximum of 16, stick to letters and
               numbers, no spaces, underscores, hyphens, etc.</small></td>
183        </tr>
184        <tr>
185            <td align="right">Confirm Password</td>
186            <td align="left"><input type="password" name="pass2" size="25"></td>
187            <td align="left"><small>Should be the same as the password.</small></td>
188        </tr>
189        <tr>
190            <td align="right">First Name</td>
191            <td align="left"><input type="text" name="first_name" size="25" maxsize="20"
               value="<?=$HTTP_POST_VARS[first_name] ?>"></td>
192            <td align="left"> </td>
```

(script continues on next page)

Script 5.6 *continued*

```
193        </tr>
194        <tr>
195           <td align="right">Last Name</td>
196           <td align="left"><input type="text" name="last_name" size="25" maxsize="20"
              value="<?=$HTTP_POST_VARS[last_name] ?>"></td>
197           <td align="left"> </td>
198        </tr>
199        <tr>
200           <td align="right">Email Address</td>
201           <td align="left"><input type="text" name="email" size="25" maxsize="60"
              value="<?=$HTTP_POST_VARS[email] ?>"></td>
202           <td align="left"><small>Use whichever email address you want to receive notices
              at.</small></td>
203        </tr>
204        <tr>
205           <td align="right">Birthdate</td>
206           <td align="left" colspan="2">
207     <?php
208     echo '<select name="birth_month">
209     <option value="">Month</option>
210     ';
211     for ($n = 1; $n <= 12; $n++) {
212         echo "<option value=\"$n\">$n</option>\n";
213     }
214     echo '</select>
215     <select name="birth_day">
216     <option value="">Day</option>
217     ';
218     for ($n = 1; $n <= 31; $n++) {
219         echo "<option value=\"$n\">$n</option>\n";
220     }
221     echo '</select>
222     <select name="birth_year">
223     <option value="">Year</option>
224     ';
225     for ($n = 1900; $n <= 2001; $n++) {
226         echo "<option value=\"$n\">$n</option>\n";
227     }
228     ?>
229            </select></td>
230        </tr>
231        <tr>
232           <td align="center" colspan="3"><input type="submit" name="Submit" value="Register!">
                    <input type="reset" name="Reset" value="Reset"></td>
233        </tr>
234     </table>
235     </form>
236     </body>
237     </html>
```

2. Cut out the bulk of the HTML form, lines 172-203, and paste these into a new HTML document, replacing the `<?=$variable` code as you go (**Script 5.7**).

```
<form name="form" action=
→ "register.php" method="post"
→ onsubmit="return CheckData()">
<table border="0" width="90%"
→ cellspacing="2" cellpadding="2"
→ align="center">
<tr>
<td align="right">Username</td>
<td align="left"><input type="text"
→ name="username" size="25"
→ maxsize="16" value="
→ <!--{username}-->"></td>
<td align="left"><small>Maximum of
→ 16 characters, stick to letters
→ and numbers, no spaces, under
→ scores, hyphens, etc.</small></td>
</tr>
<tr>
<td align="right">Password</td>
<td align="left"><input type=
→ "password" name="pass1" size="25">
→ </td>
<td align="left"><small>Minimum of 8
→ characters, maximum of 16, stick to
→ letters and numbers, no spaces,
→ underscores, hyphens, etc.</small>
→ </td>
</tr>
<tr>
<td align="right">Confirm
→ Password</td>
<td align="left"><input type=
→ "password" name="pass2" size="25">
→ </td>
<td align="left"><small>Should be the
→ same as the password.</small></td>
```

```
</tr>
<tr>
<td align="right">First Name</td>
<td align="left"><input type="text"
→ name="first_name" size="25"
→ maxsize="20" value=
→ "<!--{first_name}-->"></td>
<td align="left"> </td>
</tr>
<tr>
<td align="right">Last Name</td>
<td align="left"><input type="text"
→ name="last_name" size="25"
→ maxsize="20" value=
→ "<!--{last_name}-->"></td>
<td align="left"> </td>
</tr>
<tr>
<td align="right">Email Address</td>
<td align="left"><input type="text"
→ name="email" size="25" maxsize="60"
→ value="<!--{email}-->"></td>
<td align="left"><small>Use whichever
→ email address you want to receive
→ notices at.</small></td>
</tr>
```

For the form to work in an OOP environment, all of the PHP needs to be removed. Most of the form contains little or no PHP and can be copied directly into a new file. The PHP code, such as `<?=$HTTP_POST_VARS[email] ?>">`, can be replaced with `<!--{email}-->">` so that the page is still in keeping with the object template format. The result will be that the file is pure HTML, but PHP can still be used—in the object—to replace these values with existing ones, as the original file did.

continues on page 198

Script 5.7 The form itself should be pulled out with any PHP replaced with the `<!–{element}–>` syntax.

```
1    <form name="form" action="register.php" method="post" onsubmit="return CheckData()">
2    <table border="0" width="90%" cellspacing="2" cellpadding="2" align="center">
3        <tr>
4            <td align="right">Username</td>
5            <td align="left"><input type="text" name="username" size="25" maxsize="16" value="
             <!--{username}-->"></td>
6            <td align="left"><small>Maximum of 16 characters, stick to letters and numbers, no
             spaces, underscores, hyphens, etc.</small></td>
7        </tr>
8        <tr>
9            <td align="right">Password</td>
10           <td align="left"><input type="password" name="pass1" size="25"></td>
11           <td align="left"><small>Minimum of 8 characters, maximum of 16, stick to letters and
             numbers, no spaces, underscores, hyphens, etc.</small></td>
12       </tr>
13       <tr>
14           <td align="right">Confirm Password</td>
15           <td align="left"><input type="password" name="pass2" size="25"></td>
16           <td align="left"><small>Should be the same as the password.</small></td>
17       </tr>
18       <tr>
19           <td align="right">First Name</td>
20           <td align="left"><input type="text" name="first_name" size="25" maxsize="20" value="
             <!--{first_name}-->"></td>
21           <td align="left"> </td>
22       </tr>
23       <tr>
24           <td align="right">Last Name</td>
25           <td align="left"><input type="text" name="last_name" size="25" maxsize="20" value="
             <!--{last_name}-->"></td>
26           <td align="left"> </td>
27       </tr>
28       <tr>
29           <td align="right">Email Address</td>
30           <td align="left"><input type="text" name="email" size="25" maxsize="60" value="
             <!--{email}-->"></td>
31           <td align="left"><small>Use whichever email address you want to receive notices at.
             </small></td>
32       </tr>
33       <tr>
34           <td align="right">Birthdate</td>
35           <td align="left" colspan="2"><select name="birth_month"><option value="">Month</option>
36               <option value="1">January</option>
```

(script continues on next page)

Script 5.7 *continued*

```
                                                           script
37              <option value="2">February</option>
38              <option value="3">March</option>
39              <option value="4">April</option>
40              <option value="5">May</option>
41              <option value="6">June</option>
42              <option value="7">July</option>
43              <option value="8">August</option>
44              <option value="9">September</option>
45              <option value="10">October</option>
46              <option value="11">November</option>
47              <option value="12">December</option></select>
48              <select name="birth_day">
49              <option value="">Day</option>
50              <option value="1">1</option>
51              <option value="2">2</option>
52              <option value="3">3</option>
53              <option value="4">4</option>
54              <option value="5">5</option>
55              <option value="6">6</option>
56              <option value="7">7</option>
57              <option value="8">8</option>
58              <option value="9">9</option>
59              <option value="10">10</option>
60              <option value="11">11</option>
61              <option value="12">12</option>
62              <option value="13">13</option>
63              <option value="14">14</option>
64              <option value="15">15</option>
65              <option value="16">16</option>
66              <option value="17">17</option>
67              <option value="18">18</option>
68              <option value="19">19</option>
69              <option value="20">20</option>
70              <option value="21">21</option>
71              <option value="22">22</option>
72              <option value="23">23</option>
73              <option value="24">24</option>
74              <option value="25">25</option>
75              <option value="26">26</option>
76              <option value="27">27</option>
77              <option value="28">28</option>
78              <option value="29">29</option>
```

(script continues on next page)

Script 5.7 *continued*

```
                                                script

79              <option value="30">30</option>
80              <option value="31">31</option></select>
81              <select name="birth_year">
82              <option value="">Year</option>
83              <option value="1901">1901</option>
84              <option value="1902">1902</option>
85              <option value="1903">1903</option>
86              <option value="1904">1904</option>
87              <option value="1905">1905</option>
88              <option value="1906">1906</option>
89              <option value="1907">1907</option>
90              <option value="1908">1908</option>
91              <option value="1909">1909</option>
92              <option value="1910">1910</option>
94              <option value="1912">1912</option>
95              <option value="1913">1913</option>
96              <option value="1914">1914</option>
97              <option value="1915">1915</option>
98              <option value="1916">1916</option>
99              <option value="1917">1917</option>
100             <option value="1918">1918</option>
101             <option value="1919">1919</option>
102             <option value="1920">1920</option>
103             <option value="1921">1921</option>
104             <option value="1922">1922</option>
105             <option value="1923">1923</option>
106             <option value="1924">1924</option>
107             <option value="1925">1925</option>
108             <option value="1926">1926</option>
109             <option value="1927">1927</option>
110             <option value="1928">1928</option>
111             <option value="1929">1929</option>
112             <option value="1930">1930</option>
113             <option value="1931">1931</option></select>
114             </select></td>
115     </tr>
116     <tr>
117         <td align="center" colspan="3"><input type="submit" name="Submit" value="Register!">
                  <input type="reset" name="Reset" value="Reset"></td>
118     </tr>
119     </table>
```

PHP AND OOP TEMPLATES

3. Re-create the birthday pull-down menus without the PHP loops.

```
<tr>
<td align="right">Birthdate</td>
<td align="left" colspan="2"><select
 → name="birth_month"><option
 → value="">Month</option>
<option value="1">January</option>
<option value="2">February</option>
<option value="3">March</option>
<option value="4">April</option>
<option value="5">May</option>
<option value="6">June</option>
<option value="7">July</option>
<option value="8">August</option>
<option value="9">September</option>
<option value="10">October</option>
<option value="11">November</option>
<option value="12">December</option>
 → </select>
<select name="birth_day">
<option value="">Day</option>
<option value="1">1</option>
<option value="2">2</option>
<option value="3">3</option>
<option value="4">4</option>
<option value="5">5</option>
<option value="6">6</option>
<option value="7">7</option>
<option value="8">8</option>
<option value="9">9</option>
<option value="10">10</option>
<option value="11">11</option>
<option value="12">12</option>
<option value="13">13</option>
<option value="14">14</option>
<option value="15">15</option>
<option value="16">16</option>
<option value="17">17</option>
<option value="18">18</option>
<option value="19">19</option>
<option value="20">20</option>
<option value="21">21</option>
<option value="22">22</option>
<option value="23">23</option>
<option value="24">24</option>
<option value="25">25</option>
<option value="26">26</option>
<option value="27">27</option>
<option value="28">28</option>
<option value="29">29</option>
<option value="30">30</option>
<option value="31">31</option>
 → </select>
<select name="birth_year">
<option value="">Year</option>
<option value="1901">1901</option>
<option value="1902">1902</option>
<option value="1903">1903</option>
<option value="1904">1904</option>
<option value="1905">1905</option>
<option value="1906">1906</option>
<option value="1907">1907</option>
<option value="1908">1908</option>
<option value="1909">1909</option>
<option value="1910">1910</option>
<option value="1911">1911</option>
<option value="1912">1912</option>
<option value="1913">1913</option>
<option value="1914">1914</option>
<option value="1915">1915</option>
<option value="1916">1916</option>
<option value="1917">1917</option>
<option value="1918">1918</option>
<option value="1919">1919</option>
<option value="1920">1920</option>
```

```
<option value="1921">1921</option>
<option value="1922">1922</option>
<option value="1923">1923</option>
<option value="1924">1924</option>
<option value="1925">1925</option>
<option value="1926">1926</option>
<option value="1927">1927</option>
<option value="1928">1928</option>
<option value="1929">1929</option>
<option value="1930">1930</option>
<option value="1931">1931</option>
→ </select>
</select></td>
</tr>
```

OK, this is the real tedious part of the plan, but cutting and pasting can expedite the coding process. I've limited the years here to a three-decade span, but you could also just create a four-character text box instead.

4. Complete the HTML form and the table.

```
<tr>
<td align="center" colspan="3"
→ ><input type="submit" name="Submit"
→ value="Register!">    
→   <input type="reset" name=
→ "Reset" value="Reset"></td>
</tr>
</table>
```

5. Save the file as `registration_form.inc`.

Once the form itself has been turned into its own PHP-free document, you can do the same for the JavaScript used to pre-process the form. I could put the JavaScript in with the form, but because I want it to appear in the head of the HTML document, it needs to be separated out.

6. Copy the JavaScript from the original form and paste it into its own document (**Script 5.8**).

Since the JavaScript contains no PHP, it is good to use as is.

continues on page 201

Script 5.8 The JavaScript screening the form will not be problematic with the template structure but should be separated as well so that I can place it within the `<head>` tags.

```
1    <script type="text/javascript" language="Javascript">
2    <!-- // Begin to hide script contents from old browsers.
3    function CheckData() {
4        if (document.form.username.value.length <= 0) {
5            alert ("Enter a username.");
6            document.form.username.value = "*** Username";
7            document.form.username.focus();
8            var problem = true;
9        }
10       if (document.form.first_name.value.length <= 0) {
11           alert ("Enter your first name.");
12           document.form.first_name.value = "*** First Name";
13           document.form.first_name.focus();
14           var problem = true;
```

(script continues on next page)

Script 5.8 *continued*

```
 15          }
 16          if (document.form.last_name.value.length <= 0) {
 17              alert ("Enter your last name.");
 18              document.form.last_name.value = "*** Last Name";
 19              document.form.last_name.focus();
 20              var problem = true;
 21          }
 22          if (document.form.email.value.length <= 0) {
 23              alert ("Enter your email address.");
 24              document.form.email.value = "*** Email Address";
 25              document.form.email.focus();
 26              var problem = true;
 27          }
 28          if (document.form.pass1.value.length < 8) {
 29              alert ("Enter a password at least 8 characters long.");
 30              var problem = true;
 31          }
 32          if (document.form.pass1.value != document.form.pass2.value) {
 33              alert ("Your confirmed password does not match the entered password.");
 34              var problem = true;
 35          }
 36          if ((document.form.birth_month.value == 0) || (document.form.birth_month.
            selectedIndex == 0)) {
 37              alert ("Please select your month of birth.");
 38              var problem = true;
 39          }
 40          if ((document.form.birth_day.value == 0) || (document.form.birth_day.selectedIndex == 0)) {
 41              alert ("Please select your day of birth.");
 42              var problem = true;
 43          }
 44          if ((document.form.birth_year.value == 0) || (document.form.birth_year.selectedIndex == 0)) {
 45              alert ("Please select your year of birth.");
 46              var problem = true;
 47          }
 48
 49          if (problem == true) {
 50              return false;
 51          } else {
 52              return true;
 53          }
 54      }
 55      //-->
 56      </script>
```

Script 5.9 The *HtmlRegistrationTemplate* class is a modification of its parent, *HtmlTemplate2* (Script 5.4), but it does not send anything to the Web browser.

```
script
1    <?php
2
3    // This class is for the registration
     page. It reads in the form,
4    // sets the different values, and returns
     it to the object.
5
6    class HtmlRegistrationTemplate extends
     HtmlTemplate2 {
7
8        var $error_message;
9
10       function SwapParameters() { // This
         function does the bulk of the work.
11
12           foreach ($this->parameters as
             $key => $value) { // Loop through
             all the parameters and set the
             variables to values.
13               $template_name = '<!--{' .
                 $key . '}-->';
14               $this->html = str_replace
                 ($template_name, $value,
                 $this->html);
15           }
16           return $this->html;
17       }
18       function CreateErrorMessages ($message) {
19           $this->$error_message = "<div align=\
             "left\"><font color=red><b>The
             following problem(s)
             occurred:</b><br></br>\n";
20           if (isarray($message)) {
21               foreach ($message as $key =>
                 $value) {
22                   $this->$error_message .= "$value
                     <br></br>\n";
23               }
24           } else {
25               $this->$error_message .=
                 "$message <br></br>\n";
26           }
27           $this->$error_message .=
             "<p></p><b>Be sure to re-enter
             your passwords and your birth
             date!</b></font></div><br></br>\n
             ";
28
29           return $this->$error_message;
30       }
31
32   }
33   ?>
```

7. Save this file as

   `registration_javascript.inc`.

   Before making the instance of the registration page, I'll create a special class for it with slightly different properties than the `HtmlTemplate2` class.

8. Create a new PHP document in your text editor (**Script 5.9**).

   `<?php`

9. Define the class.

   `class HtmlRegistrationTemplate`
   `→ extends HtmlTemplate2 {`

   This class is an extension of the *HtmlTemplate2* class, which means it will build on the original's methods and attributes.

10. Add a new property to the class.

    `var $error_message;`

    The `$error_message` variable will be new to this class and will logically store the generated error message(s).

11. Create a function.

    `function SwapParameters() {`

    `foreach ($this->parameters as`
    `→ $key => $value) { $template_name =`
    `→ '<!--{' . $key . '}-->';`

    `$this->html = str_replace`
    `→ ($template_name, $value,`
    `→ $this->html);`

    `}`

    `return $this->html;`

    `}`

    The `SwapParameters()` function is a combination of the `SetParameter()` and `CreatePage()` methods of the parent class. Since this file will be used explicitly to replace sections of code with new values, you want it to be returning the new HTML, not sending it to the browser, which `CreatePage()` does.

    continues on next page

PHP AND OOP TEMPLATES

12. Write the error message function.

```
function CreateErrorMessages
→ ($message) {
$this->$error_message = "<div
→ align=\"left\"><font color=red>
→ <b>The following problem(s)
→ occurred:</b><br></br>\n";
if (isarray($message)) {
foreach ($message as $key =>
→ $value) {
$this->$error_message .= "$value
→ <br></br>\n";
}
} else {
$this->$error_message .= "$message
→ <br></br>\n";
}
$this->$error_message .= "<p>
→ </p><b>Be sure to re-enter your
→ passwords and your birthdate!</b>
→ </font></div><br></br>\n";
return $this->$error_message;
}
```

The `CreateErrorMessages()` function in this class overrides the similarly named function in the parent. The difference between the two is that this method can take either a single-string message or an array of messages. It will turn either into a properly formatted error message string, which gets returned to the object.

13. Close the class and the PHP.

```
}
?>
```

14. Save the file as `HtmlRegistration Template.class`

Finally, now that the registration page has been broken down into its form, its

JavaScript, and its own class, you can make an object of it, which does most of the PHP work.

15. Open the original `register.php` (Script 5.6) in your text editor.

16. Copy lines 1-64 of the original script and paste them into a new PHP document (**Script 5.10**). Add a line to the birthday conditional while you are at it.

```
$birthday = "$HTTP_POST_VARS
→ [birth_year]-$HTTP_POST_VARS
→ [birth_month]-$HTTP_POST_VARS
→ [birth_day]";
```

For the most part, the original PHP form validation lines will be used as they were before. One change will be the turning of the three birthday variables into one, for easier insertion into the database.

If you think about it, `register.php` started by handling the form, then displayed the form. The same thing is occurring now, except that objects are used to display the form.

17. Query the database to see if the username has already been taken.

```
$query = "select user_id from users
→ where username='$username'";
$query_db = @mysql_query($query,
→ $db_connection);
$row = @mysql_fetch_array
→ ($query_db);
```

To check if it is OK to use a particular username, the database is queried to retrieve something, in this case the *user_id*, where that username exists. The result will be turned into the variable `$row`. I suppress any error messages with the @ symbol because the query could return nothing, making `$row` empty.

continues on page 206

Script 5.10 Finally, the instance of `register.php` is built upon two objects. The included files that store the JavaScript and form are brought into the object and altered accordingly.

```
1   <?php
2
3   require_once ("../config.inc"); // Include the class.
4
5   if (isset($HTTP_POST_VARS[Submit])) { // If the form was submitted, process it.
6
7       // Check the username.
8       if (eregi ("^[[:alnum:]]+$", $HTTP_POST_VARS[username])) {
9           $a = TRUE;
10      } else {
11          $a = FALSE;
12          $message[] = "Please enter a username that consists only of letters and numbers.";
13      }
14
15      // Check to make sure the password is long enough and of the right format.
16      if (eregi ("^[[:alnum:]]{8,16}$", $HTTP_POST_VARS[pass1])) {
17          $b = TRUE;
18      } else {
19          $b = FALSE;
20          $message[] = "Please enter a password that consists only of letters and numbers, between
                8 and 16 characters long.";
21      }
22
23      // Check to make sure the password matches the confirmed password.
24      if ($HTTP_POST_VARS[pass1] == $HTTP_POST_VARS[pass2]) {
25          $c = TRUE;
26          $password = crypt ($HTTP_POST_VARS[pass1]); // Encrypt the password.
27      } else {
28          $c = FALSE;
29          $message[] = "The password you entered did not match the confirmed password.";
30      }
31
32      // Check to make sure they entered their first name and it's of the right format.
33      if (eregi ("^([[:alpha:]]|-|')+$", $HTTP_POST_VARS[first_name])) {
34          $d = TRUE;
35      } else {
36          $d = FALSE;
37          $message[] = "Please enter a valid first name.";
38      }
39
40      // Check to make sure they entered their last name and it's of the right format.
41      if (eregi ("^([[:alpha:]]|-|')+$", $HTTP_POST_VARS[last_name])) {
42          $e = TRUE;
43      } else {
44          $e = FALSE;
```

(script continues on next page)

Script 5.10 *continued*

```
                                              script
45              $message[] = "Please enter a valid last name.";
46          }
47
48          // Check to make sure they entered a valid email address.
49          if (eregi("^([[:alnum:]]|_|\.|-)+@([[:alnum:]]|\.|-)+(\.)([a-z]{2,4})$",
            $HTTP_POST_VARS[email])) {
50              $f = TRUE;
51          } else {
52              $f = FALSE;
53              $message[] = "Please enter a valid email address.";
54          }
55
56          // Check to make sure they entered a valid birth date.
57          if (checkdate ($HTTP_POST_VARS[birth_month], $HTTP_POST_VARS[birth_day],
            $HTTP_POST_VARS[birth_year])) {
58              $birthday = "$HTTP_POST_VARS[birth_year]-$HTTP_POST_VARS[birth_month]-
                $HTTP_POST_VARS[birth_day]";
59              $g = TRUE;
60          } else {
61              $g = FALSE;
62              $message[] = "Please enter a valid birth date.";
63          }
64
65          //  If the data passes all the tests, check to ensure a unique member name, then register
            them.
66          if ($a AND $b AND $c AND $d AND $e AND $f AND $g) {
67
68              $query = "select user_id from users where username='$username'";
69              $query_db = @mysql_query($query, $db_connection);
70              $row = @mysql_fetch_array($query_db);
71              if ($row) {
72                  $message[] = "That username is already taken. Please select another.";
73              } else {
74                  $query2 = "insert into users values ('0', '$HTTP_POST_VARS[username]', '$password',
                    '$HTTP_POST_VARS[first_name]', '$HTTP_POST_VARS[last_name]',
                    '$HTTP_POST_VARS[email]', '$birthday)";
75                  $query_db2 = mysql_query($query2,$db_connection) or die (mysql_error());
76                  if ($query_db2) {
77                      $mailto = $HTTP_POST_VARS[email];
78                      $mailfrom = "From: Registration@Community.Com";
79                      $subject = "Registration Confirmation";
80                      $body = "Thank you for registering with the Community.\nYour username is
                        $HTTP_POST_VARS[username].\nYour password is $HTTP_POST_VARS[password].";
81                      mail ($mailto, $subject, $body, $mailfrom);
82                      $message="You have been successfully registered. You will receive an email
                        confirmation of your username and password.";
83                      $m = urlencode ($message);
```

(script continues on next page)

Script 5.10 *continued*

```
84                    header ("Location: index2.php?good_message=$m");
85                    exit;
86              } else {
87                    $message="You could not be successfully registered due to a system error. Please
                      contact the Webmaster  at webmaster@community.com to have this corrected.";
88                    $m = urlencode ($message);
89                    header ("Location: index2.php?error_message=$m");
90                    exit;
91              }
92          }
93
94      }
95
96
97  } // End of Submit if.
98
99  require_once "classes/HtmlTemplate2.class"; // Include the class.
100 require_once "classes/HtmlRegistrationTemplate.class"; // Include the class.
101
102 $page = new HtmlTemplate2 ("templates/main_template.inc"); // Create an instance.
103
104 $page->SetParameter("PAGE_TITLE", "Register!");
105
106 $javascript = implode ("\n", (file ("includes/registration_javascript.inc")) );
107 $page->SetParameter("JAVASCRIPT", $javascript);
108
109 if ($message) {
110     $content = HtmlRegistrationTemplate::CreateErrorMessages($message);
111 }
112
113 $form = new HtmlRegistrationTemplate ("includes/registration_form.inc");
114 $form->SetParameter ("username", $HTTP_POST_VARS[username]);
115 $form->SetParameter ("first_name", $HTTP_POST_VARS[first_name]);
116 $form->SetParameter ("last_name", $HTTP_POST_VARS[last_name]);
117 $form->SetParameter ("email", $HTTP_POST_VARS[email]);
118 $content .= $form->SwapParameters();
119 unset($form);
120 $page->SetParameter("PAGE_CONTENT", $content);
121
122
123 $footer = "Last modified " . (date("l, F j, Y", filemtime("modified.txt")));
124 $page->SetParameter("PAGE_FOOTER", $footer);
125
126 $page->CreatePage(); // Send the page to the browser.
127 unset ($page);
128 ?>
```

18. Create a conditional based on the result of the database query.

```
if ($row) {
$message[] = "That username is
→ already taken. Please select
→ another.";
} else {
```

If $row has a value, then the username already exists because a *user_id* was returned. Therefore, you'll need to prompt the user to enter a different name. Otherwise, it is safe to proceed.

19. Enter the data into the database.

```
$query2 = "insert into users values
→ ('0', '$HTTP_POST_VARS[username]',
→ '$password',
→ '$HTTP_POST_VARS[first_name]',
→ '$$HTTP_POST_VARS[last_name]',
→ '$HTTP_POST_VARS[email]',
→ '$birthday')";
$query_db2 = mysql_query
→ ($query2,$db_connection) or die
→ (mysql_error());
```

20. If the information was successfully entered, email the user.

```
if ($query_db2) {
$mailto = $HTTP_POST_VARS[email];
$mailfrom = "From:
→ Registration@Community.Com";
$subject = "Registration
→ Confirmation";
$body = "Thank you for registering
→ with the Community.\nYour username
→ is $HTTP_POST_VARS[username].\n
→ Your password is $HTTP_POST_VARS
→ [password].";
mail ($mailto, $subject, $body,
→ $mailfrom);
```

This is a minimalist email, but it is best to send newly registered users something confirming their information. For added security, you could run the user-submitted *username* and password values through the `EscapeShellCmd()`, `strip_tags()`, or `htmlspecialchars()` functions to purify it before using the `mail()` function.

21. Create a message reporting the success and redirect the user to the home page.

```
$message="You have been successfully
→ registered. You will receive an
→ email confirmation of your
→ username and password.";
$m = urlencode ($message);
header ("Location: index.php
→ ?good_message=$m");
exit;
```

I use the term *good_message* here because I want to distinguish, on the index page, between error messages and successful ones.

22. Complete the database conditional and close the main conditional.

```
} else {
$message="You could not be
→ successfully registered due to a
→ system error. Please contact the
→ Webmaster  at webmaster@
→ community.com to have this
→ corrected.";
$m = urlencode ($message);
header ("Location:
→ index.php?error_message=$m");
exit;
}
}
```

Here I use the *error_message* term to report a problem back to the user. The `CreateErrorMessage()` function will be used to handle these two messages, as indicated by the code in Script 5.5.

23. Begin creating the actual registration object by including the two required classes.

```
require_once "classes/
→ HtmlTemplate2.class";

require_once "classes/
→ HtmlRegistrationTemplate.class";
```

Remember to include both classes because `register.php` will use information from the `HtmlRegistration-Template.class` as well as the original *HtmlTemplate2* class.

24. Start the register object.

```
$page = new HtmlTemplate2
→ ("templates/main_template.inc");
$page->SetParameter("PAGE_TITLE",
→ "Register!");
```

25. Set the JavaScript in the object.

```
$javascript = implode ("\n",
→ (file ("includes/registration_
→ javascript.inc")) );
$page->SetParameter("JAVASCRIPT",
→ $javascript);
```

Since the JavaScript was placed in a separate document, it can easily be read into an array, using `file()`, and then that array will be turned into a

string using `implode()`. The end result is one long string formatted as the original file was. This string will replace the `<!--{JAVASCRIPT}-->` code in the main template.

26. Report any error messages.

```
if ($message) {
$content = HtmlRegistration
→ Template::CreateErrorMessages
→ ($message);
}
```

Any error messages that the user would see here would be generated from the form processing code at the beginning of the script. It could be an array of miscues or one simple problem (as in the username is already taken). The `CreateErrorMessages()` function from the new *HtmlRegistrationTemplate* class will handle either.

27. Create a new object to manage the registration form itself.

```
$form = new HtmlRegistrationTemplate
→ ("includes/registration_form.inc");
```

Because the registration form is special—that is, you'll want to insert existing form values into it, if applicable—you'll create a new instance, based on the new class, with `registration_form.inc` as the template. Remember that the *Html-RegistrationTemplate* class never prints anything out to the browser, so it is ideal for use here.

continues on next page

28. Set all of the form parameters based on existing values.

```
$form->SetParameter ("username",
→ $HTTP_POST_VARS[username]);

$form->SetParameter ("first_name",
→ $HTTP_POST_VARS[first_name]);

$form->SetParameter ("last_name",
→ $HTTP_POST_VARS[last_name]);

$form->SetParameter ("email",
→ $HTTP_POST_VARS[email]);
```

The process here functions just as it does when replacing the page title or content, except the replaceable elements are within the registration form and the replaced values are derived from any existing values, as stored in $HTTP_POST_VARS. Since $form is an object based on the *HtmlRegistrationTemplate*, which in itself is a child of the *HtmlTemplate2* class, you can still access the SetParameter() function from the parent.

29. Add the form data to the content, delete the $form object, and set the page content.

```
$content .= $form->SwapParameters();

unset($form);

$page->SetParameter("PAGE_CONTENT",
→ $content);
```

The SwapParameters() method will replace all of the different elements in the form of <!--{element}--> with their corresponding value and return the resulting string. This string will then be appended to any existing content—consisting of error messages, that is. To clear the resources used by the object, the $form variable is deleted and finally the page content for the actual $page object can be assigned.

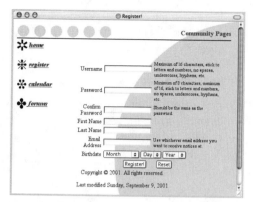

Figure 5.15 The registration form now appears within the context of the OOP design.

Figure 5.16 The JavaScript for the form still works as it originally had.

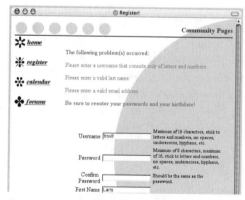

Figure 5.17 If any problems occur during the processing of the form, the errors are reported and the entered values are retained—all as it worked before.

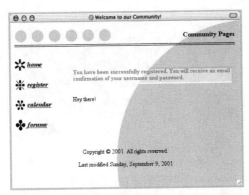

Figure 5.18 If users were successfully registered, they will be sent back to the index page and a nice message will be displayed.

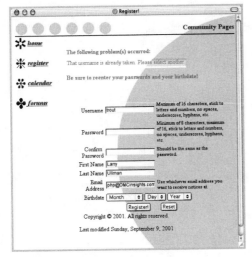

Figure 5.19 If the username is already taken, an appropriate message is displayed and the user is kept on the registration page.

30. Create and set the footer, then create the HTML page and delete the object.

```
$footer = "Last modified " .
→ (date("l, F j, Y", filemtime
→ ("modified.txt")));
$page->SetParameter("PAGE_FOOTER",
→ $footer);
$page->CreatePage();
unset ($page);
?>
```

31. Save this file as `register.php` and upload it, along with `registration_form.inc` (Script 5.7), `registration_javascript.inc` (Script 5.8)—both in the *includes* directory, and `HtmlRegistration-Template.class` (Script 5.9), stored in the *classes* directory. Test in your Web browser (**Figures 5.15**, **5.16**, **5.17**, **5.18** and **5.19**).

Sessions

One of the many very useful additions to PHP is built-in session support. Because HTTP is in itself a stateless protocol—in other words, nothing can be remembered about the user's history without some assistance—developers use different techniques such as cookies and sessions to create a sense of what the user has experienced. Where the user has been, the values of variables, and so forth can be stored on the server and associated with the user. A session, in short, is like a log of a user's visit to a site.

Previously, to create sessions, a programmer had to write an entire library of code that created a unique session name, stored information in a database or text file, sent and read a cookie, and retrieved the stored data. Even though the PHP Base Library, or PHPLib (**Figure 5.20**), simplified this process some, PHP 4's session support is a wonderful addition.

The question may arise: Why use sessions at all when cookies work just fine? First of all, sessions are more secure in that all of the recorded information is stored on the server and not continually sent back and forth between the server and the client. The stored information is harder to steal or alter. Second of all, some users reject cookies or turn them off completely. Sessions, while designed to work with a cookie, can function easily without them, as you'll see in the next section of this chapter.

I will use sessions to handle users once they have logged into the Web application. The login.php page written below will take the user-submitted username and password, and if confirmed, will log them in and create the session.

Figure 5.20 The PHP Base Library, available at http://phplib.sourceforge.net, is the best way to use sessions if you do not have access to PHP 4's built-in version.

SESSIONS

Script 5.11 The login.php page was designed to receive values from a form, check them against the database, and create a session upon successful log in.

```
1    <?php
2    // This page receives a username and
     password and checks it against the stored
3    // information to validate the log in.
4
5    require_once ("../config.inc");
6
7    if ( (ereg ("^[[:alnum:]]+$",
     $HTTP_POST_VARS[username])) AND
     (eregi ("^[[:alnum:]]{8,16}$",
     $HTTP_POST_VARS[password])) )
     { // Check the submitted info.
8
9        $query = "SELECT user_id, first_name,
         password FROM users WHERE username=
         '$HTTP_POST_VARS[username]'";
10       $query_result = mysql_query
         ($query, $db_connection) or die
         (mysql_error());
11       $result = @mysql_fetch_array
         ($query_result);
12       if ( (crypt($password, $result
         [password])) == $result[password]) {
13           session_start();
14           $user_id = $result[0];
15           $first_name = $result[1];
16           session_register ('user_id');
17           session_register ('first_name');
18           header ("Location: index.php");
19           exit;
20       } else {
21           $message = urlencode ("The
             username and password submitted
             do not match those on file.
             Please try again.");
22       }
23   } else {
24       $message = urlencode ("Please enter
         your username and password to log
         in.");
25   }
26   header ("Location: index.php?error_
     message=$message");
27   exit;
28   ?>
```

To use sessions:

1. Create a new PHP document in your text editor (**Script 5.11**) and include the configuration file.

   ```
   <?php
   require_once ("../config.inc");
   ```
   Because this page will access the database, the configuration file, which stores the database information, is necessary.

2. Confirm that a username and password have been submitted, testing them against expected forms.

   ```
   if ( (ereg ("^[[:alnum:]]+$",
   → $HTTP_POST_VARS[username])) AND
   → (eregi ("^[[:alnum:]]{8,16}$",
   → $HTTP_POST_VARS[password])) ) {
   ```
   It's important that you don't assume the validity of the username and password submitted by the user. If the data does not pass both of these tests, there's no cause to continue processing the log in.

3. Query the database.

   ```
   $query = "SELECT user_id,
   → first_name, password FROM users
   → WHERE username='$HTTP_POST_VARS
   → [username]'";
   $query_result = mysql_query
   → ($query, $db_connection) or die
   → (mysql_error());
   $result = @mysql_fetch_array
   → ($query_result);
   ```
   The query will try to retrieve the user's ID, first name, and password from the table where the username field matches the submitted username.

   The returned result can at most be one row since the username value has to be unique. Because it is possible for there to be no match, the @ symbol is used to suppress any errors that occur when trying to turn the result into an array.

continues on next page

SESSIONS

211

4. Encrypt the submitted password and compare it to the stored version.

```
if ( (crypt($password, $result
→ [password])) == $result
→ [password]) {
```

The `crypt()` function makes use of a string called the *salt*. The salt acts somewhat like a key in determining the encrypted resulting string. One option when using `crypt()` is to store the salt with the password so that you can use the same salt when comparing strings. Or, you could do what I have done here, which is use the encrypted password as the salt, which works just as well.

5. If the passwords match, the user can be logged in, so create the session.

```
session_start();
$user_id = $result[0];
$first_name = $result[1];
session_register ('user_id');
session_register ('first_name');
```

Sessions are begun with the obvious `session_start()` function. This call will create a new session of data stored on the server, giving it a random session name. The session name will automatically be sent to the Web browser in the form of a cookie so that subsequent pages can access the same session.

To store any piece of information in the session, refer to the corresponding variable's name without the initial dollar sign. Because PHP programmers are so accustomed to using the dollar sign with a variable name, this is a common cause for errors (using `session_register ('$user_id')` would store an empty value). In this example, I am recording the users' ID (which will be used when they post events) and their first name (for greeting purposes). I could have stored the entire `$result` array in the session by

calling `session_register ('result')`, but I would prefer to have separate `$first_name` and `$user_id` variables, which is why I used the intermediary step of assigning `$result[0]` and `$result[1]`.

6. Redirect the logged-in user to the home page.

```
header ("Location: index.php");
exit;
```

7. Complete the conditional.

```
} else {
$message = urlencode ("The username
→ and password submitted do not
→ match those on file. Please try
→ again.");
}
```

8. Complete the main conditional.

```
} else {
$message = urlencode ("Please enter
→ your username and password to
→ log in.");
}
```

9. Redirect the user back to the index page.

```
header ("Location: index.php?error_
→ message=$message");
exit;
```

If a problem occurred and the user has not already been redirected, the user will be sent back to the index page with the appropriate error message. The `exit` statement is not required but is always a good idea after a `header()` call.

10. Close the PHP.

```
?>
```

11. Save the page as `login.php`.

Now that the log-in processing script has been written, it's time to add a log-in form. The header section of the `index.php` page will display the log-in form, assuming the user is not logged in. I'll modify `index.php` accordingly.

12. Open `index.php` (Script 5.5) in your text editor.

13. Add a line that starts the session (**Script 5.12**).

```
session_start();
```

For the page to access any variable stored in the session, you must use a call to `session_start()`. This is another common problem programmers experience when using sessions—failure to start the session on a page. You could forcibly guarantee use of the `session_start()` function by placing it inside of the `config.inc` file instead.

continues on next page

Script 5.12 The `index.php` script has been modified to display the log-in form if the user is not logged in (Figure 5.21).

```
1    <?php
2
3    // This is the index page that uses the HtmlTemplate2 class.
4
5    session_start();
6    require_once "classes/HtmlTemplate2.class"; // Include the class.
7
8    $page = new HtmlTemplate2 ("templates/main_template.inc"); // Create an instance.
9
10   $page->SetParameter("PAGE_TITLE", "Welcome to our Community!");
11
12   // Greet them if they are logged in or show the log-in form.
13   if ($HTTP_SESSION_VARS[first_name]) {
14       $header= "Greetings, $HTTP_SESSION_VARS[first_name]!";
15   } else {
16       $header = '<form action="login.php" method="post">
17   Username <input type="text" name="username" size="16" maxlength="16" />
18   Password <input type="password" name="password" size="16" maxlength="16" />
19   <input type="submit" name="Submit" value="Go!" />
20   </form>';
21   }
22   $page->SetParameter("PAGE_HEADER", $header);
23
24   if ($error_message) {
25       $content = $page->CreateErrorMessages($error_message);
26   } elseif ($good_message) {
27   $content = '<div align="left"><font color="blue"><b>' . urldecode ($good_message) .
     '</b></font></div><br></br>';
28
29   }
30
31   $content .= "Hey there!";
32   $page->SetParameter("PAGE_CONTENT", $content);
33
34
35   $footer = "Last modified " . (date("l, F j, Y", filemtime("modified.txt")));
36   $page->SetParameter("PAGE_FOOTER", $footer);
37
38   $page->CreatePage(); // Send the page to the browser.
39   unset ($page);
40   ?>
```

SESSIONS

14. Add the following code anywhere before the CreatePage() call.

```
if ($HTTP_SESSION_VARS
→ [first_name]) {
$header= "Greetings, $HTTP_
→ SESSION_VARS[first_name]!";
} else {
$header = '<form action="login.php"
→ method="post">
Username <input type="text"
→ name="username" size="16"
→ maxlength="16" />
Password <input type="password"
→ name="password" size="16"
→ maxlength="16" />
```

```
<input type="submit" name="Submit"
→ value="Go!" />
</form>';
}
$page->SetParameter("PAGE_HEADER",
→ $header);
```

If the user is logged in, the *first_name* value within the session will have a value and therefore the user should be greeted. Otherwise, the log-in form itself will be displayed.

15. Save the page as index.php.

16. Repeat these steps for register.php (**Script 5.13**).

continues on page 217

SESSIONS

Script 5.13 The same changes have been made to register.php that were made to index.php to indicate the new log in session system.

```
1   <?php
2
3   require_once ("../config.inc"); // Include the class.
4
5   if (isset($HTTP_POST_VARS[Submit])) { // If the form was submitted, process it.
6
7       // Check the username.
8       if (eregi ("^[[:alnum:]]+$", $HTTP_POST_VARS[username])) {
9           $a = TRUE;
10      } else {
11          $a = FALSE;
12          $message[] = "Please enter a username that consists only of letters and numbers.";
13      }
14
15      // Check to make sure the password is long enough and of the right format.
16      if (eregi ("^[[:alnum:]]{8,16}$", $HTTP_POST_VARS[pass1])) {
17          $b = TRUE;
18      } else {
19          $b = FALSE;
20          $message[] = "Please enter a password that consists only of letters and numbers, between
            8 and 16 characters long.";
21      }
22
23      // Check to make sure the password matches the confirmed password.
24      if ($HTTP_POST_VARS[pass1] == $HTTP_POST_VARS[pass2]) {
25          $c = TRUE;
26          $password = crypt ($HTTP_POST_VARS[pass1]); // Encrypt the password.
27      } else {
28          $c = FALSE;
29          $message[] = "The password you entered did not match the confirmed password.";
30      }
```

(script continues on next page)

214

Script 5.13 *continued*

```
                                        script

31
32        // Check to make sure they entered their first name and it's of the right format.
33        if (eregi ("^([[:alpha:]]|-|')+$", $HTTP_POST_VARS[first_name])) {
34            $d = TRUE;
35        } else {
36            $d = FALSE;
37            $message[] = "Please enter a valid first name.";
38        }
39
40        // Check to make sure they entered their last name and it's of the right format.
41        if (eregi ("^([[:alpha:]]|-|')+$", $HTTP_POST_VARS[last_name])) {
42            $e = TRUE;
43        } else {
44            $e = FALSE;
45            $message[] = "Please enter a valid last name.";
46        }
47
48        // Check to make sure they entered a valid email address.
49        if (eregi("^([[:alnum:]]|_|\.|-)+@([[:alnum:]]|\.|-)+(\.)([a-z]{2,4})$",
          $HTTP_POST_VARS[email])) {
50            $f = TRUE;
51        } else {
52            $f = FALSE;
53            $message[] = "Please enter a valid email address.";
54        }
55
56        // Check to make sure they entered a valid birth date.
57        if (checkdate ($HTTP_POST_VARS[birth_month], $HTTP_POST_VARS[birth_day],
          $HTTP_POST_VARS[birth_year])) {
58            $birthday = "$HTTP_POST_VARS[birth_year]-$HTTP_POST_VARS[birth_month]-
              $HTTP_POST_VARS[birth_day]";
59            $g = TRUE;
60        } else {
61            $g = FALSE;
62            $message[] = "Please enter a valid birth date.";
63        }
64
65        //  If the data passes all the tests, check to ensure a unique member name, then register them.
66        if ($a AND $b AND $c AND $d AND $e AND $f AND $g) {
67
68            $query = "select * from users where username='$username'";
69            $query_db = @mysql_query($query, $db_connection);
70            $row = @mysql_fetch_object($query_db);
71            if ($row) {
72                $message[] = "That username is already taken. Please select another.";
73            } else {
74                $query2 = "insert into users values ('0', '$HTTP_POST_VARS[username]', '$password',
                  '$HTTP_POST_VARS[first_name]', '$HTTP_POST_VARS[last_name]',
                  '$HTTP_POST_VARS[email]', '$birthday')";
75                $query_db2 = mysql_query($query2,$db_connection) or die (mysql_error());
76                if ($query_db2) {
77                    $mailto = $HTTP_POST_VARS[email];
78                    $mailfrom = "From: Registration@Community.Com";
79                    $subject = "Registration Confirmation";
80                    $body = "Thank you for registering with the Community.\nYour username is
                      $HTTP_POST_VARS[username].\nYour password is $HTTP_POST_VARS[password].";
81                    mail($mailto,$subject,$body,$mailfrom);
82                    $message="You have been successfully registered. You will receive an email
                      confirmation of your username and password.";
```

(script continues on next page)

Script 5.13 *continued*

```
                                              script

83                      $m = urlencode ($message);
84                      header ("Location: index.php?good_message=$m");
85                      exit;
86              } else {
87                      $message="You could not be successfully registered due to a system error. Please
                        contact the Webmaster  at webmaster@community.com to have this corrected.";
88                      $m = urlencode ($message);
89                      header ("Location: index.php?error_message=$m");
90                      exit;
91              }
92          }
93
94      }
95
96
97  } // End of Submit if.
98
99  require_once "classes/HtmlTemplate2.class"; // Include the class.
100 require_once "classes/HtmlRegistrationTemplate.class"; // Include the class.
101
102 session_start();
103
104 $page = new HtmlTemplate2 ("templates/main_template.inc"); // Create an instance.
105
106 $page->SetParameter("PAGE_TITLE", "Register!");
107
108 $javascript = implode ("\n", (file ("includes/registration_javascript.inc")) );
109 $page->SetParameter("JAVASCRIPT", $javascript);
110
111 // Greet them if they are logged in or show the log-in form.
112 if ($HTTP_SESSION_VARS[firstname]) {
113     $header= "Greetings, $HTTP_SESSION_VARS[firstname]!";
114 } else {
115     $header = '<form action="login.php" method="post">
116 Username <input type="text" name="username" size="16" maxlength="16" />
117 Password <input type="password" name="password" size="16" maxlength="16" />
118 <input type="submit" name="Submit" value="Go!" />
119 </form>';
120 }
121 $page->SetParameter("PAGE_HEADER", $header);
122
123 if ($message) {
124     $content = HTMLRegistrationTemplate::CreateErrorMessages($message);
125 }
126
127 $page2 = new HtmlRegistrationTemplate ("includes/registration_form.inc");
128 $page2->SetParameter ("username", $HTTP_POST_VARS[username]);
129 $page2->SetParameter ("first_name", $HTTP_POST_VARS[first_name]);
130 $page2->SetParameter ("last_name", $HTTP_POST_VARS[last_name]);
131 $page2->SetParameter ("email", $HTTP_POST_VARS[email]);
132 $content .= $page2->SwapParameters();
133 unset($page2);
134 $page->SetParameter("PAGE_CONTENT", $content);
135
136
137 $footer = "Last modified " . (date("l, F j, Y", filemtime("modified.txt")));
138 $page->SetParameter("PAGE_FOOTER", $footer);
139
140 $page->CreatePage(); // Send the page to the browser.
141 unset ($page);
142 ?>
```

SESSIONS

17. Upload the files to your server and test in your Web browser (**Figures 5.21**, **5.22**, **5.23**, and **5.24**).

✔ Tips

■ Because sessions will normally send and read cookies, you should always try to begin them as early in the script as possible. Doing so will help you avoid the problem of attempting to send a cookie after the headers (HTML or white space) have already been sent.

continues on next page

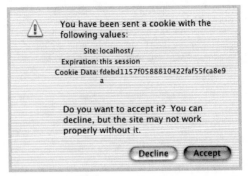

Figure 5.21 Upon first arriving at the page, the session will try to send a cookie that stores the session name.

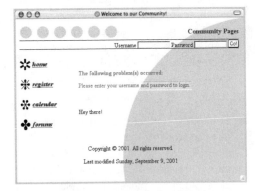

Figure 5.23 The `login.php` script is set to return an error message if any problems occur.

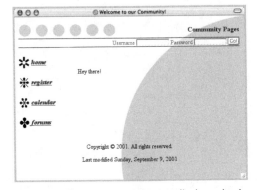

Figure 5.22 The `index.php` page now displays a log-in form if the user is not already logged in.

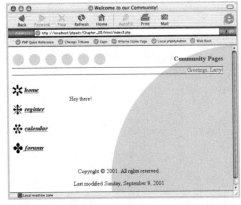

Figure 5.24 If the user is validated and logged in, the pages will now display a user-specific greeting.

SESSIONS

- If you want, you can set `session.auto_start` (**Figure 5.25**) in the `php.ini` file to *1*, making it unnecessary to use `session_start()` on each page.

- To set the name of the session (perhaps to make a more user-friendly form), use the `session_name()` function.

  `session_name('Your Session');`

  Create some system to ensure unique sessions names, though, such as using the username or some combination of the date and another piece of data.

- The `session_set_cookie_params()` function allows you to change the different attributes of the session cookie: expiration time, path, and domain. Use it as you would the `setcookie()` function, for example:

  `session_set_cookie_params(time +` `→ (60 * 60), "", www.community.com);`

- Remember that, as stated in Chapter 2, you can store objects or arrays in sessions, just as you can strings. Items stored in sessions are automatically serialized and unserialized to protect the data in transit.

Figure 5.25 There are several session-related parameters that can be set in the `php.ini` file, including where the session information should be stored and if sessions should automatically be started.

Using Sessions Without Cookies

One of the problems with sessions is that, as it stands, they rely on the use of a cookie to work properly. When a session is started, it sends a cookie that resides in the user's Web browser, which contains the session name (Figure 5.21). Every subsequent page that calls `session_start()` makes use of the cookie to know to use an existing session and to not create a new one. The problem is that users may have cookies turned off in their Web browser or may not accept the cookie because they do not understand its purpose. If this is the case, PHP will create a new session for each page and none of the registered variables will be accessible.

You can use sessions without cookies by passing along the session name from page to page. This is simple enough to do, but if you forget to pass the session in only one instance, the entire process is shot. To pass the session name from page to page, you use the `SID` constant, which stands for *sessionID*. If this value is appended to every URL within the site, the sessions will still work even if the user did not accept the cookie.

To use sessions without cookies:

1. Open `main_template.inc` in your text editor (Script 5.2).

2. Amend the four lines that refer to a URL to have a SID option (**Script 5.14**).

```
<td width="200" valign="top">
→ <a href="index.php<!--{SID}-->">
→ <img name="img1" src="images/
→ image1.gif" vspace="3" border="0"
→ align="absmiddle" width="30"
→ height="30" /><b> <i><big>home
→ </big></i></b></a><br>
→ </br>

<a href="register.php<!--{SID}-->">
→ <img name="img2" src="images/
→ image10.gif" vspace="3"
→ border="0" align="absmiddle"
→ width="30" height="30" /><b>
→ <i><big>register</big></i></b>
→ </a><br></br>

<a href="calendar.php<!--{SID}-->">
→ <img name="img3" src="images/
→ image4.gif" vspace="3" border="0"
→ align="absmiddle" width="30"
→ height="30" /><b> <i><big>calendar
→ </big></i></b></a><br></br>

<a href="forum/index.php<!--{SID}--
→ >"><img name="img4" src="images/
→ image7.gif" vspace="3" border="0"
→ align="absmiddle" width="30"
→ height="30" /><b> <i><big>forums
→ </big></i></b></a><br></br></td>
```

As it stands, only these four lines use URLs. I'll put the `<!--{SID}-->` placeholder into the template now and will then have PHP replace each of these with the sessionID. If objects were not being used, the direct way of doing this would be to change each URL to, for example, `index.php?<?=SID ?>`.

3. Save the template as `main_SID_template.inc`.

   Now you will need to make minor changes to `index.php` and `register.php` to finish the process.

4. Open `index.php` in your text editor (Script 5.12).

5. Change line 8 to use the new template (**Script 5.15**).

```
$page = new HtmlTemplate2
→ ("templates/main_SID_template.inc");
```

6. Add the SID lines somewhere before the CreatePage() call.

```
$sid_value = "?" . SID;
$page->SetParameter("SID",
→ $sid_value);
```

   The first step is to set a temporary variable, `$sid_value`, to a question mark followed by the value of the constant `SID`. `SID` will actually be equal to a string like *PHPSESSID=09e8c745e02080208d557566 e03b8235*. The question mark appended to the URL turns this into a link-like `index.php?PHPSESSID=09e8c745e02080208 d557566e03b8235`.

7. Add the session ID as a hidden value in the log-in form.

```
<input type="hidden" name="PHPSESSID"
→ value="' . session_id() . '" />
```

   The `login.php` form also needs to keep track of the session so it will receive the ID as a hidden value in the form. The *PHPSES-SID* value will be assigned something like *09e8c745e02080208d557566e03b8235*, which the `session_id()` function returns.

8. Save the script as `index.php`.

9. Make the same changes to `register.php` (**Script 5.16**).

continues on page 226

Script 5.14 In case the user does not accept the session cookie, the session ID will be passed along with each URL.

```
1    <!DOCTYPE html PUBLIC "-//W3C//DTD XHTML 1.0 Transitional//EN"
2        "http://www.w3.org/TR/2000/REC-xhtml1-20000126/DTD/xhtml1-transitional.dtd">
3    <html xmlns="http://www.w3.org/1999/xhtml">
4    <head>
5        <title><!--{PAGE_TITLE}--></title>
6    <!--{JAVASCRIPT}-->
7    </head>
8    <body background="images/bg1.jpg" link="#0033FF" alink="#0033FF" vlink="#0033FF">
9    <table border="0" width="600" height="320" cellpadding="0" cellspacing="0">
10       <tr>
11           <td width="50%">
12               <img border="0" src="images/dot.jpg" width="36" height="36" /><img border="0" src=
                 "images/dot.jpg" hspace="10" width="36" height="36" /><img border="0" src="images/
                 dot.jpg" width="36" height="36" /><img border="0" src="images/dot.jpg" hspace="10"
                 width="36" height="36" /><img border="0" src="images/dot.jpg" width="36" height="36"
                 /><img border="0" src="images/dot.jpg" hspace="10" width="36" height="36" />
13   </td>
14           <td width="50%" align="right"><big><b><font color="#0033FF">Community
             Pages</font></b></big></td>
15       </tr>
16       <tr>
17           <td width="600" colspan="2" height="2"><img src="images/line.gif" width="600"></td>
18       </tr>
19       <tr>
20           <td width="600" colspan="2" height="2" align="right"><!--{PAGE_HEADER}--></td>
21       </tr>
22       <tr>
23           <td width="600" colspan="2" height="2"><img src="images/line.gif" width="600"></td>
24       </tr>
25       <tr>
26           <td width="600" colspan="2">
27               <table border="0" cellspacing="0" cellpadding="0">
28                   <tr>
29                       <td width="200" valign="top"><a href="index.php<!--{SID}-->"> <img
                         name="img1" src="images/image1.gif" vspace="3" border="0" align="absmiddle"
                         width="30" height="30" /><b> <i><big>home</big></i></b></a><br></br>
30                       <a href="register.php<!--{SID}-->"> <img name="img2" src="images/image10.gif"
                         vspace="3" border="0" align="absmiddle" width="30" height="30" /><b>
                         <i><big>register</big></i></b></a><br></br>
31                       <a href="calendar.php<!--{SID}-->"> <img name="img3" src="images/image4.gif"
                         vspace="3" border="0" align="absmiddle" width="30" height="30" /><b>
                         <i><big>calendar</big></i></b></a><br></br>
32                       <a href="forum/index.php<!--{SID}-->"><img name="img4" src="images/
                         image7.gif" vspace="3" border="0" align="absmiddle" width="30" height="30"
                         /><b> <i><big>forums</big></i></b></a><br></br></td>
33                       <td width="610" valign="top"><br></br><!--{PAGE_CONTENT}--></td>
34                   </tr>
35               </table>
36       </tr>
37   </table>
38   <table border="0" cellspacing="0" cellpadding="0" width="600">
39       <tr>
40           <td align="center">Copyright &copy; 2001. All rights reserved.<br></br>
             <!--{PAGE_FOOTER}--><br></br></td>
41       </tr>
42   </table>
43   </body>
44   </html>
```

Script 5.15 The `index.php` script will replace each instance of `<!--{SID}-->` with the code PHPSESSID=....

```
1    <?php
2
3    // This is the index page that uses the HtmlTemplate2 class.
4
5    session_start();
6    require_once "classes/HtmlTemplate2.class"; // Include the class.
7
8    $page = new HtmlTemplate2 ("templates/main_SID_template.inc"); // Create an instance.
9
10   $page->SetParameter("PAGE_TITLE", "Welcome to our Community!");
11
12   // Greet them if they are logged in or show the log-in form.
13   if ($HTTP_SESSION_VARS[first_name]) {
14       $header= "Greetings, $HTTP_SESSION_VARS[first_name]!";
15   } else {
16       $header = '<form action="login.php" method="post">
17   Username <input type="text" name="username" size="16" maxlength="16" />
18   Password <input type="password" name="password" size="16" maxlength="16" />
19   <input type="hidden" name="PHPSESSID" value="' . session_id() . '" />
20   <input type="submit" name="Submit" value="Go!" />
21   </form>';
22   }
23   $page->SetParameter("PAGE_HEADER", $header);
24
25   if ($error_message) {
26       $content = $page->CreateErrorMessages($error_message);
27   } elseif ($good_message) {
28       $content = '<div align="left"><font color="blue"><b>' . urldecode ($good_message) .
             '</b></font></div><br></br>';
29
30   }
31
32   $content .= "Hey there!";
33   $page->SetParameter("PAGE_CONTENT", $content);
34
35
36   $footer = "Last modified " . (date("l, F j, Y", filemtime("modified.txt")));
37   $page->SetParameter("PAGE_FOOTER", $footer);
38
39   $sid_value = "?" . SID;
40   $page->SetParameter("SID", $sid_value);
41
42   $page->CreatePage(); // Send the page to the browser.
43   unset ($page);
44   ?>
```

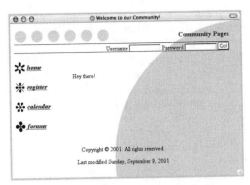

Figure 5.26 The index.php page looks exactly the same as it had, but by viewing the code (Figure 5.27), you can see how the session ID has been incorporated.

Figure 5.27 See how the session ID is assigned to the *PHPSESSID* variable in both the links and the log-in form by viewing the HTML source code.

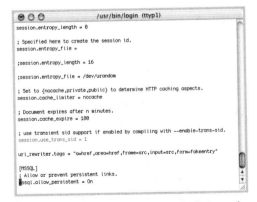

Figure 5.28 You can have PHP automatically append the session ID to URLs by either setting this in the php.ini file or adding it during PHP configuration.

11. Upload the new index.php, the new register.php, the modified login.php, and main_SID_template.inc to your server and run in your Web browser (**Figures 5.26** and **5.27**).

✔ Tips

- If you have access to your php.ini file and are using PHP 4, you can set --enable-trans-sid to *On* (**Figure 5.28**). Doing so will have PHP automatically append the session ID to the URL as you manually have done here. It will slow down execution of the scripts though, as PHP will need to check every page for URLs.

continues on next page

Using Sessions Without Cookies

- Depending on the Web browser being used by the client, a session may be either browser-specific or window-specific. If the latter is the case, a pop-up window in your site will not be part of the same session unless it is passed the sessionID.

- Sessions can be ended using the session_destroy() function, or you can delete all the variables without destroying the session with session_unset(). Lastly, you can delete a particular variable with session_unregister() or check to see if a particular variable is set with session_is_registered().

- Because destroying a session is so simple, I won't go over an example in detail. However, **Script 5.18** shows a log-out form that could be used with this Web application. Just add to every page a Logout button generated by this code:

```
<form action="logout.php"
→ method="post">

<input type="hidden" name="PHPSESSID"
→ value=" . session_id() . '" />

<input type="submit" name="Submit"
→ value="Logout" />

</form>
```

When the user submits this form, he or she will be taken to Script 5.18, which will end the session.

Script 5.18 This script can act as the log-out form for the Web application. It destroys the session that contains all of the user's information.

```
1   <?php
2   // This page logs the user out by
    destroying the session.
3
4   session_start();
5   session_destroy();
6
7   $message = urlencode ("You have been
    logged out.");
8
9   header ("Location:
    index.php?good_message=$message");
10  exit;
11  ?>
```

Table 5.4 You've probably encountered most of these before, but in a code-addled state, sometimes it's helpful to have the common PHP errors listed out.

Common PHP Errors

ERROR	LIKELY CAUSE
Parse Error	Missing semicolon
Parse Error	Unbalanced braces, parentheses, or quotation marks
Parse Error	Use of unescaped quotation marks in a string.
Cannot Open File	Wrong file permissions set
Cannot Open File	Wrong fopen() parameter
Empty Variable Value	Forgot initial $
Empty Variable Value	Misspelled variable name
Empty Variable Value	Mis-capitalized variable name
Empty Variable Value	Inappropriate variable scope
Undefined Function	Misspelled function name
Undefined Function	Function is defined after it is used (PHP 3 only)
Undefined Function	Document that contains the function definition is not properly included
Cannot Redeclare Function	Document that contains the function definition is included twice
Headers Already Sent	White space exists in the script before the PHP tags

Debugging

Every programmer is constantly on the lookout for a better way to minimize errors and problems in their scripts. Unfortunately, most programmers learn debugging through sheer trial and error—and lots of it. Here are some tips for debugging your scripts:

◆ View the HTML source when a problem happens. Some browsers—for example, Netscape Navigator—will show a blank page even when a PHP error occurs toward the end of a page. Viewing the source may be the only way to see what the issue is.

◆ Use a text editor that checks for balanced parentheses, braces, tags, quotation marks, and more.

◆ Use reverse testing when logical errors occur. Reverse testing is the method of switching your conditionals. For example,

`if ($variable = 5) { …`

may not seem incorrect among 500 lines of code but still causes problems because that condition is always TRUE. Changing it to

`if (5 = $variable) { …`

will immediately send up a red flag.

Table 5.4 lists the likely causes of the most common PHP errors.

DEBUGGING

Error Logging and Reporting

By now most programmers know that errors are going to happen. The key is how to best handle them.

The first recommendation is to incorporate @ and die() in your scripts. The former is used for function calls that could not work but which you do not want to stop the execution of your script. Examples would be a case where nothing is returned from a database query or a file could not be opened. The latter, die(), should be used with any action for which an unsuccessful execution essentially renders the progression of the script moot. If you cannot connect to a database or query it, there is probably no need to continue. The great benefit of die() is that you can use it to not only stop the script but also report an error.

```
mysql_select_db ($db_info[dbname],
→ $db_connection) or die
→ (mysql_error());
```

This use of die() will print out the error that MySQL returned. The following will also print out the database name that was being used:

```
mysql_select_db ($db_info[dbname],
→ $db_connection) or die (mysql_error()
→ . $db_info[dbname]);
```

To understand how best to use die(), realize that it acts like a combination of exit() and echo(). Modify your code accordingly so that when errors happen, informative messages are printed to the Web browser.

My second recommendation is to add the following code, or your own version of this, to your config.inc files:

```
function ReportErrors ($error_number,
→ $error_message) {

global $level;

if ($level = "development") {

echo "Error reported:
→ $error_number $error_message
→ <br></br>\n";

} elseif ($level == "live") {

echo "An error occurred. We
→ apologize for any inconvenience.
→ <br></br>\n";

mail ("webmaster@site.com",
→ "Error Reported", "Error:
→ $error_number $error_message");

}

set_error_handler (ReportErrors);

$level = "development";

// $level = "live"; // Uncomment to go
→ live.
```

The set_error_handler() determines what function handles errors, including your own defined one. In the example above, by setting a global variable to the level of error reporting—development or live—you can determine how errors across the site are managed. If you are still coding, they will just be printed to the browser. If the site is live, a user will get a friendlier response, but you will be instantly emailed to know that there is a problem.

✔ Tips

- If your `php.ini` file has `--track-errors` set to *1*, every error that occurs will automatically be stored in an array called `$php_errormsg`. This information can be emailed to you or written to an error log.

- The `@` symbol will work only on expressions. You cannot use `@` before conditionals, loops, function definitions, and so forth.

- As part of your configuration file, you can set the `error_reporting()` there so that it has a sitewide effect. See the manual for more information.

- If you want, you can incorporate two more predefined constants into your error management: `__FILE__` and `__LINE__`. The one states what file the error occurred in and the other specifies the line number.

E-COMMERCE

Despite all of the recent dot-com failures, the need for e-commerce done right is greater than ever. The term e-commerce can refer to many things, from marketing to customer service to internal corporate uses to straight-up sales of products. What these all have
in common is an aim to make (or save) a company money. Each type of e-commerce Web site therefore has its own considerations in terms of aesthetic, features, goals, and programming.

In this chapter, we are going to develop a Web site explicitly for selling products. The information you learn here will help you to understand the mechanics of an online store while giving you some viable code to begin using. The example will focus on the PHP coding itself, along with the database requirements, and it will lead you to the point of implementing a payment system. Due to the vast number of online payment systems, attempting to demonstrate any one would be of limited use.

Instead of selling the common widget which can be purchased just about anywhere (it seems to be the default example product), this chapter's store, Waponi Woo, will sell bubureau (a mineral used to make superconductors) and orange soda—it's a diverse market. Bubureau will come in regular and light formats while orange soda will be available in 12-ounce, 16-ounce, and 2-liter sizes. The specifics of these products are irrelevant; all I'm really trying to do is establish real-world variables for what might be sold. You could also sell shirts in small, medium, and large that come in different colors or music available on Compact Disc, cassette tape, LP, or 8-Track. Rarely will you get the chance to develop a site that sells only a handful of items each in a singular format so I'm introducing representational diversity with bubureau and orange soda.

Even the most basic e-commerce site requires multiple features that must be programmed in order to function properly. For example, an administrator should be able to add new products and edit existing ones, and customers need to be able to browse through the products offered and order different quantities. I'll go over the PHP code to manage each of these tasks, along with the corresponding database design. Other features you might consider adding are:

◆ Customer registration and login

◆ Administrator's capability to view or search orders

◆ Display of a customer's order history

◆ Inventory reporting

Because the core of this application will be an OOP class, you can take what you learn here and quickly tailor it to your needs. Additional information and code relating to this chapter is available on the companion Web site (www.DMCinsights.com/phpadv).

Creating the Database

The foundation for the store will be a database containing all the tables required for recording the customers, products, and transactions. Because databases are significantly more secure than flat files, you always want to use them for e-commerce applications so that the store and user information is safely kept away from curious eyes.

The first table you'll need—and the easiest to design—is for the customers (or *users*), detailed in **Table 6.1**.

This is a straightforward template for containing all of the customer information. I like to make the zip code and phone numbers text rather than number formats to allow for parentheses and dashes. This table also assumes only United States clients, but you can easily add a country field as well. One important concept is that I am not planning on storing the customer's credit card information. This means a slight inconvenience to the user (in having to reenter a credit card for each order) but it also significantly decreases the security risks involved. If you want to store credit card information, you must do so in an encrypted form, preferably in a database that is not on a machine connected to the Internet. There have been too many cases of hackers breaking into major e-commerce sites and pilfering the credit card information therein. Trust is at the heart of any business, and part of trust is security.

The next-easiest table to make is the one that records the transactions. I'll make mine like **Table 6.2**.

Table 6.1 The users table keeps a list of every customer the site has. One update to the database would be to make the information in this table more international in scope by allowing for less Americentric addresses.

Table Users

COLUMN	DATA TYPE
user_id	number
username	text
password	text (encrypted)
first_name	text
last_name	text
email_address	text
address1	text
address2	text
city	text
state	text
zip	text
phone	text

Table 6.2 The orders table records the user (via the customer's ID), the total amount of the order, the last four digits of the credit card used, the date and time the order was placed, and the contents of the shopping cart.

Table Orders

COLUMN	DATA TYPE
order_id	number
user_id	number
total	number (floating point)
credit_card_number	number
date_ordered	date and time
shopping_cart	text

I know what you are thinking: didn't I just say I wasn't going to store the credit card information? Yes, I did. All that the `credit_card_number` field in this table plans on storing is the last four digits of the credit card used by the customer for that order. By recording this information, customers can review their orders and see they used card number ************1234, which will mean something to them but nothing to a potential thief.

The other field I'd like to discuss in this table is `shopping_cart`. The shopping cart developed in this chapter will be an object containing an array of each item purchased and in what quantity. The easiest way to store this information is to serialize the array or object representing a customer's shopping cart and storing it directly in the database. The downside of this system is you cannot perform searches on the `orders` table by products purchased, but each order can be reviewed by retrieving and unserializing the array or object. The step of storing the user's order will not be discussed in this chapter—as it would take place after payment processing—but the requisite code, along with explication, will be made available online.

This table could also include the shipping information for products that are to be shipped to a non-billing address. Also, depending upon the system used to actually process the order, you could store the order result here too. Some billing systems return a code indicating the success of the order. Storing this code would allow you to separate out successful orders from unsuccessful ones.

The third table will manage the different products the store offers (**Table 6.3**). If you understand database design you'll see that this is the most taxing of the categories. The end result of such a table should be that each unique product must have its own ID, or *SKU*, in retail terms. By referring to the SKU, you can retrieve inventory, pricing, and more. Selling books, music, and videos is relatively straightforward, as these industries provide item-specific SKUs for the vendor (e.g., each book has its own ISBN number and the hardcover edition has a different ISBN than the paperback).

For a more complex understanding of listing products, consider selling clothes. A blue turtleneck is different than a red one, and a large blue turtleneck is not the same as a medium blue turtleneck. But to the customer they all fall under the product name of *turtlenecks*. In the Waponi Woo situation, there are two products, one that comes in three sizes and one that comes in two formats. How do you design a database that allows for all these possibilities?

My answer is to begin with one table that stores each product, along with its price and a virtual SKU for each possible variant of the item.

Table 6.3 The `products` table, in conjunction with `product_names`, `product_sizes`, and `product_formats`, does the bulk of the store's work.

Table Products	
COLUMN	DATA TYPE
product_id	number
name_id	number
size_id	number
format_id	number
price	number (floating point)
available	Yes/No
picture	text

Table 6.4 The `product_names` table lists the general terms for the individual products.

Table Product_Names	
COLUMN	DATA TYPE
product_name_id	number
product_name	text

Table 6.5 The size options for the wares will be stored in the `product_sizes` table.

Table Product_Sizes	
COLUMN	DATA TYPE
product_size_id	number
product_size	text

Table 6.6 Because bubureau will come in either light or regular, I've made a `product_formats` table to list the options.

Table Product_Formats	
COLUMN	DATA TYPE
product_format_id	number
product_format	text

Each row in this table will represent a particular product, based upon the name, size, and format. The `product_id` will be the SKU and the remaining three ID fields are each foreign keys, referring to separate tables (**Tables 6.4, 6.5,** and **6.6**). The `name_id` will indicate, in this case, either bubureau or orange soda, allowing the customer to view all the options each has to offer at one time. In another use, the `name_id` could mean turtleneck, t-shirt, or sweater. The `size_id` will dictate what size the product comes in: orange soda is available in 12 ounce, 16 ounce, or 2 liter sizes; bubureau comes in only one size. Similarly, bubureau will come in two formats but orange soda only one.

Using multiple tables and foreign keys helps distinguish one product from another. Each individual product can now be specifically priced and inventoried. I've just created a field stating whether or not a product is currently available for sale, but this column could be used to reflect current inventory instead. Finally, you could put in a picture of the item or a textual description. These last two optional fields may go with the Product Names table instead—you could use the same description for every orange soda option or the same picture for every form of bubureau.

Once you have all of the tables sketched out on paper, you can create them in your database. I'll be using MySQL, so if you use another RDMS, change the SQL and instructions below as needed.

To create the database:

1. Connect to your server via a command line interface and connect to MySQL (**Figure 6.1**).

2. Create the database (**Figure 6.2**).

   CREATE DATABASE waponi_woo;

   If your database has already been created for you, skip this step.

3. Choose the database (**Figure 6.3**).

   USE waponi_woo;

4. Create the users table (**Figure 6.4**).

   ```
   CREATE TABLE users (
   user_id INT UNSIGNED NOT NULL
   ⇢ AUTO_INCREMENT,
   username VARCHAR(16) NOT NULL,
   password VARCHAR(13) NOT NULL,
   first_name VARCHAR(20),
   last_name VARCHAR(40),
   email VARCHAR(60),
   address1 VARCHAR(80),
   address2 VARCHAR(80),
   city VARCHAR(40),
   state VARCHAR(2),
   zip VARCHAR(10),
   phone VARCHAR(20),
   PRIMARY KEY (user_id),
   INDEX (username),
   UNIQUE (username)
   );
   ```

This is an expansion upon Table 6.1 using the *VARCHAR* field type almost everywhere for improved performance and database size. The user_id will be the primary key (automatically incremented) but username will also be unique and indexed. Although you won't directly use this table within the confines of this chapter, it's a viable part of any e-commerce site and it would be remiss of me not to include it.

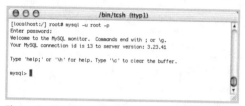

Figure 6.1 If you are using a Web-based RDMS interface, such as phpMyAdmin, you won't need to use a command-line interface like I use here.

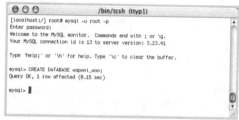

Figure 6.2 The first step is to create the database itself, unless one has already been created for you.

Figure 6.3 After you've established the database, tell MySQL that you want to use it—a step that's easy to forget.

Figure 6.4 The first table I've created is users, established accordingly to the guidelines set in Table 6.1.

CREATING THE DATABASE

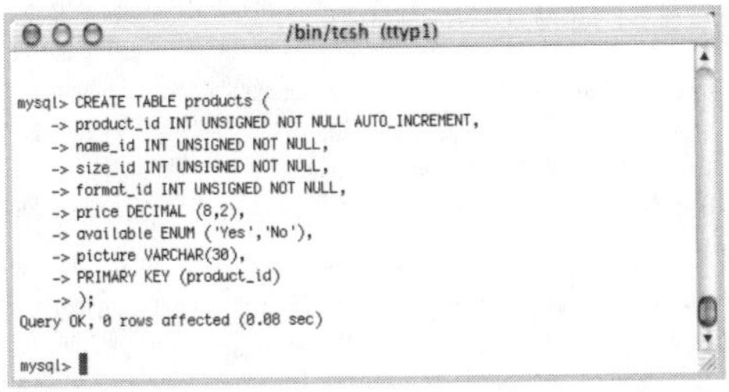

```
mysql> CREATE TABLE products (
    -> product_id INT UNSIGNED NOT NULL AUTO_INCREMENT,
    -> name_id INT UNSIGNED NOT NULL,
    -> size_id INT UNSIGNED NOT NULL,
    -> format_id INT UNSIGNED NOT NULL,
    -> price DECIMAL (8,2),
    -> available ENUM ('Yes','No'),
    -> picture VARCHAR(30),
    -> PRIMARY KEY (product_id)
    -> );
Query OK, 0 rows affected (0.08 sec)

mysql>
```

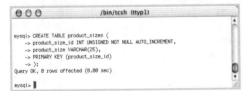

Figure 6.5 The products table will suffice as is but it also has ample room for you to modify it for specific purposes.

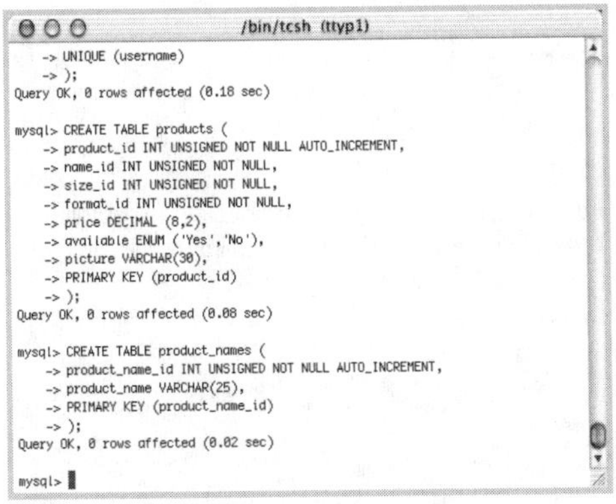

```
    -> UNIQUE (username)
    -> );
Query OK, 0 rows affected (0.18 sec)

mysql> CREATE TABLE products (
    -> product_id INT UNSIGNED NOT NULL AUTO_INCREMENT,
    -> name_id INT UNSIGNED NOT NULL,
    -> size_id INT UNSIGNED NOT NULL,
    -> format_id INT UNSIGNED NOT NULL,
    -> price DECIMAL (8,2),
    -> available ENUM ('Yes','No'),
    -> picture VARCHAR(30),
    -> PRIMARY KEY (product_id)
    -> );
Query OK, 0 rows affected (0.08 sec)

mysql> CREATE TABLE product_names (
    -> product_name_id INT UNSIGNED NOT NULL AUTO_INCREMENT,
    -> product_name VARCHAR(25),
    -> PRIMARY KEY (product_name_id)
    -> );
Query OK, 0 rows affected (0.02 sec)

mysql>
```

Figure 6.6 Along with the products table, you'll need to create the three related ones: product_names, product_sizes (Figure 6.7), and product_formats (Figure 6.8).

```
mysql> CREATE TABLE product_sizes (
    -> product_size_id INT UNSIGNED NOT NULL AUTO_INCREMENT,
    -> product_size VARCHAR(25),
    -> PRIMARY KEY (product_size_id)
    -> );
Query OK, 0 rows affected (0.00 sec)

mysql>
```

Figure 6.7 The product_sizes table follows a simple two-column structure.

5. Create the products table (**Figure 6.5**).

```
CREATE TABLE products (
product_id INT UNSIGNED NOT NULL
→ AUTO_INCREMENT,
name_id INT UNSIGNED NOT NULL,
size_id INT UNSIGNED NOT NULL,
format_id INT UNSIGNED NOT NULL,
price DECIMAL (8,2),
available ENUM ('Yes', 'No'),
picture VARCHAR(30),
PRIMARY KEY (product_id)
);
```

If you want to add a description of your products, put a *text* or large *varchar* field here. If you want to turn the availability into an inventory, change the column's name and make it an *integer*.

6. Create the product_names table (**Figure 6.6**).

```
CREATE TABLE product_names (
product_name_id INT UNSIGNED NOT
→ NULL AUTO_INCREMENT,
product_name VARCHAR(25),
PRIMARY KEY (product_name_id)
);
```

7. Create the product_sizes table (**Figure 6.7**).

```
CREATE TABLE product_sizes (
product_size_id INT UNSIGNED NOT
→ NULL AUTO_INCREMENT,
product_size VARCHAR(25),
PRIMARY KEY (product_size_id)
);
```

continues on next page

8. Create the `product_formats` table (**Figure 6.8**).

```
CREATE TABLE product_formats (
product_format_id INT UNSIGNED NOT
→ NULL AUTO_INCREMENT,
product_format VARCHAR(25),
PRIMARY KEY (product_format_id)
);
```

Figure 6.8 Finally, the `product_formats` table rounds out the product definitions tables.

9. Create the `orders` table (**Figure 6.9**).

```
CREATE TABLE orders (
order_id INT UNSIGNED NOT NULL
→ AUTO_INCREMENT,
user_id INT UNSIGNED NOT NULL,
total DECIMAL (10,2),
credit_card_number INT UNSIGNED,
date_ordered DATETIME,
shopping_cart TEXT,
PRIMARY KEY (order_id)
);
```

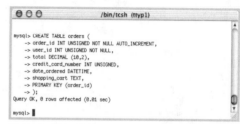

Figure 6.9 This table, `orders`, is used at the completion of the ordering process, to store each transaction.

10. Confirm all the tables exist (**Figure 6.10**).

```
SHOW TABLES;
```

✔ Tip

■ If you decide to try a different store that sells other products, be sure to analyze all of the store's requirements before creating and using this database structure. Each e-commerce application has its own considerations that should be reflected in your database design.

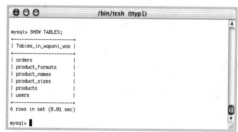

Figure 6.10 Check that every required table is present by running `SHOW TABLES`. (Better to catch such a problem now rather than when programming.)

Script 6.1 The config.inc file is essentially the same as that written in Chapter 5, Developing Web Applications.

```
         script
1   <?php
2
3   // ***** config.inc *****
4   // Developed by Larry E. Ullman
5   // Contact: php@DMCinsights.com
6   // Created  October 8, 2001
7   // Last modified October 8, 2001
8   // This is the configuration file for the
9   // Waponi Woo
10  // Web site.
11  // Base url = http://www.waponiwoo.com
12
13  // Database-specific information:
14  $db_info[username] = "username";
15  $db_info[password] = "password";
16  $db_info[host] = "localhost";
17  $db_info[dbname] = "waponi_woo";
18  $db_connection = mysql_connect
        ($db_info[host], $db_info[username],
        $db_info[password]) or die
        (mysql_error());
19  mysql_select_db ($db_info[dbname],
        $db_connection) or die (mysql_error());
20  ?>
```

Administration

Once the structure of the database has been created, you can make the administration side wherein the store owner can establish products, set prices, and so forth. There's nothing too novel here, but I'll go through the scripts so you can better understand how the database relates to the virtual store and how the whole should be administered.

On account of the structure of the products table—the only one ultimately controlled by the administrator—the proper order is to fill in the product_names, product_sizes, and product_formats tables first, and then define individual products. I'll write one page that adds to these three tables and another that uses them to create a product. A third script will allow for editing an item.

To administer the store:

1. Create the configuration file in your text editor (**Script 6.1**) and save it as config.inc.

```
<?php
$db_info[username] = "username";
$db_info[password] = "password";
$db_info[host] = "localhost";
$db_info[dbname] = "waponi_woo";
$db_connection = mysql_connect
→ ($db_info[host], $db_info
→ [username], $db_info[password])
→ or die (mysql_error());
mysql_select_db ($db_info[dbname],
→ $db_connection) or die
→ (mysql_error());
?>
```

continues on next page

This is just a basic configuration file where I've stored all the required database information for the site. Depending upon how particular you (and PHP) are, you might want to enclose each array index within single or double quotation marks to be formal.

2. Create a header document (**Script 6.2**) and save it as admin_header.inc.

```
<!DOCTYPE html PUBLIC "-//W3C//DTD
→ XHTML 1.0 Transitional//EN"
"http://www.w3.org/TR/2000/REC-
→ xhtml1-20000126/DTD/xhtml1-
→ transitional.dtd">
<html xmlns="http://www.w3.org/
→ 1999/xhtml">
<head>
<title><?=$page_title ?></title>
</head>
<body>
```

I'm going to use a very, very simple HTML page layout for the administration side of the store. However, I'll write header and footer documents so that I can quickly change the layout at a later date.

The only variable in the layout is the page title, placed automatically by PHP.

3. Create a footer document (**Script 6.3**), saving it as admin_footer.inc.

```
</body>
</html>
```

4. Write the index page (**Script 6.4**), saving it as index.php.

```
<?php
$page_title = 'Administer The
→ Store';
require_once
→ ("includes/admin_header.inc");
?>
<div align="center">
```

Script 6.2 The admin_header.inc document (the name distinguishes it from the public_header.inc file you'll write later) contains the beginnings of an HTML page.

```
1    <!DOCTYPE html PUBLIC "-//W3C//DTD XHTML
     1.0 Transitional//EN"
2    "http://www.w3.org/TR/2000/REC-xhtml1-
     20000126/DTD/xhtml1-transitional.dtd">
3    <html xmlns="http://www.w3.org/1999/
     xhtml">
4    <head>
5        <title><?=$page_title ?></title>
6    </head>
7    <body>
```

Script 6.3 The admin_footer.inc file completes the HTML begun in admin_header.inc.

```
1    </body>
2    </html>
```

Script 6.4 The home page for the administration side uses the two HTML includes for formatting and lists the options that will be available to the administrator.

```
1    <?php
2
3    // This is a basic home page for the
     administration side of the site.
4
5    $page_title = 'Administer The Store';
6    require_once
     ("includes/admin_header.inc");
     // Include the HTML formatting.
7
8    // *********************************
9    // Page specific content begins here
10   // *********************************
11
12   ?>
13   <div align="center">
14   <big><b>Administration Options
15   </b></big></div>
16   <br />
```

(script continues on next page)

Script 6.4 *continued*

```
                    script
17   <b>General:</b>
18   <ul>
19       <li>Add a new <a
         href="add_item.php?item=name">
         product line</a></li>
20       <li>Add a new <a
         href="add_item.php?item=size">
         product size</a></li>
21       <li>Add a new <a
         href="add_item.php?item=format">
         product format</a></li>
22   </ul>
23   <p></p>
24   <br />
25   <b>Specific:</b>
26   <ul>
27       <li>Add a new <a href=
         "add_product.php">product</a></li>
28       <li>Edit an <a href=
         "edit_product.php">existing product
         </a></li>
29   </ul>
30   <?php
31
32   // *********************************
33   // End of page specific content
34   // *********************************
35
36   require_once
     ("includes/admin_footer.inc");
     // Finish the HTML formatting.
37   ?>
```

```
<big><b>Administration Options
</b></big></div>
<br />
<b>General:</b>
<ul>
<li>Add a new <a href="add_item.php?
→ item=name">product line</a></li>
<li>Add a new <a href="add_item.php?
→ item=size">product size</a></li>
<li>Add a new <a href="add_item.php?
→ item=format">product format</a>
→ </li>
</ul>
<p></p>
<br />
<b>Specific:</b>
<ul>
<li>Add a new <a href=
→ "add_product.php">product</a>
→ </li>
<li>Edit an <a href=
→ "edit_product.php">existing
→ product</a></li>
</ul>
<?php
require_once
→ ("includes/admin_footer.inc");
?>
```

The index page uses the header and footer for the layout (separating most of the HTML from the PHP as every administration page does) and lists every available option. Right now the administrator can fill up the database with product specifications and particular products and also edit existing ones. You may want to add the capability to view all the orders, update inventory, and so forth.

continues on next page

This administration system will require instructing the store owner on how to properly create products: first by defining sizes, names, and formats; and then by adding a particular item.

The links on this page are to a mere three files, as the add_item.php script can be used redundantly for each of the product_* tables.

5. Create add_item.php—the page that fills in the product_names, product_sizes, and product_formats tables (**Script 6.5**).

```php
<?php
$page_title = 'Add To The Store';
require_once
→ ("includes/admin_header.inc");
require_once ("../../config.inc");
$tablename = 'product_' . $item . 's';
$columnname = 'product_' . $item .
→ '_id';
if (isset($HTTP_POST_VARS
→ ['submit'])) {
```

```php
$query = "insert into $tablename
→ values ";
if ($HTTP_POST_VARS['value1']) {
$query .= "('0', '$HTTP_POST_VARS
→ [value1]')";
}
if ($HTTP_POST_VARS['value2']) {
$query .= ", ('0', '$HTTP_POST_VARS
→ [value2]')";
}
if ($HTTP_POST_VARS['value3']) {
$query .= ", ('0', '$HTTP_POST_VARS
→ [value3]')";
}
mysql_query ($query, $db_connection)
→ or die (mysql_error());
}
echo "<table>\n";
$query = "select * from $tablename
→ order by $columnname";
```

continues on page 246

Script 6.5 Since the three supporting product_* tables have similar structures and usage, one page can handle adding data to any of them.

```
1    <?php
2
3    // This page adds data to the db tables.
4
5    $page_title = 'Add To The Store';
6    require_once ("includes/admin_header.inc"); // Include the HTML formatting.
7
8    require_once ("../../config.inc"); // Include the configuration file.
9
10   // *************************************************************
11   // Page specific content begins here
12   // *************************************************************
13
14   // Identify the table and column.
15   $tablename = 'product_' . $item . 's';
16   $columnname = 'product_' . $item . '_id';
17
```

(script continues on next page)

Script 6.5 *continued*

```
                              script

18   if (isset($HTTP_POST_VARS['submit'])) {
19       $query = "insert into $tablename values ";
20       if ($HTTP_POST_VARS['value1']) {
21           $query .= "('0', '$HTTP_POST_VARS[value1]')";
22       }
23       if ($HTTP_POST_VARS['value2']) {
24           $query .= ", ('0', '$HTTP_POST_VARS[value2]')";
25       }
26       if ($HTTP_POST_VARS['value3']) {
27           $query .= ", ('0', '$HTTP_POST_VARS[value3]')";
28       }
29       mysql_query ($query, $db_connection) or die (mysql_error());
30   }
31
32   echo "<table>\n";
33
34   $query = "select * from $tablename order by $columnname";
35   $db_query = mysql_query ($query, $db_connection) or die (mysql_error());
36
37   while ($row = mysql_fetch_array ($db_query)) {
38       echo "<tr><td align=\"left\">$row[1]</td></tr>\n";
39   }
40
41   ?>
42   <tr><td align="center">Add a new product <?=$item ?>:</td></tr>
43   <form action="add_item.php" method="post">
44   <tr><td align="left"><input type="text" name="value1" size="25" maxlength="25"></td></tr>
45   <tr><td align="left"><input type="text" name="value2" size="25" maxlength="25"></td></tr>
46   <tr><td align="left"><input type="text" name="value3" size="25" maxlength="25"></td></tr>
47   <tr><td align="left"><input type="submit" name="submit" value="Submit!"></td></tr>
48   <input type="hidden" name="item" value="<?=$item ?>">
49   </form>
50   </table>
51   <?php
52
53   // ***********************************
54   // End of page specific content
55   // ***********************************
56
57   require_once ("includes/admin_footer.inc"); // Finish the HTML formatting.
58   ?>
```

```
$db_query = mysql_query ($query,
→ $db_connection) or die
→ (mysql_error());
while ($row = mysql_fetch_array
→ ($db_query)) {
echo "<tr><td align=\"left\">
→ $row[1]</td></tr>\n";
}
?>
<tr><td align="center">Add a new
→ product <?=$item ?>:</td></tr>
<form action="add_item.php"
→ method="post">
<tr><td align="left"><input type=
→ "text" name="value1" size="25"
→ maxlength="25"></td></tr>
<tr><td align="left"><input type=
→ "text" name="value2" size="25"
→ maxlength="25"></td></tr>
<tr><td align="left"><input type=
→ "text" name="value3" size="25"
→ maxlength="25"></td></tr>
<tr><td align="left"><input type=
→ "submit" name="submit"
→ value="Submit!"></td></tr>
```

```
<input type="hidden" name="item"
→ value="<?=$item ?>">
</form>
</table>
<?php
require_once
→ ("includes/admin_footer.inc");
?>
```

In short this page takes the $item variable which it receives to display the existing values for that table (be it product_names, product_sizes, or product_formats). It then produces a form that allows the administrator to enter in up to three new values. These values in turn will be inserted into the proper table.

6. Write the script—add_product.php—for adding a particular product (**Script 6.6**).

```
<?php
$page_title = 'Add A Product';
require_once
→ ("includes/admin_header.inc");
require_once ("../../config.inc");
```

continues on page 249

Script 6.6 By letting MySQL do most of the hard work—with an exquisitely written query (line 52), I've taken advantage of the relational database structure.

```
1   <?php
2
3   // This is the main page for adding products.
4
5   $page_title = 'Add A Product';
6   require_once ("includes/admin_header.inc"); // Include the HTML formatting.
7
8   require_once ("../../config.inc"); // Include the configuration file.
9
10  // ************************************************************
11  // Page specific content begins here
12  // ************************************************************
13
```

(script continues on next page)

Script 6.6 *continued*

```
                              script
14   function make_product_select_row ($which) {
15
16      global $db_connection;
17
18      echo '<tr><td align="right">Product ' . ucfirst ($which) . ':</td><td align="left">
        <select name="' . $which . '_id">
19      ';
20
21      $tablename = 'product_' . $which . 's';
22      $columnname = 'product_' . $which . '_id';
23      $query = "select * from $tablename order by $columnname";
24      $db_query = mysql_query ($query, $db_connection) or die (mysql_error());
25
26      while ($row = mysql_fetch_array ($db_query)) {
27          echo "<option value=\"$row[0]\">$row[1]</option>\n";
28      }
29
30      echo '</select></td></tr>
31      ';
32   }
33
34   // Submit the query if the form has been submitted.
35   if (isset($HTTP_POST_VARS['submit'])) {
36      $query = "insert into products values ('0', '$HTTP_POST_VARS[name_id]',
        '$HTTP_POST_VARS[size_id]', '$HTTP_POST_VARS[format_id]', '$HTTP_POST_VARS[price]',
        '$HTTP_POST_VARS[available]', '')";
37      mysql_query ($query, $db_connection) or die (mysql_error());
38   }
39
40   // Display the current products.
41   echo '<table>
42      <tr>
43         <td align="center"><b>SKU</b></td>
44         <td align="center"><b>Product Name</b></td>
45         <td align="center"><b>Product Size</b></td>
46         <td align="center"><b>Product Format</b></td>
47         <td align="center"><b>Price Per Unit</b></td>
48         <td align="center"><b>Product Availability</b></td>
49      </tr>
50      ';
51
```

(script continues on next page)

ADMINISTRATION

Script 6.6 *continued*

```
┌─────────────────────────────────────── script ───────────────────────────────────────┐
52  $query = "select products.product_id, product_names.product_name AS NAME,
        product_sizes.product_size AS SIZE, product_formats.product_format AS FORMAT,
        products.price, products.available from products, product_names, product_sizes,
        product_formats where products.name_id = product_names.product_name_id and
        products.size_id = product_sizes.product_size_id and products.format_id =
        product_formats.product_format_id order by product_id";
53  $db_query = mysql_query ($query, $db_connection) or die (mysql_error());
54
55  while ($row = mysql_fetch_array ($db_query)) {
56      echo "<tr>
57          <td align=\"center\">$row[product_id]</td>
58          <td align=\"center\">$row[NAME]</td>
59          <td align=\"center\">$row[SIZE]</td>
60          <td align=\"center\">$row[FORMAT]</td>
61          <td align=\"center\">\$$row[price]</td>
62          <td align=\"center\">$row[available]</td>
63      </tr>\n";
64  }
65
66  echo '</table>';
67  echo '<br />
68  <table>
69  <tr><td align="center">Add a new product:</td></tr>
70  <form action="add_product.php" method="post">
71  ';
72
73  // Make a form for adding a new product.
74  make_product_select_row ('name');
75  make_product_select_row ('size');
76  make_product_select_row ('format');
77
78  echo ' <tr><td align="right">Price Per Unit:</td><td align="left"><input type="text"
        name="price" size="10"></td></tr>
79      <tr><td align="right">Available:</td><td align="left"><select name="available"><option
        value="Yes">Yes</option><option value="No">No</option></td></tr>
80      <tr><td align="center" colspan="2"><input type="submit" name="submit" value="Add
        Product"></td></tr>
81  </form>
82  </table>';
83
84  // *************************************************************
85  // End of page specific content
86  // *************************************************************
87
88  require_once ("includes/admin_footer.inc"); // Finish the HTML formatting.
89  ?>
```

ADMINISTRATION

Because this script is more complex, I'll go over it in greater detail. The first few lines just incorporate the necessary required files.

7. Define a function for creating a pull-down menu for each of the product_* tables.

```
function make_product_select_row
→ ($which) {
global $db_connection;
echo '<tr><td align="right">
→ Product ' . ucfirst ($which) . ':
→ </td><td align="left"><select
→ name="' . $which . '_id">
';
$tablename = 'product_' . $which .
→ 's';
$columnname = 'product_' . $which .
→ '_id';
$query = "select * from $tablename
→ order by $columnname";
$db_query = mysql_query ($query,
→ $db_connection) or die
→ (mysql_error());
while ($row = mysql_fetch_array
→ ($db_query)) {
echo "<option value=\"$row[0]\">
→ $row[1]</option>\n";
}
echo '</select></td></tr>
';
}
```

To save space and cut down on redundancy, I'm writing one function that will be called three times. Because each product is comprised of a combination of name, size, and format (along with its price and availability), I'll need to generate pull-down menus so that the administrator can choose amongst the existing values—which is why the data has to be

added to these tables prior to adding any specific products. The make_product_select_row() function (a long but descriptive name) creates a table row with one column being *Product * (Name, Size, Format)* and the next column the select box.

8. If the form has been submitted, process it.

```
if (isset($HTTP_POST_VARS
→ ['submit'])) {
$query = "insert into products
→ values ('0',
→ '$HTTP_POST_VARS[name_id]',
→ '$HTTP_POST_VARS[size_id]',
→ '$HTTP_POST_VARS[format_id]',
→ '$HTTP_POST_VARS[price]',
→ '$HTTP_POST_VARS[available]', '')";
mysql_query ($query, $db_connection)
→ or die (mysql_error());
}
```

9. Display all of the existing products.

```
echo '<table>
<tr>
<td align="center"><b>SKU</b></td>
<td align="center"><b>Product
→ Name</b></td>
<td align="center"><b>Product
→ Size</b></td>
<td align="center"><b>Product
→ Format</b></td>
<td align="center"><b>Price Per
→ Unit</b></td>
<td align="center"><b>Product
→ Availability</b></td>
</tr>
';
```

continues on next page

ADMINISTRATION

```
$query = "select products.product_id,
→ product_names.product_name AS
→ NAME, product_sizes.product_size
→ AS SIZE, product_formats.product_
→ format AS FORMAT, products.price,
→ products.available from products,
→ product_names, product_sizes,
→ product_formats where products.
→ name_id = product_names.product_
→ name_id and products.size_id =
→ product_sizes.product_size_id and
→ products.format_id = product_
→ formats.product_format_id order
→ by product_id";
$db_query = mysql_query ($query,
→ $db_connection) or die
→ (mysql_error());
while ($row = mysql_fetch_array
→ ($db_query)) {
echo "<tr>
<td align=\"center\">$row
→ [product_id]→ </td>
<td align=\"center\">$row[NAME]
→ </td>
<td align=\"center\">$row[SIZE]
→ </td>
<td align=\"center\">$row[FORMAT]
→ </td>
<td align=\"center\">\$$row[price]
→ </td>
<td align=\"center\">$row[available]
→ </td>
</tr>\n";
}
echo '</table>';
```

This process is more direct than the verbose query would indicate. I'm selecting everything from the products table, but at the same time I am turning the different *_id fields into their English language

counterpart. For example, I am selecting the product_name field from the product_names table where product_names_id is equal to the name_id field in the products table. That part of the query alone will turn, for example, *1* into *Orange Soda*.

10. Create the form for adding a new product and finish out the page.

```
echo '<br />
<table>
<tr><td align="center">Add a new
→ product:</td></tr>
<form action="add_product.php"
→ method="post">
';
make_product_select_row ('name');
make_product_select_row ('size');
make_product_select_row ('format');
echo ' <tr><td align="right">Price
→ Per Unit:</td><td align="left">
→ <input type="text" name="price"
→ size="10"></td></tr>
<tr><td align="right">Available:
→ </td><td align="left"><select
→ name="available"><option value=
→ "Yes">Yes</option><option value=
→ "No">No</option></td></tr>
<tr><td align="center" colspan="2">
→ <input type="submit" name=
→ "submit" value="Add Product">
→ </td></tr>
</form>
</table>';
require_once
→ ("includes/admin_footer.inc");
?>
```

11. Write the file for editing existing products (**Script 6.7**), edit_product.php.

```
<?php
$page_title = 'Edit A Product';
require_once
 ("includes/admin_header.inc");
require_once ("../../config.inc");
function make_product_select_row
 ($which, $value) {
global $db_connection;
echo '<tr><td align="right">
 Product ' . ucfirst ($which) . ':
 </td><td align="left"><select
 name="' . $which . '_id">
';
$tablename = 'product_' . $which .
 's';
$columnname = 'product_' . $which .
 '_id';
$query = "select * from $tablename
 order by $columnname";
```

```
$db_query = mysql_query ($query,
 $db_connection) or die
 (mysql_error());
while ($row = mysql_fetch_array
 ($db_query)) {
if ($row[0] == $value) {
$selected = 'SELECTED';
} else {
$selected = '';
}
echo "<option value=\"$row[0]\"
 $selected>$row[1]</option>\n";
}
echo '</select></td></tr>
';
}
```

continues on page 255

Script 6.7 The edit_product.php script displays every product in the products table, allowing the user to edit each product's particulars.

```
1   <?php
2
3   // This page allows the admin to alter the product specifications.
4
5   $page_title = 'Edit A Product';
6   require_once ("includes/admin_header.inc"); // Include the HTML formatting.
7
8   require_once ("../../config.inc"); // Include the HTML formatting.
9
10  // ************************************************************
11  // Page specific content begins here
12  // ************************************************************
13
14
```

(script continues on next page)

Script 6.7 *continued*

```
                              script

15   function make_product_select_row ($which, $value) {

16

17       global $db_connection;

18

19       echo '<tr><td align="right">Product ' . ucfirst ($which) . ':</td><td align="left">
         <select name="' . $which . '_id">

20       ';

21

22       $tablename = 'product_' . $which . 's';

23       $columnname = 'product_' . $which . '_id';

24       $query = "select * from $tablename order by $columnname";

25       $db_query = mysql_query ($query, $db_connection) or die (mysql_error());

26

27       while ($row = mysql_fetch_array ($db_query)) {

28           if ($row[0] == $value) {

29               $selected = 'SELECTED';

30           } else {

31               $selected = '';

32           }

33           echo "<option value=\"$row[0]\" $selected>$row[1]</option>\n";

34       }

35

36       echo '</select></td></tr>

37       ';

38   }

39

40

41   function display_products () {

42

43       global $db_connection;

44

45       echo '<table>

46           <tr>

47               <td align="center"><b>SKU</b></td>

48               <td align="center"><b>Product Name</b></td>

49               <td align="center"><b>Product Size</b></td>

50               <td align="center"><b>Product Format</b></td>

51               <td align="center"><b>Price Per Unit</b></td>

52               <td align="center"><b>Product Availability</b></td>

53           </tr>

54       ';

55
```

(script continues on next page)

ADMINISTRATION

Script 6.7 *continued*

```
                                      script

56    $query = "select products.product_id, product_names.product_name AS NAME,
      product_sizes.product_size AS SIZE, product_formats.product_format AS FORMAT,
      products.price, products.available from products, product_names, product_sizes,
      product_formats where products.name_id = product_names.product_name_id and
      products.size_id = product_sizes.product_size_id and products.format_id =
      product_formats.product_format_id order by product_id";
57    $db_query = mysql_query ($query, $db_connection) or die (mysql_error());
58
59    while ($row = mysql_fetch_array ($db_query)) {
60       echo "<tr>
61          <td align=\"center\"><a href=\"edit_product.php?pid=$row[product_id]\">
             $row[product_id]</a></td>
62          <td align=\"center\">$row[NAME]</td>
63          <td align=\"center\">$row[SIZE]</td>
64          <td align=\"center\">$row[FORMAT]</td>
65          <td align=\"center\">\$$row[price]</td>
66          <td align=\"center\">$row[available]</td>
67       </tr>\n";
68    }
69
70    echo '</table>
71    <br />Click on a SKU to edit that product.
72    ';
73
74
75 }
76
77
78 if (isset($HTTP_POST_VARS['submit'])) { // Update the product
79
80    $query = "update products set name_id='$HTTP_POST_VARS[name_id]',
      size_id='$HTTP_POST_VARS[size_id]', format_id='$HTTP_POST_VARS[format_id]',
      price='$HTTP_POST_VARS[price]', available='$HTTP_POST_VARS[available]' where
      product_id='$HTTP_POST_VARS[product_id]'";
81    mysql_query ($query, $db_connection) or die (mysql_error());
82
83    display_products ();
84
85 } elseif (isset($HTTP_GET_VARS['pid'])) { // Show the product
86
87    $query = "select * from products where products.product_id='$HTTP_GET_VARS[pid]'";
88    $db_query = mysql_query ($query, $db_connection) or die (mysql_error());
89    $row = mysql_fetch_array ($db_query);
90
```

(script continues on next page)

ADMINISTRATION

Script 6.7 *continued*

```
 91      echo '<table>
 92      <form action="edit_product.php" method="post">
 93      ';
 94
 95      make_product_select_row ('name', $row[1]);
 96      make_product_select_row ('size', $row[2]);
 97      make_product_select_row ('format', $row[3]);
 98
 99      echo ' <tr><td align="right">Price Per Unit:</td><td align="left"><input type="text"
         name="price" size="10" value="'. $row[4] . '"></td></tr>
100          <tr><td align="right">Available:</td><td align="left"><select name="available">
             <option value="Yes"';
101
102      if ($row[5] == 'Yes') {
103          echo ' SELECTED';
104      }
105
106      echo '>Yes</option><option value="No"';
107
108      if ($row[5] == 'No') {
109          echo ' SELECTED';
110      }
111
112      echo '>No</option></td></tr>
113          <tr><td align="center" colspan="2"><input type="submit" name="submit"
             value="Edit Product"></td></tr>
114      <input type="hidden" name="product_id" value="' . $HTTP_GET_VARS['pid'] . '">
115      </form>
116      </table>';
117
118 } else { // List all products
119
120      display_products();
121
122 }
123
124 // ************************************************************
125 // End of page specific content
126 // ************************************************************
127
128 require_once ("includes/admin_footer.inc"); // Finish the HTML formatting.
129 ?>
```

Again I'll go through this script in some detail, considering its more involved structure. The beginning is familiar except that the `make_product_row()` function has been modified to indicate the current value. This will come in handy editing a product.

12. Write a function for displaying the current products.

```
function display_products () {
global $db_connection;
echo '<table>
<tr>
<td align="center"><b>SKU</b></td>
<td align="center"><b>Product
→ Name</b></td>
<td align="center"><b>Product
→ Size</b></td>
<td align="center"><b>Product
→ Format</b></td>
<td align="center"><b>Price Per
→ Unit</b></td>
<td align="center"><b>Product
→ Availability</b></td>
</tr>
';
$query = "select products.product_id,
→ product_names.product_name AS
→ NAME, product_sizes.product_size
→ AS SIZE, product_formats.product_
→ format AS FORMAT, products.price,
→ products.available from products,
→ product_names, product_sizes,
→ product_formats where products.
→ name_id = product_names.product_
→ name_id and products.size_id =
→ product_sizes.product_size_id
→ and products.format_id = product_
→ formats.product_format_id order
→ by product_id";
```

```
$db_query = mysql_query ($query,
→ $db_connection) or die
→ (mysql_error());
while ($row = mysql_fetch_array
→ ($db_query)) {
echo "<tr>
<td align=\"center\"><a href=
→ \"edit_product.php?pid=$row
→ [product_id]\">$row[product_id]
→ </a></td>
<td align=\"center\">$row[NAME]
→ </td>
<td align=\"center\">$row[SIZE]
→ </td>
<td align=\"center\">$row[FORMAT]
→ </td>
<td align=\"center\">\$$row[price]
→ </td>
<td align=\"center\">$row[available]
→ </td>
</tr>\n";
}
echo '</table>
<br />Click on a SKU to edit that
→ product.
';
}
```

continues on next page

This function just displays every existing product, almost exactly as the code in `add_product.php` does (Script 6.6). One addition here is that each SKU, or `product_id`, is turned into a link that allows the user to edit that particular item.

13. Handle the form if it has been submitted.

```
if (isset($HTTP_POST_VARS
→ ['submit'])) {
$query = "update products set
→ name_id='$HTTP_POST_VARS
→ [name_id]', size_id='$HTTP_POST_
→ VARS[size_id]', format_id=
→ '$HTTP_POST_VARS[format_id]',
→ price='$HTTP_POST_VARS[price]',
→ available='$HTTP_POST_VARS
→ [available]' where product_id=
→ '$HTTP_POST_VARS[product_id]'";
mysql_query ($query, $db_connection)
→ or die (mysql_error());
display_products ();
```

This script will have three steps to it. Upon first seeing the page, the user will view every existing product. When they click on a SKU (which is a link of the form `edit_product.php?pid=x`), they will return back to this page and begin step two—editing of that particular item. Upon submitting the form in step two, they will return here again at which time the changes will be recorded in the database. Afterwards, the list of products will be displayed again to start the steps over.

14. Create the second step.

```
} elseif (isset($HTTP_GET_VARS
→ ['pid'])) {
$query = "select * from products
→ where products.product_id=
→ '$HTTP_GET_VARS[pid]'";
$db_query = mysql_query ($query,
→ $db_connection) or die
→ (mysql_error());
$row = mysql_fetch_array
→ ($db_query);
echo '<table>
<form action="edit_product.php"
→ method="post">
';
make_product_select_row ('name',
→ $row[1]);
make_product_select_row ('size',
→ $row[2]);
make_product_select_row ('format',
→ $row[3]);
echo ' <tr><td align="right">Price
→ Per Unit:</td><td align="left">
→ <input type="text" name="price"
→ size="10" value="'. $row[4] . '">
→ </td></tr>
<tr><td align="right">Available:
→ </td><td align="left"><select
→ name="available"><option value=
→ "Yes"';
if ($row[5] == 'Yes') {
echo ' SELECTED';
}
echo '>Yes</option><option value=
→ "No"';
if ($row[5] == 'No') {
echo ' SELECTED';
}
echo '>No</option></td></tr>
```

```
<tr><td align="center" colspan="2">
→ <input type="submit" name=
→ "submit" value="Edit Product">
→ </td></tr>
<input type="hidden" name=
→ "product_id" value="' .
→ $HTTP_GET_VARS['pid'] . '">
</form>
</table>';
```

The second step, as mentioned above, will list the details of the product in its current form. Each attribute will be available for modification, except for the SKU (product_id).

15. Finish the page.

```
} else { // List all products
display_products();
}
require_once
→ ("includes/admin_footer.inc");
→ // Finish the HTML formatting.
?>
```

16. Upload the pages to your server. **Figure 6.11** shows my configuration.

17. Test the scripts in your Web browser by adding all the requisite data (**Figures 6.12**, **6.13**, **6.14**, **6.15**, **6.16**, **6.17**, and **6.18**), and then creating and editing the individual products (**Figures 6.19**, **6.20**, **6.21**, **6.22**, **6.23**, and **6.24**).

Figure 6.11 This is a pictorial view of how I've placed the administration files on my server, in a directory called d4dm1n (as an added level of security).

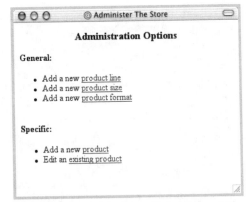

Figure 6.12 The administration-side index page lists the current options for managing the store.

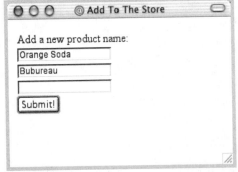

Figure 6.13 I can, as administrator, begin by adding the two product lines my store will carry. Figure 6.14 shows the result.

ADMINISTRATION

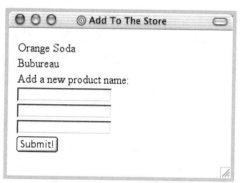

Figure 6.14 *Orange Soda* and *Bubureau* have been added to my product names table and I can now add more, should I choose.

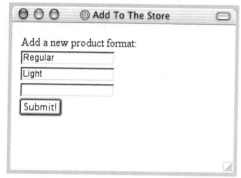

Figure 6.17 Since bubureau will come in two formats, I'll add those to the database as a last step before adding particular products.

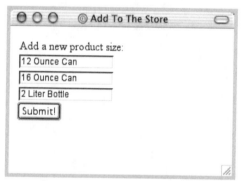

Figure 6.15 The same add_product.php script can be used for adding product names (Figure 6.13), product sizes (here), and product formats (Figure 6.17).

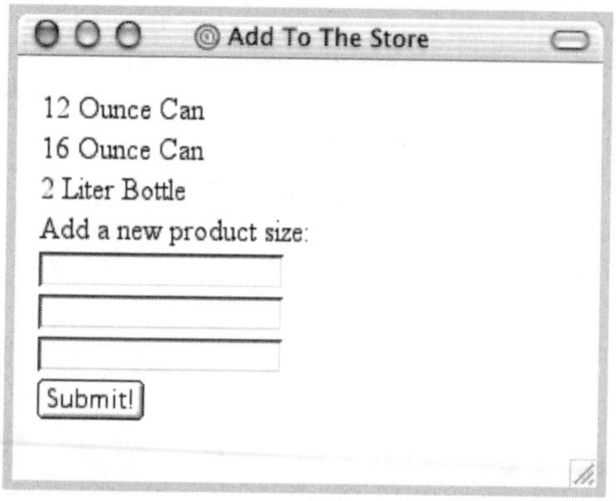

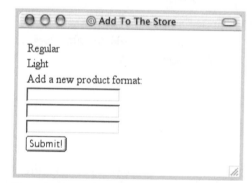

Figure 6.18 The *Regular* and *Light* formats have been added to the database, but I'll need to add an *n/a* category, too, as orange soda doesn't have a format.

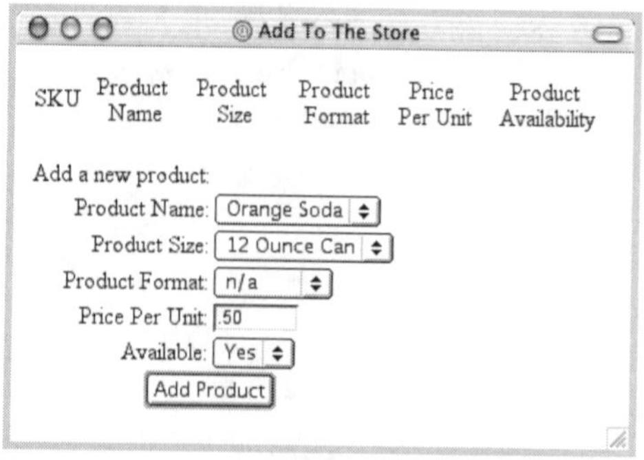

Figure 6.16 After the form is submitted, the script will immediately reflect the additions to the database. I'll now need to add an n/a option since bubureau does not come in any particular size.

Figure 6.19 The add_product.php page starts by showing the current products, of which there are none. Then it creates a form showing every possible parameter used to define an individual product.

ADMINISTRATION

Add To The Store

SKU	Product Name	Product Size	Product Format	Price Per Unit	Product Availability
1	Orange Soda	12 Ounce Can	n/a	$0.50	Yes

Add a new product:
Product Name: Orange Soda
Product Size: 16 Ounce Can
Product Format: n/a
Price Per Unit:
Available: Yes
[Add Product]

Figure 6.20 After adding one product (Figure 6.19), it is reflected in the list of products and the page creates the form again.

Add To The Store

SKU	Product Name	Product Size	Product Format	Price Per Unit	Product Availability
1	Orange Soda	12 Ounce Can	n/a	$0.50	Yes
2	Orange Soda	16 Ounce Can	n/a	$0.75	Yes
3	Orange Soda	2 Liter Bottle	n/a	$1.25	Yes
4	Bubureau	n/a	Regular	$8.00	Yes
5	Bubureau	n/a	Light	$10.00	Yes

Add a new product:
Product Name: Orange Soda
Product Size: 12 Ounce Can
Product Format: Regular
Price Per Unit:
Available: Yes
[Add Product]

Figure 6.21 After using the form several times, I've now entered all the products I'm interested in displaying.

Edit A Product

SKU	Product Name	Product Size	Product Format	Price Per Unit	Product Availability
1	Orange Soda	12 Ounce Can	n/a	$0.50	Yes
2	Orange Soda	16 Ounce Can	n/a	$0.75	Yes
3	Orange Soda	2 Liter Bottle	n/a	$1.00	Yes
4	Bubureau	n/a	Regular	$8.00	Yes
5	Bubureau	n/a	Light	$10.00	Yes

Click on a SKU to edit that product.

Figure 6.22 The edit_product.php page starts by listing every item in the products table. Clicking on the SKU brings you to a form where you can edit that item (Figure 6.23).

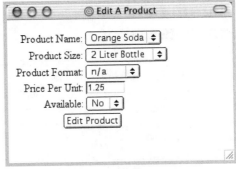

Edit A Product

Product Name: Orange Soda
Product Size: 2 Liter Bottle
Product Format: n/a
Price Per Unit: 1.25
Available: No
[Edit Product]

Figure 6.23 I've decided to raise the price of the 2-liter bottle of orange soda and make it currently unavailable. The changes made here will be immediately reflected (Figure 6.24).

Edit A Product

SKU	Product Name	Product Size	Product Format	Price Per Unit	Product Availability
1	Orange Soda	12 Ounce Can	n/a	$0.50	Yes
2	Orange Soda	16 Ounce Can	n/a	$0.75	Yes
3	Orange Soda	2 Liter Bottle	n/a	$1.25	No
4	Bubureau	n/a	Regular	$8.00	Yes
5	Bubureau	n/a	Light	$10.00	Yes

Click on a SKU to edit that product.

Figure 6.24 Since the third size of orange soda is marked as unavailable, it will not be listed as an option for customers to purchase.

Showing the Products Online

Now that the database exists and there are products therein, you can create the HTML and database-interaction that allows users to view the different products. Again, there's not too much new here (the most important part of the application will be in the next two sections), but I'll go through it so you understand how the whole operates. All of the scripts and images—should you decide to follow this same format—are available on the companion Web site.

To create the store:

1. Create the header file in your text editor (**Script 6.8**).

   I won't go over this script in detail except to point out that it creates a table consisting of three rows: the top header, the middle content, and the bottom footer (which is in the `public_footer.inc` document). The second row consists of four columns: the first containing all the links, the second and fourth being spacers, and the third containing each page's content. The page includes JavaScript for different image effects and, like the administration side header file, uses PHP to set the page title.

continues on page 263

Script 6.8 Instead of using OOP to manage the HTML of the site, I'm using the simpler trick of placing the majority of the formatting into header and footer files.

```
script
1   <!DOCTYPE html PUBLIC "-//W3C//DTD XHTML 1.0 Transitional//EN"
2        "http://www.w3.org/TR/2000/REC-xhtml1-20000126/DTD/xhtml1-transitional.dtd">
3   <html xmlns="http://www.w3.org/1999/xhtml">
4   <head>
5      <title><?=$page_title ?></title>
6   <script language="JavaScript">
7   <!-
8
9   function newImage(arg) {
10     if (document.images) {
11        rslt = new Image();
12        rslt.src = arg;
13        return rslt;
14     }
15  }
16
```

(script continues on next page)

Script 6.8 *continued*

```
                                    script

17    function changeImages() {
18        if (document.images && (preloadFlag == true)) {
19            for (var i=0; i<changeImages.arguments.length; i+=2) {
20                document[changeImages.arguments[i]].src = changeImages.arguments[i+1];
21            }
22        }
23    }
24
25    var preloadFlag = false;
26    function preloadImages() {
27        if (document.images) {
28            register_over = newImage("images/register_over.gif");
29            register_down = newImage("images/register_down.gif");
30            login_over = newImage("images/login_over.gif");
31            login_down = newImage("images/login_down.gif");
32            products_over = newImage("images/products_over.gif");
33            products_down = newImage("images/products_down.gif");
34            cart_over = newImage("images/cart_over.gif");
35            cart_down = newImage("images/cart_down.gif");
36            checkout_over = newImage("images/checkout_over.gif");
37            checkout_down = newImage("images/checkout_down.gif");
38            preloadFlag = true;
39        }
40    }
41
42    // -->
43    </script>
44    </head>
45    <body bgcolor="#FFFFFF" onload="preloadImages();" leftmargin="0" topmargin="0"
      marginwidth="0" marginheight="0">
46    <table width="480" border="0" cellpadding="0" cellspacing="0">
47        <tr>
48            <td><img src="images/topleft.gif" width="110" height="61"></td>
49            <td colspan="3"><a href="index.php"><img src="images/title.gif" width="370" height="61"
              border="0"></a></td>
50        </tr>
51        <tr>
52            <td><img src="images/lei1.gif" width="110" height="29"></td>
53            <td colspan="3"><img src="images/lei2.gif" width="370" height="29"></td>
54        </tr>
55        <tr>
56            <td bgcolor="#000000" valign="top" align="center"><table width="110" border="0"
              cellpadding="0" cellspacing="0" valign="top" align="center">
```

(script continues on next page)

Script 6.8 *continued*

```
 57          <tr>
 58            <td><a href="register.php" onmouseover="changeImages('register',
              'images/register_over.gif'); return true;" onmouseout="changeImages('register',
              'images/register.gif'); return true;" onmousedown="changeImages('register',
              'images/register_down.gif'); return true;" onmouseup="changeImages('register',
              'images/register_over.gif'); return true;"><img name="register"
              src="images/register.gif" width="110" height="33" border="0"></a></td>
 59          </tr>
 60          <tr>
 61            <td><a href="login.php" onmouseover="changeImages('login',
              'images/login_over.gif'); return true;" onmouseout="changeImages('login',
              'images/login.gif'); return true;" onmousedown="changeImages('login',
              'images/login_down.gif'); return true;" onmouseup="changeImages('login',
              'images/login_over.gif'); return true;"><img name="login" src="images/login.gif"
              width="110" height="27" border="0"></a></td>
 62          </tr>
 63          <tr>
 64            <td><a href="products.php" onmouseover="changeImages('products',
              'images/products_over.gif'); return true;" onmouseout="changeImages('products',
              'images/products.gif'); return true;" onmousedown="changeImages('products',
              'images/products_down.gif'); return true;" onmouseup="changeImages('products',
              'images/products_over.gif'); return true;"><img name="products"
              src="images/products.gif" width="110" height="29" border="0"></a></td>
 65          </tr>
 66          <tr>
 67            <td><a href="cart.php" onmouseover="changeImages('cart',
              'images/cart_over.gif'); return true;" onmouseout="changeImages('cart',
              'images/cart.gif'); return true;" onmousedown="changeImages('cart',
              'images/cart_down.gif'); return true;" onmouseup="changeImages('cart',
              'images/cart_over.gif'); return true;"><img name="cart" src="images/cart.gif"
              width="110" height="29" border="0"></a></td>
 68          </tr>
 69          <tr>
 70            <td><a href="checkout.php" onmouseover="changeImages('checkout',
              'images/checkout_over.gif'); return true;" onmouseout="changeImages('checkout',
              'images/checkout.gif'); return true;" onmousedown="changeImages('checkout',
              'images/checkout_down.gif'); return true;" onmouseup="changeImages('checkout',
              'images/checkout_over.gif'); return true;"><img name="checkout"
              src="images/checkout.gif" width="110" height="29" border="0"></a></td>
 71          </tr></table></td>
 72      <td width="5"> </td>
 73        <td>
```

Script 6.9 The footer file finishes the second row of the layout table, makes the third row, and completes the page.

```
script
1          <td width="5"> </td>
2          </td>
3       </tr>
4       <tr>
5          <td><img src="images/volcano.gif"
           width="110" height="112"></td>
6          <td width="5"> </td>
7          <td>Copyright blah, blah,
           blah.</td>
8          <td width="5"> </td>
9       </tr>
10    </table>
11    </body>
12    </html>
```

2. Create the corresponding footer file in your text editor (**Script 6.9**).

3. Create the index page (**Script 6.10**), saving it as index.php.

```
<?php
$page_title ='Welcome To Waponi Woo!';
require_once ("includes/public_
→ header.inc");
?>
Welcome to our store.<br />
Please use the links at left to shop
→ here.
<?php
require_once ("includes/public_
→ footer.inc"); // Finish the HTML
→ formatting.
?>
```

continues on next page

Script 6.10 The home page is rather bland but serves its purpose just fine.

```
script
1    <?php
2
3    // This is the home page for the site.
4
5    $page_title = 'Welcome To Waponi Woo!';
6    require_once ("includes/public_header.inc"); // Include the HTML formatting.
7
8    // ************************************************************
9    // Page specific content begins here
10   // ************************************************************
11
12   ?>
13
14   Welcome to our store.<br />
15   Please use the links at left to shop here.
16
17   <?php
18
19   // ************************************************************
20   // End of page specific content
21   // ************************************************************
22
23   require_once ("includes/public_footer.inc"); // Finish the HTML formatting.
24   ?>
```

SHOWING THE PRODUCTS ONLINE

263

4. Write the page for displaying products,
products.php (**Script 6.11**).

```php
<?php
$page_title = 'View The Products';
require_once ("includes/public_
→ header.inc");
require_once ("../config.inc");
```

This script will have two steps to it, allowing the customer to browse through the available products. The first step will display all the product lines (orange soda and bubureau) and the second will show the particulars of each line (sizes or formats).

continues on page 266

Script 6.11 The customer can browse through all of the available products via the products.php script. First it will display every product line, then the specifics within that line (once the user clicks on a product name).

```
                                       script
1    <?php
2
3    // This page displays the products.
4
5    $page_title = 'View The Products';
6    require_once ("includes/public_header.inc"); // Include the HTML formatting.
7
8    require_once ("../config.inc"); // Include the HTML formatting.
9
10   // ***********************************************************
11   // Page specific content begins here
12   // ***********************************************************
13
14   if (isset($HTTP_GET_VARS['nid'])) { // Show the specific product.
15
16       echo '<table>';
17
18       $query = "select products.product_id, product_names.product_name AS NAME,
             product_sizes.product_size AS SIZE, product_formats.product_format AS FORMAT,
             products.price, products.available from products, product_names, product_sizes,
             product_formats where products.name_id = product_names.product_name_id and
             products.size_id = product_sizes.product_size_id and products.format_id =
             product_formats.product_format_id and products.name_id='$HTTP_GET_VARS[nid]' and
             available='Yes'";
```

(script continues on next page)

Script 6.11 *continued*

```
                                                         script

19     $db_query = mysql_query ($query, $db_connection) or die (mysql_error());
20     while ($row = mysql_fetch_array ($db_query)) {
21         echo "<tr>
22             <td align=\"center\">$row[NAME]</td>";
23
24         if ($row['SIZE'] != 'n/a') {
25             echo "<td align=\"center\">$row['SIZE']</td>";
26         }
27
28         if ($row['FORMAT'] != 'n/a') {
29             echo "<td align=\"center\">$row['FORMAT']</td>";
30         }
31
32         echo "<td align=\"center\">\$$row['price']</td>
33             <td align=\"center\"><a href=\"cart.php?pid=$row['product_id']&do=Add\">Add To
               Cart</a></td>
34         </tr>\n";
35     }
36
37     echo '</table>';
38
39 } else { // List all products.
40
41     $query = "select products.name_id, product_names.product_name AS NAME, products.available
         from products, product_names where products.name_id = product_names.product_name_id and
         available='Yes' group by name_id";
42     $db_query = mysql_query ($query, $db_connection) or die (mysql_error());
43
44     while ($row = mysql_fetch_array ($db_query)) {
45         echo "<a href=\"products.php?nid=$row['name_id']\">$row[NAME]</a><br />\n";
46     }
47
48     echo '<br />Click on a product to see more information.
49     ';
50
51 }
52
53 // ***********************************************************
54 // End of page specific content
55 // ***********************************************************
56
57 require_once ("includes/public_footer.inc"); // Finish the HTML formatting.
58 ?>
```

5. Code for step 2 of the browse process.

```
if (isset($HTTP_GET_VARS['nid'])) {
echo '<table>';

$query = "select products.product_id,
→ product_names.product_name
→ AS NAME, product_sizes.product_size
→ AS SIZE, product_formats.product_
→ format AS FORMAT, products.price,
→ products.available from products,
→ product_names, product_sizes,
→ product_formats where products.
→ name_id = product_names.product_
→ name_id and products.size_id =
→ product_sizes.product_size_id and
→ products.format_id = product_
→ formats.product_format_id and
→ products.name_id='$HTTP_GET_VARS
→ [nid]' and available='Yes' ";
$db_query = mysql_query ($query,
→ $db_connection) or die
→ (mysql_error());
while ($row = mysql_fetch_array
→ ($db_query)) {
echo "<tr>
<td align=\"center\">$row[NAME]
→ </td>";
if ($row['SIZE'] != 'n/a') {
echo "<td align=\"center\">$row
→ ['SIZE']</td>";
}
if ($row['FORMAT'] != 'n/a') {
echo "<td align=\"center\">
→ $row['FORMAT']</td>";
}
echo "<td align=\"center\">
→ \$$row['price']→ </td>
<td align=\"center\"><a href=
→ \"cart.php?pid=$row['product_id']
→ &do=Add\">Add To Cart</a></td>
</tr>\n";
}
echo '</table>';
```

The query and format of this code is much like that in the add_product.php and edit_product.php scripts on the administration side. The query turns the different *_id fields into their English language equivalent and displays each available product. The items are linked to the cart.php page, which you'll write next, so that customers can add items to their carts.

6. Write step 1 of the product-browsing process and complete the page.

```
} else {
$query = "select products.name_id,
→ product_names.product_name
→ AS NAME, products.available from
→ products, product_names where
→ products.name_id = product_names.
→ product_name_id and available=
→ 'Yes' group by name_id";
$db_query = mysql_query ($query,
→ $db_connection) or die
→ (mysql_error());
while ($row = mysql_fetch_array
→ ($db_query)) {
echo "<a href=\"products.php?nid=
→ $row['name_id']\">$row[NAME]</a>
→ <br />\n";
}
echo '<br />Click on a product to
→ see more information.
';
}
require_once ("includes/public_
→ footer.inc");
?>
```

Figure 6.25 The public side of the Waponi Woo store is now available for viewing!

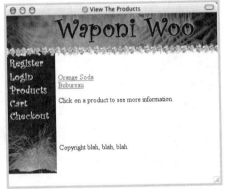

Figure 6.26 When customers click on the *Products* link, the first thing they will see is a listing of the available product names.

Figure 6.27 Clicking on the *Orange Soda* link in Figure 6.26 brings the customer to the detailed page listing the particular sizes and prices of orange soda. Since the 2-liter bottle was made unavailable, it does not appear as an option here.

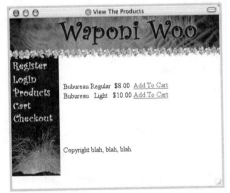

Figure 6.28 Clicking on the *Bubureau* link in Figure 6.26 brings the customer back to products.php, this time with the two different bubureau formats listed.

By adding `group by name_id` to the query, the database will return only the product lines, not every individual product, creating a multi-tiered method of browsing through the online catalog.

7. Save this file as `product.php` and upload it, along with `index.php` (Script 6.10), `public_header.inc` (Script 6.8), and `public_footer.inc` (Script 6.9), to your server. Test in your Web browser (**Figures 6.25**, **6.26**, **6.27**, and **6.28**).

✔ Tip

■ The `register.php` and `login.php` scripts are just applications of similar code developed in Chapter 4, Security, and Chapter 5, Developing Web Applications. You can write these yourself or download them from the companion Web site.

Writing a Shopping Cart

The most important aspect of the e-commerce site is the shopping cart itself. There are many types of carts out there, from a programming perspective, for many different purposes. What I'm going to write here is a generic cart class that can be adapted towards other e-commerce uses. But first, let's think about what a shopping cart should do:

♦ Allow the customer to add items to the cart

♦ Allow for different quantities of each item

♦ Allow the customer to alter the quantities of an item

♦ Allow the customer to remove an item

I'm going to write a shopping cart class that does all of this as well as displays the cart's contents. This last feature might also be placed in an extended class, as its particulars may change from application to application.

To make a shopping cart class:

1. Create a new PHP document in your text editor (**Script 6.12**).

   ```
   <?php
   ```

2. Define the class.

   ```
   class ShoppingCart {
   ```

3. Initialize your attributes.

   ```
   var $items = array();
   ```

   The only variable required by this class is the $items array. It will store the product SKU and quantity while sessions will be used to match each cart up with the particular user.

4. Write a method for adding items to the cart.

   ```
   function AddItem ($item) {
   if ($this->items[$item]) {
   $this->items[$item] = $this->items
   → [$item] + 1;
   } else {
   $this->items[$item] = 1;
   }
   }
   ```

continues on page 271

Script 6.12 The code that is at the heart of this, or any, e-commerce application is in the ShoppingCart.class file. This class defines an object, which handles the basics of online shopping.

```
                                        script
1    <?php
2
3    class ShoppingCart {
4
5        var $items = array(); // One variable
6
7        // Function to add an item to the cart.
8        function AddItem ($item) {
9            if ($this->items[$item]) {
10               $this->items[$item] = $this->items[$item] + 1;
11           } else {
12               $this->items[$item] = 1;
13           }
```

(script continues on next page)

Script 6.12 *continued*

```
14        }
15
16        // Function to delete an item from the cart.
17        function DropItem ($item) {
18           $this->items[$item] = 0;
19        }
20
21        // Function to alter quantities.
22        function ChangeQuantity ($item, $quantity) {
23           if ($quantity == 0) {
24              $this->DropItem($item);
25           } else {
26              $this->items[$item] = $quantity;
27           }
28
29        }
30
31        // Function to display the cart contents.
32        function DisplayCart () {
33
34           global $db_connection;
35
36           // Display a table and start the form.
37           echo '<form action="cart.php?do=Change" method="post">
38           <table>
39              <tr>
40                 <td align="center"><b>Product Name</b></td>
41                 <td align="center"><b>Product Size</b></td>
42                 <td align="center"><b>Product Format</b></td>
43                 <td align="center"><b>Price Per Unit</b></td>
44                 <td align="center"><b>Quantity</b></td>
45                 <td align="center"><b>Total</b></td>
46                 <td align="center"><b>Delete</b></td>
47              </tr>
48              ';
49
50           // Loop through the cart.
51           foreach ($this->items as $key => $value) {
52
53              $was_one = FALSE; // Dummy variable
54              if ($value != 0) {
55
56                 $was_one = TRUE;
57
```

(script continues on next page)

WRITING A SHOPPING CART

Script 6.12 *continued*

```
                                                                          script

58              $query = "select products.product_id, product_names.product_name AS NAME,
                product_sizes.product_size AS SIZE, product_formats.product_format AS FORMAT,
                products.price, products.available from products, product_names, product_sizes,
                product_formats where products.name_id = product_names.product_name_id and
                products.size_id = product_sizes.product_size_id and products.format_id =
                product_formats.product_format_id and products.product_id = '$key'";
59              $db_query = mysql_query ($query, $db_connection) or die (mysql_error());
60
61              $row = mysql_fetch_array ($db_query);
62              $sub_total = sprintf ("%01.2f", ($value * $row['price']));
63              $total += $sub_total;
64              echo "<tr>
65                  <td align=\"center\">$row[NAME]</td>
66                  <td align=\"center\">$row[SIZE]</td>
67                  <td align=\"center\">$row[FORMAT]</td>
68                  <td align=\"center\">\$$row[price]</td>
69                  <td align=\"center\"><input type=\"text\" name=\"pid[$key]\" size=\"2\"
                    maxsize=\"3\" value=\"$value\"></td>
70                  <td align=\"center\">\$$sub_total</td>
71                  <td align=\"center\"><a href=\"cart.php?pid=$key&do=Drop\">Delete</a></td>
72              </tr>\n";
73
74          }
75      }
76
77      // Complete the table and form.
78      echo '<tr>
79              <td align="right" colspan="5">Total</td>
80              <td align="center">$';
81      printf ("%01.2f", $total);
82      echo '</td>
83              <td align="center"> </td>
84          </tr>
85          <input type="hidden" name="do" value="Change">
86      </table>
87      Alter the quantities by changing the above values and clicking here <input
        type="submit" name="submit" value="Change Quantities">
88      <input type="hidden" name="do" value="Change">
89      </form>';
90
91      if (!$was_one) {
92          echo '<br /><font color="#CC0000"><big>Your shopping cart is currently
            empty.</big></font>';
93      }
94
95  } // End of the DisplayCart() function.
96
97  } // End of the class.
98
99  ?>
```

This function receives one argument, the `$item` (which will come in the form of a SKU, although it does not know that). If the item is already in the cart, then another is added. Otherwise, one copy of that item is placed in the virtual shopping basket.

5. Create a method for deleting items from the cart.

```
function DropItem ($item) {
$this->items[$item] = 0;
}
```

This method is very simple, setting the quantity of that particular item to *0*. To make myself clear, this cart uses an array of the form `$items[$key] = $value` where $key will be the SKU and $value will be the quantity. The `DropItem()` method merely sets the value of `$items[$key]` to *0*.

6. Write a method that will alter the quantities of an item in the cart.

```
function ChangeQuantity ($item,
→ $quantity) {
if ($quantity == 0) {
$this->DropItem($item);
} else {
$this->items[$item] = $quantity;
}
}
```

This method takes two arguments, the SKU and the new quantity. If the new quantity is *0*, the item will be dropped. If not, the value of the array at that item/key will be set to the new quantity.

7. Create one last method for displaying the cart.

```
function DisplayCart () {
global $db_connection;
```

This method will need to access the database, so be sure to include the database connection global variable, as defined in the `config.inc` (Script 6.1) file.

8. Start the form and table for the shopping cart.

```
echo '<form action="cart.php?do=
→ Change" method="post">
<table>
<tr>
<td align="center"><b>Product
→ Name</b></td>
<td align="center"><b>Product
→ Size</b></td>
<td align="center"><b>Product
→ Format</b></td>
<td align="center"><b>Price Per
→ Unit</b></td>
<td align="center"><b>Quantity</b>
→ </td>
<td align="center"><b>Total</b>
→ </td>
<td align="center"><b>Delete</b>
→ </td>
</tr>
';
```

The table generated by this cart will list the products ordered, as well as how many and at what price. It will be created as an HTML form allowing the customer to alter the quantities or delete an item altogether. The recipient of the form will be the `cart.php` script, which you'll write next.

continues on next page

9. Loop through each item in the cart, displaying it as you go.

```
foreach ($this->items as $key =>
→ $value) {
$was_one = FALSE;
if ($value != 0) {
$was_one = TRUE;
$query = "select products.product_id,
→ product_names.product_name
→ AS NAME, product_sizes.product_
→ size AS SIZE, product_formats.
→ product_format AS FORMAT, products.
→ price, products.available from
→ products, product_names, product_
→ sizes, product_formats where
→ products.name_id = product_names.
→ product_name_id and products.
→ size_id = product_sizes.product_
→ size_id and products.format_id =
→ product_formats.product_format_id
→ and products.product_id =
→ '$key'";
$db_query = mysql_query ($query,
→ $db_connection) or die
→ (mysql_error());
$row = mysql_fetch_array
→ ($db_query);
$sub_total = sprintf ("%01.2f",
→ ($value * $row['price']));
$total += $sub_total;
echo "<tr>
<td align=\"center\">$row[NAME]
→ </td>
<td align=\"center\">$row[SIZE]
→ </td>
<td align=\"center\">$row[FORMAT]
→ </td>
<td align=\"center\">\$$row[price]
→ </td>
<td align=\"center\"><input type=\
→ "text\" name=\"pid[$key]\" size=\
→ "2\" maxsize=\"3\" value=\"$value\">
→ </td>
```

```
<td align=\"center\">\$$sub_total
→ </td>
<td align=\"center\"><a href=
→ \"cart.php?pid=$key&do=Drop\">
→ Delete</a></td>
</tr>\n";
}
}
```

The loop goes through the $items array, and if the quantity of a product is not *0* (in other words, it has not been deleted) it will list the product in the table. The long query is based on the query used on the products.php page.

This version of the cart totals each order on the fly, rather than totaling it once and storing that amount. The rationale behind this decision is that if the total is always recalculated and the prices are retrieved from the database, the ability for a malicious user to scam the store is negated. There is a trade-off in terms of performance, but I think the improved security makes it worthwhile

Finally, I'll point out that I use the $was_one variable here to confirm that there was at least one item in the cart, or else I'll display a *Your cart is currently empty* message later on in the script.

10. Complete the table and form.

```
echo '<tr>
<td align="right" colspan="5">
→ Total</td>
<td align="center">$';
printf ("%01.2f", $total);
echo '</td>
<td align="center"> </td>
</tr>
<input type="hidden" name="do"
→ value="Change">
</table>
```

Alter the quantities by changing
→ the above values and clicking
→ here <input type="submit"
→ name="submit" value="Change
→ Quantities">
<input type="hidden" name="do"
→ value="Change">
</form>';
if (!$was_one) {
echo '
<font color="#CC0000">
→ <big>Your shopping cart is
→ currently empty.</big></font>';
}
}

Depending upon how particular you want to be, you might consider coding the 'Alter the quantities...' line so that it only shows up if there are products in the cart.

11. Complete the class and the PHP.

```
}
?>
```

12. Save this script as ShoppingCart.class and upload it to your server, in the classes directory.

Now that the class itself is written, I'll write the primary page that makes use of it.

13. Create a new PHP document in your text editor (**Script 6.13**).

```
<?php
require_once ("../config.inc");
require_once ("classes/
→ ShoppingCart.class");
session_start();
$page_title = 'Your Shopping Cart';
require_once ("includes/public_
→ header.inc");
```

continues on page 275

Script 6.13 The oft-mentioned cart.php script creates an instance of the ShoppingCart class and manipulates it according to the data it receives. The page also handles session management, leaving the shopping cart on the server.

```
1   <?php
2
3   // This is a basic home page for the administration side of the site.
4
5   require_once ("../config.inc"); // Include the Configuration file.
6   require_once ("classes/ShoppingCart.class"); // Include the class.
7   session_start(); // Start the session.
8
9   $page_title = 'Your Shopping Cart';
10  require_once ("includes/public_header.inc"); // Include the HTML formatting.
11
12  // ************************************************************
13  // Page specific content begins here
14  // ************************************************************
15
16  if (isset ($HTTP_SESSION_VARS['cart'])) { // If there's already a session/object...
```

(script continues on next page)

Script 6.13 *continued*

```
17      $cart = $HTTP_SESSION_VARS['cart'];
18  } else {
19      $cart = new ShoppingCart();
20  }
21
22  switch ($HTTP_GET_VARS['do']) {
23
24      case "Add":
25          $cart->AddItem ($HTTP_GET_VARS['pid']);
26          $cart->DisplayCart();
27          break;
28
29      case "Drop":
30          $cart->DropItem ($HTTP_GET_VARS['pid']);
31          $cart->DisplayCart();
32          break;
33
34      case "Change":
35          foreach ($HTTP_POST_VARS['pid'] as $key => $value) {
36              $cart->ChangeQuantity ($key, $value);
37          }
38          $cart->DisplayCart();
39          break;
40
41      case "Display":
42          $cart->DisplayCart();
43          break;
44
45      default:
46          $cart->DisplayCart();
47          break; // Same as display.
48
49  }
50
51  session_register ('cart');
52
53  // ************************************************************
54  // End of page specific content
55  // ************************************************************
56
57  require_once ("includes/public_footer.inc"); // Finish the HTML formatting.
58  ?>
```

This page requires inclusion of the ShoppingCart.class file and will use sessions to track the user. Be sure to place the session_start() line as near to the top of the script so that no HTML gets to the browser before session_start() attempts to send the session ID cookie. Also, if your session is storing an object—as this one is—it's best to include the class file before starting the session.

14. Create a shopping cart object.

```
if (isset ($HTTP_SESSION_VARS
→ ['cart'])) {
$cart = $HTTP_SESSION_VARS['cart'];
} else {
$cart = new ShoppingCart();
}
```

If the user has already placed an item in the shopping cart (which means that he or she has been to this page before), a session will already exist. Therefore, the script should use the existing, stored cart (the $cart = $HTTP_SESSION_ → VARS['cart']; line is not technically required but I like having it there). If the cart session variable does not exist, then a new shopping cart should be created.

15. Create a switch conditional based upon what action the page should take.

```
switch ($HTTP_GET_VARS['do']) {
case "Add":
$cart->AddItem ($HTTP_GET_VARS
→ ['pid']);
$cart->DisplayCart();
break;
case "Drop":
$cart->DropItem
→ ($HTTP_GET_VARS['pid']);
$cart->DisplayCart();
break;
```

```
case "Change":
foreach ($HTTP_POST_VARS['pid'] as
→ $key => $value) {
$cart->ChangeQuantity ($key,
→ $value);
}
$cart->DisplayCart();
break;
case "Display":
$cart->DisplayCart();
break;
default:
$cart->DisplayCart();
break;
}
```

Two of the public pages created up to this point refer to the cart.php script in one way or another. The products.php page has a link in the form of cart.php?pid= x&do=Add. The ShoppingCart.class script has a link in the form of cart.php? pid=x&do=Drop for deleting items. Also, the form in the DisplayCart() function of the class refers to cart.php and stores a hidden variable of do, which is equal to *Change*. So, based upon the value of do, the shopping cart will have an item added to it, have an item deleted from it, and have possibly multiple items change in quantity. The proper object method is called for each case and then the newly altered cart is displayed.

16. Store the cart object in the session.

```
session_register ('cart');
```

17. Finish the PHP page.

```
require_once ("includes/public_
→ footer.inc");
?>
```

continues on next page

WRITING A SHOPPING CART

18. Save the script as `cart.php`, upload it to your server, and test it in your Web browser (**Figures 6.29**, **6.30**, **6.31**, **6.32**, and **6.33**).

✔ Tips

■ Another option you might want to add to your shopping cart class is the capability to record the purchase price of each item. This way, if the product's price changes over time in the database, the price the customer paid is still recorded.

■ I mentioned in Chapter 2, Object Oriented Programming and it's worth reiterating here that an object is automatically serialized and unserialized when stored in sessions.

Figure 6.29 After clicking on *Add To Cart* on products.php (Figure 6.28), the cart.php page reflects the updated cart.

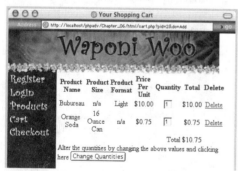

Figure 6.30 By browsing through the products and adding a 16-ounce can of orange soda, my cart now contains two products.

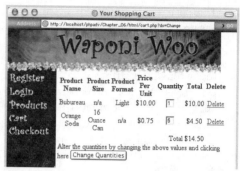

Figure 6.31 Using the *Change Quantities* button, I've altered my order to make it a 6-pack of orange soda.

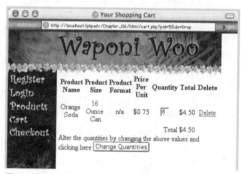

Figure 6.32 After much consideration, I've decided that I currently have enough buburO and used the *Delete* link to remove it.

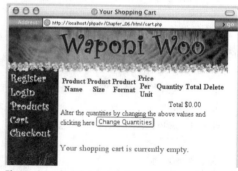

Figure 6.33 If I delete every item or click on the *Cart* link before adding anything, the page indicates that my cart is currently empty.

NETWORKING
WITH PHP

All of the examples in the chapters up to this point have dealt with building larger-scale Web applications. PHP has been used to interact with databases and file structures, send emails, provide a secure means of registering users, handle e-commerce, and more. Although these different PHP programs have been very utilitarian, they still lack a certain dynamism that PHP has to offer.

Not only can PHP write to text files and retrieve information from a database, it can also interact with other Web sites, secretly learn more about the current user, send complex emails and even FTP files. In this chapter, I'll discuss and demonstrate a couple of network-related PHP functions and capabilities. In the next chapter, PHP and the Server, I'll give comparable treatment on how PHP interacts with the machine on which it is running.

Because a lot of what is being discussed here has been well developed by other programmers over the years, one example in this chapter will use an object-oriented programming class already available. Further, although I do show you how to write your own code for other examples, they too have been significantly regimented in third-party classes and in PEAR (which you'll learn more about in Chapter 12, Extending PHP). In short, most of PHP's networking capability has been finely written into existing code, but it is certainly worth your while to comprehend the underpinnings of how these work. This chapter will give you the basics of the many network-related functions in PHP, demonstrate how to use two existing network classes, and indicate what other resources exist for similar uses.

NETWORKING WITH PHP

277

Browser Detection

The PHP programmer is almost spoiled when it comes to Web development because PHP is largely browser- and platform-independent. This means that the code you write functions similarly regardless of the operating system of the computer on which it is running or the Web browser that the client (the person/computer viewing the Web site) is using.

The same cannot be said for other aspects of Web development. HTML code will look slightly different from one browser to the next. Sections of JavaScript code will work or not work depending upon whether the page is being viewed with Internet Explorer 5 on a Macintosh or on Windows. And with the two major browsers being controlled by megacorporations less interested in supporting standards than in promoting their own cause, this fact is not likely to change. But enough with the diatribe. How can you work around these inconsistencies?

With JavaScript alone you can detect what version of Web browser the client is using, but the same can be done directly in PHP, too (and without the client-side limitation as to what you can do with that knowledge). Two choices you have for detecting the Web browser are making use of the `browscap.ini` file or using a PHP class such as phpSniff.

For the first option, you will need to download the `browscap.ini` file, available from `http://www.cyscape.com/browscap` (**Figure 7.1**). This document contains several thousand lines of text describing the different browsers. **Script 7.1** shows a fraction of the file. It is kept current by CyScape and Microsoft and, at the time of printing, the latest version is 2.5, put out in February 2000.

Once the `browscap.ini` file has been installed and you've told `php.ini` where to find it (**Figure 7.2**), you can use the PHP function

continues on page 280

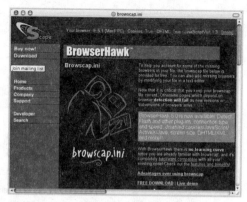

Figure 7.1 CyScape, one of the companies that manages `browscap.ini`, also offers up BrowserHawk, a more elaborate (but commercial) browser detection system.

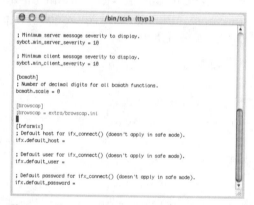

Figure 7.2 If you are using the `browscap.ini` system, be sure to tell your `php.ini` file where to find the document.

Script 7.1 The browscap.ini file details every possible permutation of Web browser over thousands of lines.

```
1    ;---------------------
2    ; Netscape 3.04
3    ; v2.1
4    ;---------------------
5    [Mozilla/3.04 * (Win95; I; 16bit)]
6    parent=Netscape 3.01
7    platform=Win16
8    minorver=#04
9
10   [Mozilla/3.04 * (Win95; I)]
11   parent=Netscape 3.01
12   platform=Win95
13   minorver=#04
14
15   [Mozilla/3.04 * (Win95; U)]
16   parent=Netscape 3.01
17   platform=Win95
18   minorver=#04
19
20   [Mozilla/3.04 * (WinNT; I)]
21   parent=Netscape 3.01
22   platform=WinNT
23   minorver=#04
24
25   [Mozilla/3.04 * (WinNT; U)]
26   parent=Netscape 3.01
27   platform=WinNT
28   minorver=#04
29
30   [Mozilla/3.04 * (Win16; I)]
31   parent=Netscape 3.01
32   platform=Win16
33   Win16=True
34   minorver=#04
```

(script continues in next column)

Script 7.1 *continued*

```
35
36   [Mozilla/3.04 * (Win16; U)]
37   parent=Netscape 3.01
38   platform=Win16
39   Win16=True
40   minorver=#04
41
42   [Mozilla/3.04 * (Macintosh; I; 68K)]
43   parent=Netscape 3.01
44   platform=Mac68K
45   minorver=#04
46
47   [Mozilla/3.04 * (Macintosh; U; 68K)]
48   parent=Netscape 3.01
49   platform=Mac68K
50   minorver=#04
51
52   [Mozilla/3.04 * (Macintosh; I; PPC)]
53   parent=Netscape 3.01
54   platform=MacPPC
55   minorver=#04
56
57   [Mozilla/3.04 * (Macintosh; U; PPC)]
58   parent=Netscape 3.01
59   platform=MacPPC
60   minorver=#04
61
62   ;--
63   [Mozilla/3.04 (Win95; I; 16bit)*]
64   parent=Netscape 3.01
65   platform=Win16
66   minorver=#04
```

get_browser() to learn everything you want to know. This function makes use of the $HTTP_USER_AGENT environmental variable (**Figure 7.3**) and will turn that into an array of information: the browser (e.g., Netscape), the version (4), the platform (Windows 95), and more. However, the downside of using this system is that it requires an up-to-date version of browscap.ini.

Another option for Web browser detection is to use a class such as phpSniff, available at http://sourceforge.net/projects/phpsniff (**Figure 7.4**). The class, as it stands, is used to detect almost everything you would want to know about the Web browser: the language being used, if the user is accessing the site via AOL or WebTV, the user's operating system, etc. (**Figure 7.5**). Again, this system will rely on the definition files being up-to-date, but that is a responsibility I would rather have in the hands of a few programmers rather than two companies.

Instead of just printing out all the data as the class itself is designed to do, I'll make some modifications so that the information it provides can be used more practically.

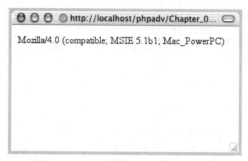

Figure 7.3 PHP's $HTTP_USER_AGENT variable has a value like this, indicating that I'm using Microsoft Internet Explorer 5.1b1 on a Macintosh.

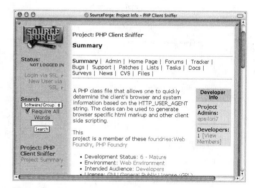

Figure 7.4 The phpSniff class, developed by Roger Raymond, accurately provides all the browser information you will need and then some (Figure 7.5).

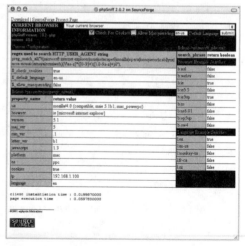

Figure 7.5 The default use of phpSniff prints out a large table of information regarding the browser with which you are viewing the page.

Figure 7.6 To start developing the browser detection system, I've placed all of phpSniff's files into a `classes` directory.

To detect a Web browser with phpSniff:

1. Download all of the `phpSniff` files from the project's Web site.

   The files are listed as the *PHPClientSniffer* package and the download itself will be a file with a name like phpSniff-x.x.x.zip.

2. Unzip the package and place every file within the `classes` directory of your Web site (**Figure 7.6**).

3. Open `phpSniff-2.0.2-class.php` in your text editor.

   If you are using a different version of phpSniff, the filename will be different.

4. Alter the second line so that the site's structure is represented (i.e., that the class files will be placed within the `classes` directory).

   ```
   if(!defined('_PHP_SNIFF_CORE_
   → INCLUDED')) include('classes/
   → phpSniff-2.0.2-core.php');
   ```

   This line needs to be changed because the file will be included from another file. If you do not do this, an error will occur upon object instantiation.

   continues on next page

BROWSER DETECTION

Now that the phpSniff class is installed and modified, it can be used in other scripts. For this purpose, I'll make a demonstration script that incorporates a different JavaScript file based on the level of JavaScript supported. The code will also print out the current browser name and version.

5. Create a new PHP document in your text editor (**Script 7.2**).

```
<?php
```

6. Include the phpSniff file.

```
if (!defined('_PHP_SNIFF_INCLUDED')) {
require_once ('classes/phpSniff-
→ 2.0.2-class.php');
}
```

This line states that if the class has not been included, then include it here. Since the phpSniff-2.0.2-class.php file (included here) will look for the phpSniff-2.0.2-core.php file, I had to change the second line of phpSniff-2.0.2-class.php (step 4).

7. Make an object from the class.

```
$browser = new phpSniff ();
$browser->check_cookies = TRUE;
$browser->init();
```

The very first step is to instantiate the object. Then I set check_cookies to TRUE, because I want to confirm that cookies are enabled. Next, I call the init() function, which does all of the work (from within the phpSniff-2.0.2-core.php file).

8. Check to see what JavaScript is enabled.

```
switch ($browser->property
→ ('javascript')) {
case "1.1":
$javascript_file = 'javascript1.js';
break;
case "1.2":
$javascript_file = 'javascript2.js';
break;
```

```
case "1.3":
$javascript_file = 'javascript3.js';
break;
default:
$javascript_file = 'javascript.js';
break;
}
```

The property() method returns the Web browser value corresponding to the submitted argument. In this case, I want to know what JavaScript version the user's browser supports. The call to $browser->property('javascript') will return a decimal like 1.1 or 1.3. This number will be used to dictate which JavaScript file the page should use.

9. Close the PHP and begin an HTML form.

```
?>
<!DOCTYPE html PUBLIC "-//W3C//DTD
→ XHTML 1.0 Transitional//EN"
"http://www.w3.org/TR/2000/REC-
→ xhtml1-20000126/DTD
→ /xhtml1-transitional.dtd">
<html xmlns="http://www.w3.org/1999/
→ xhtml">
<head>
<title>Browser Detection</title>
<script src="javascripts/
→ <?=$javascript_file ?>"
→ type="text/javascript"
→ language="Javascript">
</script>
</head>
<body>
```

Using this system, you can tailor the JavaScript according to what the user's Web browser specifically supports. The value that phpSniff returns for the *javascript* property dictates the file used, which PHP will enter here.

continues on page 284

Script 7.2 Using the phpSniff class as its base, this script will determine some of the client's Web browser settings and report or act on them accordingly.

```
1    <?php
2
3    // Include the class files.
4    if (!defined('_PHP_SNIFF_INCLUDED')) {
5        require_once ('classes/phpSniff-2.0.2-class.php');
6    }
7
8    // Create a new object.
9    $browser = new phpSniff ();
10   $browser->_check_cookies = TRUE; // Check for cookies.
11   $browser->init();
12
13   switch ($browser->property('javascript')) {
14       case "1.1":
15           $javascript_file = 'javascript1.js';
16           break;
17       case "1.2":
18           $javascript_file = 'javascript2.js';
19           break;
20       case "1.3":
21           $javascript_file = 'javascript3.js';
22           break;
23       default:
24           $javascript_file = 'javascript.js';
25           break;
26   }
27   ?>
28   <!DOCTYPE html PUBLIC "-//W3C//DTD XHTML 1.0 Transitional//EN"
29   "http://www.w3.org/TR/2000/REC-xhtml1-20000126/DTD/xhtml1-transitional.dtd">
30   <html xmlns="http://www.w3.org/1999/xhtml">
31   <head>
32       <title>Browser Detection</title>
33   <script src="javascripts/<?=$javascript_file ?>" type="text/javascript" language="Javascript">
34   </script>
35   </head>
36   <body>
37   <?php
38   echo 'Browser Type: ' . $browser->property('browser') . '<br></br>';
39   echo 'Browser Version: ' . $browser->property('version') . '<br></br>';;
40   echo 'Are Cookies Enabled? ';
41   echo $browser->property('cookies') ? 'Yes' : 'No';
42   echo '</body>
43   </html>';
44
45   unset ($browser);
46   ?>
```

10. Use PHP to print other values.

```php
<?php
echo 'Browser Type: ' . $browser->
→ property('browser') . '<br></br>';
echo 'Browser Version: ' .
→ $browser->property('version') .
→ '<br></br>';;
echo 'Are Cookies Enabled? ';
echo $browser->property('cookies') ?
→ 'Yes' : 'No';
echo '</body>
</html>';
```

You can look at how phpSniff operates to determine all of the possible properties. Here I am using *browser*, *version*, and *cookies* to see what application is being used (e.g., Internet Explorer or Netscape), the version (4.7 or 5.1), and whether are not cookies are enabled.

11. Delete the object and close the page.

```php
unset ($browser);
?>
```

12. Save the file as `determine_browser.php` and upload it to the Web server in the same directory as the `classes` folder.

13. Create the different JavaScript pages and place them within a `javascripts` directory. For our purposes here, I've just written files like **Script 7.3**.

Script 7.3 This JavaScript page is only for demonstration purposes. Applicable uses of the browser detection process would allow for each page to have JavaScript-specific functionality.

```
script
1    <!--
2    // JavaScript for JS 1.3 Browers
3    // -->
```

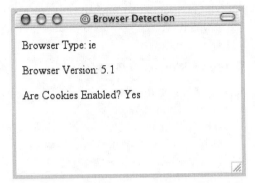

Figure 7.7 This is the result of using detect_browser.php with Internet Explorer 5.1.

Figure 7.8 The JavaScript page used for this page—however mundane it may currently be—will cater to the version of JavaScript supported by my browser.

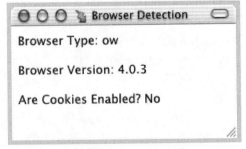

Figure 7.9 Using OmniWeb, a less common browser, has no effect on the accuracy of phpSniff.

Figure 7.10 Because OmniWeb only supports basic JavaScript, the default JavaScript file is included.

14. Test in your Web browser (**Figures 7.7** and **7.8**). If possible, test in multiple browsers (**Figures 7.9** and **7.10**).

✔ Tips

- The get_browser() function takes an optional user_agent parameter that sets what factor is used to determine browser. If you would like to use something other than the default $HTTP_USER_AGENT, you can set it here.

- Web browser detection can establish whether or not frames can be used—if the session name will not be stored in a cookie and therefore ought to be appended to each URL—and what platform the user is on. Understanding these values can allow you to better customize your site for enhanced viewing experience.

Accessing Other Web Sites with PHP

Even though PHP itself is normally used to create Web sites, it can also access and interact with Web pages on its own. This can be useful for retrieving information, writing spiders (applications that scour the Internet for particular data), and more. Surprisingly, you can access other Web sites in much the same way you would access a text file on your hard drive: by using fopen().

```
fopen ("http://www.dmcinsights.com/
→ phpadv/", "r");
```

The fopen() function used for opening files can also open Web pages because they are, after all, just files on a server. The parameters for using fopen() are the same (r, w, and a), although you will be limited to opening a file only for reading unless the file's permissions are open. One caveat, though, is that you must use a trailing slash after a directory because fopen() will not support redirects.

The above example and this one are fine:

```
fopen ("http://www.dmcinsights.com/
→ index.php", "r");
```

But this will fail:

```
fopen ("http://www.dmcinsights.com/
→ phpadv", "r");
```

Once you have opened a file, you can treat it as you otherwise would, using file(), fgets(), etc., to retrieve (or place) the data.

I'll demonstrate this by making use of Yahoo!'s financial pages to return New York Stock Exchange quotes for different stocks. Before proceeding, I should state that the legality of retrieving information from another Web site may be an issue you would want to investigate. Most sites

contain copyrighted information and the use of which without permission would be a violation.

To read a Web site with PHP:

1. Create a new PHP document in your text editor (**Script 7.4**).

```
<!DOCTYPE html PUBLIC "-//W3C//
→ DTD XHTML 1.0 Transitional//EN"
"http://www.w3.org/TR/2000/
→ REC-xhtml1-20000126/DTD/
→ xhtml1-transitional.dtd">
<html xmlns="http://www.w3.org/
→ 1999/xhtml">
<head>
<title>Get Stock Quotes</title>
</head>
<body>
```

2. Begin the PHP section by checking if the form has been submitted.

```
<?php
if (isset($HTTP_POST_VARS
→ ['submit'])) {
```

3. Confirm that a stock symbol was entered.

```
if (isset($HTTP_POST_VARS
→ ['symbol'])) {
```

4. Define the URL to be opened.

```
$url = 'http://quote.yahoo.com/d/
→ quotes.csv?s=' . $HTTP_POST_VARS
→ ['symbol'] . '&f=sl1d1t1c1ohgv
→ &e=.csv';
```

The most important consideration when accessing and reading other Web pages is to know exactly what data will be there and in what form. In other words, unless you are merely copying the entire contents of a file, you'll need to develop some system for gleaning the parts of the page you want based on how the data is structured.

continues on page 288

Script 7.4 The code in this example will retrieve stock quotes by opening up Yahoo!'s quote page and parsing the data therein.

```
1    <!DOCTYPE html PUBLIC "-//W3C//DTD XHTML 1.0 Transitional//EN"
2        "http://www.w3.org/TR/2000/REC-xhtml1-20000126/DTD/xhtml1-transitional.dtd">
3    <html xmlns="http://www.w3.org/1999/xhtml">
4    <head>
5        <title>Get Stock Quotes</title>
6    </head>
7    <body>
8    <?php
9    if (isset($HTTP_POST_VARS['submit'])) { // Handle the form.
10
11       if (isset($HTTP_POST_VARS['symbol'])) {
12
13           $url = 'http://quote.yahoo.com/d/quotes.csv?s=' . $HTTP_POST_VARS['symbol'] .
                 '&f=sl1d1t1c1ohgv&e=.csv';
14           $fp = fopen ($url, 'r') or die ('Cannot access Yahoo!.');
15           $read = fgetcsv ($fp, 30);
16           fclose ($fp);
17
18           echo '<div align="center">The current value for ' . $HTTP_POST_VARS["symbol"] . ' is
                 <b>$' . $read[1] . '</b>.</div><br></br>';
19
20       } else {
21           echo '<div align="center"><font color="red">Please enter a symbol before submitting the
                 form!</font></div><br></br>';
22       }
23   }
24   ?>
25   <form action="get_quote.php" method="post">
26   <table border="0" cellspacing="2" cellpadding="2" align="center">
27       <tr align="center" valign="top">
28           <td align="center" valign="top" colspan="2">Enter a NYSE stock symbol to get the latest
                 price:</td>
29       </tr>
30       <tr align="center" valign="top">
31           <td align="right" valign="top">Symbol:</td>
32           <td align="left" valign="top"><input type="text" name="symbol" size="5"
                 maxlength="5"></td>
33       </tr>
34       <tr>
35           <td align="center" valign="top" colspan="2"><input type="submit" name="submit"
                 value="Fetch the Quote!"></td>
36       </tr>
37   </table>
38   </form>
39   </body>
40   </html>
```

ACCESSING OTHER WEB SITES WITH PHP

In this example, a URL such as `http://quote.yahoo.com/d/quotes.csv?s=CSCO&f=sl1d1t1c1ohgv&e=.csv` returns the page in **Figure 7.11**. Once I know that this is a comma-delineated list of the: stock symbol, current value, date, time, change, low, high, asking price, volume, I can then retrieve exactly what I am looking for (in this case, the current value). More complex Web pages might require use of regular expressions to retrieve the particular pieces you want. You'll see an example of this in Chapter 8, PHP and the Server.

5. Open the Web page and read in the data.

```
$fp = fopen ($url, 'r') or die
→ ('Cannot access Yahoo!.');
$read = fgetcsv ($fp, 30);
fclose ($fp);
```

Now that the URL is defined, I can open the file for reading. Since I am looking to get only the current value, I just need to read in (`fgetcsv()`) the first 30 characters of the file. I use `fgetcsv()` as it will automatically turn the line it reads into an array, using commas as the delimiter. Then I close the file pointer. Note that if the URL was a proper HTML document (this one is not), the first 30 characters would be something like `<!DOCTYPE html PUBLIC "-//W3C/`.

6. Print the stock's value.

```
echo '<div align="center">The current
→ value for ' . $HTTP_POST_VARS
→ ["symbol"] . ' is <b>$' . $read[1]
→ . '</b>.</div><br></br>';
```

I take the information retrieved (e.g., "CSCO",11.43,"9/27/2001","3:11) and turn it into an array. The second element in the array is the current stock value.

7. Complete the `$HTTP_POST_VARS` `['symbol']` conditional.

```
} else {
```

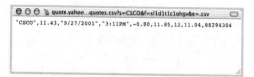

Figure 7.11 The URL, with all of the appended values that dictate formatting, returns one line of text, without any HTML code.

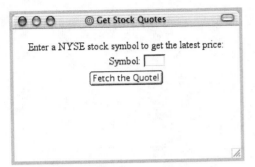

Figure 7.12 The form takes a stock symbol (NYSE only) and will return the current value of that stock (Figure 7.13).

Figure 7.13 The script has determined, by opening the Yahoo! page, that Cisco is currently at $11.47.

Figure 7.14 General Electric is worth $35.80.

```
echo '<div align="center"><font
→ color="red">Please enter a symbol
→ before submitting the
→ form!</font></div><br></br>';
}
```

8. Complete the `$HTTP_POST_VARS['submit']` conditional and the PHP section.

```
}
?>
```

9. Create the HTML form.

```
<form action="get_quote.php"
→ method="post">
<table border="0" cellspacing="2"
→ cellpadding="2" align="center">
<tr align="center" valign="top">
<td align="center" valign="top" col
→ span="2">Enter a NYSE stock symbol
→ to get the latest price:</td>
</tr>
<tr align="center" valign="top">
<td align="right" valign="top">
→ Symbol:</td>
<td align="left" valign="top"><input
→ type="text" name="symbol" size="5"
→ maxlength="5"></td>
</tr>
<tr>
<td align="center" valign="top"
→ colspan="2"><input type="submit"
→ name="submit" value="Fetch the
→ Quote!"></td>
</tr>
</table>
</form>
</body>
</html>
```

10. Save the file as get_quote.php, upload it to your server, and test in your Web browser (**Figures 7.12**, **7.13**, and **7.14**).

continues on next page

ACCESSING OTHER WEB SITES WITH PHP

✔ Tips

- Snoopy, a PHP class available at `http://snoopy.sourceforge.net` (**Figure 7.15**), allows you to do a lot of Web site-related things (like access particular parts of a frame-based site) with ease.

- The PEAR (PHP Extension and Application Repository) series of classes that come with PHP 4 have built-in code for dealing with the cURL (client URL) library (**Figure 7.16**), a tool for accessing sites via HTTP, FTP, and so forth.)

- With PHP you can also access Whois? servers (to find out if a domain name is available), newsgroups, and almost anything else that is online and publicly available.

Figure 7.15 Snoopy is a very advanced class for networking with PHP and may be worth your time to investigate.

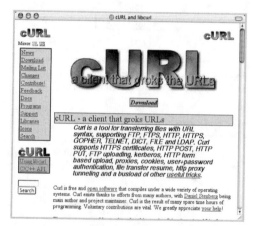

Figure 7.16 cURL is a library that's nearly limitless in its networking ability and support for cURL has grown in PHP 4. You can find out more at `http://curl.haxx.se`.

Using fsockopen()

The fopen() function is one way to access Web pages, but a more sophisticated method would be to use fsockopen(). This function opens sockets—a channel of communication—on a server.

```
$fp = fsockopen ("www.DMCinsights.com",
→ 80, &$errno, &$errstr, 30);
```

You use fsockopen() to establish a file pointer as you would use fopen(). The parameters the function takes are the URL, the port (here, 80), an error number variable, an error string variable, and the timeout. The last three arguments are optional. In layman's terms, a port is the door through which different protocols (methods of communication) go. For Web pages, the port is normally 80. The error number and string variables are interesting in that they are not really sent to the function (as they have no value initially) so much as they are returned by the function should an error occur. They ought to be passed by reference instead of by value because you are really sending the function an empty variable by that name and it is returning the updated version. Finally, the timeout simply states for how many seconds the function should try to connect.

Once the file has been successfully opened, you can again use fputs(), fgets(), and so forth to manipulate the data.

Another function I'll explain before writing the fsockopen() example is parse_url().

```
$url_pieces = parse_url ($url);
```

This function takes a URL and turns it into an associate array by breaking the structure into its parts. The primary pieces of the URL will be scheme, host, port, path, and query. For example:

```
$url_pieces = parse_url ("http://www.
→ dmcinsights.com/view.php?week=1");

echo $url_pieces["scheme"]; // http://

echo $url_pieces["host"];
→ // www.dmcinsights.com

echo $url_pieces["path"]; // /view.php

echo $url_pieces["query"]; // week=1
```

The parse_url() function can be handy in all sorts of instances. I'll demonstrate one example in the following script. The code developed below will run through a database of URLs and check each to make sure they are still valid.

continues on next page

USING FSOCKOPEN()

To use fsockopen():

1. Create a new HTML document in your text editor (**Script 7.5**):

```
<!DOCTYPE html PUBLIC "-//W3C//DTD
→ XHTML 1.0 Transitional//EN"
"http://www.w3.org/TR/2000/
→ REC-xhtml1-20000126/DTD/
→ xhtml1-transitional.dtd">
<html xmlns="http://www.w3.org/1999/
→ xhtml">
<head>
<title>Validate URLs</title>
</head>
<body>
```

2. Create the PHP section and include the configuration file.

```
<?php
require_once ("../../../config.inc");
```

Since I'll need to access the database to retrieve the URLs, I must use the config.inc file, which connects to the database. I assume you've already written your own appropriate config.inc, like the one in Chapter 5, Developing Web Applications.

3. Define the check_url() function.

```
function check_url ($url) {
```

4. Parse the URL.

```
$url_pieces = parse_url ($url);
$path = ($url_pieces['path']) ?
→ $url_pieces['path'] :  "/";
```

```
$port = ($url_pieces['port']) ?
→ $url_pieces['port'] : 80;
```

I want to make sure that I've got the right path and port when testing the connection later on so I first break the URL down into its parts. Then I set the $path variable to be either the existing path, if any, or a slash, as the default. The same treatment is given to the $port, although the default will be 80.

5. Attempt to connect using fsockopen().

```
if ($fp = fsockopen ($url_pieces
→ ['host'], $port, &$errno,
→ &$errstr, 5)) {
```

6. If a connection is established, place some data in the file.

```
fputs ($fp, "HEAD $path
→ HTTP/1.1\r\n\r\n");
fputs($fp, "HOST:
→ $url_pieces[host]\r\n");
fputs($fp, "CONNECTION:
→ close\r\n\r\n");
```

These lines may seem confusing, but what they are essentially doing is sending a simple HTTP header to the file to initiate communication.

7. Retrieve and return the response code.

```
$data = fgets ($fp,128);
fclose($fp);
$array = explode (" ", $data);
return $array[1];
```

continues on page 294

Script 7.5 The check_urls() function, defined here, will try to access a URL and will return either the status code or the fsockopen() error message.

```
1    <!DOCTYPE html PUBLIC "-//W3C//DTD XHTML 1.0 Transitional//EN"
2        "http://www.w3.org/TR/2000/REC-xhtml1-20000126/DTD/xhtml1-transitional.dtd">
3    <html xmlns="http://www.w3.org/1999/xhtml">
4    <head>
5        <title>Validate URLs</title>
6    </head>
7    <body>
8    <?php
9
10   // Include the configuration file.
11   require_once ("../../../config.inc");
12
13   // This function will try to connect to a URL.
14   function check_url ($url) {
15
16       // Break the URL down into its parts.
17       $url_pieces = parse_url ($url);
18       $path = ($url_pieces['path']) ? $url_pieces['path'] :  "/";
19       $port = ($url_pieces['port']) ? $url_pieces['port'] : 80;
20
21       // Connect.
22       if ($fp = fsockopen ($url_pieces['host'], $port, &$errno, &$errstr, 5)) {
23
24           fputs ($fp, "HEAD $path HTTP/1.1\r\n\r\n");
25           fputs($fp, "HOST: $url_pieces[host]\r\n");
26           fputs($fp, "CONNECTION: close\n\n\r\n");
27           $data = fgets ($fp,128);
28           fclose($fp);
29           $array = explode (" ", $data);
30           return $array[1]; // Return the HTTP code.
31
32       } else {
33           return "$errstr ($errno)"; // Return the error message.
34       }
35
36   }
37
38   // Query the database.
39   $query = "select * from php_links order by id";
40   $query_result = mysql_query ($query, $db_connection);
41
42   // Create a table.
43   echo '<table border="1" cellspacing="2" cellpadding="2" align="center">';
44   echo '<tr><td align="left"><b>Site Name</b></td><td align="left"><b>URL</b></td><td
     align="left"><b>HTTP Code</b></td></tr>';
45
46   // Check each URL.
47   while ($row = mysql_fetch_object ($query_result)) {
48       $check = check_url ($row->url);
49       echo '<tr><td align="left">' . $row->name . '</td><td align="left"><a href="'. $row->url . '"
         target="_new">' . $row->url . '</a></td><td align="left">' . $check . '</td></tr>';
50   }
51   ?>
52   </table>
53   </body>
54   </html>
```

Once the URL has been hit with a header it will respond with its own http headers. The code will read in the first 128 characters of the response, then break this down into an array. The second element returned will be the HTTP code. **Table 7.1** lists some of the possible response codes.

8. Finish the conditional and the function.

```
} else {
return "$errstr ($errno)";
}
}
```

If a socket connection was not made, the returned error message and number will be sent back from the check_urls() function.

9. Run the database query and check each URL, printing the result.

```
$query = "select * from php_links
→ order by id";
$query_result = mysql_query ($query,
→ $db_connection);
echo '<table border="1"
→ cellspacing="2" cellpadding="2"
→ align="center">';
echo '<tr><td align="left"><b>Site
→ Name</b></td><td align="left">
→ <b>URL</b></td><td align="left">
→ <b>HTTP Code</b></td></tr>';
while ($row = mysql_fetch_object
→ ($query_result)) {
$check = check_url ($row->url);
echo '<tr><td align="left">' .
→ $row->name . '</td><td align=
→ "left"><a href="'. $row->url . '"
→ target="_new">' . $row->url .
→ '</a></td><td align="left">' .
→ $check . '</td></tr>';
}
```

Table 7.1 I've broken down the bulk of the HTTP status codes into this table. In sum, 200s and 300s are good, 400s and 500s are bad.

HTTP Status Codes	
CODE	**MEANING**
2xx	OK
3xx	Redirected successfully
400	Bad request
401	Unauthorized
403	Forbidden
404	File not found
5xx	Miscellaneous errors

USING FSOCKOPEN()

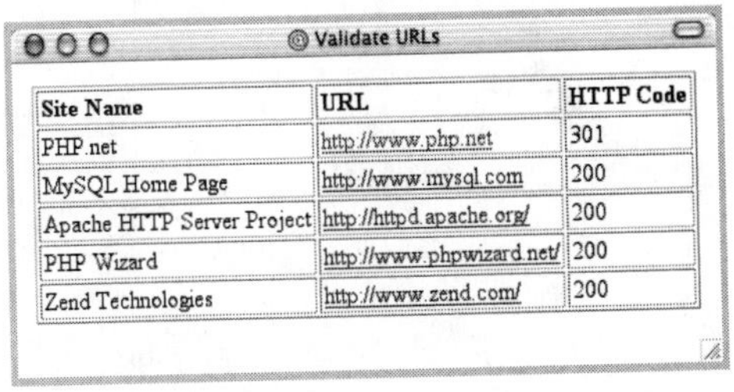

Site Name	URL	HTTP Code
PHP.net	http://www.php.net	301
MySQL Home Page	http://www.mysql.com	200
Apache HTTP Server Project	http://httpd.apache.org/	200
PHP Wizard	http://www.phpwizard.net/	200
Zend Technologies	http://www.zend.com/	200

Figure 7.17 Each of the URLs that I ran through the first trial returned a good status.

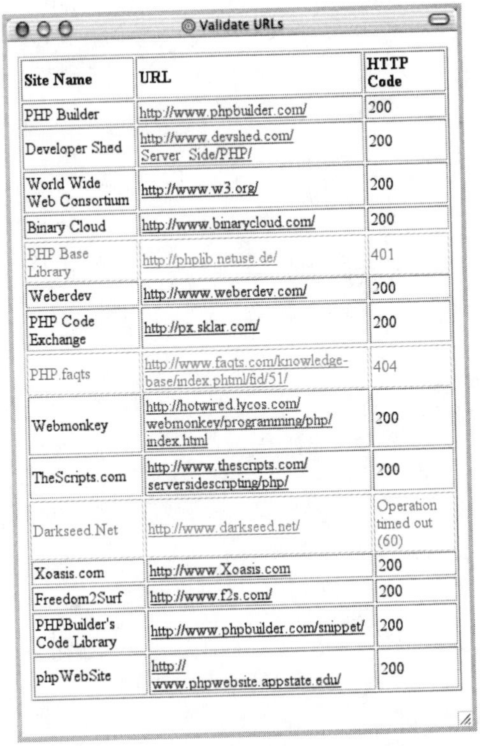

Site Name	URL	HTTP Code
PHP Builder	http://www.phpbuilder.com/	200
Developer Shed	http://www.devshed.com/Server_Side/PHP/	200
World Wide Web Consortium	http://www.w3.org/	200
Binary Cloud	http://www.binarycloud.com/	200
PHP Base Library	http://phplib.netuse.de/	401
Weberdev	http://www.weberdev.com/	200
PHP Code Exchange	http://px.sklar.com/	200
PHP.faqts	http://www.faqts.com/knowledge-base/index.phtml/fid/51/	404
Webmonkey	http://hotwired.lycos.com/webmonkey/programming/php/index.html	200
TheScripts.com	http://www.thescripts.com/serversidescripting/php/	200
Darkseed.Net	http://www.darkseed.net/	Operation timed out (60)
Xoasis.com	http://www.Xoasis.com	200
Freedom2Surf	http://www.f2s.com/	200
PHPBuilder's Code Library	http://www.phpbuilder.com/snippet/	200
phpWebSite	http://www.phpwebsite.appstate.edu/	200

Figure 7.18 These 15 URLs had varied responses. One timed out and two others had negative codes in the 400s.

10. Finish the PHP and the HTML.

```
?>
</table>
</body>
</html>
```

11. Save the file as `check_urls.php`, upload it to your server, and test in your Web browser (**Figures 7.17** and **7.18**).

✔ Tips

- If you have need to find out either the IP address or the host name of a Web site, use the corresponding `gethostbyaddr()` and `gethostbyname()` functions. The former will return the name if provided an IP address and the latter will do just the opposite.
- If a URL might be on multiple servers, the `gethostbynamel()` function returns all the possible IP addresses. You can then check one or every IP.

PHP AND THE SERVER

Most of the exercises in the first six chapters have taken advantage of PHP's capability to dynamically generate Web content. Chapter 7, Networking With PHP, added some more behind-the-scenes features of the language. Continuing along this vein, there are a plethora of possibilities when it comes to PHP interacting with the server itself.

A lot of very standard PHP actions, such as communicating with databases and sending emails, actually occur between applications on the server and PHP. Of course, the most important server-side process is the relationship between the Web server application (Apache or IIS) and PHP itself. If you are using a CGI version of PHP, then PHP is simply an application that is called by the Web server whenever it encounters the appropriate content. (The other version of PHP, the module, is built into the server and acts as an extension of that application.)

As PHP is increasingly used for advanced applications and not simply to generate Web content, its ability to manipulate and use the services the server has to offer becomes more important. In fact, PHP 4's support for using Component Object Model (COM) on Windows—which you'll use in this chapter—plugs one of the last gaps between ASP (Active Server Pages, frequently written in Microsoft Visual Basic) and PHP.

This chapter will show you how to better take advantage of the other services and applications that your server may already be running. In this chapter, you will learn how to have PHP scripts automatically executed, compress files, and use COM technology. Two of the examples in this chapter will be operating system-specific, with the focus being on the Unix (including Linux and Mac OS X) and Windows (98, Me, NT, 2000) families.

This script simply sends an email message to every registered user. It assumes that a configuration file exists with the database access information and that there is a table called *users* that contains a field *email*. There is nothing here that would count as new or advanced PHP knowledge (hopefully).

One thing to note is that because this script will not be viewed by anyone (it will be run automatically by the server) there's no need to include the HTML, echo statements, etc. I've left those in here as I'll probably view it once or twice in my Web browser first to make sure the script works properly. There's no harm in writing this script either as a standard Web page (like I've done) or as a minimalist PHP script (without the HTML, etc.).

2. Save the file as `cron.php` and upload it to your server. It must be stored within the Web document root because it will be accessed by a Web browser (namely Wget).

Now that the script itself exists, you can have cron execute it. First you'll write a dummy *cronjob* file, then add this to the actual crontab.

3. Create a new document in your text editor (**Script 8.2**).

```
1 0 * * 5 wget http://www.
→ DMCinsights.com/cron.php >
→ /dev/null
```

Make sure you press Enter/Return once at the end of the line. The Wget application will attempt to save the file to the disk, so the use of `> /dev/null` will nullify this effect. Also, Wget does not spawn a new browser with each use as Lynx does, which is why I'm using, it but it really does not matter one way or the other.

Script 8.2 This line will add the task defined in cronjob1 to the crontab file.

```
1    0 * * 5 wget http://www.DMCinsights.com/
     |cron.php > /dev/null
```

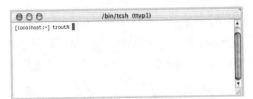

Figure 8.1 Use a command-line interface to work with cron and crontab.

Figure 8.2 This line will add the task defined in cronjob1 to the crontab file.

Figure 8.3 The command `crontab -l` will allow you to view the current cron information, but you should not make changes in this file.

4. Save this file as `cronjob1` (without any extension) and upload it to the server in a convenient location (not necessarily within the Web document root).

5. Access your server via a command-line interface (**Figure 8.1**).

6. Enter the following code and then press Enter/Return once:

`crontab /path/to/cronjob1`

In my example (**Figure 8.2**), cronjob1 is stored on the desktop of user *trout*. The path is `/Users/trout/Desktop/cronjob1`. Replace that part of the code with the applicable location of your `cronjob1` file on the server.

7. Confirm the cron task list by viewing the crontab file. Enter this code at the command line, then press Enter/Return once:

`crontab -l`

This command will show you all the relevant crontab information (**Figure 8.3**): what file was installed and when, the version of cron running, and the task itself.

continues on next page

The unfortunate fact regarding this example is that you will not know for sure that it worked until 1 a.m. on Friday. If you are looking for more immediate gratification, try this first:

8. Open cron.php (Script 8.1) in your text editor.

9. Add the following line just before the mail() function (**Script 8.3**):

$email = 'you@enteryouraddress.com';

Now, although the script will still retrieve all of the email addresses, it will actually email only you (assuming you put your email address there instead).

10. Open cronjob1 (Script 8.2) in your text editor.

11. Change the first and only line and save the file as cronjob2 (**Script 8.4**):

0 * * * * wget http://www.
→ DMCinsights.com/cron_test.php >
→ /dev/null

Now the cron will be run every hour on the hour (turn the first value into an asterisk to be deluged with emails every minute).

12. Save both files and upload them again to your server.

Script 8.3 I've modified Script 8.1 so that I can test it more immediately.

```
1   <!DOCTYPE html PUBLIC "-//W3C//DTD XHTML
    1.0 Transitional//EN"
2       "http://www.w3.org/TR/2000/
        REC-xhtml1-20000126/DTD/xhtml1-
        transitional.dtd">
3   <html xmlns="http://www.w3.org/
    1999/xhtml">
4   <head>
5       <title>Email Notice</title>
6   </head>
7   <body>
8   <?php
9
10  require_once ("../config.inc");
11
12  $query = "select email from users";
13  $query_db = mysql_query ($query,
    $db_connection);
14
15  while ($data = mysql_
    fetch_array($query_db)) {
16
17      $email .= $data[0] . ', ';
18  }
19
20  $subject = "Your Weekly Update";
21
22  $body = "Things you ought to know:
23  Blah
24  Blah
25  Blah
26
27  Sincerely,
28  The Web People";
29
30  echo "$email <br></br>$subject<br></br>
    <pre>$body</pre><br></br>Result: ";
31  $email = you@enteryouraddress.com';
32  echo mail ($email, $subject, $body,
    "From: webmaster@site.com");
33  ?>
34  </body>
35  </html>
```

Script 8.4 The new cronjob2 file will call cron_test.php every hour on the hour.

```
1   0 * * * * wget http://www.DMCinsights.
    com/cron test.php > /dev/null
```

Figure 8.4 Use `crontab -r` to clear cron's memory.

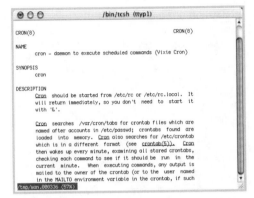

Figure 8.5 The cron manual explains how it works in greater detail than I have here.

13. Clear the current cron memory (**Figure 8.4**).

`crontab -r`

14. Enter the new cron.

`crontab /path/to/cronjob2`

Once you are satisfied with how it works, clear the cron's memory again and reapply the original—or some new—job.

✔ Tips

■ To see more information about using cron, type `man cron` in the command line (**Figure 8.5**). You can also view `man crontab` and `man 5 crontab`.

■ The PHP example demonstrated here is the kind of thing that used to be, and one could argue is more naturally, accomplished using Perl. But if you do not know Perl or would prefer to stay within the PHP world, now you have a viable option.

■ Because cron runs from memory, not by rechecking the crontab file, you must enter `crontab -r` to clear a job (in fact, all the jobs) from cron. You cannot add more tasks or edit existing ones merely by altering the crontab file after typing `crontab -l`. You could, however, edit the crontab file using `crontab -e`.

Executing a PHP Script

Depending on your PHP and server configuration, you can make a PHP file executable. This option is a more direct way of having PHP scripts run automatically, without the use of the server's Web browser. To make your PHP script executable you must be running a CGI version of PHP, not a Web server module (again, this is within the Unix family of operating systems).

Assuming that you have a CGI version of PHP installed, the first step is to make your PHP script look more like its Perl brethren by adding the following line to the top of the code:

```
#!/path/to/php
```

Perl scripts that are meant to be executable begin with (assuming the Perl binary is in the /usr/local/bin directory):

```
#!/usr/local/bin/perl
```

Thus, your PHP script will be, as an example:

```
#!/usr/local/bin/php
<?php
// Normal PHP script.
?>
```

To find where the PHP binary is installed, run this command:

```
find / -name 'php'
```

In the end you will probably discover PHP installed in a bin or sbin folder (since the *bin* stands for *binary*, i.e., an application).

Once you've modified your PHP script accordingly, you must then store the file on your server, outside of the Web document root. This file will not, nor should not, be accessible via a Web browser.

Finally, change the permissions on the file to either 333 or 777 (universal read-execute or universal read-write-execute). The file will need to be readable and executable by all categories of user. Thus the permissions are *2* (read) plus *1* (execute) plus an optional *4* (write) for owner, group, others. This wide-open permission scheme is why the file should not be available via HTTP (i.e., the Web browser).

Save this file as `php_script.php` or whatever name you would like to give it. Now go through the same steps as the example in this section to add the task to the crontab file. Assuming you have stored this file in /home/username, then cronjob1 would look like so:

```
1 0 * * 5 /home/username/php_script.php
```

Figure 8.6 The zlib library adds compression capability to your server (and therefore PHP).

Compressing Files with PHP

Most users are familiar with client-based GUI compression utilities such as WinZip or StuffIt, which will compress and decompress files. Thanks to the zlib, available from `www.gzip.org/zlib` (**Figure 8.6**), you can have PHP automatically compress files as well. The zlib library was written by two of the major compression/decompression developers as a patent-free, lossless data-compression tool. Zlib is available on every major platform (even for Palm handhelds!) and is frequently built into a server's configuration. I would be surprised if a Unix-brand of operating system did not include zlib, and you can use a Dynamic Link Library (DLL) version of the library on Windows.

Once zlib is installed, you can use it to compress or decompress files (using `gzcompress()` and `gzuncompress()`), but in this example I'll have PHP create a compressed file on the fly. The PHP script itself will retrieve all of the data stored in a database and will create files listing said data in tab-delineated format.

To compress a file:

1. Start with an HTML header as part of a new PHP document (**Script 8.5**).

   ```
   <!DOCTYPE html PUBLIC "-//W3C//DTD
   → XHTML 1.0 Strict//EN"
   "http://www.w3.org/TR/2000/
   → REC-xhtml1-20000126/DTD/
   → xhtml1-strict.dtd">
   <html xmlns="http://www.w3.org/
   → 1999/xhtml">
   <head>
   <title>Database Backup</title>
   </head>
   <body>
   ```

2. Begin the PHP section and include the configuration file.

   ```
   <?php
   require_once ('../config.inc');
   ```

   The config.inc file stores my database information safely out of the Web document structure.

3. Define and submit the query.

   ```
   $query = "show tables";
   $query_result = mysql_query ($query,
   → $db_connection);
   ```

   Assuming that a database has already been selected (using mysql_select_db()), this query will return a list of every table in that database.

4. Loop through the query result.

   ```
   while ($row = mysql_fetch_array
   → ($query_result)) {
   ```

5. Define and open the file.

   ```
   $filename = "../backup/$row[0]_" .
   → time() . ".txt.gz";
   $fp = gzopen ($filename, 'w9');
   ```

Script 8.5 This very useful script will back up a database, table by table, to a compressed, tab-delineated text file.

```
1    <!DOCTYPE html PUBLIC "-//W3C//DTD XHTML
     1.0 Strict//EN"
2    "http://www.w3.org/TR/2000/REC-xhtml1-
     20000126/DTD/xhtml1-strict.dtd">
3    <html xmlns="http://www.w3.org/
     1999/xhtml">
4    <head>
5        <title>Database Backup</title>
6    </head>
7    <body>
8    <?php
9    // This page will back up all the data in
     a database to a compressed text file.
10
11   require_once ('../config.inc');
12
13   $query = "show tables";
14   $query_result = mysql_query ($query,
     $db_connection);
15   while ($row = mysql_fetch_array
     ($query_result)) {
16
17       $filename = "../backup/$row[0]_" .
         time() . ".txt.gz"; // Identify the
         filenameœone per table.
18       $fp = gzopen ($filename, 'w9'); //
         Open the file.
19
20       $query1 = "select * from $row[0]";
21       $query_result1 = mysql_query
         ($query1, $db_connection);
22
23       while ($row1 = mysql_fetch_row
         ($query_result1)) { // Retrieve each
         row in the table.
24
25           foreach ($row1 as $key =>
             $value) {
26               gzwrite ($fp, "'$value'\t");
                 // Write the data as a tab-
                 delineated row.
27           }
28           gzwrite ($fp, "\n"); // Add a new
             line to each row.
29       }
30
31       gzclose ($fp); // Close the file.
32
33       echo "Table $row[0] Backed Up
     <br></br>\n"; // Print the success.
34   }
35   ?>
36   </body>
37   </html>
```

Each table will be backed up to its own file, the name of which is derived from the table name ($row[0]), the current time stamp, and a .txt.gz extension. All of the files will be written to a backup folder, which must have open permissions on it.

The gzopen() function takes two parameters: the filename and the mode of opening. The modes correspond directly to fopen()'s modes (*w*, *r*, *a* along with *b* for writing binary data) but can also indicate a level of compression, 9 being a reasonable value in this case. The acceptable compression levels are on a scale from 1 (minimal compression) to 9 (maximum) with a trade-off between compression and performance. For relatively small files like these text documents, maximum compression is fine.

6. Retrieve all of the table's data, and write it to the file.

```
$query1 = "select * from $row[0]";
$query_result1 = mysql_query
→ ($query1, $db_connection);
while ($row1 = mysql_fetch_row
→ ($query_result1)) {
foreach ($row1 as $key => $value) {
gzwrite ($fp, "'$value'\t"); }
gzwrite ($fp, "\n");
}
```

This loop will take every row out of the table and write that to a text file in the format 'VALUE'[TAB]. Instead of using the fwrite() function that you are familiar with, you have gzwrite(), which works just the same.

continues on next page

7. Close the file and print a message to the browser.

```
gzclose ($fp);
echo "Table $row[0] Backed Up
→ <br></br>\n";
```

8. Close the main loop, the PHP, and the HTML.

```
}
?>
</body>
</html>
```

9. Save the file as backup_db.php, upload it to your server, and test in your Web browser (**Figures 8.7** and **8.8**). Do not forget to create the backup folder with 777 permissions.

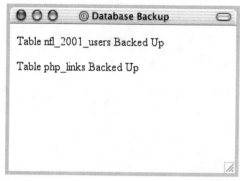

Figure 8.7 The browser will display what tables were backed up by the backup_db.php script.

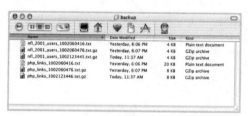

Figure 8.8 The script has created compressed backup files of the database and stored them in the backup folder.

Script 8.6 To tell how much impact compression has on the file size, rewrite Script 8.5 like so.

```
1    <!DOCTYPE html PUBLIC "-//W3C//DTD XHTML
     1.0 Strict//EN"
2         "http://www.w3.org/TR/2000/
          REC-xhtml1-20000126/DTD/xhtml1-
          strict.dtd">
3    <html xmlns="http://www.w3.org/
     1999/xhtml">
4    <head>
5        <title>Database Backup</title>
6    </head>
7    <body>
8    <?php
9    // This page will back up all the data in
     a database to a compressed text file.
10
11   require_once ('../config.inc');
12
13   $query = "show tables";
14   $query_result = mysql_query ($query,
     $db_connection);
15   while ($row = mysql_fetch_array
     ($query_result)) {
16
17       $filename = "../backup/$row[0]_" .
         time() . ".txt"; // Identify the
         filename—one per table.
18       $fp = fopen ($filename, 'w9'); //
         Open the file.
19
20       $query1 = "select * from $row[0]";
21       $query_result1 = mysql_query
         ($query1, $db_connection);
22
23       while ($row1 = mysql_fetch_row
         ($query_result1)) { // Retrieve each
         row in the table.
24
25           foreach ($row1 as $key =>
             $value) {
26               fwrite ($fp, "'$value'\t");
                 // Write the data as a tab-
                 delineated row.
27           }
28           fwrite ($fp, "\n"); // Add a new
             line to each row.
29       }
30
31       fclose ($fp); // Close the file.
32
33       echo "Table $row[0] Backed Up
         <br></br>\n"; // Print the success.
34   }
35   ?>
36   </body>
37   </html>
```

✔ Tips

■ This quick and dirty backup script turns an entire database into a few text files. Because their filenames are derived partially from a time stamp, you will always be able to see which is the most recent copy. A tab-delineated file can always be used later to restore the data in a database, should a problem occur.

■ The backup_db.php file would be an excellent candidate for routinely calling from a cron. You could even add a line so that the files are automatically emailed to you, ensuring that the database information is backed up offline.

■ To see the effect that compression has on your file, rewrite backup_db.php to use fopen(), fwrite(), and fclose() instead (**Script 8.6**). On one table that contained about 150 rows of 6 columns each, the compressed file was 40 percent of the size of the noncompressed form.

Using COM with PHP

New to PHP 4 is support for COM on Windows operating systems. COM, which stands for Component Object Module, is a technology developed by Microsoft to control its applications via a programming language, notably Visual Basic. It is related to other Microsoft systems such as OLE (Object Linking and Embedding) and ActiveX.

Microsoft has defined every function and attribute that an application—such as Word or Excel—has as an object with methods and properties. Using the proper notation you can then control the application with Visual Basic or, in your case, PHP. You begin by creating a new object using the name of the application and PHP's com() function.

```
$word = new COM("word.application");
```

You can set the application to run either visibly on the server or invisibly by setting the *Visible* value (this step is not required).

```
$word->Visible = 1; // Visible
```

Once the application is running, you begin by creating a new document.

```
$word->Documents->Add();
```

Now, in the case of a Word document, you can start adding text to the page.

```
$word->Selection->TypeText
↦ ("mmmm...COM....");
```

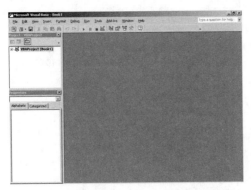

Figure 8.9 The Visual Basic Editor, part of Microsoft Office, may be your most useful tool when using PHP with COM.

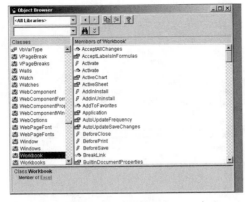

Figure 8.10 The Visual Basic Object Browser is a great reference for the possible objects, methods, and attributes available.

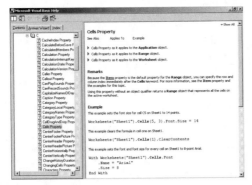

Figure 8.11 The Visual Basic Help application has a lot of information for doing different things in an application via a COM interface.

Finally, save the document and quit Word.

```
$word->Documents[1]->SaveAs("com.doc");
```

```
$word->Quit();
```

Accessing COM with PHP is fairly simple and direct; the most complicated issue will be understanding what objects are available in an application and how exactly you should refer to them. You have several options. The first would be to pick up a book that covers COM for the specific application you are using. The second solution is to learn Visual Basic, which will help with knowing the different objects available. The third possibility is to use the Visual Basic Help aspect of the application itself.

Once you have opened the application, press ALT + F11 to bring up the Visual Basic editor (**Figure 8.9**). Then press F2 to view the Object Browser (**Figure 8.10**). By clicking and viewing the different elements in the Object Browser, you can see how the different objects, methods, and attributes you'll need relate. To get a jump-start on understanding COM for an application, use the Visual Basic Help application (**Figure 8.11**).

As an example of using COM technology with PHP, I'll write a script that downloads URLs from Yahoo!, then stores them in an Excel spreadsheet on the server.

To use COM with PHP:

1. Create a new PHP document in your text editor, beginning with the HTML header (**Script 8.7**).

```
<!DOCTYPE html PUBLIC "-//W3C//DTD
→ XHTML 1.0 Strict//EN"
"http://www.w3.org/TR/2000/
→ REC-xhtml1-20000126/DTD/xhtml1-
→ strict.dtd">
<html xmlns="http://www.w3.org/
→ 1999/xhtml">
<head>
<title>Excel COM</title>
</head>
<body>
```

2. Start the PHP script.

```
<?php
```

3. Increase the allowable time limit for script execution.

```
set_time_limit(90);
```

The set_time_limit() function determines, in seconds, at what point the script has taken too long. Because this script will need to open, write to, save from, and quit an application, the default time limit—probably 30 seconds, depending on the setting in your php.ini file—needs to be increased. A minute and a half should be adequate, but there would also be little harm in doubling or tripling that value, depending on the complexity of the script.

continues on page 314

Script 8.7 This script will retrieve URLs from a Web page and store them in an Excel spreadsheet, using PHP 4's COM functions.

```
1   <!DOCTYPE html PUBLIC "-//W3C//DTD XHTML 1.0 Strict//EN"
2       "http://www.w3.org/TR/2000/REC-xhtml1-20000126/DTD/xhtml1-strict.dtd">
3   <html xmlns="http://www.w3.org/1999/xhtml">
4   <head>
5       <title>Excel COM</title>
6   </head>
7   <body>
8   <?php
9
10  // This page retrieves URLs from a Web site and stores them in an Excel file.
11
12  set_time_limit(90); // Increase the PHP time limit.
13
14  $excel = new COM ("excel.application") or die ("Cannot start Excel for you.");
15
16  echo "Loaded Excel Version $excel->Version<br></br>\n";
17
18  $excel->Visible = 0; // Don't show the application.
19
20  $workbook = $excel->Workbooks->Add(); // Create a new workbook.
21  $worksheet = $workbook->Worksheets("Sheet1");
22  $worksheet->Activate; // Activate the top worksheet.
23
```

(script continues on next page)

Script 8.7 *continued*

```
                              script
24   // Now retrieve the URLs.
25   $url = "http://dir.yahoo.com/Computers_and_Internet/Programming_Languages/Python/";
26   $fp = fopen ($url, 'r') or die ("Cannot get through to Yahoo!"); // Open the URL.
27
28   // Some formatting stuff.
29   echo "<pre>";
30   $pattern = "[0-9]+/\*http://(.+)\">(.+)</a>(.+)"; // The regex pattern to match.
31
32   while ($one_line = fgets ($fp, 1024)) { // Fetch every line.
33
34       if (eregi ($pattern, $one_line, $urls)) {
35
36           $n++; // Counter.
37
38           // Select and activate each cell.
39           $cell = $worksheet->Cells($n,1);
40           $cell->Activate;
41           $cell->Value = $urls[1];
42           $cell = $worksheet->Cells($n,2);
43           $cell->Activate;
44           $cell->Value = $urls[2];
45           $cell = $worksheet->Cells($n,3);
46           $cell->Activate;
47           $cell->Value = substr ($urls[3], 3, strlen($urls[3]));
48
49           // Print the result.
50           echo "$n $urls[1] $urls[2] " . substr ($urls[3], 3, strlen($urls[3]));
51           echo "<p></p>";
52
53       }
54
55   } // Close the while loop
56
57   // Close the file and the formatting.
58   echo "</pre><br></br>";
59   fclose ($fp);
60
61   // Save the spreadsheet and quit Excel.
62   $workbook->SaveAs('C:\files\urls.xls');
63   $excel->Quit();
64
65   // Delete every object.
66   unset ($cell);
67   unset ($worksheet);
68   unset ($workbook);
69   unset ($excel);
70   ?>
71   </body>
72   </html>
```

USING COM WITH PHP

4. Create an instance of the COM object.

```
$excel = new COM ("excel.application")
→ or die ("Cannot start Excel for
→ you.");
echo "Loaded Excel Version
→ $excel->Version<br></br>\n";
$excel->Visible = 0;
```

You may need to change the name of the application if your system has trouble with *excel.application*. (I am running this script on a server with Windows 2000 and Office XP.) Just for the heck of it, I'm going to print the version of Excel loaded to the Web browser so that I know it's working but I'll make the whole process (of opening and using Excel) invisible so that it runs in the background.

It may function differently on your server, but in my case, each call of new COM will open up a new copy of that application, so be careful not to overburden the server when using COM.

5. Create a new workbook and worksheet.

```
$workbook = $excel->Workbooks->Add();
$worksheet = $workbook->Worksheets
→ ("Sheet1");
$worksheet->Activate;
```

These lines are what the application will essentially do on its own when you open it up: create a workbook containing one worksheet called Sheet1, which is the active worksheet by default.

6. Retrieve the URLs from Yahoo!.

```
$url = "http://dir.yahoo.com/
→ Computers_and_Internet/
→ Programming_Languages/Python/";
$fp = fopen ($url, 'r') or die
→ ("Cannot get through to Yahoo!");
echo "<pre>";
$pattern = "[0-9]+/\*http://(.+)\">
→ (.+)</a>(.+)";
while ($one_line = fgets ($fp,
→ 1024)) {
if (eregi ($pattern, $one_line,
→ $urls)) {
```

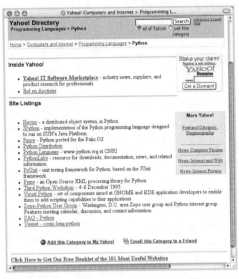

Figure 8.12 This is the Yahoo! page that I will be parsing for URLs.

For this example, I'll generate a file of links related to the Python programming language, which Yahoo! keeps organized at `http://dir.yahoo.com/Computers_and_Internet/Programming_Languages/Python` (**Figure 8.12**). (Yahoo! currently does not have a page dedicated to PHP, which is strange.)

I'm going to go through the page, line by line, fetching every appropriate URL. The pattern defined correlates to how this particular page lists each item (**Script 8.8** shows a clip of the page source). If my pattern is found, the matched part will be stored in the `$urls` array.

continues on next page

Script 8.8 The source code for the page I will be accessing helps me understand what pattern I should be using in my regular expressions.

```
script
1    <li><a href="http://srd.yahoo.com/drst/2298437/*http://www.python.org/workshops/1996-
     06/papers/d.arnold/paper.html">Hector</a> - a distributed object system, in Python.
2    <li><a href="http://srd.yahoo.com/drst/12733902/*http://www.jpython.org/">JPython</a> -
     implementation of the Python programming language designed to run on SUN's Java Platform.
3    <li><a href="http://srd.yahoo.com/drst/39855194/*http://www.endeavors.com/pippy/">Pippy</a> -
     Python ported for the Palm OS.
4    <li><a href="http://srd.yahoo.com/drst/79885/*http://www.cwi.nl/ftp/python/">Python
     Distribution</a>
5    <li><a href="http://srd.yahoo.com/drst/79886/*http://www.python.org/">Python Language</a> -
     www.python.org at CNRI
6    <li><a href="http://srd.yahoo.com/drst/35254779/*http://www.pythonlabs.com/">PythonLabs</a> -
     resource for downloads, documentation, news, and related information.
7    <li><a href="http://srd.yahoo.com/drst/30512084/*http://pyunit.sourceforge.net/">PyUnit</a> -
     unit testing framework for Python, based on the JUnit framework.
8    <li><a href="http://srd.yahoo.com/drst/27361825/*http://www.digitome.com/pyxie.html">Pyxie</a>
     - an Open Source XML processing library for Python.
9    <li><a href="http://srd.yahoo.com/drst/79893/*http://www.python.org/workshops/1995-12/">Third
     Python Workshop</a> - 4-6 December 1995
10   <li><a href="http://srd.yahoo.com/drst/30972132/*http://www.thekompany.com/projects/vp/">Visual
     Python</a> - set of components aimed at GNOME and KDE application developers to enable them to
     add scripting capabilities to their applications.
11   <li><a href="http://srd.yahoo.com/drst/45444126/*http://www.zpug.org/">Zope-Python User
     Group</a> - Washington, D.C. area Zope user group and Python interest group. Features meeting
     calendar, discussion, and contact information.
12   <li><a href="http://srd.yahoo.com/drst/6582814/*http://www.python.org/doc/FAQ.html">FAQ -
     Python</a>
```

7. Place the data into the Excel spreadsheet.

```
$n++;
$cell = $worksheet->Cells($n,1);
$cell->Activate;
$cell->Value = $urls[1];
$cell = $worksheet->Cells($n,2);
$cell->Activate;
$cell->Value = $urls[2];
$cell = $worksheet->Cells($n,3);
$cell->Activate;
$cell->Value = substr ($urls[3], 3,
→ strlen($urls[3]));
```

Unfortunately, because of syntactical differences between COM (which uses dot-syntax, e.g., Worksheets("Sheet1"). Cells(1,1)) and PHP, sometimes you have to take several steps to accomplish a simple task. Here I first define the cell based on the row (using $n as a counter) and column numbers. Then I activate this cell and finally set its value. I repeat this for three cells per row: the URL itself, the URL name, and the URL description, as parsed from the Yahoo! page. (I also cut the space-dash-space off of the beginning of the description (see Script 8.8)).

It is possible to define a range of cells and place all of the data at once, but I'm trying to keep this as straightforward as possible.

8. Print the matched URL to the Web browser.

```
echo "$n $urls[1] $urls[2] " . substr
→ ($urls[3], 3, strlen($urls[3]));
```

9. Close the loops, finish the HTML formatting, and close the file.

```
echo "<p></p>";
}
}
echo "</pre><br></br>";
fclose ($fp);
```

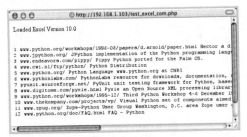

Figure 8.13 The script indicates to me what URLs were found, which should be stored in the spreadsheet file (Figure 8.15).

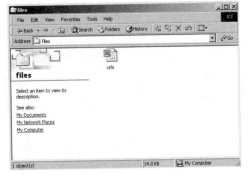

Figure 8.14 The newly created urls.xls file is stored in the files directory.

Figure 8.15 This is the spreadsheet created by PHP as viewed afterward in Excel (with some slight formatting adjustments).

10. Save the spreadsheet and quit Excel.

```
$workbook->SaveAs('C:\files\
→ urls.xls');

$excel->Quit();
```

The new file will be saved as urls.xls in the C:\files directory. It is best to use absolute file paths here, and you might want to consider creating unique file-names because the application will insist on confirming with you before it over-writes an existing file.

For the SaveAs command to work, the files directory must have open permis-sions and the overall security on the machine must be such that the operat-ing system will not block the request or demand authentication. This is more of an issue on NT servers.

11. Destroy every object and complete the page.

```
unset ($cell);

unset ($worksheet);

unset ($workbook);

unset ($excel);

?>

</body>

</html>
```

This step is not required, but it is best to be tidy.

12. Save the file as test_excel_com.php, upload it to your server, and test in your Web browser (**Figures 8.13**, **8.14**, and **8.15**).

continues on next page

✔ Tips

- Within the Unix family of operating systems you can connect to other applications using a `popen()` and `pclose()`, which create pipes—avenues of communication.

- There is even support in PHP 4 for DCOM, Dynamic Component Object Modules. This extension allows for use of COM over networks.

- Another way to see what COM properties you'll need is to record a macro in the application that does what you intend to do. Then view this macro in the macro editor to see what terminology it uses.

- There are already COM classes available such as the Excel class at `http://sourceforge.net/projects/psxlsgen`.

XML AND PHP

Extensible Markup Language, or XML, is the next big thing—and has been for some time. It has been quickly embraced as one of the best ways to manage information in today's networked environment. XML was written to be able to transfer data with better consistency. Since XML is used to define what pieces of data are, the end result is that the data will be transmittable across different platforms and systems without losing its integrity. XML, like HTML, is based on Standard Generalized Markup Language, or SGML, which means that you'll see numerous similarities between the two. PHP supported XML even in earlier versions, and PHP 4 promises even better integration. In this chapter I will give a basic introduction to what XML is, how you use it and why, and then go through an example of using PHP with XML. There are two technical requirements for this chapter: a text editor (which you already have) and PHP 4, which includes XML support (although you can build XML capability into PHP 3). This chapter, more so than any of the others, will be largely explanation of the technology but should also provide you with the groundwork for using XML with PHP today. Appendix C, General Resources, lists numerous references for more XML information.

What Is XML?

XML, which is controlled by the World Wide Web Consortium (W3C) (**Figure 9.1**), was created with several goals in mind:

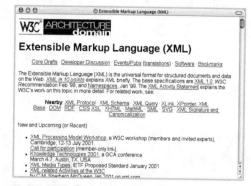

Figure 9.1 The World Wide Web Consortium (located at www.w3c.org) controls the XML standard among other standards.

◆ To be a regulated standard, not the proprietary technology of any one company

◆ To act as a highly flexible way to store nearly any type of information

◆ To be easily readable by humans and usable by computers

◆ To be able to check itself for validity and integrity

While XML itself is not actually a markup language—despite its name—it provides a foundation for you to manufacture your own markup language. A markup language is used to help define or describe pieces of information. For example, the HTML code `<b>Giant</b>` indicates that the word *Giant* should be displayed in bold text.

With XML you use tags to encapsulate pieces of information in defined chunks. XML tags (or *elements* as they are formally called) are the opposite of HTML tags in that they define what something is but do not reveal how that something should be displayed. HTML tags, conversely, can indicate how a string should be treated in a Web browser but cannot reveal anything about what type of information that string represents.

The power of XML is that you are not limited to any predetermined set of tags and you can actually use XML to come up with your own. Once you have created your markup language (your own definition of elements), you can begin to store data formatted within the newly defined tags.

An example of XML code might be

```
<album>

<title>Moon Safari</title>

<artist>Air</artist>

<review>Air's debut album marks a hip
→ redefinition of what muzak can be.
→ </review>

</album>
```

Because XML is still relatively in its infancy, the current technology most users possess (like Web browsers) does not fully support what XML can do. As an example, controlling how XML information should be formatted requires the use of Extensible Stylesheet Language, or XSL. XSL is like a Cascading Style Sheet, or CSS, in its ability to control the look of an entire site with just one page, but it is not completely usable by the major Web browsers yet. Despite this minor limitation, XML seems to be where the industry is moving and it is worth your understanding for that very reason. In fact, as you'll see later in the chapter, using PHP to turn XML into a browser-friendly format is one common use of both technologies.

WHAT IS XML?

XML Syntax

The primary thing you must understand before doing anything with XML is how XML documents themselves are structured. An XML document, which is just an organized text file, contains three parts:

- The prolog or XML declaration
- The document type declaration
- The element(s)/content

The XML prolog (which is to say, *prologue*) is the first line of every XML file and should be in the form of

```
<?xml version="1.0"?>
```

The next step, the document type declaration, is where you define your primary (or root) element.

```
<!DOCTYPE name

...

>
```

This is similar to HTML documents that begin with `<!DOCTYPE html`, stating that the overarching element of the file is the `html` tag. Within the document type declaration, you can define your elements or you can reference an external document (called a Document Type Definition, or DTD) that contains these definitions. I would recommend the latter and will demonstrate how to do this in the next section. First, to point to (or include) the external file, your document type declaration would be

```
<!DOCTYPE name SYSTEM "/path/to/
  filename.dtd">
```

where `filename.dtd` is the included file and `/path/to` is a Uniform Resource Indicator,

or URI, pinpointing where that file is on the server.

The third part of the XML document is the content itself. This section, like an HTML page, begins and ends with the root element, as defined in your document type declaration. Within that field will be the various pieces of information bound by their respective tags. The previous section of the chapter showed an example using music albums, but another might involve products for an e-commerce store:

```
<product>

<name>bubureau</name>

<size></size>

<price>12.00</price>

<picture filename="bubureau.jpg" />

</product>
```

The XML rules for listing items insist upon the following:

- XML tags must be balanced in that they open and close (for every `<tag>` there must be a `</tag>`). An exception to this is the `<picture>` tag, which has an attribute (the `filename`) but no content per se. Examples like `<picture>` (or the HTML `<br>`) use a space followed by a slash to indicate closure: `<picture />`. For the record, `<picture … />` is the same as `<picture …></picture>`.

- Elements cannot be intertwined. HTML will let you get away with a construct like `<b><i>Soul Mining</b></i>`, but XML will not.

To start down the XML path, I'll write my first XML document: a partial listing of a compact disc collection.

Script 9.1 This is a basic XML document containing three compact discs from a collection.

```
1    <?xml version="1.0"?>
2    <!DOCTYPE collection SYSTEM
     "collection.dtd">
3    <collection>
4    <album>
5        <title>Moon Safari</title>
6        <artist>Air</artist>
7        <review>Air's debut album marks a hip
         redefinition of what muzak can
         be.</review>
8    </album>
9    <album>
10       <title>The Hour Of
         Bewilderbeast</title>
11       <artist>Badly Drawn Boy</artist>
12       <review>One of the best records of
         the year...</review>
13   </album>
14   <album>
15       <title>Lazer Guided Melodies</title>
16       <artist>Spiritualized</artist>
17       <review></review>
18   </album>
19   </collection>
```

To write XML:

1. Create a new XML document in your text editor (**Script 9.1**).

   ```
   <?xml version="1.0"?>
   ```

2. Write the document type declaration.

   ```
   <!DOCTYPE collection SYSTEM
   → "collection.dtd">
   ```

   This line indicates that the root element of the document will be collection and that the DTD file is collection.dtd, stored in the same directory as this file.

3. Open with the root element.

   ```
   <collection>
   ```

   For a file to be proper XML it must begin with the XML declaration, be followed by the document type declaration, and then use the root element. All of the content of the page will be stored between the opening and closing tags of this element.

4. Add an album to the file.

   ```
   <album>
   <title>Moon Safari</title>
   <artist>Air</artist>
   <review>Air's debut album marks a
   → hip redefinition of what muzak can
   → be.</review>
   </album>
   ```

   These tags themselves will be defined in the DTD in the next section. Notice here that the entire section is bounded by the album tags and that it is safe to use white space outside of elements but not within the tags or between them (XML is generally sensitive to white space).

continues on next page

XML SYNTAX

5. Add more albums.

```
<album>
<title>The Hour Of
➝ Bewilderbeast</title>
<artist>Badly Drawn Boy</artist>
<review>One of the best records of
➝ the year...</review>
</album>
<album>
<title>Lazer Guided Melodies</title>
<artist>Spiritualized</artist>
<review></review>
</album>
```

With XML it is acceptable to have elements that contain no data—as `review` does in this last example—but you must still use the tags regardless, depending upon how your DTD is structured, as you'll see.

6. Close the XML document.

```
</collection>
```

7. Save this file as `albums1.xml`. If you want, upload the file to your server and view in your Web browser (**Figures 9.2** and **9.3**). Depending on your browser's support for XML, you will see different results. Technically the document is an invalid XML page, as the referenced DTD does not yet exist.

✔ Tips

- XML, unlike HTML, is case-sensitive and affected by extraneous white space.

- You can place comments within an XML file—for your own use, not for any technical purposes—by using the same syntax as HTML:

```
<!-- This is my comment. -->
```

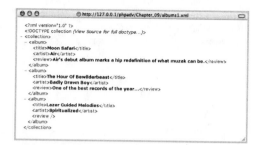

Figure 9.2 Internet Explorer 5.1 (for Macintosh) automatically parses an XML document to display it in a meaningful form.

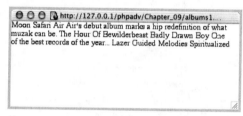

Figure 9.3 Opera 5.0 Beta (also for Macintosh) shows XML files as plain text, dropping the tags altogether.

Table 9.1 These are the three main element types, although an element can also consist of other elements or mixed data.

Element Types	
TYPE	ASSOCIATION
(#PCDATA)	Generally text (specifically Parsed-Character Data)
EMPTY	Nothing
ANY	Anything

Document Type Definitions

XML involves two primary steps: defining your tags (or elements) and using those tags. In the previous script you referenced elements such as `album` and `artist`. Here you will learn how to give those labels meaning.

With HTML, the tags have already been defined for you, but XML allows you to create your own. You can do this either within the document type declaration section of your XML file or in a separate DTD file, as I would recommend. This process is called document modeling, because you are creating a paradigm for how your files should be written. A DTD defines every element and attribute for your markup language.

The syntax for defining an element is

`<!ELEMENT name TYPE>`

where `name` is the name of the new tag and it will contain content of type `TYPE`. Element names must begin with a letter or underscore but can contain numbers and hyphens.

Table 9.1 lists the three primary element types and their meanings.

Applying this to my e-commerce example, I could define some of the elements like so:

`<!ELEMENT name (#PCDATA)>`

`<!ELEMENT size (#PCDATA)>`

`<!ELEMENT price (#PCDATA)>`

`<!ELEMENT picture EMPTY>`

The last element, picture, is of type `EMPTY` because it has no per se content (it has an attribute of `filename`). You'll see how this works shortly.

continues on next page

DOCUMENT TYPE DEFINITIONS

The rules set here seem to fill the bill, but there are still a couple of missing pieces. First, there's another element used, that of `product`, which contains all of the other elements. To define it, I write

```
<!ELEMENT product (name, size, price,
→ picture)>
```

Here I've stated that `product` contains four other elements in the order of `name`, `size`, `price`, and `picture`. I can be more flexible in my definition by using regular expression-like syntax.

```
<!ELEMENT product (name, size*, price,
→ picture?)>
```

This line indicates that `product` can contain up to four elements. One element, `size`, can be listed anywhere from zero to multiple times. Another element, `picture`, is entirely optional but, if present, there can be only one. **Table 9.2** lists the pertinent characters for defining elements.

You can extend this even further by dictating that an element contain other elements, parsed-character data, or nothing.

```
<!ELEMENT thing (other_element |
→ #PCDATA | EMPTY)>
```

The second problem with the current model is that the `picture` element, which is empty should take an argument, namely the `filename`. Elements can have attributes, even multiple attributes. You've seen this before with HTML tags such as `<table>`, which has attributes like `border`, `cellspacing`, and `width`. It is perfectly acceptable for an element to have many attributes as long as each attribute has a different name.

Table 9.2 The four symbols here reflect their regular expression counterparts when used to define an element.

Element Type Symbols	
SYMBOL	MEANING
?	Optional (zero or one)
+	At least one
*	Zero or more
|	Or

Table 9.3 There are more options for your attribute type field, but these four cover the basics.

Element Attribute Types

TYPE	MEANING	EXAMPLE
CDATA	Character Data	General text
NMTOKEN	Name Token	String (without white space)
NMTOKENS	Several Name Tokens	NMTOKENS separated by white spaces (e.g., "Nick Kelsey Jude")
ID	Unique Identifier	Text or numerical, but it must be unique for each element

To allow elements to have attributes, you make an attribute list within your DTD. You must do this after defining the elements (or at least, the attributes of an element must be defined after the element itself has been defined).

```
<!ATTLIST element_name

attribute_name attribute_type
→ attribute_description

>
```

The `attribute_name` field is simply a text string like *color* or *alignment*. The `attribute_type` indicates the format of the attribute. **Table 9.3** lists the possibilities.

Another possibility is for an attribute to be an enumerated list.

```
<!ATTLIST element_name

attribute_name  (value1 | value2 |
→ value3)

>
```

The third parameter for an attribute—the attribute's description—allows you to further define how it will function. Possibilities include #REQUIRED, meaning that an element must use that attribute; #IMPLIED, which means that the attribute is optional; and #FIXED, indicating that the attribute will always have the same value. To round out the definition of the `picture` element, I would add an attribute.

```
<!ATTLIST picture

filename NMTOKEN #REQUIRED

>
```

continues on next page

You can also specify the possible values of an attribute instead of identifying a type.

```
<!ATTLIST element_name

attribute_name  (value1 | value2)
→ "value1"

>
```

The above code says that element_name takes an attribute of attribute_name with possible values of value1 or value2, the former being the default.

Now that you understand the foundation of defining elements, you can write the Document Type Definition that corresponds to albums1.xml.

To write a Document Type Definition:

1. Create a new XML document in your text editor (**Script 9.2**).

2. Define the album element.

```
<!ELEMENT album (title, artist,
→ song*, review*, cover_image?)>
```

This tag will contain up to five other tags: title and artist—which are required; song and review, which are optional and can be listed numerous times; and cover_image, which is optional but can occur only once.

3. Define the title, artist, song, and review elements.

```
<!ELEMENT title (#PCDATA)>
<!ELEMENT artist (#PCDATA)>
<!ELEMENT song (#PCDATA)>
<!ELEMENT review (#PCDATA)>
```

If you would like to add extra data to the XML document, add more elements here. However, be sure to include these new elements in the album definition. As a rule, you want a separate element defined for each type of information that your XML file will contain.

Script 9.2 The DTD file will establish all the rules that my XML pages must abide by.

```
1    <!ELEMENT album (title, artist, song*,
     review*, cover_image?)>
2    <!ELEMENT title (#PCDATA)>
3    <!ELEMENT artist (#PCDATA)>
4    <!ELEMENT song (#PCDATA)>
5    <!ELEMENT review (#PCDATA)>
6    <!ELEMENT cover_image EMPTY>
7
8    <!ATTLIST cover_image
9    filename NMTOKEN #REQUIRED
10   >
11
12   <!ATTLIST song
13   length NMTOKEN #IMPLIED
14   track NMTOKEN #IMPLIED
15   >
```

4. Define the `cover_image` element.

`<!ELEMENT cover_image EMPTY>`

This one field is different from the others because the tags themselves will not encapsulate any data (the element will be empty). The information for this element will be stored in the attribute.

5. Define the attribute for `cover_image`.

`<!ATTLIST cover_image`
`filename NMTOKEN #REQUIRED`

`>`

The `cover_image` element will take one mandatory attribute, the `filename` of type `NMTOKEN`, which means it will be a string (e.g., "image.jpg"). Keep in mind that the element itself is not required, as defined in the `album` tag. So the XML file should either include `cover_image` in a listing with a `filename` attribute or not include it at all.

6. Define the attributes for `song`.

`<!ATTLIST song`
`length NMTOKEN #IMPLIED`
`track NMTOKEN #IMPLIED`

`>`

The `song` element will have two attributes—`length` and `track`—both of which are optional.

7. Save this file as `collection.dtd` and upload it to your server in the same directory as `albums1.xml`.

continues on next page

DOCUMENT TYPE DEFINITIONS

Now that I have done my document modeling, I'll take another look at my XML file to see how it matches up. One of the benefits of XML is that you can do quite a bit of validating by eye. I'm going to make a couple of changes to my XML file to better reflect and utilize the DTD.

8. Open albums1.xml in your text editor (Script 9.1).

9. Add a couple of songs to the second album (**Script 9.3**, lines 12 and 13).

   ```
   <song length="5:18" track="1">The
   → Shining</song>

   <song length="3:40" track="2">
   → Everybodys Stalking</song>
   ```

   As the DTD states, the song element is optional but can be listed multiple times. The element takes two possible attributes, both of which I'm using here.

10. Remove the review from the last listing and add an image.

    ```
    <cover_image filename="lgm.jpg" />
    ```

    Since the review element is defined as optional, I can just go ahead and delete the blank listing. In its stead I'll place a cover_image element with an attribute of the image filename.

11. Save the file with these new changes (I've also changed its name to album2.xml, to keep the different versions straight). Upload it to your server and view in your Web browser (**Figure 9.4**).

Script 9.3 I've updated the original album1.xml (Script 9.1) to incorporate the structure defined in my DTD (Script 9.2).

```
1   <?xml version="1.0"?>
2   <!DOCTYPE collection SYSTEM
    "collection.dtd">
3   <collection>
4   <album>
5   <title>Moon Safari</title>
6   <artist>Air</artist>
7   <review>Air's debut album marks a hip
    redefinition of what muzak can
    be.</review>
8   </album>
9   <album>
10  <title>The Hour Of Bewilderbeast</title>
11  <artist>Badly Drawn Boy</artist>
12  <song length="5:18" track="1">The
    Shining</song>
13  <song length="3:40" track="2">Everybodys
    Stalking</song>
14  <review>One of the best records of the
    year...</review>
15  </album>
16  <album>
17  <title>Lazer Guided Melodies</title>
18  <artist>Spiritualized</artist>
19  <cover_image filename="lgm.jpg" />
20  </album>
21  </collection>
```

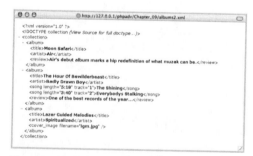

Figure 9.4 My Web browser displays the XML file in a colorful format (assuming it supports XML). This is the modified version of the first XML data file.

Script 9.4 If I wanted to establish all of my elements in my XML file, I could remove the DTD reference and place the element definitions there instead.

```
1    <?xml version="1.0"?>
2    <!DOCTYPE collection [
3    <!ELEMENT album (title, artist, song*,
     review*, cover_image?)>
4    <!ELEMENT title (#PCDATA)>
5    <!ELEMENT artist (#PCDATA)>
6    <!ELEMENT song (#PCDATA)>
7    <!ELEMENT review (#PCDATA)>
8    <!ELEMENT cover_image EMPTY>
9    <!ATTLIST cover_image
10   filename NMTOKEN #REQUIRED
11   >
12   <!ATTLIST song
13   length NMTOKEN #IMPLIED
14   track NMTOKEN #IMPLIED
15   >
16   ]>
17   <collection>
18   <album>
19   <title>Moon Safari</title>
20   <artist>Air</artist>
21   <review>Air's debut album marks a hip
     redefinition of what muzak can
     be.</review>
22   </album>
23   <album>
24   <title>The Hour Of Bewilderbeast</title>
25   <artist>Badly Drawn Boy</artist>
26   <song length="5:18" track="1">The
     Shining</song>
27   <song length="3:40" track="2">Everybodys
     Stalking</song>
28   <review>One of the best records of the
     year...</review>
29   </album>
30   <album>
31   <title>Lazer Guided Melodies</title>
32   <artist>Spiritualized</artist>
33   <cover_image filename="lgm.jpg" />
34   </album>
35   </collection>
```

✔ Tips

■ One of the great things about XML is that you can write your own DTDs or make use of document models created by others, which are freely available online. Developers have already written models for books, recipes, and more.

■ If you get into developing complex XML applications, you may want to learn about namespaces, which is another way to group elements. Check an XML reference for more information. (Appendix C is a place to start.)

■ Another way to accomplish document modeling is by using XML Schema, which defines documents by example.

■ XML also supports entities, which are like constants you define that can be used to replace values within an XML file.

■ **Script 9.4** shows albums2.xml (Script 9.3) if I decided to define all of the elements within the document instead of using an external DTD.

DOCUMENT TYPE DEFINITIONS

Parsing XML with PHP and Expat

There's more to XML than just composing XML documents and DTD files, although that certainly would be sufficient. One thing you can do with XML is parse it. Parsing XML is a matter of using an application or library to access XML files and check to make sure they are well-formed (free of errors) and valid. At the same time, the information can be transformed to suit other purposes. I'll explain all this in better detail.

A parser, in short, takes XML files and breaks them down into their various pieces. As an example, the code `<artist>Air</artist>` consists of the opening tag (`<artist>`), the content (*Air*) and the closing tag (`</artist>`). While this distinction is obvious to the human eye, it's a great feature of XML for a computer to be able to recognize the same when looking at text files.

There are two types of XML parsers: event-based and tree-based. The former goes into action when an event occurs. An example of an event would be encountering an opening tag in an XML file. By reading an entire file and doing things at each event, this type of parser—also called a SAX (Simple API for XML)—manages the entire XML document. The second parser views an XML file and creates a tree-like representation of the entire thing that can then be manipulated. A subset of the tree parsers would be DOM (Document Object Model) systems such as libxml, which can be compiled into PHP.

Parsers, as part of what they do, confirm that the XML data is well-formed, meaning that the information is presented as the parser expects it to be based on the rules of XML as outlined at the very beginning of this chapter. Ensuring well-formed files is one of the keys to XML's success: the thinking being that a zero-tolerance policy increases compatibility across multiple systems. Secondarily, some parsers also check to see if an XML file is valid, which requires that it is well-formed in XML terms and follows the rules of the DTD. Expat, the SAX parser most commonly used with PHP (it's part of Apache these days, too), does not validate XML files; it checks to see only if they are well-formed.

Ensuring the validity of an XML document is what makes it so powerful and universally acceptable. HTML in comparison is forgiving to a fault. Failure to omit closing `</tr>` tags will normally be overlooked. Some browsers are more generous than others, resulting in inconsistent appearance depending on the system being used by the user.

Using Expat with PHP is a four-step process:

1. Create a new parser.

2. Identify the functions to use for handling events.

3. Parse the file.

4. Free up the resources used by the parser.

The first step is accomplished using `xml_parse_create()`.

`$parser = xml_parser_create();`

The second step is the most important. Because Expat is an event-handler parser, it makes exclusive use of call-back functions when encountering events. The primary events that occur are when the parser finds an opening tag, content (the data between tags), and a closing tag. You need to tell PHP what user-defined functions should be called when each of these events occurs.

```
xml_set_element_handler ($parser,
→ 'open_element_function',
→ 'close_element_function');
```

```
xml_set_character_data_handler ($parser,
→ 'data_function');
```

Now, when the parser encounters the different events, it will automatically send that content to the proper function.

Parsing the file requires the use of the `xml_parse()` function, which takes two (and an optional third) arguments.

```
xml_parse ($parser, $data,
→ $stopping_point);
```

This function is first fed the pointer or reference to the parser, then the information to be parsed. The third argument tells the parser when to stop working.

Finally, you should free up the resources used by the parser by calling

```
xml_parser_free ($parser);
```

One of the best uses of PHP and XML is to turn XML documents into HTML so that the information can be displayed in the browser (especially because most of the currently available browsers will not do this automatically). As an example, I'll write a PHP script that uses Expat to make a legible Web page from an XML file. Further explanation of this entire process will be given while I write the code.

To parse XML with PHP:

1. Create a new HTML document in your text editor (**Script 9.5**).

   ```
   <!DOCTYPE html PUBLIC "-//W3C//DTD
   → XHTML 1.0 Transitional//EN"
   "http://www.w3.org/TR/2000/
   → REC-xhtml1-20000126/DTD/xhtml1-
   → transitional.dtd">
   <html xmlns="http://www.w3.org/
   → 1999/xhtml">
   <head>
   <title>XML Parser</title>
   </head>
   <body>
   <pre>
   ```

   I add the <pre> tag here because I'll be using spaces throughout the page to align my code and I want the Web browser to honor them.

2. Create a section of PHP and define the necessary constants.

   ```
   <?php
   define ('LT', '<font
   → color="blue">&lt;</font>');
   define ('GT', '<font
   → color="blue">&gt;</font>');
   ```

   My script will mimic what the built-in Internet Explorer parser does with XML files (see Figure 9.2). To this end, I'll frequently be printing out the greater than and less than symbols in a blue font. By establishing them as constants here, it will make maintenance and use of the script easier.

3. Write the function for handling opening tags.

   ```
   function handle_open_element ($p,
   → $element, $attributes) {
   ```

   ```
   $element = strtolower($element);
   switch ($element) {
   case 'cover_image':
   $image = @getimagesize
   → ($attributes['FILENAME']);
   echo "<img src=\"{$attributes
   → ['FILENAME']}\" $image[3]
   → border=\"0\"><br />\n";
   break;
   case 'song':
   echo '        ' . LT . '<font color=
   → "red">' . $element . '</font>';
   foreach ($attributes as $key =>
   → $value) {
   echo ' <font color="green">' .
   → strtolower($key) . '="' . $value .
   → '"</font>';
   }
   echo GT;
   break;
   case 'collection':
   echo LT . '<font color="red">' .
   → $element . '</font>' . GT .
   → '<br />';
   break;
   case 'album':
   echo LT . '<font color="red">' .
   → $element . '</font>' . GT .
   → '<br />';
   break;
   default:
   echo '    ' . LT . '<font color=
   → "red">' . $element . '</font>' .
   → GT;
   break;
   }
   }
   ```

continues on page 337

Script 9.5 This script uses PHP in conjunction with the Expat library to parse XML documents, turning them into HTML pages.

```
                                    script
1    <!DOCTYPE html PUBLIC "-//W3C//DTD XHTML 1.0 Transitional//EN"
2        "http://www.w3.org/TR/2000/REC-xhtml1-20000126/DTD/xhtml1-transitional.dtd">
3    <html xmlns="http://www.w3.org/1999/xhtml">
4    <head>
5        <title>XML Parser</title>
6    </head>
7    <body>
8    <pre>
9    <?php
10
11   // This script will parse an XML file, which it takes as an argument.
12
13   // Define some constants to represent the greater than and less than symbols.
14   define ('LT', '<font color="blue">&lt;</font>');
15   define ('GT', '<font color="blue">&gt;</font>');
16
17   // Define the functions required for handling the different pieces.
18   function handle_open_element ($p, $element, $attributes) {
19       $element = strtolower($element);
20       switch ($element) {
21           case 'cover_image':
22               $image = @getimagesize ($attributes['FILENAME']);
23               echo "<img src=\"{$attributes['FILENAME']}\" $image[3] border=\"0\"><br />\n";
24               break;
25           case 'song':
26               echo '      ' . LT . '<font color="red">' . $element . '</font>';
27               foreach ($attributes as $key => $value) {
28                   echo ' <font color="green">' . strtolower($key) . '="' . $value . '"</font>';
29               }
30               echo GT;
31               break;
32           case 'collection':
33               echo LT . '<font color="red">' . $element . '</font>' . GT . '<br />';
34               break;
35           case 'album':
36               echo LT . '<font color="red">' . $element . '</font>' . GT . '<br />';
37               break;
```

(script continues on next page)

Script 9.5 *continued*

```
                                                    script

38          default:
39              echo '   ' . LT . '<font color="red">' . $element . '</font>' . GT;
40              break;
41      }
42  }
43
44  function handle_close_element ($p, $element) {
45      $element = strtolower($element);
46      if ($element != 'cover_image') {
47          echo LT . '<font color="red">/' . $element . '</font>' . GT . '<br />';
48      }
49  }
50
51  function handle_character_data ($p, $cdata) {
52      echo "<b>$cdata</b>";
53  }
54
55  // End of the functions.
56
57  // Create the parser and set the handling functions.
58  $p = xml_parser_create();
59  xml_set_element_handler ($p, 'handle_open_element', 'handle_close_element');
60  xml_set_character_data_handler ($p, 'handle_character_data');
61
62  // Read the file.
63  $fp = @fopen ($file, 'r') or die ("Could not open a file called: $file");
64  while ($data = fread ($fp, filesize($file))) {
65      xml_parse ($p, $data, feof($fp));
66  }
67
68  // Free up the parser.
69  xml_parser_free($p);
70  ?>
71  </pre>
72  </body>
73  </html>
```

The function that will be called whenever an opening tag is encountered by the parser will be `handle_open_element()`. This function will naturally receive from the parser the parser reference, the name of the element, and an associative array of any attributes that element contains. As an example, the song element has both `length` and `track` attributes. Upon encountering that tag, the parser will send this function the values `$p` (for the parser), `song` (the name of the element), and an array that could be defined like so:

```
$attributes = array ("LENGTH" =>
→ "3:22", "TRACK", "2");
```

(One oddity is that every element and attribute name is received in all upper-case letters, so I use the `strtolower()` function to turn them back into a lower-case form.)

Now, depending on the element received, the PHP will do different things. Working from the bottom of the `switch` statement up, the default is to print three spaces, followed by the `LT` constant (as defined earlier), followed by the element name in red, followed by the `GT` constant.

If the element received is either `album` or `collection`, I'll do the same but without printing initial spaces and instead will make a break at the end of the line.

For the `song` element, I'll want to loop through the `$attributes` array, printing each name/value pair (or key/value pair).

Lastly (or first, according to the `switch` statement), if the element is the `cover_image`, I'll place the image itself in the page in lieu of referring to the textual name of the element or its attributes.

4. Write the function for handling any closing elements.

```
function handle_close_element ($p,
→ $element) {
$element = strtolower($element);
if ($element != 'cover_image') {
echo LT . '<font color="red">/' .
→ $element . '</font>' . GT .
→ '<br />';
}
}
```

This function is more straightforward than its predecessor. All this does is send a formatted version of the tag to the browser, assuming the tag is not the closing `cover_image` tag.

5. Script the final function.

```
function handle_character_data
→ ($p, $cdata) {
echo "<b>$cdata</b>";
}
```

The `handle_character_data()` function will be used for the information between the opening and closing tags. It will be printed in bold. Note that the parser does not capitalize this information as it does the element and attribute names.

6. Create a new parser and identify the functions to use.

```
$p = xml_parser_create();
xml_set_element_handler ($p,
→ 'handle_open_element',
→ 'handle_close_element');
xml_set_character_data_handler
→ ($p, 'handle_character_data');
```

continues on next page

7. Read and parse the XML file.

```
$fp = @fopen ($file, 'r') or die
→ ("Could not open a file called:
→ $file");
while ($data = fread ($fp,
→ filesize($file))) {
xml_parse ($p, $data, feof($fp));
}
```

To parse the file I first try to open it using fopen(). My intention is to pass the filename along to the script via the URL. Then I loop through the file and send the retrieved data to the parser. The main loop stops once the entire file has been read, and the parser is told to stop once the end of the file has been reached.

8. Free up the parser and complete the page.

```
xml_parser_free($p);
?>
</pre>
</body>
</html>
```

9. Save the file as **parse.php**, upload it to your server, and test in your Web browser, appending **?file=albums2.xml** to your URL (**Figure 9.5** and **9.6**).

✔ Tips

- Remember when working with XML to always use formal PHP tags (<?php and ?>) that will not conflict with XML tags.

- As I mentioned earlier, PHP supports using DOM for parsing XML, but it is still in an experimental stage (not to mention it can be more resource-hungry to use).

Figure 9.5 Running albums2.xml through the PHP-Expat parser generates this HTML page, viewable in any browser.

Figure 9.6 I put together another albums.xml document and ran it through the parser as well. Notice that the third listing makes use of the optional attributes for each song.

XML Error Handling

One final alteration you'll probably want to make to the `parse.php` script is to take into account error handling. Because part of the purpose of parsing XML files is to check that they are well-formed (free of errors), you'll want to devise a system for making note of any issues. There are two primary XML error-handling functions to use.

```
xml_get_error_code($parser);
```

```
xml_error_string($error_code);
```

The first function takes the `$parser` reference as its argument and will report the error code associated with the parser, when an error occurs. The second function can take this code and turn it into a string version of the problem.

Almost every resource I've seen discussing PHP and Expat uses some variation on the following for error reporting.

```
printf("An XML error occurred on
→ line %d: %s.", xml_get_current_
→ line_number($p), xml_error_string
→ (xml_get_error_code($p)));
```

The `printf()` function, as you might know, takes a number of arguments and formats

the whole into a string it prints. Here I am telling PHP to print *An XML error occurred on line*, followed by the line number (as determined by `xml_get_current_line_number()`), followed by a colon and the error string itself.

This code is normally integrated with the `xml_parse()` line in one of two ways: as an or `die()` or as the result of a conditional. The first option would look like

```
xml_parse ($p, $data, feof($fp)) or
→ die (printf("An XML error occurred
→ on line %d: %s.",
xml_get_current_line_number($p),
→ xml_error_string(xml_get_error_
→ code($p))));
```

The second option, which I'll use in my script, is

```
if (!xml_parse ($p, $data, feof($fp))) {
printf("An XML error occurred on
→ line %d: %s.", xml_get_current_
→ line_number($p), xml_error_string
→ (xml_get_error_code($p)));
}
```

As the last of the steps in working with XML and PHP, I'll place this error-management code into my `parse.php` script.

To incorporate error handling:

1. Open parse.php in your text editor (Script 9.5).

2. Change line 65 to the following (**Script 9.6**):

   ```
   if (!xml_parse ($p, $data,
   → feof($fp))) {
   printf("An XML error occurred on
   → line %d: %s.", xml_get_current_
   → line_number($p), xml_error_string
   → (xml_get_error_code($p)));
   }
   ```

   If the parser runs into a problem, it will now print an error message indicating what the problem was and where it occurred. As long as the parser works without issue, the printf() line will never be called.

3. Save the file, upload it to your server, and test in your Web browser (**Figure 9.7**).

4. Alter your XML file by omitting a tag or creating some other error, then run parse.php in your Web browser again (**Figure 9.8**).

Figure 9.7 The parse.php file works the same as it did before, assuming there are no problems with your XML file.

Figure 9.8 Now, if parse.php does encounter an error, it will report the problem to you in sufficient detail.

Script 9.6 This slight modification of Script 9.5 now includes XML error management.

```
     script
1    <!DOCTYPE html PUBLIC "-//W3C//DTD XHTML 1.0 Transitional//EN"
2          "http://www.w3.org/TR/2000/REC-xhtml1-20000126/DTD/xhtml1-transitional.dtd">
3    <html xmlns="http://www.w3.org/1999/xhtml">
4    <head>
5        <title>XML Parser</title>
6    </head>
7    <body>
8    <pre>
9    <?php
10
11   // This script will parse an XML file which it takes as an argument.
12
13   // Define some constants to represent the greater than and less than symbols.
14   define ('LT', '<font color="blue">&lt;</font>');
15   define ('GT', '<font color="blue">&gt;</font>');
16
17   // Define the functions required for handling the different pieces.
18   function handle_open_element ($p, $element, $attributes) {
19       $element = strtolower($element);
20       switch ($element) {
21           case 'cover_image':
22               $image = @getimagesize ($attributes['FILENAME']);
23               echo "<img src=\"{$attributes['FILENAME']}\" $image[3] border=\"0\"><br />\n";
24               break;
25           case 'song':
26               echo '        ' . LT . '<font color="red">' . $element . '</font>';
27               foreach ($attributes as $key => $value) {
28                   echo ' <font color="green">' . strtolower($key) . '="' . $value . '"</font>';
29               }
30               echo GT;
31               break;
32           case 'collection':
33               echo LT . '<font color="red">' . $element . '</font>' . GT . '<br />';
34               break;
35           case 'album':
36               echo LT . '<font color="red">' . $element . '</font>' . GT . '<br />';
37               break;
```

(script continues on next page)

Script 9.6 *continued*

```
38              default:
39                   echo '   ' . LT . '<font color="red">' . $element . '</font>' . GT;
40                   break;
41          }
42      }
43
44      function handle_close_element ($p, $element) {
45          $element = strtolower($element);
46          if ($element != 'cover_image') {
47              echo LT . '<font color="red">/' . $element . '</font>' . GT . '<br />';
48          }
49      }
50
51      function handle_character_data ($p, $cdata) {
52          echo "<b>$cdata</b>";
53      }
54
55      // End of the functions.
56
57      // Create the parser and set the handling functions.
58      $p = xml_parser_create();
59      xml_set_element_handler ($p, 'handle_open_element', 'handle_close_element');
60      xml_set_character_data_handler ($p, 'handle_character_data');
61
62      // Read the file
63      $fp = @fopen ($file, 'r') or die ("Could not open a file called: $file");
64      while ($data = fread ($fp, filesize($file))) {
65          if (!xml_parse ($p, $data, feof($fp))) {
66              printf("An XML error occurred on line %d: %s.", xml_get_current_line_number($p),
                    xml_error_string(xml_get_error_code($p)));
67          }
68      }
69
70      // Free up the parser.
71      xml_parser_free($p);
72      ?>
73      </pre>
74      </body>
75      </html>
```

IMAGE GENERATION

As you certainly know by now, Web pages are created out of a judicious use of text, HTML, and images. Just as you can use PHP to generate text and HTML, you can also use it to make images on the fly, assuming your PHP installation has been configured properly.

This chapter will demonstrate how to use the capabilities of PHP and the GD Graphics Library to extend the functionality of your Web applications. Needless to say, using PHP to compose images is not a viable across-the-board replacement for a sense of graphic design and a copy of Adobe Photoshop, but if you have a need for images that are made instantaneously, possibly upon changing data, PHP can do that.

To follow the examples in this chapter, you will need to install the GD library, available from www.boutell.com/gd. Fortunately, it comes built into PHP 4 and is generally one of the most popular libraries on most servers. Along with the GD library, you will need: zlib (www.gzip.org/zlib) for compression—another common library; the JPEG library (www.ijg.org) for creating JPEG images; the PNG library (www.libpng.org/pub/png) for making PNGs; and FreeType (www.freetype.org) to be able to use TrueType fonts. Incorporating all of these libraries into your PHP installation is not as complicated as it may sound, and you may be surprised which features you can already use without adding any new software yourself. Also, the existence of one library or another dictates only which features you can and cannot use and does not rule out creating images altogether. (To determine what image types your PHP configuration can safely generate, use the imagetypes() function, detailed in the PHP manual.)

Before I get into the heart of the chapter, I should take a moment to talk about the four main image types you'll use:

◆ GIF (Graphics Interface Format)

◆ JPEG (Joint Photographic Experts Group)

◆ PNG (Portable Network Graphics)

◆ WBMP (Wireless Bitmap)

GIFs are primarily used for graphics that contain large fields of solid colors where details are not important, such as with graphs, icons, and cartoon-like characters. JPEGs, or JPGs, are best for photographs and other highly detailed images. For years, these were the two primary formats for Web sites.

Now, as a result of legal complications with GIFs, the nature of Web graphics is changing. The LZV algorithm used for compressing GIFs is patented by Unisys Corp., which means that only companies that purchase the use of this algorithm should have software that makes GIF images (e.g., Adobe pays for this right for Photoshop). In response to this, two things relevant to the Web developer occurred. First, the GD library, as of version 1.6, no longer supports the ability to create GIFs. Second, the Web community has created a new format, PNG, explicitly designed to display images in a high-quality but small file size format. PNG would be the absolute choice for all images on the Web except for the fact that a large number of Web browsers—including

the two biggies, Netscape Navigator and Microsoft Internet Explorer—do not support PNG images, at least not consistently across all platforms. And what's the point of using graphics that some of your users can't see?

The fourth image option, Wireless Bitmaps, are for use with Web sites designed with the wireless user in mind.

As it stands now, you have four options for creating images with PHP: find an older version of GD (older versions are not available through Boutell's site) and illegally make GIFs, find an older version of GD and pay Unisys for the right to make GIFs, generate PNG images with the understanding that some of your site's users will not be able to see the image, or make JPEGs that will be uniformly accepted but not of the quality or size that PNG can produce. It is not an ideal situation, but for demonstration purposes here, I've chosen to create PNGs in a quixotic gesture toward supporting the technology. Even though I'll be coding with PNG in mind, by changing only two lines of code, you can make these scripts turn out JPEGs instead. You could also use the techniques in Chapter 7, Networking with PHP, to identify the capabilities of the user's Web browser and display a JPEG or PNG accordingly.

As a side note, the patent on the GIF algorithm runs out in 2003, meaning it may be legal and inexpensive to make GIFs again at that time. On the other hand, browser support for PNG should be improved by then.

Creating a Simple Image

For the first example in this chapter, you'll create a simple image: text on a colored background. To be able to do so, you will only need use of the GD, zlib, and either the JPEG or PNG libraries, depending upon which format you want to create. Most installations of PHP should not have difficulty with the following script.

Making images with PHP is straightforward: You begin the process, you paint your picture, then you send the image to the Web browser (the images in the first three sections of the chapter will be created in memory and sent to the Web browser; the images in the final section will be saved on the server). It all starts with the `imagecreate()` function, which takes the width and height of the image, in pixels, as its arguments.

```
$image = imagecreate (100, 100);
```

The resulting variable, `$image`, is akin to a pointer used to refer to an open file or the link to a database connection. It will be used from here on out to refer to the image being created. It will be mandatory for every image function called from here on out.

Once the image is created and before you add shapes or text, you need to identify the colors being used, preferably by assigning them to variables. The `imagecolorallocate()` function turns values on the RGB (red, green, blue) scale into corresponding colors.

```
$black = imagecolorallocate
→ ($image, 0, 0, 0);
```

For this function to work, it must receive the image pointer. You cannot assign the colors before an image is created (or after it is destroyed). The RGB scale is numbered from 0 to 255 with all Web-safe colors being a multiple of 51: 0, 51, 102, 153, 204, 255. Black is 0 red, 0 green, and 0 blue. White is 255 red, 255 green, and 255 blue. **Table 10.1** lists 15 colors and their RGB values for you to use. A fuller, color version of the table is available through the book's supporting Web site (www.DMCinsights.com/phpadv).

Once the image has been created and a color assigned, you can create shapes and lines or place text. To add text to an image, you use the imagestring() function.

```
imagestring ($image, $font, $x, $y,
→ "Text", $color);
```

Again, this function requires the image pointer first. The font specified, when not using TrueType or PostScript fonts, is a built-in GD font on a scale of 1 to 5. These are listed in **Table 10.2**.

The x- and y-coordinates refer to where the string should begin in the image, from the starting point of the upper-left corner (which is always the reference point in any image). Thus, coordinates of 10, 50 means that the upper-right portion of the first character in the string will begin 10 pixels in from the left side and 50 pixels down from the top. Each string added to the image can be printed in its own color, too.

Table 10.1 This list of 15 somewhat random colors should be enough to get you started making images.

RBG Color Values

Color	Red	Green	Blue
Black	0	0	0
Blue	51	51	255
Blue-Green	51	153	153
Green	51	255	51
Dark Gray	102	102	102
Gray	153	153	153
Light Purple	153	153	255
Light Blue	153	255	255
Light Gray	204	204	204
Red	255	51	51
Purple	255	51	255
Orange	255	153	51
Pink	255	153	153
Yellow	255	255	51
White	255	255	255

Table 10.2 The built-in fonts are crude in appearance but work effectively enough. The height and width for each font refers to the number of pixels that a standard letter (M being the standard) will take up.

GD Fonts

Font Number	Name	Size (Height, Width)
1	gdFontTiny	8, 5
2	gdFontSmall	13, 6
3	gdFontMediumBold	13, 7
4	gdFontLarge	15, 8
5	gdFontGiant	15, 9

After you have created the image, you can send it to the Web browser using these two lines of code:

```
header ("Content-type: image/png");

imagepng ($image);
```

The first line tells the browser to expect a PNG image. Naturally, since this is a header() call, nothing can be sent prior to this line. The second line turns the image in memory into an actual PNG.

If you want to create GIFs, use

```
header ("Content-type: image/gif");

imagegif ($image);
```

If you want to create JPEGs, use

```
header ("Content-type: image/jpeg");

imagejpeg ($image);
```

Those are the only changes you'll ever need to make to distinguish what type of image you make (assuming no transparency is involved, as will be the case in this chapter's scripts).

Lastly, just as you have to close a file pointer, you ought to eliminate the resources the image is taking up.

```
imagedestroy ($image);
```

Failure to include this line can crash a server rather quickly as the images take up more and more memory. Always double-check to ensure the image is destroyed at the end of your script!

Now that you understand the basics of image creation, you'll write a script that generates a text-based image from data submitted in an HTML form.

To create a simple image:

1. Create a new PHP document in your text editor (**Script 10.1**).

```
<?php
```

2. Write a function for managing the colors.

```
function color_allocate ($image,
→ $color) {
switch ($color) {
case "white":
$red = 255;
$green = 255;
$blue = 255;
break;
case "red":
$red = 255;
$green = 51;
$blue = 51;
break;
case "orange":
$red = 255;
$green = 153;
$blue = 51;
break;
case "yellow":
$red = 255;
$green = 255;
$blue = 51;
break;
case "green":
$red = 51;
$green = 255;
$blue = 51;
break;
case "blue":
$red = 51;
$green = 51;
$blue = 255;
break;
case "purple":
```

```
$red = 255;
$green = 51;
$blue = 255;
break;
case "black":
$red = 0;
$green = 0;
$blue = 0;
break;
}
return imagecolorallocate ($image,
→ $red, $green, $blue);
}
```

This is just one way of separating out some of the redundant code into its own function. Check the PHP manual and other online resources for different ways of identifying colors.

3. Check to see if the form has been submitted.

```
if (isset($HTTP_GET_VARS
→ ['submit'])) {
```

4. Validate the incoming data.

```
if ( (isset($HTTP_GET_VARS
→ ['background_color'])) AND
→ (isset($HTTP_GET_VARS['text']))
→ AND (isset($HTTP_GET_VARS
→ ['text_color'])) ) {
```

5. Set the constants that will be used.

```
define ("FONT_TO_USE", 4);
define ("WIDTH", (strlen($HTTP_
→ GET_VARS['text']) * 10) );
if (WIDTH < 35) {
define ("HEIGHT", (WIDTH * 2) );
} elseif (WIDTH  < 70) {
define ("HEIGHT", round (WIDTH/2) );
} else {
define ("HEIGHT", round (WIDTH/4) );
}
```

continues on page 352

CREATING A SIMPLE IMAGE

Script 10.1 This form takes three factors from the user—a text string, the text color, and the background color—and turns that into an image (Figure 10.2).

```
1    <?php
2    // This page creates a simple image based on user-submitted information.
3
4       // This function turns color names into their actual values on the RGB scale.
5    function color_allocate ($image, $color) {
6         switch ($color) {
7             case "white":
8                 $red = 255;
9                 $green = 255;
10                $blue = 255;
11                break;
12            case "red":
13                $red = 255;
14                $green = 51;
15                $blue = 51;
16                break;
17            case "orange":
18                $red = 255;
19                $green = 153;
20                $blue = 51;
21                break;
22            case "yellow":
23                $red = 255;
24                $green = 255;
25                $blue = 51;
26                break;
27            case "green":
28                $red = 51;
29                $green = 255;
30                $blue = 51;
31                break;
32            case "blue":
33                $red = 51;
34                $green = 51;
35                $blue = 255;
36                break;
37            case "purple":
38                $red = 255;
39                $green = 51;
40                $blue = 255;
41                break;
42            case "black":
43                $red = 0;
44                $green = 0;
45                $blue = 0;
46                break;
47        }
48        return imagecolorallocate ($image, $red, $green, $blue);
```

(script continues on next page)

Script 10.1 *continued*

```
          script

49    }
50
51    if (isset($HTTP_GET_VARS['submit'])) { // Handle the form.
52
53        if ( (isset($HTTP_GET_VARS['background_color'])) AND (isset($HTTP_GET_VARS['text']))  AND
          (isset($HTTP_GET_VARS['text_color'])) ) {
54
55            // Set the font and size info.
56            define ("FONT_TO_USE", 4); // Number from 1-5.
57            define ("WIDTH", (strlen($HTTP_GET_VARS['text']) * 10) ); // Number of pixels.
58            if (WIDTH < 35) {
59                define ("HEIGHT", (WIDTH * 2) ); // Number of pixels.
60            } elseif (WIDTH  < 70) {
61                define ("HEIGHT", round (WIDTH/2) ); // Number of pixels.
62            } else {
63                define ("HEIGHT", round (WIDTH/4) ); // Number of pixels.
64            }
65
66            // Make and send the image.
67            header ("Content-type: image/png");
68            $image = @imagecreate (WIDTH, HEIGHT) or die ("A problem occurred trying to create the
          image.");
69
70            $background_color = color_allocate ($image, $HTTP_GET_VARS['background_color']);
71            $text_color = color_allocate ($image, $HTTP_GET_VARS['text_color']);
72
73            imagefill ($image, 0, 0, $background_color); // Not necessary but good form.
74            imagestring ($image, FONT_TO_USE, (WIDTH/10), (HEIGHT/4), $HTTP_GET_VARS['text'],
          $text_color);
75
76            imagepng ($image);
77            imagedestroy ($image); // Destroy the image.
78
79        } else {
80            echo "You either forgot to select a background color, a text color or you forgot to enter
          the text itself.\n";
81        }
82
83    } else {
84        // Display the form.
85    ?>
86    <!DOCTYPE html PUBLIC "-//W3C//DTD XHTML 1.0 Transitional//EN"
87        "http://www.w3.org/TR/2000/REC-xhtml1-20000126/DTD/xhtml1-transitional.dtd">
88    <html xmlns="http://www.w3.org/1999/xhtml">
89    <head>
90        <title>Create An Image</title>
91    </head>
92    <body>
```

(script continues on next page)

Script 10.1 *continued*

```
script
93    <form action="image_form.php" method="get">
94    <table border="0" width="80%" cellspacing="2" cellpadding="2" align="center">
95        <tr align="center" valign="top">
96            <td align="center" valign="top" colspan="2">Fill out the form to have your image
              created!</td>
97        </tr>
98        <tr align="center" valign="top">
99            <td align="right" valign="top">Enter the image text:</td>
100           <td align="left" valign="top"><input type="text" name="text" size="20"
              maxlength="40"></td>
101       </tr>
102       <tr align="center" valign="top">
103           <td align="right" valign="top">Select the text color:</td>
104           <td align="left" valign="top"><select name="text_color">
105   <option value="white">White</option>
106   <option value="red">Red</option>
107   <option value="orange">Orange</option>
108   <option value="yellow">Yellow</option>
109   <option value="green">Green</option>
110   <option value="blue">Blue</option>
111   <option value="purple">Purple</option>
112   <option value="black">Black</option>
113   </select></td>
114       </tr>
115       <tr align="center" valign="top">
116           <td align="right" valign="top">Select the background color:</td>
117           <td align="left" valign="top"><select name="background_color">
118   <option value="white">White</option>
119   <option value="red">Red</option>
120   <option value="orange">Orange</option>
121   <option value="yellow">Yellow</option>
122   <option value="green">Green</option>
123   <option value="blue">Blue</option>
124   <option value="purple">Purple</option>
125   <option value="black">Black</option>
126   </select></td>
127       </tr>
128       <tr align="center" valign="top">
129           <td align="center" valign="top" colspan="2"><input type="submit" name="submit"
              value="Make The Image!"></td>
130       </tr>
131   </table>
132   </form>
133   </body>
134   </html>
135   <?php
136   } // Close the SUBMIT conditional.
137   ?>
```

To determine the dimensions of the image, I first find the length of the submitted string. I multiply this by 10 to create enough space for the text.

The height will be based on the width. If the width is really small—fewer than four letters—I'll need a larger height. If the width is kind of small—fewer than seven letters—I can cut the width in half. Otherwise, one-fourth of the width will suffice for the height. The numbers here were based on trial and error using the number 4 GD font.

6. Send the header and start the image.

```
header ("Content-type: image/png");
$image = @imagecreate (WIDTH, HEIGHT)
→ or die ("A problem occurred trying
→ to create the image.");
```

I prefer to put the header() up front, but you can place it later in the script. Because debugging image creation can be difficult, you may want to place the header() call as the penultimate line before using imagepng() or imagejpeg(). The complication stems from the fact that once the browser is expecting an image, it will not print PHP errors properly. Commenting out the header() call will allow you to debug. Conversely, if the header() call is later in your script and any white space gets sent to the browser, that will also be a problem.

I've also added a die() statement to the initial imagecreate() call, which will stop execution if there are problems (with the libraries, for example).

7. Set the two colors.

```
$background_color = color_allocate
→ ($image, $HTTP_GET_VARS
→ ['background_ color']);

$text_color = color_allocate ($image,
→ $HTTP_GET_VARS['text_color']);
```

The written version of the selected colors will be turned into numeric values, then allocated forms, by the color_allocate() function defined above. Each is assigned to the appropriate variable, but you could also change the next line to

```
imagefill ($image, 0, 0, color_
→ allocate ($image, $HTTP_GET_VARS
→ ['background_color']);
```

if you were looking to conserve space.

8. Fill the image with the background color.

```
imagefill ($image, 0, 0,
→ $background_color);
```

It turns out that the first allocated color—the background color—will be used as the background on some configurations even if you do not include this line. It is proper to have it here nonetheless.

9. Print the text.

```
imagestring ($image, FONT_TO_USE,
→ (WIDTH/10), (HEIGHT/4), $HTTP_GET_
→ VARS['text'], $text_color);
```

I used two rough calculations—*WIDTH* divided by 10 and *HEIGHT* divided by 4—to roughly center the text on the image. It works pretty well, although in the next section, you'll see a better system for centering TrueType fonts.

10. Create the image and then destroy it.

```
imagepng ($image);
imagedestroy ($image);
```

I'm creating a PNG image, so I used the imagepng() function. If you would like to make a JPEG instead, change this line to imagejpeg ($image) and also change the header() line earlier in the script.

11. Complete the validation conditional.

```
} else {
echo "You either forgot to select a
→ background color, a text color
→ or you forgot to enter the text
→ itself.\n";
}
```

12. Complete the page itself by showing an HTML form.

```
} else {
?>
<!DOCTYPE html PUBLIC "-//W3C//
→ DTD XHTML 1.0 Transitional//EN"
"http://www.w3.org/TR/2000/
→ REC-xhtml1-20000126/DTD/
→ xhtml1-transitional.dtd">
<html xmlns="http://www.w3.org/
→ 1999/xhtml">
<head>
<title>Create An Image</title>
</head>
<body>
<form action="image_form.php"
→ method="get">
<table border="0" width="80%"
→ cellspacing="2" cellpadding="2"
→ align="center">
<tr align="center" valign="top">
<td align="center" valign="top"
→ colspan="2">Fill out the form to
→ have your image created!</td>
</tr>
```

```
<tr align="center" valign="top">
<td align="right" valign="top">Enter
→ the image text:</td>
<td align="left" valign="top"><input
→ type="text" name="text" size="20"
→ maxlength="40"></td>
</tr>
<tr align="center" valign="top">
<td align="right"
→ valign="top">Select the text
→ color:</td>
<td align="left" valign="top">
→ <select name="text_color">
<option value="white">White</option>
<option value="red">Red</option>
<option value="orange">Orange
→ </option>
<option value="yellow">Yellow
→ </option>
<option value="green">Green</option>
<option value="blue">Blue</option>
<option value="purple">Purple
→ </option>
<option value="black">Black</option>
</select></td>
</tr>
<tr align="center" valign="top">
<td align="right" valign="top">
→ Select the background color:</td>
<td align="left" valign="top">
→ <select name="background_color">
<option value="white">White</option>
<option value="red">Red</option>
<option value="orange">Orange
→ </option>
<option value="yellow">Yellow
→ </option>
<option value="green">Green</option>
<option value="blue">Blue</option>
```

continues on next page

```
<option value="purple">Purple
→ </option>
<option value="black">Black</option>
</select></td>
</tr>
<tr align="center" valign="top">
<td align="center" valign="top"
→ colspan="2"><input type="submit"
→ name="submit" value="Make The
→ Image!"></td>
</tr>
</table>
</form>
</body>
</html>
```

The form is very simple and needs no explanation. Notice that I placed the entire result of the conditional outside of the PHP tags so that I do not need to use print() or echo(). Doing so still works because the PHP conditional dictates behavior even if the behavior is not formally within PHP.

13. Close the PHP page and the conditional.

```
<?php
}
?>
```

14. Save the file as image_form.php, upload it to your server, and test in your Web browser (**Figures 10.1**, **10.2**, **10.3**, and **10.4**).

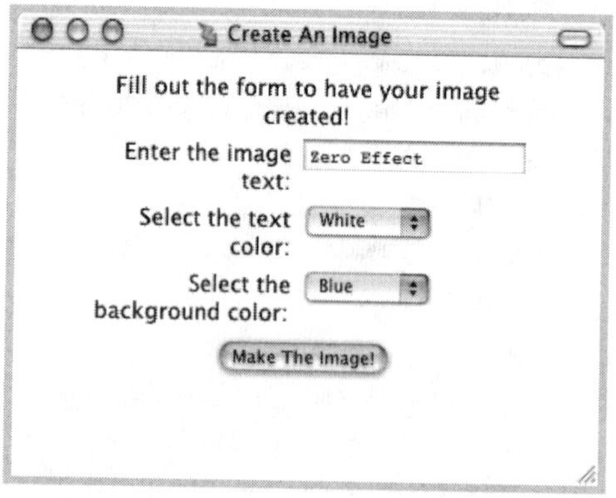

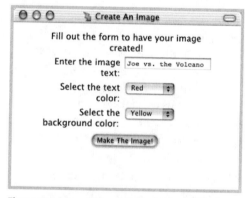

Figure 10.1 This basic form allows the user to choose the image's parameters.

Zero Effect

Figure 10.2 The grayscale versions of the images printed in the text don't accurately represent the generated image itself but do reflect the success of the operation. (Also, to save space, I've cut out the Web browser itself, which displays only this one image anyway.)

Figure 10.3 Because the generated image size is based on the length of the submitted string, longer text will result in larger images (Figure 10.4).

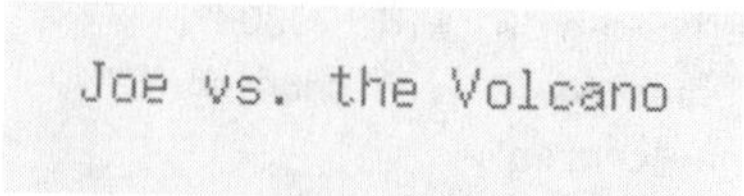

Joe vs. the Volcano

Figure 10.4 The entered string is roughly centered on the image and displayed in the color of the user's choosing.

✔ Tips

- Because functions in PHP are case-insensitive, some programmers prefer to use the format `ImageCreate()` and `ImageColorAllocate()` rather than all lowercase as I have done here. The decision is really up to you because either will work.

- As a rough gauge, most operating systems use a key of 72 pixels per inch (although now Windows is moving toward 96 pixels per inch) for displaying images. Thus, an image 144 pixels wide is about 2 inches in size to the viewer.

- If you are more comfortable with the HTML format for colors (e.g., *#00000* or *#FFFFFF*), you can use this syntax:

  ```
  imagecolorallocate ($image, 0xFF,
  → 0xFF, 0xFF);
  ```

- The `imagestring()` function used in this example is for writing text horizontally. The `imagestringup()` function will place the text vertically.

Using TrueType Fonts

The font options available to you when creating simple images as you did in the previous example can be limiting: five fixed-size and crude fonts. There are two other font options for creating images: PostScript fonts and TrueType fonts. PostScript fonts were designed for improved printing and are therefore more suited for straight text documents rather than Web images, in my opinion. It is an option for those more accustomed to them, but I'll stick to TrueType fonts in my examples here.

Without going into unnecessary font details, suffice it to say that TrueType fonts are the default fonts on most operating systems because they render higher-quality text (they are anti-aliased, which is to say not jagged) than their predecessors' bitmapped fonts (GD's built-in fonts are more like a bitmap). TrueType fonts are also more flexible in terms of sizing and offer more possibilities for bold print, italics, and other treatments.

To use TrueType fonts instead of the standard GD fonts, you will need two things: the FreeType library installed on your server and the font file itself. The former is freely available and the latter can be found all over the place, including the fonts directory on your own computer (search for files named *.ttf) or Web sites such as www.FontFreak.com. Some fonts are free and others are commercial products, so pay attention to licensing when using them.

There are only two relevant PHP functions for using TrueType fonts: imagettftext() and imagettfbbox(). The first function prints out a string onto the image.

```
imagettftext ($image, $font_size,
→ $angle, $x, $y, $text_color,
→ $font_file, "Text");
```

Table 10.3 The `imagettfbbox()` function, when called, returns an array of points indicating the x and y coordinates of the rectangle a string will be placed in.

Imagettfbbox Array	
KEY	**VALUE**
0	Lower-left corner, x
1	Lower-left corner, y
2	Lower-right corner, x
3	Lower-right corner, y
4	Upper-right corner, x
5	Upper-right corner, y
6	Upperleft corner, x
7	Upper-left corner, y

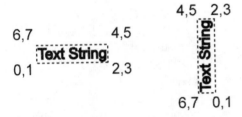

Figure 10.5 This image shows how the array returned by the TrueType functions represent the bounding box of the string.

The `$font_size` value is an integer indicating the number of pixels per character in terms of height. The `$angle` indicates the direction of the text: 0 (horizontal from left to right), 90 (vertical from bottom to top—i.e., rotated 90 degrees counterclockwise from 0), 180 (horizontal from right to left, upside down), and so forth. The `$font_file` value should refer to the file of the font being used. It needs to indicate that font's location on the server relative to the current script, just as you would refer to a JavaScript file, perhaps, or an image in your HTML code.

The companion function to `imagettftext()`, `imagettfbbox()`, does not add anything to the image but rather returns an array of eight items (technically, `imagettftext()` returns the same array but does place the text on the image). This array corresponds to the four points of an imaginary box that the text will take up (an x and a y for each corner). Hence, the *bbox* of the function name refers to the string's bounding box—the rectangle that contains the entire string.

This is useful because you can accurately determine how much space the text will take up—both horizontally and vertically—without altering the image. **Table 10.3** lists the array keys and values returned by these two functions, and **Figure 10.5** gives a pictorial representation of it as well. The array always begins in the lower-left corner of the text string, regardless of the angle or direction of the text string.

Keeping this information in mind, I'll rewrite the `image_form.php` page to make use of TrueType fonts. At the same time, I'll add code that will fix the image to a set size, fitting the text in accordingly.

USING TRUETYPE FONTS

To use TrueType fonts:

1. Open `image_form.php` (Script 10.1) in your text editor.

2. Change the constants for this script (**Script 10.2**).

   ```
   $font_size = 50;
   define ("WIDTH", 300);
   define ("HEIGHT", 100);
   ```

   The actual font size will be calculated later in the script based on the length of the string entered. I'll start it off with a high value and the script will work from there down. The image size will be fixed, unlike the previous images, which were based on the text entered.

3. Add the lines that calculate the font size.

   ```
   $type_space = imagettfbbox
   → ($font_size, 0, "arial.ttf",
   → $HTTP_GET_VARS['text']);
   while ( ( ( ($type_space[7] -
   → $type_space[1]) + 10 ) >= HEIGHT)
   → OR ( ( ($type_space[2] - $type_
   → space[0]) + 5) >= WIDTH) ) {
   $font_size--;
   $type_space  = imagettfbbox
   → ($font_size, 0, "arial.ttf",
   → $HTTP_GET_VARS['text']);
   }
   ```

   The first line will make an imaginary box containing the entered text. Using the returned array, the current height

   ($type_space[7] - $type_space[1]) and width ($type_space[2] - $type_space[0]) of the box, plus a small buffer in each case, will be compared against the size of the image. If either is larger than the image itself—in other words, the text will not print within the confines of the image, the font size will be reduced by one, the bounding box will be recalculated, and the loop will be retested. Once the size of the text string fits comfortably within the image, you know that the font size is safe to use.

4. Fix the starting x- and y-coordinates for the text.

   ```
   $x = round ( (WIDTH -  ($type_space
   → [2] - $type_space[0])) / 2);
   $y = round ( (HEIGHT - ($type_space
   → [7] - $type_space[1])) / 2);
   ```

   These two lines will establish the starting points for the text, based on the size of the bounding box. The width and height of the text are subtracted from the image dimensions and the resulting number is divided by 2, then rounded off. This will place the text roughly centered within the image.

5. Add the TrueType text to the image.

   ```
   imagettftext ($image, $font_size, 0,
   → $x, $y, $text_color, "arial.ttf",
   → $HTTP_GET_VARS['text']);
   ```

continues on page 362

Script 10.2 Using TrueType fonts in your images will give you cleaner, more consistent results than the built-in fonts.

```php
1    <?php
2    // This page creates a simple image based on user-submitted information.
3
4    // This function turns color names into their actual values on the RGB scale.
5    function color_allocate ($image, $color) {
6        switch ($color) {
7            case "white":
8                $red = 255;
9                $green = 255;
10               $blue = 255;
11               break;
12           case "red":
13               $red = 255;
14               $green = 51;
15               $blue = 51;
16               break;
17           case "orange":
18               $red = 255;
19               $green = 153;
20               $blue = 51;
21               break;
22           case "yellow":
23               $red = 255;
24               $green = 255;
25               $blue = 51;
26               break;
27           case "green":
28               $red = 51;
29               $green = 255;
30               $blue = 51;
31               break;
32           case "blue":
33               $red = 51;
34               $green = 51;
35               $blue = 255;
36               break;
37           case "purple":
38               $red = 255;
39               $green = 51;
40               $blue = 255;
41               break;
42           case "black":
43               $red = 0;
44               $green = 0;
45               $blue = 0;
46               break;
47       }
48       return imagecolorallocate ($image, $red, $green, $blue);
49   }
50
```

(script continues on next page)

Script 10.2 *continued*

```
      script

51    if (isset($HTTP_GET_VARS['submit'])) { // Handle the form.
52
53        if ( (isset($HTTP_GET_VARS['background_color'])) AND (isset($HTTP_GET_VARS['text'])) AND
          (isset($HTTP_GET_VARS['text_color'])) ) {
54
55            // Set the font and size info.
56            $font_size = 50; // Number of pixels.
57            define ("WIDTH", 300); // Number of pixels.
58            define ("HEIGHT", 100); // Number of pixels.
59
60            // Make and send the image.
61            header ("Content-type: image/png");
62            $image = @imagecreate (WIDTH, HEIGHT) or die ("A problem occurred trying to create the
              image.");
63
64            $background_color = color_allocate ($image, $HTTP_GET_VARS['background_color']);
65            $text_color = color_allocate ($image, $HTTP_GET_VARS['text_color']);
66
67            // Set the TrueType font size.
68            $type_space = imagettfbbox ($font_size, 0, "arial.ttf", $HTTP_GET_VARS['text']);
69
70            while ( ( ( ($type_space[7] - $type_space[1]) + 10 ) >= HEIGHT) OR ( ( ($type_space[2] -
              $type_space[0]) + 5) >= WIDTH) ) {
71                $font_size--;
72                $type_space = imagettfbbox ($font_size, 0, "arial.ttf", $HTTP_GET_VARS['text']);
73            }
74
75            $x = round ( (WIDTH - ($type_space[2] - $type_space[0])) / 2);
76            $y = round ( (HEIGHT - ($type_space[7] - $type_space[1])) / 2);
77            imagefill ($image, 0, 0, $background_color); // Not necessary but good form.
78            imagettftext ($image, $font_size, 0, $x, $y, $text_color, "arial.ttf",
              $HTTP_GET_VARS['text']);
79
80            imagepng ($image);
81            imagedestroy ($image); // Destroy the image.
82
83        } else {
84            echo "You either forgot to select a background color, a text color or you forgot to enter
              the text itself.\n";
85        }
86
87    } else {
88        // Display the form.
89    ?>
90    <!DOCTYPE html PUBLIC "-//W3C//DTD XHTML 1.0 Transitional//EN"
91        "http://www.w3.org/TR/2000/REC-xhtml1-20000126/DTD/xhtml1-transitional.dtd">
92    <html xmlns="http://www.w3.org/1999/xhtml">
93    <head>
94        <title>Create An Image</title>
95    </head>
```

(script continues on next page)

Script 10.2 *continued*

```
                                    script
96    <body>
97    <form action="image_tt_form.php" method="get">
98    <table border="0" width="80%" cellspacing="2" cellpadding="2" align="center">
99        <tr align="center" valign="top">
100           <td align="center" valign="top" colspan="2">Fill out the form to have your image
              created!</td>
101       </tr>
102       <tr align="center" valign="top">
103           <td align="right" valign="top">Enter the image text:</td>
104           <td align="left" valign="top"><input type="text" name="text" size="20"
              maxlength="40"></td>
105       </tr>
106       <tr align="center" valign="top">
107           <td align="right" valign="top">Select the text color:</td>
108           <td align="left" valign="top"><select name="text_color">
109   <option value="white">White</option>
110   <option value="red">Red</option>
111   <option value="orange">Orange</option>
112   <option value="yellow">Yellow</option>
113   <option value="green">Green</option>
114   <option value="blue">Blue</option>
115   <option value="purple">Purple</option>
116   <option value="black">Black</option>
117   </select></td>
118       </tr>
119       <tr align="center" valign="top">
120           <td align="right" valign="top">Select the background color:</td>
121           <td align="left" valign="top"><select name="background_color">
122   <option value="white">White</option>
123   <option value="red">Red</option>
124   <option value="orange">Orange</option>
125   <option value="yellow">Yellow</option>
126   <option value="green">Green</option>
127   <option value="blue">Blue</option>
128   <option value="purple">Purple</option>
129   <option value="black">Black</option>
130   </select></td>
131       </tr>
132       <tr align="center" valign="top">
133           <td align="center" valign="top" colspan="2"><input type="submit" name="submit"
              value="Make The Image!"></td>
134       </tr>
135   </table>
136   </form>
137   </body>
138   </html>
139   <?php
140   } // Close the SUBMIT conditional.
141   ?>
```

6. Change the form `action` attribute.

```
<form action="image_tt_form.php"
→ method="get">
```

Since I'm going to be changing the name of the file, I have to remember to change the form, too.

7. Save the file as `image_tt_form.php`, upload it to your Web server along with the font file, and test in your Web browser (**Figures 10.6**, **10.7**, **10.8**, and **10.9**).

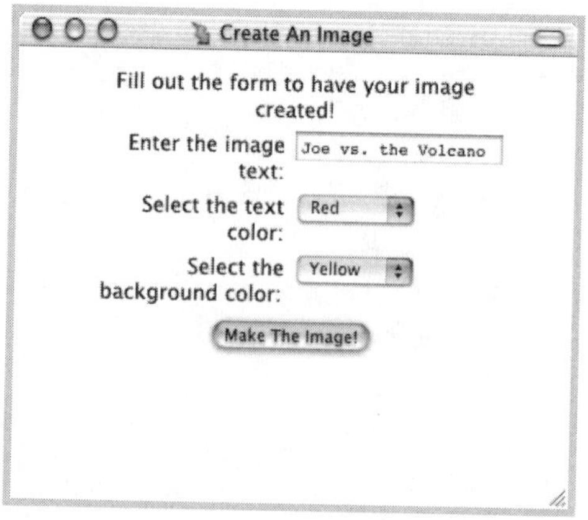

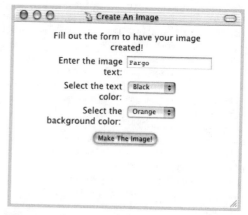

Figure 10.6 The form itself is the same, but the results are much improved. Compare Figures 10.4 and 10.7.

Figure 10.8 If a short string is submitted, the font on the image will be larger (Figure 10.9) than it was for a longer string (Figure 10.7).

Figure 10.7 Besides the fact that the text is smoother, the images created with the TrueType system are of uniform size.

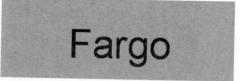

Figure 10.9 The script will display the text almost as large as it can and will do a good, albeit not perfect, job of centering it, too.

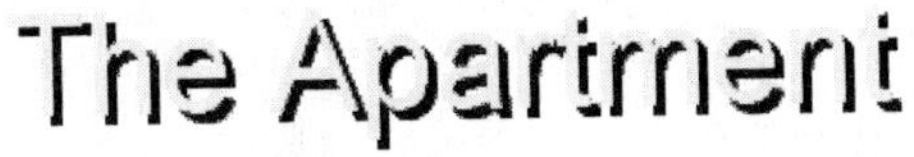

The Apartment

Figure 10.10 Sending two lines of the same text to an image, slightly offset and with different colors, creates a drop-shadow effect.

✔ Tips

- Rasmus Lerdorf, PHP's creator, wrote a two-page article, available at `http://PHPBuilder.com`, that discusses how he uses a script similar to this to make Web site images on the fly. Once the image-generation script is written, your HTML could include lines such as `<img src="image_tt_form.php?text=Home&text_color=blue&background_color=red" width="300" height="100">`, which would create and place the image when the page is viewed. It's a great trick that's worth checking out.

- To create a drop-shadow effect with a string, repeat the `imagettftext()` line using all the same values, but offset the x- and y-coordinates by a couple of pixels and use a gray or black text color (**Figure 10.10**). Call the shadow line prior to the main text line so it is written first (and therefore behind).

Creating a Database-Driven Graph

Now that I've covered the basics of image generation with PHP, which is surprisingly easy, I'll develop a more advanced application that creates a graph derived from stored data.

The example I'll use will be based on the sports pool application developed back in Chapter 1, Advanced PHP Programming. At the time, I wrote a script that created an array of how each player was doing to date. In this section and the next, you'll create a graph for each week's results instead. In the process, you'll see how to create different shapes in your image, including rectangles, dashed lines, and circles.

There are two functions for creating rectangles: imagerectangle() and imagefilledrectangle(). The latter obviously makes the entire rectangle the same color, whereas the former makes a rectangle with only a border of the desired color.

```
imagerectangle ($image, $x1, $y1, $x2,
→ $y2, $color);
```

```
imagefilledrectangle ($image, $x1, $y1,
→ $x2, $y2, $color);
```

To create a rectangle, you need to provide all four coordinates—two x and two y. It does not matter which coordinates you use and in what order, as long as you use opposite corners.

Similarly, there are two functions for creating a straight line, both imageline() and imagedashedline().

```
imageline ($image, $x1, $y1, $x2, $y2,
→ $color);
```

```
imagedashedline ($image, $x1, $y1, $x2,
→ $y2, $color);
```

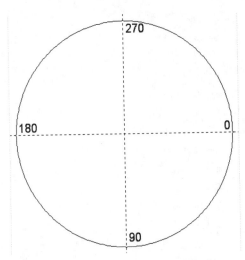

270

180 ———————————————— 0

90

Figure 10.11 The trickiest aspect to generating images is knowing where strings and shapes begin. Arcs and circles start at 0 on this image and go clockwise.

These are self-explanatory; to use them you only need to stipulate both points that define the line (and the color, naturally).

The `imagearc()` function is not as straightforward in naming or use as the previous four. Its intention is to create arcs—an arc being a segment of a circle or ellipse.

```
imagearc ($image, $x, $y, $width,
→ $height, $start, $end, $color);
```

The x- and y-coordinates represent where the center of the circle is going to be, even if you are just creating a part of that circle. The width and height dictate how far along the x and y axes the arc travels. Thus, you can create an arc that is part of a theoretical ellipse and not a perfect circle if these two numbers are different (in other words, if it travels more along one axis than it does the other). The `$start` and `$end` variables represent the degree at which the arc begins and the degree at which it stops, using the far-right side of the circle as 0 and continuing clockwise (**Figure 10.11**). If your start and end-points are 0 and 360, a complete circle will be created.

Finally, if you are using a version of PHP prior to 4.0.6, you cannot use the `imagefilledarc()` function and must manually fill in the created space to make a full circle (`imagearc()` alone will create a hollow circle). To fill in any space, arc or otherwise, use the `imagefilltoborder()` function.

```
imagefilltoborder ($image, $x, $y,
→ $border_color, $fill_color);
```

This function takes a starting point, as indicated by the x- and y-coordinates. From there it will expand out, like the Blob, changing the color of the entire image to the `$fill_color` until it runs into a border of `$border_color`. It can fill a circle, a rhombus, or any generic polygon you want.

CREATING A DATABASE-DRIVEN GRAPH

Now I'll apply all of this information in a script that will make a graph based on data stored in a text file (although it could just as easily retrieve this data from a database). If you recall, the sports pool application stored each week's results in a text file called `results_1_.txt`, which in turn is in the `2001` directory. This information will be the foundation for the graph on a week-by-week basis.

To create a data-generated graph:

1. Create a new PHP document in your text editor (**Script 10.3**).

```
<?php
```

2. Code the `color_allocate()` function or copy it from a previous script.

```
function color_allocate ($image,
→ $color) {
switch ($color) {
case "white":
$red = 255;
$green = 255;
$blue = 255;
break;
case "red":
$red = 255;
$green = 51;
$blue = 51;
break;
case "orange":
$red = 255;
$green = 153;
$blue = 51;
break;
case "yellow":
$red = 255;
$green = 255;
$blue = 51;
break;
case "green":
$red = 51;
$green = 255;
$blue = 51;
break;
case "blue":
$red = 51;
$green = 51;
$blue = 255;
break;
case "purple":
$red = 255;
$green = 51;
$blue = 255;
break;
case "black":
$red = 0;
$green = 0;
$blue = 0;
break;
case "gray":
$red = 153;
$green = 153;
$blue = 153;
break;
}

return imagecolorallocate ($image,
→ $red, $green, $blue);
}
```

This function is the same as it was before, although I've added a *gray* option.

continues on page 370

Script 10.3 This script makes a graph indicating each player's winning percentage for the week.

```
1    <?php
2    // This page creates a graph based on data stored in text files.
3
4    // This function turns color names into their actual values on the RGB scale.
5    function color_allocate ($image, $color) {
6        switch ($color) {
7            case "white":
8                $red = 255;
9                $green = 255;
10               $blue = 255;
11               break;
12           case "red":
13               $red = 255;
14               $green = 51;
15               $blue = 51;
16               break;
17           case "orange":
18               $red = 255;
19               $green = 153;
20               $blue = 51;
21               break;
22           case "yellow":
23               $red = 255;
24               $green = 255;
25               $blue = 51;
26               break;
27           case "green":
28               $red = 51;
29               $green = 255;
30               $blue = 51;
31               break;
32           case "blue":
33               $red = 51;
34               $green = 51;
35               $blue = 255;
36               break;
37           case "purple":
38               $red = 255;
39               $green = 51;
40               $blue = 255;
41               break;
42           case "black":
```

(script continues on next page)

Script 10.3 *continued*

```
                                      script
43              $red = 0;
44              $green = 0;
45              $blue = 0;
46              break;
47          case "gray":
48              $red = 153;
49              $green = 153;
50              $blue = 153;
51              break;
52      }
53      return imagecolorallocate ($image, $red, $green, $blue);
54  }
55
56  // Set the font and size info.
57  $font_size = 10; // Number in pixels.
58  $font_file = "arial.ttf";
59  define ("WIDTH", 400); // Number of pixels = (17 weeks * 20 pixels) + (10-pixel spacer * 2) + 40.
60  define ("HEIGHT", 260); // Number of pixels = 200-pixel scale + (10-pixel spacer * 2) + 40.
61
62  // Make and send the image.
63  header ("Content-type: image/png");
64  $image = @imagecreate (WIDTH, HEIGHT) or die ("A problem occurred trying to create the image.");
65
66  // Set the main colors.
67  $background_color = color_allocate ($image, 'gray');
68  $text_color = color_allocate ($image, 'black');
69  $line_color = color_allocate ($image, 'black');
70  $rectangle_color = color_allocate ($image, 'white');
71
72  // Set the user colors.
73  $people_color['Brian'] = color_allocate ($image, 'blue');
74  $people_color['Juan'] = color_allocate ($image, 'red');
75  $people_color['Larry'] = color_allocate ($image, 'orange');
76  $people_color['Michael'] = color_allocate ($image, 'green');
77
78  // Create the main image.
79  imagefill ($image, 0, 0, $background_color); // Not necessary but good form.
80  imagerectangle ($image, 0, 0, (WIDTH-1), (HEIGHT-1), $line_color); // Border for the image.
81  imagefilledrectangle ($image, 50, 10, 390, 210, $rectangle_color);
82  imagerectangle ($image, 50, 10, 390, 210, $line_color); // Border for the graph.
83
84  // Make the graph lines.
```

(script continues on next page)

(left margin) CREATING A DATABASE-DRIVEN GRAPH

Script 10.3 *continued*

```
                              script
85   imagedashedline ($image,50,50,390,50,$line_color);
86   imagedashedline ($image,50,90,390,90,$line_color);
87   imagedashedline ($image,50,130,390,130,$line_color);
88   imagedashedline ($image,50,170,390,170,$line_color);
89
90   // Number the graph.
91   imagettftext ($image, $font_size, 0, 40, 215, $text_color, $font_file, '0');
92   imagettftext ($image, $font_size, 0, 35, 175, $text_color, $font_file, '20');
93   imagettftext ($image, $font_size, 0, 35, 135, $text_color, $font_file, '40');
94   imagettftext ($image, $font_size, 0, 35, 95, $text_color, $font_file, '60');
95   imagettftext ($image, $font_size, 0, 35, 55, $text_color, $font_file, '80');
96   imagettftext ($image, $font_size, 0, 30, 15, $text_color, $font_file, '100');
97
98   for ($i = 1; $i <= 17; $i++) {
99       $x = ($i * 20) + 40; // Each week is 20 pixels; 40-pixel offset.
100      imagettftext ($image, $font_size, 0, $x, 220, $text_color, $font_file, "$i");
101  }
102
103  imagettftext ($image, ($font_size * 2), 90, 20, 180, $text_color, $font_file, 'Percentage');
104  imagettftext ($image, ($font_size * 2), 0, 180, 250, $text_color, $font_file, 'Week');
105
106  // Read the data.
107  $x = ($HTTP_GET_VARS[week] * 20) + 42;
108  $file_name = 'results_' . $HTTP_GET_VARS['week'] . '_.txt';
109
110  if ($data = @file ("2001/$file_name")) {
111      foreach ($data as $key => $value) {
112          if ($key != 0) {
113              $line = explode ("\t", $value);
114              $winning_percentage = round ( ($line[1] / ($line[1] + $line[2]) ) * 100);
115              $y = ((100 - $winning_percentage) * 2) + 10;
116              imagearc ($image, $x, $y, 10, 10, 0, 360, $people_color["$line[0]"]);
117              imagefilltoborder ($image, $x, $y, $people_color["$line[0]"],
                 $people_color["$line[0]"]);
118          }
119      }
120  }
121
122  // Finished!
123  imagepng ($image);
124  imagedestroy ($image); // Destroy the image.
125  ?>
```

CREATING A DATABASE-DRIVEN GRAPH

3. Set the defaults.

```
$font_size = 10;
$font_file = "arial.ttf";
define ("WIDTH", 400);
define ("HEIGHT", 260);
```

The font size will be smaller here than in previous examples because there will be a lot of information displayed. The font itself is stored in a variable, listing not the font name (e.g., *Arial*), but the name and location of the file where it can be found. Here, arial.ttf should be in the same folder as this script will be.

The height and width are based on a certain scale—the full percentage being displayed on the y axis in double terms (i.e., 100 percent over 200 pixels) and each of the 17 weeks is given 20 pixels. Added to each is some buffer room, resulting in an image 400 by 260 pixels.

4. Send the header and create the image pointer.

```
header ("Content-type: image/png");
$image = @imagecreate (WIDTH, HEIGHT)
→ or die ("A problem occurred trying
→ to create the image.");
```

5. Assign the colors.

```
$background_color = color_allocate
→ ($image, 'gray');
$text_color = color_allocate
→ ($image, 'black');
$line_color = color_allocate
→ ($image, 'black');
$rectangle_color = color_allocate
→ ($image, 'white');
$people_color['Brian'] = color_
→ allocate ($image, 'blue');
$people_color['Juan'] = color_
→ allocate ($image, 'red');
$people_color['Larry'] = color_
→ allocate ($image, 'orange');
$people_color['Michael'] = color_
→ allocate ($image, 'green');
```

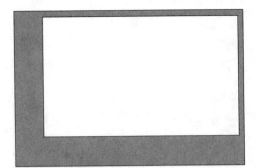

Figure 10.12 The image currently consists of two filled-in rectangles and two empty rectangles for borders.

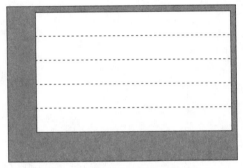

Figure 10.13 Dashed lines have been added to the image to mark the y axis across the entire x axis.

I want each player to be represented by his or her own color, so I've created one array, indexed by the player name, to contain them all. This is one step in which the script is not completely independent of the data it represents. If you would like to make it more independent—so that it allows for a variable number of participants, perhaps—create an array of colors and then assign a unique color to each participant.

6. Create the image.

```
imagefill ($image, 0, 0,
→ $background_color);

imagerectangle ($image, 0, 0,
→ (WIDTH-1), (HEIGHT-1), $line_color);

imagefilledrectangle ($image, 50,
→ 10, 390, 210, $rectangle_color);

imagerectangle ($image, 50, 10, 390,
→ 210, $line_color);
```

The first line simply makes the whole image gray. The second line creates a black border around the whole image. The third line places a white rectangle inside the image that will be the graph itself (the remaining space in the image will be for text labels). The fourth line gives this graph rectangle a black border. **Figure 10.12** shows the image created to this point.

7. Add lines to the graph.

```
imagedashedline
→ ($image,50,50,390,50,$line_color);

imagedashedline
→ ($image,50,90,390,90,$line_color);

imagedashedline
→ ($image,50,130,390,130,$line_color);

imagedashedline
→ ($image,50,170,390,170,$line_color);
```

I want to give a rough sense of the values across the entire graph, so I've added dashed lines. **Figure 10.13** shows the graph now.

continues on next page

CREATING A DATABASE-DRIVEN GRAPH

8. Place the corresponding numbers and labels on the graph.

```
imagettftext ($image, $font_size, 0,
→ 40, 215, $text_color, $font_file,
→ '0');
imagettftext ($image, $font_size, 0,
→ 35, 175, $text_color, $font_file,
→ '20');
imagettftext ($image, $font_size, 0,
→ 35, 135, $text_color, $font_file,
→ '40');
imagettftext ($image, $font_size, 0,
→ 35, 95, $text_color, $font_file,
→ '60');
imagettftext ($image, $font_size, 0,
→ 35, 55, $text_color, $font_file,
→ '80');
imagettftext ($image, $font_size, 0,
→ 30, 15, $text_color, $font_file,
→ '100');
for ($i = 1; $i <= 17; $i++) {
$x = ($i * 20) + 40;
imagettftext ($image, $font_size, 0,
→ $x, 220, $text_color, $font_file,
→ "$i");
}
imagettftext ($image, ($font_size *
→ 2), 90, 20, 180, $text_color,
→ $font_file, 'Percentage');
imagettftext ($image, ($font_size *
→ 2), 0, 180, 250, $text_color,
→ $font_file, 'Week');
```

Using some basic math and a *for* loop, I'm quickly able to label each axis. Notice also that the *Percentage* text is written vertically (**Figure 10.14**).

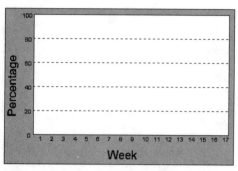

Figure 10.14 The structure of the graph is now complete, including labels, and the image is now ready for the user marks (Figure 10.15).

Script 10.4 The results files were created automatically by the PHP scripts written in Chapter 1, Advanced PHP Programming.

	script		
1	User	Wins	Losses
2	Brian	10	5
3	Juan	9	6
4	Larry	11	4
5	Michael	12	3

9. Retrieve each user's results and use that information to plot the user's winning percentage.

```php
$x = ($HTTP_GET_VARS[week] * 20) + 42;
$file_name = 'results_' . $HTTP_
→ GET_VARS['week'] . '_.txt';
if ($data = @file ("2001/$file_
→ name")) {
foreach ($data as $key => $value) {
if ($key != 0) {
$line = explode ("\t", $value);
$winning_percentage = round
→ (($line[1] / ($line[1] +
→ $line[2]) ) * 100);
$y = ((100 - $winning_percentage) *
→ 2) + 10;
imagearc ($image, $x, $y, 10, 10, 0,
→ 360, $people_color["$line[0]"]);
imagefilltoborder ($image, $x, $y,
→ $people_color["$line[0]"],
→ $people_color["$line[0]"]);
}
}
}
```

The x-coordinate for each player will be the same, as determined by the week number times 20 (each week gets 20 pixels) with a little guesstimated buffer of 42 pixels thrown in to line it up with the numbering along the x axis.

Afterward, the results file is read into an array. Each line of the array is broken up into its own subarray. (This is done only if it is not the first, dummy line. See **Script 10.4**, line 1.) The structure of the results files indicate that the resulting array, $line, contains the user's name, wins, and losses.

continues on next page

The y-coordinate of each player is based on the player's winning percentage for that week, calculated as wins divided by the total number of games, multiplied by 100 and rounded to the nearest integer. This number (the player's winning percentage) is then subtracted from 100, because I want to determine how far down from 100 I ought to place the player's marker. Because the scale is doubled and because the graph itself starts 10 pixels down, I need to double the number (100 minus the winning percentage) and add 10.

As an example, Juan went 9 and 6: 9 divided by 15 (9 + 6) is 0.6, times 100 is 60. This number is rounded and then is subtracted from 100, leaving 40. That means that Juan's y value should be down 40 from the top of the graph. The top of the graph is at 10, and 40 is actually 80 on the double scale, so Juan's final y value is 90.

Once the x- and y-coordinates for a player have been determined, a circle can be created using the player's color at the appropriate location. The circle is then filled in with the same color.

10. Finish the image and destroy it.

```
imagepng ($image);
imagedestroy ($image);
?>
```

11. Save the file as `generate_graph.php`, upload it to your server, and test in your Web browser, appending a week value to the URL—e.g., `www.DMCinsights.com/generate_graph.php?week=1` (**Figure 10.15**).

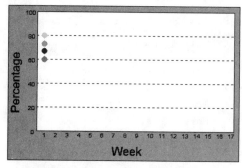

Figure 10.15 The final graph has plotted all four participants' winning percentages for the week based on data retrieved from a text file.

✔ Tips

■ PHP 4.0.6 now has extended capabilities in terms of filling in arcs as they are created and generating ellipses. If you are using this version or later (and the new functions also require version 2.0.2 or greater of the GD library), read the manual for more information.

■ I didn't do so here, but you probably would want to create a key for the image, too. One option would be to print out each user's name across the bottom or top in his or her respective color.

Saving and Building on Existing Images

Up to this point every image has been created in memory and immediately sent to the browser. You also have the option with PHP and GD to build on existing images and to save them to the server. The three relevant functions are

```
$image = imagecreatefromgif ($file_name);
```

```
$image = imagecreatefrompng ($file_name);
```

```
$image = imagecreatefromjpg ($file_name);
```

Each of these functions would be used in lieu of the imagecreate() function. Note that which function you use should be based on the format of the source image, not the final one. You could theoretically build on a GIF or JPEG to create a PNG, although the quality of the image itself will suffer. Which function you can use is also dependent on the version of the GD library installed (since GIF support was dropped and PNG support added at various stages).

Just as you have the option to start with an existing image rather than from scratch, you can also save a created image instead of just sending it to the browser and destroying it.

The same image used for creating an image in the Web browser can create the image as a file on the server; you just need to provide it with a name.

```
imagepng ($image, "pingpong.png");
```

I'll build on the existing generate_graph. php script so that each week the previous week's graph is opened, the new week's data is appended, and the file is saved. Before I do, though, I'd like to mention two more functions: imagepolygon() and imagefilledpolygon().

The imagepolygon() function is used to create a many-sided shape. To use it you must first create an array of coordinates for each point in the polygon. Then you feed this array to imagepolygon() along with the number of points the shape should have. This code will make an equilateral triangle:

```
$points[0] = 100; // x1
```

```
$points[1] = 0; // y1
```

```
$points[2] = 150; // x2
```

```
$points[3] = 100; // y2
```

```
$points[4] = 50; // x3
```

```
$points[5] = 100; // y3
```

```
imagepolygon ($image, $points, 3,
→ $color);
```

Using the imagepolygon() function, I'll give each user his or her own unique shape as well as color since I'm already remaking the script.

To save and build on existing images:

1. Open generate_graph.php (Script 10.3) in your text editor.

2. Turn the height, width, and image-creation lines from the original script (lines 59-64) into a week-specific conditional (**Script 10.5**).

```
if ($HTTP_GET_VARS['week'] == 1) {
define ("WIDTH", 400);
define ("HEIGHT", 260);
header ("Content-type: image/png");
$image = @imagecreate (WIDTH, HEIGHT)
→ or die ("A problem occurred trying
→ to create the image.");
} else {
$old_image_name = 'graphs/week_' .
→ ($HTTP_GET_VARS['week'] - 1) .
→ '_graph.png';
header ("Content-type: image/png");
$image = @imagecreatefrompng
→ ($old_image_name) or die ("I
→ couldn't open the original image
→ $old_image_name.");
}
```

I'm going to write this script so that the first week it will make the entire image from scratch and the remaining weeks it will open and build on the previous week's graph. There will be a handful of conditionals like this one added to the original script to reflect this change.

3. Enclose the code for creating the graph structure and labels within another conditional.

```
if ($HTTP_GET_VARS['week'] == 1) {
imagefill ($image, 0, 0,
→ $background_color);
imagerectangle ($image, 0, 0,
→ (WIDTH-1), (HEIGHT-1), $line_color);
imagefilledrectangle ($image, 50, 10,
→ 390, 210, $rectangle_color);
imagerectangle ($image, 50, 10, 390,
→ 210, $line_color);
imagedashedline ($image,50,50,390,50,
→ $line_color);
imagedashedline ($image,50,90,390,90,
→ $line_color);
imagedashedline ($image,50,130,390,
→ 130,$line_color);
imagedashedline ($image,50,170,390,
→ 170,$line_color);
imagettftext ($image, $font_size,
→ 0, 40, 215, $text_color,
→ $font_file, '0');
imagettftext ($image, $font_size,
→ 0, 35, 175, $text_color,
→ $font_file, '20');
imagettftext ($image, $font_size,
→ 0, 35, 135, $text_color,
→ $font_file, '40');
imagettftext ($image, $font_size,
→ 0, 35, 95, $text_color,
→ $font_file, '60');
imagettftext ($image, $font_size,
→ 0, 35, 55, $text_color, $font_file,
→ '80');
imagettftext ($image, $font_size,
→ 0, 30, 15, $text_color, $font_file,
→ '100');
for ($i = 1; $i <= 17; $i++) {
$x = ($i * 20) + 40;
imagettftext ($image, $font_size,
→ 0, $x, 220, $text_color,
→ $font_file, "$i");
}
imagettftext ($image, ($font_size *
→ 2), 90, 20, 180, $text_color,
→ $font_file, 'Percentage');
imagettftext ($image, ($font_size *
→ 2), 0, 180, 250, $text_color,
→ $font_file, 'Week');
}
```

continues on page 381

Script 10.5 The final version of the graph generator will create a new image or build on an existing one depending on which week it is. A version of the image is also stored to the server each week as well as sent to the Web browser.

```
script
1    <?php
2    // This page creates a graph based on data stored in text files.
3
4    // This function turns color names into their actual values on the RGB scale.
5    function color_allocate ($image, $color) {
6        switch ($color) {
7            case "white":
8                $red = 255;
9                $green = 255;
10               $blue = 255;
11               break;
12           case "red":
13               $red = 255;
14               $green = 51;
15               $blue = 51;
16               break;
17           case "orange":
18               $red = 255;
19               $green = 153;
20               $blue = 51;
21               break;
22           case "yellow":
23               $red = 255;
24               $green = 255;
25               $blue = 51;
26               break;
27           case "green":
28               $red = 51;
29               $green = 255;
30               $blue = 51;
31               break;
32           case "blue":
33               $red = 51;
34               $green = 51;
35               $blue = 255;
36               break;
37           case "purple":
38               $red = 255;
39               $green = 51;
40               $blue = 255;
41               break;
42           case "black":
43               $red = 0;
44               $green = 0;
45               $blue = 0;
46               break;
47           case "gray":
48               $red = 153;
49               $green = 153;
```

(script continues on next page)

Script 10.5 *continued*

```
50              $blue = 153;
51              break;
52          }
53      return imagecolorallocate ($image, $red, $green, $blue);
54  }
55
56  // Set the font and size info.
57  $font_size = 10; // Number in pixels.
58  $font_file = "arial.ttf";
59
60  if ($HTTP_GET_VARS['week'] == 1) { // Create the image only once.
61
62      define ("WIDTH", 400); // Number of pixels = (17 weeks * 20 pixels) +
        (10-pixel spacer * 2) + 40.
63      define ("HEIGHT", 260); // Number of pixels = 200-pixel scale + (10-pixel spacer * 2) + 40.
64
65      // Make and send the image.
66      header ("Content-type: image/png");
67      $image = @imagecreate (WIDTH, HEIGHT) or die ("A problem occurred trying to create the
        image.");
68
69  } else {
70
71      $old_image_name = 'graphs/week_' . ($HTTP_GET_VARS['week'] - 1) . '_graph.png';
72
73      // Make and send the image.
74      header ("Content-type: image/png");
75      $image = @imagecreatefrompng ($old_image_name) or die ("I couldn't open the original image
        $old_image_name.");
76
77  }
78
79  // Set the main colors.
80  $background_color = color_allocate ($image, 'gray');
81  $text_color = color_allocate ($image, 'black');
82  $line_color = color_allocate ($image, 'black');
83  $rectangle_color = color_allocate ($image, 'white');
84
85  // Set the user colors.
86  $people_color['Brian'] = color_allocate ($image, 'blue');
87  $people_color['Juan'] = color_allocate ($image, 'red');
88  $people_color['Larry'] = color_allocate ($image, 'orange');
89  $people_color['Michael'] = color_allocate ($image, 'green');
90
91  if ($HTTP_GET_VARS['week'] == 1) { // Create the image only once.
92
93      // Create the main image.
94      imagefill ($image, 0, 0, $background_color); // Not necessary but good form.
95      imagerectangle ($image, 0, 0, (WIDTH-1), (HEIGHT-1), $line_color); // Border for the image.
96      imagefilledrectangle ($image, 50, 10, 390, 210, $rectangle_color);
```

(script continues on next page)

Script 10.5 *continued*

```
 97      imagerectangle ($image, 50, 10, 390, 210, $line_color); // Border for the graph.
 98
 99      // Make the graph lines.
100      imagedashedline ($image,50,50,390,50,$line_color);
101      imagedashedline ($image,50,90,390,90,$line_color);
102      imagedashedline ($image,50,130,390,130,$line_color);
103      imagedashedline ($image,50,170,390,170,$line_color);
104
105      // Number the graph.
106      imagettftext ($image, $font_size, 0, 40, 215, $text_color, $font_file, '0');
107      imagettftext ($image, $font_size, 0, 35, 175, $text_color, $font_file, '20');
108      imagettftext ($image, $font_size, 0, 35, 135, $text_color, $font_file, '40');
109      imagettftext ($image, $font_size, 0, 35, 95, $text_color, $font_file, '60');
110      imagettftext ($image, $font_size, 0, 35, 55, $text_color, $font_file, '80');
111      imagettftext ($image, $font_size, 0, 30, 15, $text_color, $font_file, '100');
112
113      for ($i = 1; $i <= 17; $i++) {
114          $x = ($i * 20) + 40; // Each week is 20 pixels; 40-pixel offset.
115          imagettftext ($image, $font_size, 0, $x, 220, $text_color, $font_file, "$i");
116      }
117
118      imagettftext ($image, ($font_size * 2), 90, 20, 180, $text_color, $font_file, 'Percentage');
119      imagettftext ($image, ($font_size * 2), 0, 180, 250, $text_color, $font_file, 'Week');
120
121  } // Close the conditional.
122
123  // Read the data.
124  $file_name = 'results_' . $HTTP_GET_VARS['week'] . '_.txt';
125  $x = ($HTTP_GET_VARS[week] * 20) + 42;
126
127  if ($data = @file ("2001/$file_name")) {
128      foreach ($data as $key => $value) {
129          if ($key != 0) {
130              $line = explode ("\t", $value);
131              $winning_percentage = round ( ($line[1] / ($line[1] + $line[2]) ) * 100);
132              $y = ((100 - $winning_percentage) * 2) + 10;
133
134              switch ($line[0]) {
135                  case "Brian":
136                      imagearc ($image, $x, $y, 10, 10, 0, 360, $people_color["$line[0]"]);
137                      imagefilltoborder ($image, $x, $y, $people_color["$line[0]"],
                         $people_color["$line[0]"]);
138                      break;
139                  case "Juan":
140                      $juans_points[0] = $x; // Diamond top x.
141                      $juans_points[1] = $y - 5; // Diamond top y.
142                      $juans_points[2] = $x + 5;      // Diamond right x.
143                      $juans_points[3] = $y;          // Diamond right y.
144                      $juans_points[4] = $x;          // Diamond bottom x.
```

(script continues on next page)

Script 10.5 *continued*

```
                                                     script

145             $juans_points[5] = $y + 5;       // Diamond bottom y.
146             $juans_points[6] = $x - 5;       // Diamond left x.
147             $juans_points[7] = $y;           // Diamond left y.
148             imagefilledpolygon ($image, $juans_points, 4, $people_color["$line[0]"]);
149             break;
150         case "Larry":
151             imagefilledrectangle ($image, ($x - 5), ($y - 5), ($x + 5), ($y + 5),
                $people_color["$line[0]"]);
152             break;
153         case "Michael":
154             $michaels_points[0] = $x; // Triangle top x.
155             $michaels_points[1] = $y - 5; // Triangle top y.
156             $michaels_points[2] = $x + 5;    // Triangle right x.
157             $michaels_points[3] = $y;        // Triangle right y.
158             $michaels_points[4] = $x - 5;    // Triangle left x.
159             $michaels_points[5] = $y;        // Triangle left y.
160             imagefilledpolygon ($image, $michaels_points, 3, $people_color["$line[0]"]);
161             break;
162         } // Close the switch.
163
164         if ($HTTP_GET_VARS['week'] != 1) { // Store this week's results if it's not week 1.
165             $y_coordinate["$line[0]"] = $y;
166         }
167     } // Close the $key conditional.
168   } // Close the foreach loop.
169 } // Close the WEEK conditional.
170
171 if ($HTTP_GET_VARS['week'] != 1) { // Connect to last week's marks.
172     $old_file_name = 'results_' . ($HTTP_GET_VARS['week'] - 1) . '_.txt';
173     $old_x = (($HTTP_GET_VARS['week'] - 1) * 20) + 42;
174
175     if ($data = @file ("2001/$old_file_name")) {
176         foreach ($data as $key => $value) {
177             if ($key != 0) {
178                 $line = explode ("\t", $value);
179                 $winning_percentage = round ( ($line[1] / ($line[1] + $line[2]) ) * 100);
180                 $old_y = ((100 - $winning_percentage) * 2) + 10;
181                 imageline ($image, $old_x, $old_y, $x, $y_coordinate["$line[0]"],
                    $people_color["$line[0]"]);
182             }
183         } // Close the $key conditional.
184     } // Close the foreach loop.
185 } // Close the WEEK conditional.
186
187 // Finished!
188 imagepng ($image);
189 $new_image_name = 'graphs/week_' . $HTTP_GET_VARS['week'] . '_graph.png';
190 imagepng ($image, $new_image_name);
191 imagedestroy ($image); // Destroy the image.
192 ?>
```

CREATING PDFs

You're probably familiar with the Portable Document Format invented by Adobe Systems Inc. that provides a reliable way to create, transmit, and read complex documents while retaining all the original formatting. With Adobe Acrobat, you can create PDFs on your computer that anyone can read by downloading and installing the freely available and widely used Adobe Acrobat Reader. What you may not know is that you can also make PDFs directly with PHP. Just as you can have PHP dynamically create graphs or buttons on the fly (as you saw in the previous chapter), you can have it generate PDF invoices for you, make reports, or manufacture contracts and documents for your clients. (PHP 4 can make Macromedia Flash and Shockwave animations via an external library, too.)

To create PDFs with PHP you will need to install one of two libraries: either the PDFlib (www.pdflib.com) or ClibPDF (www.fastio.com). Neither is free for all uses, so be sure to check each license and documentation to determine the applicable fee. The PDFlib is more tightly integrated and supported in PHP and will therefore be the one we use here. Also required are two image libraries: JPEG (www.ijg.org), which was necessary for Chapter 10, Image Generation, and TIFF (www.libtiff.org).

I should say upfront that making a simple PDF with PHP can be difficult. However, making a complex PDF (involving graphics, images, different fonts, and so forth) is not that much more challenging. This oddity is because installing PDFlib can be tricky and its usage has varied remarkably between PHP 3 and 4 and between PDFlib 3 and 4. A number of functions that worked in earlier versions of PHP have been deprecated, meaning that there are newer functions you ought to be using. That being said, PHP's support for the PDFlib is solid and reliable now and will continue to remain so in future developments.

The key to successfully using this library is to try to work with the most recent version of PHP (of course) and with the latest PDFlib. For this chapter, I recommend you work with at least version 4.0.5 of PHP and version 4.0.1 of the PDFlib (there's a major bug in PDFlib 4.0.0, so you should either be using 3.x or 4.0.1). A lot of the recommended functions changed with PHP 4.0.5, so if you are using an older version, I will try to suggest all of the appropriate deprecated functions to use instead. Before getting into this chapter make a note of what version of PHP and PDFlib you have. If you run into problems with a script, check the different manuals to see what changes might be necessary.

In this chapter I'll make a highly usable and very practical application of the PDF technology: an automatic invoice generator that takes values from an HTML form and churns out a PDF invoice. You could, instead, use Forms Data Format to simplify this process. An FDF is like a PDF with the added ability for users to directly enter information into specific fields from Acrobat Reader. Unfortunately, creating FDFs requires Adobe Acrobat, although PHP can work with them once they are created. Since I am focusing on a Web-based solution, I'll stick to the HTML-form PDFlib system.

At some point in time, if you plan to develop a lot of PDF documents, it would be worth your while to read the manual that comes with PDFlib (which will be far more informative than the PHP manual section on PDF functions) as well as look at some of the other online resources. The PDF format is well supported within the Internet community and Appendix C, General Resources, lists some varied avenues for PDF information.

Creating a Simple PDF

To begin with, I'm going to create a blank PDF. This may seem like a waste of time, but it does, in fact, serve two purposes. First, it will allow me adequate space to give each function enough coverage. Second, it will give you an opportunity to test your PDF installation. Because of the slightly complicated nature of the format, most problems in generating or viewing a PDF are likely to happen during the simple act of creation, rather than during what might seem to be the more complicated steps. Once you've successfully run this script, you'll know where you stand for the more involved ones later in the chapter.

You will see numerous similarities between creating PDFs and creating images, which you did in the previous chapter. For example, the very first step for creating a PDF must be to create a new PDF object.

```
$pdf = pdf_new();
```

This object will act like an image or file pointer in that every function will use it as a reference. Note that as of version 4 of PHP and PDFlib, every function as described in the PDFlib manual has the same name and use in PHP, although the PDFlib manual uses slightly different syntax for describing them.

Once the object has been created, you need to open the PDF.

```
pdf_open_file ($pdf, $file_name);
```

If you will be creating the PDF in memory and sending it to the Web browser, no filename is required. If you intend to save the file to the server, enter the name of the file here. I'll demonstrate saving a PDF to the server in the last section of this chapter.

With older versions of PHP, you were supposed to use just **pdf_open()**. If you are using a version of PHP before 4.0.5, one change you

continues on next page

will need to make in this chapter's scripts is to replace the previous two lines with

```
$pdf = pdf_open();
```

Once the initial object has been established, you can set some of the file's information.

```
pdf_set_info ($pdf, "Author",
→ "Larry E. Ullman");
```

The `pdf_set_info()` function defines the document's properties—such as author, creator, title, and subject—which are not visible in the document itself. Its use is not strictly required but worth doing.

Now it is safe to create the first page of the document.

```
pdf_begin_page ($pdf, $width, $height);
```

PDFs use PostScript points as the unit of measurement. There are 72 points per inch, as a rule (there's some room for modifying this ratio, if you want to get really involved with PDFs). A standard 8.5–by–11-inch page will have dimensions of 612 points by 792. **Table 11.1** lists a few common page sizes and their corresponding point dimensions.

When you have finished working with a page, you can close it with

```
pdf_end_page ($pdf);
```

In the first couple of examples, I will be working with one-page documents. Later in the chapter, I will create a multiple-page PDF. While each PDF should have only one `pdf_new()` call, each page will require its own `pdf_begin_page()` and `pdf_end_page()`.

Once you are finished with the PDF and have ended the final page, you can close the object.

```
pdf_close ($pdf);
```

At this point what you have created is a PDF document in the server's memory. It can now be sent to the Web browser.

Table 11.1 These are the most common formats and sizes of documents, but PDFs can be of nearly any dimension. Check the PDFlib manual for what limits exist.

Page Sizes in PostScript Points		
FORMAT	WIDTH	HEIGHT
Letter	612	792
Legal	612	1008
A0	2380	3368
A1	1684	2380
A2	1190	1684
A3	842	1190
A4	595	842
A5	421	595
A6	297	421

Sending a PDF to a browser is a three-step process. First you must assign the PDF in memory to a variable.

```
$buffer = pdf_get_buffer ($pdf);
```

This variable is now a string that contains all of the PDF data.

Second you have to prepare the Web browser to receive a PDF document. To do so, I send the browser three headers: the type of content, the length of the content, and the disposition of the content.

```
header ("Content-type: application/pdf");
```

```
header ("Content-Length: " .
→ strlen($buffer));
```

```
header ("Content-Disposition: inline;
→ filename=filename.pdf");
```

There is a little room to play with these headers to prepare the browser how you want, but the content-type is required and the other two are best to include.

Now that the browser is prepared, you send it the content and then delete the object to free up the resources it is using from the server's memory.

```
echo $buffer;
```

```
pdf_delete ($pdf);
```

I'll write a script that will demonstrate these steps, generating a blank PDF. If you are using an earlier version of PHP or PDFlib, you'll need to make the recommended changes above and move the header() lines to the top of the script, removing everything else after pdf_close(). Earlier versions of PHP immediately sent the PDF to the browser as it was created, which means that the headers had to be sent first, and closing the object was sufficient for completing the page. PHP is directly incorporated into PDFlib 4 so the methodology has changed.

To create a simple PDF document:

1. Create a new PHP script in your text editor (**Script 11.1**):

   ```php
   <?php
   ```

2. Set the page height and width as constants based on the desired document size.

   ```php
   define ("PAGE_WIDTH", 612);
   define ("PAGE_HEIGHT",792);
   ```

   This PDF will be a standard letter size.

3. Create the PDF object and open it.

   ```php
   $pdf = pdf_new();
   pdf_open_file ($pdf, "");
   ```

4. Set the desired PDF information.

   ```php
   pdf_set_info ($pdf, "Author",
   → "Larry E. Ullman");
   pdf_set_info ($pdf, "Title", "Invoice
   → for " . $HTTP_POST_VARS['client']);
   pdf_set_info ($pdf, "Creator",
   → "See Author");
   ```

   None of these is required and there are more options, so use whichever settings you would prefer.

5. Begin and end the only page.

   ```php
   pdf_begin_page ($pdf, PAGE_WIDTH,
   → PAGE_HEIGHT);
   pdf_end_page ($pdf);
   ```

6. Close the document.

   ```php
   pdf_close ($pdf);
   ```

7. Send the PDF to the Web browser.

   ```php
   $buffer = pdf_get_buffer ($pdf);
   header ("Content-type:
   → application/pdf");
   header ("Content-Length: " .
   → strlen($buffer));
   header ("Content-Disposition:
   → inline; filename=filename.pdf");
   echo $buffer;
   ```

Script 11.1 This script will create a blank PDF that will allow you to test if your system is properly configured for PDF creation.

```php
1    <?php
2    // This page creates a blank PDF.
3
4    // Set the constants and variables.
5    define ("PAGE_WIDTH", 612); // 8.5
     inches.
6    define ("PAGE_HEIGHT",792); // 11 inches.
7
8    // Make the invoice.
9    $pdf = pdf_new();
10   pdf_open_file ($pdf, "");
11
12   // Set the different PDF values.
13   pdf_set_info ($pdf, "Author", "Larry E.
     Ullman");
14   pdf_set_info ($pdf, "Title", "Invoice for
     " . $HTTP_POST_VARS['client']);
15   pdf_set_info ($pdf, "Creator", "See
     Author");
16
17   // Create the page.
18   pdf_begin_page ($pdf, PAGE_WIDTH,
     PAGE_HEIGHT);
19
20   // Finish the page.
21   pdf_end_page ($pdf);
22
23   // Close the PDF.
24   pdf_close ($pdf);
25
26   // Send the PDF to the browser.
27   $buffer = pdf_get_buffer ($pdf);
28   header ("Content-type: application/pdf");
29   header ("Content-Length: " .
     strlen($buffer));
30   header ("Content-Disposition: inline;
     filename=filename.pdf");
31   echo $buffer;
32
33   // Free the resources.
34   pdf_delete ($pdf);
35   ?>
```

CREATING A SIMPLE PDF

Adding Text to PDFs

Obviously, you'll want to do more with your PDFs than just generate blank documents. The most important thing to be able to do is to add text, which you'll learn here.

Placing text within PDF documents is not nearly as easy or straightforward as you might think. Text cannot just be written down the page from left to right, top to bottom, as you can in your text editor or Web browser. Text in PDFs must be placed on the page as you would place points and lines on a graph. In fact, you can place the text in nearly any order and result in the same page (assuming no overlaps), but I still find it makes the most sense to code your way from the top down.

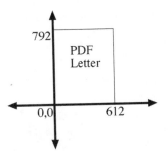

Figure 11.6 The origin of every page in a PDF is the lower-left corner, not the top-left corner as you might expect.

One of the trickier aspects of PDF generation is that the lower-left corner of the page is the point of origin, so text placed at the top of the page would be at coordinates of maybe 100, 700. As a visualization technique, consider that your PDF page is like the top-right quadrant in a standard graph (**Figure 11.6**).

Before you can use any of the functions for placing text, you need to establish the font type and size. The current method for setting the font is to start by assigning to a variable the font name, encoding and embedding.

```
$font = pdf_findfont ($pdf, $font_name,
→ $encoding);
```

Table 11.2 The 14 fonts listed here are always available when making PDFs and require no special treatment.

Built-in PDF Fonts
Courier
Courier-Bold
Courier-Bold Oblique
Courier-Oblique
Helvetica
Helvetica-Bold
Helvetica-Bold Oblique
Helvetica-Oblique
Symbol
Times-Bold
Times-Bold Italic
Times-Italic
Times-Roman
Zapf Dingbats

The font name is simply *Courier* or *Helvetica-Bold* or so forth. **Table 11.2** lists the fonts that come built-in with the PDFlib. These are part of every Acrobat Reader application and do not need to be embedded within the PDF itself (but you must name the font exactly as it appears in the table or else the PDFlib will not be able to use it). If you want to use other PostScript fonts, you will need to add the font file to the server and embed the font into the

continues on next page

PDF document. See the PDFlib manual for more information on embedding fonts.

A font's encoding has to do with what kind of operating system the font is prepared for. **Table 11.3** lists the possibilities.

It may seem that the host encoding type would be preferred, but it can run into problems with large-scale uses. As a rule, it is safe to use the *winansi* encoding except with Symbol, Zapf Dingbats, or similar fonts (that are symbol, rather than character, based) which require the *builtin* encoding.

Now that the font has been established using the `pdf_findfont()` function, you can set it as the font to use, indicating the font size at that time.

```
pdf_setfont ($pdf, $font, $font_size);
```

The **$font** variable should be the variable assigned during a `pdf_findfont()` call (like a font pointer) and the size is in PostScript points. Since there are 72 points per inch, a font set to 36 points will be half an inch tall on the page (the font size refers to the height of standard letter).

(If you are using older versions of PHP or PDFlib, you'll need to use this line instead:

```
$font = pdf_set_font ($pdf, $font,
→ $font_size, $encoding);)
```

After the font has been found and set, you are ready to print text to the PDF. Your options for doing so are: `pdf_show_xy()`, `pdf_show()`, `pdf_continue_text()`, and `pdf_show_boxed()`. All of these functions should work with your server configuration except for `pdf_show_boxed()`, which is new to PHP 4.0.0.

Table 11.3 Each font must be encoded in a certain manner to function properly. Using the *winansi* encoding is the best general-purpose choice.

Font Encodings	
ENCODING	DESCRIPTION
winansi	Windows
macroman	Mac Roman (Macintosh default)
ebcdic	EBCDIC, used on IBM AS/400 and S/390 systems
builtin	Coding built into the font itself
host	System-specific coding: macroman on the Mac, ebcdic on EBCDIC-based systems, and winansi on all others.

I'll indicate how each function is used:

- ♦ pdf_show_xy ($pdf, $x, $y, $text);

  This function will print $text in the current font starting at the coordinates x, y and working toward the right. It will continue to print the entire string even if it goes off the page (it will not automatically wrap the text).

- ♦ pdf_show ($pdf, $text);

  This function works exactly like pdf_show_xy() but will print $text in the current font at the current position within the document.

- ♦ pdf_continue_text ($pdf, $text);

  This function will print $text in the current font on the next line.

- ♦ pdf_show_boxed ($pdf, $text, $x, $y, → $width, $height, $mode);

  This function will create a virtual text box (without a border) of size $width and $height. The text will be wrapped from one line to the next, formatted according to the mode. Valid modes are *left, right, center, justify*, and *fulljustify*. It is very important to understand two things about this function: the x- and y-coordinates refer to the lower-left corner of the box, not the top left as you might expect; and, the box will not necessarily be large enough to print the entire text string as is. The function will return the number of characters cut off from a text box that is too small. These are very strange considerations, but as you'll see shortly, there are workarounds.

The pdf_show_boxed() function takes an optional eighth parameter, *feature*. If *feature* is set to *blind*, then the function will be called without actually printing the text. You can assign the returned value of the function to a variable and if that variable is equal to 0, all of the text can be printed within the confines of that box.

```
$leftovers = pdf_show_boxed ($pdf,
→ $text, $x, $y, $width, $height,
→ "justify", "blind");
```

If $leftovers is greater than 0, the box needs to be resized or a smaller font ought to be used. In the script you'll write shortly, I'll show you how to use a loop to resize the box appropriately.

You may ask how one knows where exactly to place text. You can track how much vertical space is taken up by text using the font's size. A string started at 100, 700 in a font 36 points large, means that the next line of text should begin no sooner than 100, 664 (700 − 36). The stringwidth() function will calculate how much horizontal space a string takes up.

```
$width = stringwidth ($pdf, $text);
```

There are several methods for sprucing up your text, including changing its color, underlining it, or using an outline form of the text. Don't forget that making text bold or italic (oblique) is determined by which font you use (e.g., *Helvetica-Bold* or *Helvetica-Oblique*).

To change the color of a font, use pdf_setvalue() before printing the text to the PDF.

```
pdf_set_value ($pdf, $type, $color_mode,
→ $color1, $color2, $color3, $color4);
```

continues on next page

ADDING TEXT TO PDFs

The available types are *stroke*, *fill*, or *both*, meaning that the coloring should apply to the line itself, the area inside of the line, or both (meaning that you can set the fill and the stroke or a character as two different colors). The possible color modes are *gray*, *RBG*, and *CMYK* (along with two others not frequently used). RGB is the same scale used in Chapter 10, Image Generation, and CMYK (cyan, magenta, yellow, black) is the default mode for printers. The colors fed to the function should relate to the appropriate mode but on a scale of 0 to 1. For example, to set the color as black, which is the default color of any PDF, use:

```
pdf_set_value ($pdf, 'both', 'rgb', 0,
→ 0, 0, 0);
```

To determine how the 0 to 255 RGB scale would translate into a 0 to 1 scale, divide each number by 255. Even when using RGB, you must include a fourth color value, set to 0, or else you will encounter errors. (If you are using an older version of PHP or PDFlib, use `pdf_setrgbcolor()` instead of `pdf_set_value()`).

You can add underlining to any text by preceding the string placement with

```
pdf_set_parameter ($pdf, "underline",
→ "true");
```

The same function allows you to turn underlining off (`pdf_set_parameter ($pdf, "underline", "false")`) and gives you the option of striking out the text (`pdf_set_parameter ($pdf, "strikeout", "true")`) or placing a line above it (`pdf_set_parameter ($pdf, "overline", "true")`).

Finally, I'll mention that you can alter how the text is displayed by setting its rendering to *fill*, *outline*, *both*, or *invisible*. (Users of older versions of PHP or PDFlib should use `pdf_set_text_rendering()` instead of `pdf_set_value()`.)

```
pdf_set_value ($pdf, "textrendering", 2);
```

Table 11.4 lists the different text rendering options and values. These options are repeated again (as numbers 4-6) with the ability to involve the text with clipping paths, but the topic of clipping paths with fonts is not covered or necessary for the examples in this chapter.

Whew! Now that I've covered a slew of functions that relate to using fonts, I'll make a fancy script that automatically generates invoices based on user-submitted data.

Table 11.4 These are the four basic text rendering options, although there are others.

Text Rendering	
OPTION	VALUE
Fill	0
Outline	1
Fill and Outline	2
Invisible	3

To use fonts in PDFs:

1. Open `create_pdf.php` (Script 11.1) in your text editor.

2. Create a conditional for handling the form (**Script 11.2**).

   ```
   if (isset($HTTP_POST_VARS
   → ['submit'])) {
   ```

   This script will be parallel in structure to those in Chapter 10 that generated images from an HTML form. The page will both display the form and handle it upon submission.

3. Validate the submitted data.

   ```
   if ( (isset($HTTP_POST_VARS
   → ['client'])) AND (isset($HTTP_POST_
   → VARS['amount'])) AND (isset($HTTP_
   → POST_VARS['invoice_number'])) ) {
   ```

   For my purposes, these three fields will be required.

4. Add two more constants to the existing two.

   ```
   define ("FONT_SIZE", 18);

   define ("INCH", 72);
   ```

   The base font will be 18 points, about one-fourth of an inch tall. I'm also setting the INCH value as a constant that will be used several places in the script (like placing text indented 1 inch from the side of the page, which PDFs do not automatically do).

5. Assign the font type, size, color, and rendering for the title.

   ```
   $helvetica_bold = pdf_findfont ($pdf,
   → "Helvetica-Bold", "winansi");

   pdf_setfont ($pdf, $helvetica_bold,
   → 36);

   pdf_set_value ($pdf, "textrendering",
   → 2);

   pdf_setcolor ($pdf, 'both', 'rgb',
   → 0.2, 0.2, 1.0, 0);
   ```

The first line on the page—a title—will be drawn in Helvetica Bold, 36 points, with rendering set to both fill and stroke, giving a bolder font appearance. The color being used will be blue, derived by taking the RGB value of blue (51, 51, 255) and dividing each number by 255.

6. Print the title.

   ```
   $width = pdf_stringwidth ($pdf, 'DMC
   → Insights, Inc.');

   $x = round ((PAGE_WIDTH - $width) /
   → 2);

   pdf_show_xy ($pdf, 'DMC Insights,
   → Inc.', $x, (PAGE_HEIGHT - INCH));
   ```

   I want the title to be centered on the page so I first determine the length of the string at the current font settings. I take this number, subtract it from the page width, and then divide the result by two. Once I round off the number, my $x value will ensure the title is centered. You have to use the exact same string in both the `pdf_stringwidth()` line and the `pdf_show_xy()` call for this to work properly.

   I display the text with the `pdf_show_xy()` function, which places the string at an exact location: my $x as previously calculated and then 1 inch from the top of the page. Since the page is upside down, so to speak (it begins at the bottom), I can work my way top down as is natural by just subtracting where I would like to place the text from the height of the page. If I want it 1 inch down, I would subtract 72 from 792, meaning that 720 (10 inches up) is where it should be.

7. Reset the color back to black.

   ```
   pdf_setcolor ($pdf, 'both', 'rgb',
   → 0, 0, 0, 0);
   ```

   If I don't include this line here, everything will be blue for the rest of the page.

continues on page 399

ADDING TEXT TO PDFS

Script 11.2 The script here displays and processes an HTML form, turning user-entered data into a PDF file.

```
        script
1    <?php
2    // This page creates an invoice based on user-submitted information.
3
4    if (isset($HTTP_POST_VARS['submit'])) { // Handle the form.
5
6        if ( (isset($HTTP_POST_VARS['client'])) AND (isset($HTTP_POST_VARS['amount']))  AND
             (isset($HTTP_POST_VARS['invoice_number'])) ) {
7
8            // Set the constants and variables.
9            define ("PAGE_WIDTH", 612); // 8.5 inches.
10           define ("PAGE_HEIGHT", 792); // 11 inches.
11           define ("FONT_SIZE", 18); // Large 0.5-inch type.
12           define ("INCH", 72);
13
14           // Make the invoice.
15           $pdf = pdf_new();
16           pdf_open_file ($pdf, "");
17
18           // Set the different PDF values.
19           pdf_set_info ($pdf, "Author", "Larry E. Ullman");
20           pdf_set_info ($pdf, "Title", "Invoice for " . $HTTP_POST_VARS['client']);
21           pdf_set_info ($pdf, "Creator", "See Author");
22
23           // Create the page.
24           pdf_begin_page ($pdf, PAGE_WIDTH, PAGE_HEIGHT);
25
26           // Print a title.
27           $helvetica_bold = pdf_findfont ($pdf, "Helvetica-Bold", "winansi");
28           pdf_setfont ($pdf, $helvetica_bold, 36);
29           pdf_set_value ($pdf, "textrendering", 2);
30           pdf_setcolor ($pdf, 'both', 'rgb', 0.2, 0.2, 1.0, 0);
31           $width = pdf_stringwidth ($pdf, 'DMC Insights, Inc.');
32           $x = round ((PAGE_WIDTH - $width) / 2);
33           pdf_show_xy ($pdf, 'DMC Insights, Inc.', $x, (PAGE_HEIGHT - INCH));
34           pdf_setcolor ($pdf, 'both', 'rgb', 0, 0, 0, 0);
35
36           // Print the subtitle.
37           $helvetica_obl = pdf_findfont ($pdf, "Helvetica-Oblique", "winansi");
38           pdf_setfont ($pdf, $helvetica_obl, 24);
39           pdf_set_value ($pdf, "textrendering", 0);
40           $width = pdf_stringwidth ($pdf, 'Invoice For Services Completed');
41           $x = round ((PAGE_WIDTH - $width) / 2);
42           pdf_show_xy ($pdf, 'Invoice For Services Completed', $x, (PAGE_HEIGHT - INCH - 36 - 18));
43
44           // Set the default font from here on out.
45           $times = pdf_findfont ($pdf, "Times-Roman", "winansi");
46           pdf_setfont ($pdf, $times, FONT_SIZE);
47
48           // Print the remaining lines.
49           pdf_set_parameter ($pdf, "underline", "true");
50           pdf_show_xy ($pdf, 'Invoice Date:', INCH, (PAGE_HEIGHT - (INCH * 3)) );
51           pdf_set_parameter ($pdf, "underline", "false");
52           pdf_show ($pdf, ' ' . date("F j, Y"));
53           $used_height = (INCH * 3) + FONT_SIZE;
54
55           pdf_set_value ($pdf, "leading", (FONT_SIZE * 2) );
56           pdf_set_parameter ($pdf, "underline", "true");
57           pdf_continue_text ($pdf, 'Invoice Number:');
58           pdf_set_parameter ($pdf, "underline", "false");
```

(script continues on next page)

Script 11.2 *continued*

```
                                         script
59        pdf_show ($pdf, ' ' . $HTTP_POST_VARS['invoice_number']);
60        $used_height += (FONT_SIZE * 3);
61
62        pdf_set_value ($pdf, "leading", (FONT_SIZE * 2) );
63        pdf_set_parameter ($pdf, "underline", "true");
64        pdf_continue_text ($pdf, 'Client:');
65        pdf_set_parameter ($pdf, "underline", "false");
66        pdf_show ($pdf, ' ' . $HTTP_POST_VARS['client']);
67        $used_height += (FONT_SIZE * 3);
68
69        pdf_set_value ($pdf, "leading", (FONT_SIZE * 2) );
70        pdf_set_parameter ($pdf, "underline", "true");
71        pdf_continue_text ($pdf, 'Amount Due:');
72        pdf_set_parameter ($pdf, "underline", "false");
73        pdf_show ($pdf, ' $' . $HTTP_POST_VARS['amount']);
74        $used_height += (FONT_SIZE * 3);
75
76        pdf_set_value ($pdf, "leading", (FONT_SIZE * 2) );
77        pdf_set_parameter ($pdf, "underline", "true");
78        pdf_continue_text ($pdf, "Description of Work:");
79        pdf_set_parameter ($pdf, "underline", "false");
80
81        // Determine the description of work box size.
82        $box_height = FONT_SIZE;
83        while ((pdf_show_boxed ($pdf, $HTTP_POST_VARS['description'], INCH, (PAGE_HEIGHT -
          $used_height - $box_height), (PAGE_WIDTH - (INCH * 2)), $box_height, "justify",
          "blind")) > 0 ) {
84            $box_height += FONT_SIZE;
85        }
86
87        // Make sure there's enough room.
88        $remaining_space = PAGE_HEIGHT - ($used_height + INCH);
89
90        $font_size = FONT_SIZE;
91        while ( $box_height > $remaining_space ) {
92            $font_size = $font_size - 2;
93            pdf_setfont ($pdf, $times, $font_size);
94
95            $box_height = $font_size;
96            while ((pdf_show_boxed ($pdf, $HTTP_POST_VARS['description'], INCH, (PAGE_HEIGHT -
              $used_height - $box_height), (PAGE_WIDTH - (INCH * 2)), $box_height, "justify",
              "blind")) > 0 ) {
97                $box_height += $font_size;
98            }
99        }
100       pdf_show_boxed ($pdf, $HTTP_POST_VARS['description'], INCH, (PAGE_HEIGHT - $used_height
          - $box_height), (PAGE_WIDTH - (INCH * 2)), $box_height, 'justify');
101
102
103       // Finish the page.
104       pdf_end_page($pdf);
105
106       // Close the PDF.
107       pdf_close($pdf);
108
109       // Send the PDF to the browser.
110       $buffer = pdf_get_buffer ($pdf);
111       header ("Content-type: application/pdf");
112       header ("Content-Length: " . strlen($buffer));
```

(script continues on next page)

ADDING TEXT TO PDFS

Script 11.2 *continued*

```
                                      script

113         header ("Content-Disposition: inline; filename=" . $HTTP_POST_VARS['invoice_number'] .
            ".pdf");
114         echo $buffer;
115
116         // Free the resources.
117         pdf_delete ($pdf);
118
119      } else {
120         echo "You either forgot to enter the client's name, the invoice number, or the amount
            due. Please go back and try again.\n";
121      }
122
123   } else {
124      // Display the form.
125   ?>
126   <!DOCTYPE html PUBLIC "-//W3C//DTD XHTML 1.0 Transitional//EN"
127   "http://www.w3.org/TR/2000/REC-xhtml1-20000126/DTD/xhtml1-transitional.dtd">
128   <html xmlns="http://www.w3.org/1999/xhtml">
129   <head>
130      <title>Create An Invoice</title>
131   </head>
132   <body>
133   <form action="create_pdf_invoice.php" method="POST">
134   <table border="0" width="80%" cellspacing="2" cellpadding="2" align="center">
135      <tr align="center" valign="top">
136         <td align="center" valign="top" colspan="2">Fill out the form to have your invoice
            created!</td>
137      </tr>
138      <tr align="center" valign="top">
139         <td align="right" valign="top">Enter the client's name:</td>
140         <td align="left" valign="top"><input type="text" name="client" size="40"
            maxlength="80"></td>
141      </tr>
142      <tr align="center" valign="top">
143         <td align="right" valign="top">Enter the invoice number:</td>
144         <td align="left" valign="top"><input type="text" name="invoice_number" size="10"
            maxlength="20"></td>
145      </tr>
146      <tr align="center" valign="top">
147         <td align="right" valign="top">Enter the amount due (without the dollar sign):</td>
148         <td align="left" valign="top"><input type="text" name="amount" size="10"
            maxlength="10"></td>
149      </tr>
150      <tr align="center" valign="top">
151         <td align="right" valign="top">Enter a description of the work:</td>
152         <td align="left" valign="top"><textarea name="description" rows="5"
            cols="40"></textarea></td>
153      </tr>
154      <tr align="center" valign="top">
155         <td align="center" valign="top" colspan="2"><input type="submit" name="submit"
            value="Make The Invoice!"></td>
156      </tr>
157   </table>
158   </form>
159   </body>
160   </html>
161   <?php
162   } // Close the SUBMIT conditional.
163   ?>
```

8. Print the subtitle.

```
$helvetica_obl = pdf_findfont ($pdf,
→ "Helvetica-Oblique", "winansi");
pdf_setfont ($pdf, $helvetica_obl,
→ 24);
pdf_set_value ($pdf,
→ "textrendering", 0);
$width = pdf_stringwidth ($pdf,
→ 'Invoice For Services Completed');
$x = round ((PAGE_WIDTH - $width) /
→ 2);
pdf_show_xy ($pdf, 'Invoice For
→ Services Completed', $x,
→ (PAGE_HEIGHT - INCH - 36 - 18));
```

The subtitle is handled like the title, except it will be italicized Helvetica, 24 points, black, with normal text rendering.

9. Set the font for the remainder of the page.

```
$times = pdf_findfont ($pdf,
→ "Times-Roman", "winansi");
pdf_setfont ($pdf, $times,
→ FONT_SIZE);
```

Every piece of text that requires a special font type, size, color, or rendering must be preceded by lines like these.

10. Print an underlined caption.

```
pdf_set_parameter ($pdf,
→ "underline", "true");
pdf_show_xy ($pdf, 'Invoice Date:',
→ INCH, (PAGE_HEIGHT - (INCH * 3)) );
```

First I set the underline parameter to *true*, then I use the pdf_show_xy() function to place the text. Every line of text after this one will be relatively placed and not absolute.

11. Print today's date afterward.

```
pdf_set_parameter ($pdf,
→ "underline", "false");
```

```
pdf_show ($pdf, ' ' . date("F j,
→ Y"));
$used_height = (INCH * 3) +
→ FONT_SIZE;
```

The first thing I need to do is turn off the underlining. Then I'm using pdf_show() to place the date immediately after the caption (but with a space in between).

Because I want to keep track of where I am on the page vertically, I now establish a variable that records how much of the page has been used up. This is calculated by taking the current text line location (INCH * 3) and adding one line of text (FONT_SIZE).

12. Adjust the leading.

```
pdf_set_value ($pdf, "leading",
→ (FONT_SIZE * 2) );
```

Leading refers to the amount of space between lines of text. By default, the leading is the same as the font size, in this case, 18 points. To increase the spacing, I double the font size. The leading must be set before each line of text if you are not intending to use the default.

13. Print the invoice number as you did the invoice date.

```
pdf_set_parameter ($pdf,
→ "underline", "true");
pdf_continue_text ($pdf,
→ 'Invoice Number:');
pdf_set_parameter ($pdf,
→ "underline", "false");
pdf_show ($pdf, ' ' . $HTTP_POST_
→ VARS['invoice_number']);
$used_height += (FONT_SIZE * 3);
```

Here I introduce the pdf_continue_text() function, which automatically begins on the next line of the PDF, vertically in line with its predecessor.

continues on next page

14. Repeat the same steps for the client's name and the amount due.

```
pdf_set_value ($pdf, "leading",
→ (FONT_SIZE * 2) );
pdf_set_parameter ($pdf,
→ "underline", "true");
pdf_continue_text ($pdf, 'Client:');
pdf_set_parameter ($pdf,
→ "underline", "false");
pdf_show ($pdf, ' ' .
→ $HTTP_POST_VARS['client']);
$used_height += (FONT_SIZE * 3);
pdf_set_value ($pdf, "leading",
→ (FONT_SIZE * 2) );
pdf_set_parameter ($pdf,
→ "underline", "true");
pdf_continue_text ($pdf,
→ 'Amount Due:');
pdf_set_parameter ($pdf,
→ "underline", "false");
pdf_show ($pdf, ' $' .
→ $HTTP_POST_VARS['amount']);
$used_height += (FONT_SIZE * 3);
```

15. Print the *Description of Work* caption.

```
pdf_set_value ($pdf, "leading",
→ (FONT_SIZE * 2) );
pdf_set_parameter ($pdf,
→ "underline", "true");
pdf_continue_text ($pdf,
→ "Description of Work:");
pdf_set_parameter ($pdf,
→ "underline", "false");
```

16. Determine how much space the description itself will take up.

```
$box_height = FONT_SIZE;
while ((pdf_show_boxed ($pdf,
→ $HTTP_POST_VARS['description'],
→ INCH, (PAGE_HEIGHT - $used_height
→ - $box_height), (PAGE_WIDTH -
→ (INCH * 2)), $box_height,
→ "justify", "blind")) > 0 ) {
```

```
$box_height += FONT_SIZE;
}
```

To create a text box large enough to contain all the description, I use this construct. I begin by setting the box height to the same size as the font, meaning that the box will contain one line of text. The loop uses the box height and the *blind* feature of pdf_show_boxed() to see if there are any leftover characters. If there are, the box height is increased by adding another line to it (one line being the font size). The loop will be repeated until the imaginary box is large enough to hold all of the text.

17. Make sure there is still enough room left on the page.

```
$remaining_space = PAGE_HEIGHT -
→ ($used_height + INCH);
$font_size = FONT_SIZE;
while ( $box_height >
→ $remaining_space ) {
$font_size = $font_size - 2;
pdf_setfont ($pdf, $times,
→ $font_size);
$box_height = $font_size;
while ((pdf_show_boxed ($pdf,
→ $HTTP_POST_VARS['description'],
→ INCH, (PAGE_HEIGHT - $used_height
→ - $box_height), (PAGE_WIDTH -
→ (INCH * 2)), $box_height,
→ "justify", "blind")) > 0 ) {
$box_height += $font_size;
}
}
```

Once I know how large the description box will be, I have to be sure that there is ample space on the page to print it all out or it will spill over the edge (a PDF will not automatically continue on a second page). To do this, I calculate the remaining vertical space by subtracting the $used_height, which the script has been tracking, from the page height, and I include the bottom inch margin, too. Then I set a variable equal to the current font size. Now I set up a loop that stops when the box size is no longer larger than the available space.

In this loop, I start by making the font size smaller. Then I go through the same loop I used earlier to determine the appropriate box size. After it has passed that test, it goes back to the original loop to see if the box is now small enough. This process will continue until the font is so small that the requisite text box will fit in the room left on the page.

18. Print out the description text.

```
pdf_show_boxed ($pdf, $HTTP
→ _POST_VARS['description'], INCH,
→ (PAGE_HEIGHT - $used_height -
→ $box_height), (PAGE_WIDTH - (INCH
→ * 2)), $box_height, 'justify');
```

After the process of determining the font size and space required for the description text, I can print it to the PDF. Because the text box starts in the lower-left corner, I determine the y value as the page height, minus the height already used, minus the requisite box height. The width of the box is simply the page width minus both margins.

19. Change the name of the file to be the invoice number.

```
header ("Content-Disposition:
→ inline; filename=" . $HTTP_POST_
→ VARS['invoice_number'] . ".pdf");
```

20. Complete the two conditionals and make the HTML form.

```
} else {
echo "You either forgot to enter the
→ client's name, the invoice number,
→ or the amount due. Please go back
→ and try again.\n";
```

```
}
} else {
?>
<!DOCTYPE html PUBLIC "-//W3C//DTD
→ XHTML 1.0 Transitional//EN"
"http://www.w3.org/TR/2000/
→ REC-xhtml1-20000126/DTD/xhtml1-
→ transitional.dtd">
<html xmlns="http://www.w3.org/
→ 1999/xhtml">
<head>
<title>Create An Invoice</title>
</head>
<body>
<form action="create_pdf_invoice.php"
→ method="POST">
<table border="0" width="80%"
→ cellspacing="2" cellpadding="2"
→ align="center">
<tr align="center" valign="top">
<td align="center" valign="top"
→ colspan="2">Fill out the form to
→ have your invoice created!</td>
</tr>
<tr align="center" valign="top">
<td align="right" valign="top">Enter
→ the client's name:</td>
<td align="left" valign="top"><input
→ type="text" name="client"
→ size="40" maxlength="80"></td>
</tr>
<tr align="center" valign="top">
<td align="right" valign="top">Enter
→ the invoice number:</td>
<td align="left" valign="top"><input
→ type="text" name="invoice_number"
→ size="10" maxlength="20"></td>
</tr>
<tr align="center" valign="top">
```

continues on next page

ADDING TEXT TO PDFS

```
<td align="right" valign="top">Enter
→ the amount due (without the dollar
→ sign):</td>
<td align="left" valign="top"><input
→ type="text" name="amount"
→ size="10" maxlength="10"></td>
</tr>
<tr align="center" valign="top">
<td align="right" valign="top">Enter
→ a description of the work:</td>
<td align="left"
→ valign="top"><textarea
→ name="description" rows="5"
→ cols="40"></textarea></td>
</tr>
<tr align="center" valign="top">
<td align="center" valign="top"
→ colspan="2"><input type="submit"
→ name="submit" value="Make The
→ Invoice!"></td>
</tr>
</table>
</form>
</body>
</html>
```

There is no need to go over this part of the script in detail: It works exactly as the compatriots in Chapter 10 did.

21. Close the PHP script and the main conditional.

```
<?php
}
?>
```

22. Save the script as create_pdf_invoice.php, upload to your server, and test in your Web browser (**Figures 11.7**, **11.8**, **11.9**, and **11.10**).

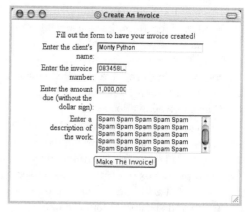

Figure 11.7 The information entered here will be turned into a PDF (Figure 11.9).

Figure 11.8 The PDF itself will be given a filename based on the invoice number.

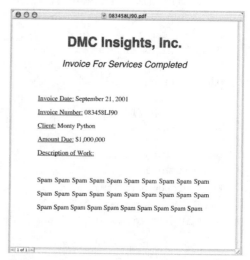

Figure 11.9 The final PDF looks like this, but if more description text is entered, that section will be resized (Figure 11.10).

ADDING TEXT TO PDFs

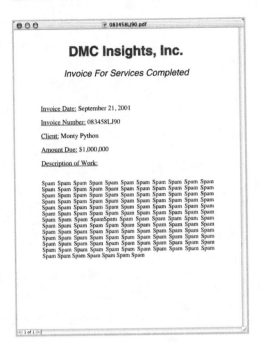

Figure 11.10 The loops in the script adjust the font size until the description will fit appropriately on the page.

✔ Tips

- The PDFlib manual tells how to reorient your pages so that they begin in the upper-left corner (see section 3.2.1, *Coordinate Systems*), but I have found that with a little thinking, it becomes easier to deal with the PDFs as they are. One thing you'll need to do if you reorient your pages is use negative font sizes because they will be drawn upside down.

- Depending on how cautious you want to be, you might create a loop like the one for the description box that ensures the client's name does not spill over the width of the page. To do so, use the `pdf_stringwidth()` function and the remaining page width. Keep decreasing the font size until the string width is less than or equal to the remaining width. Further, you might want to add a conditional to the second loop ensuring a positive font size.

- You can also use TrueType fonts with PDFs, if you prefer. I use PostScript fonts since they are native to the format and better for printing.

Drawing Shapes

Since you now understand how to use fonts, it's time to add a little graphical flare to the PDF. With just a few functions, you can make lines, rectangles, circles, polygons, arcs, and more. There are numerous factors you can adjust, including the line width and color.

The only thing you really need to understand about drawing shapes in PDFs is that the process takes two steps: defining the path and then stroking it. This may sound familiar to anyone who has used a vector-based graphics program such as Adobe Illustrator. First you define a path by identifying points along it—a line requires two, a rectangle four, and a circle a whole, whole lot. Defining the path (or clipping path as its formally called) does not actually create the shape, it just provides a template for it. Then the path is painted in by stroking it.

First, here are some functions for defining paths:

* `pdf_lineto ($pdf, $x, $y);`

  This function creates a line (in path form) from the current position to x, y. You can set the current position—i.e., the origin of the line—using `pdf_moveto()`.

* `pdf_moveto ($pdf, $x, $y);`

  This function does nothing more than place the location of the imaginary cursor to x, y, allowing you to draw a line from that point (or place text using `pdf_show()`).

* `pdf_rect ($pdf, $x, $y, $width,`
  `↪ $height);`

  Naturally, `pdf_rect()` draws a rectangle starting at x, y (the lower-left corner of the box). The rectangle will be drawn along the y axis for `$height` points and along the x axis for `$width` points.

- pdf_circle ($pdf, $x, $y, $radius);

  The pdf_circle() function makes a circle centered at x, y with a radius of $radius.

- pdf_arc ($pdf, $x, $y, $radius,
  → $begin, $end);

  This is the most complicated of the functions. It draws, as a path, an arc (part of a circle) whose center is x, y, has a radius of $radius, and goes from $begin degrees to $end degrees. The center is the center of the circle, if the arc were complete. The degrees start at 0, which is the positive end of the x axis (the same was true when designing images). So 0 degrees is like 3 o'clock (as is 360 degrees); 90 is 12 o'clock; 180 is 9 o'clock; and 270 degrees is 6 o'clock.

Once a path is defined, be it a circle, rectangle, line, or arc, you can turn it into a graphical thing on the page by stroking it.

pdf_stroke ($pdf);

Use of this function paints the established path and clears it from memory.

There are a number of ways you adjust the properties of the mythical brush used to stroke the paths.

The pdf_setlinewidth() function does just as it's named.

pdf_setlinewidth ($pdf, 3);

The default line width in a PDF is 1, which can be overridden with pdf_setlinewidth(). Once this value is set, it will remain set (unlike leading), which could affect your fonts later in a script unexpectedly. Its best to always reset the line width after your graphics are complete.

The pdf_setlinejoin() function affects how two lines or paths meet up—whether the junction is rounded, mitered, or beveled. Examples of each can be found in the PDFlib manual.

pdf_setlinejoin ($pdf, 1); // Rounded

The pdf_setlinecap() function dictates how lines end, generally square (0) or rounded (1). Again, the PDFlib manual gives pictorial examples.

pdf_setlinecap ($pdf, 1); // Rounded

Finally, there is pdf_setdash(), which means that the next stroked path should be a dashed line.

pdf_setdash ($pdf, $filled, $blank);

The $filled and $blank variables are integers in points specifying how long each dash ($filled) and gap ($blank) should be.

I'll make two last notes on drawing shapes before I go back to the script. First, because some functions that define a path will automatically connect to any existing paths (pdf_arc() does this), it's a good idea to apply pdf_stroke() after each complete path has been created. Second, you will get errors if you attempt to adjust the line settings (using pdf_setlinewidth(), pdf_setlinejoin(), etc.) after a path is created and before it has been stroked. The proper order would be to set the line parameters (if necessary), create a path, then stroke it.

I'll demonstrate these functions by adding some nice and some silly graphics to the PDF invoice-generating script.

To draw shapes in a PDF:

1. Open `generate_pdf_invoice.php`
   (Script 11.2) in your text editor.

2. After the `pdf_begin_page()` line, add the
   code to draw a watermark (**Script 11.3**).

   ```
   pdf_setlinewidth ($pdf, 3);
   pdf_setcolor ($pdf, 'both', 'rgb',
   → 0.8, 0.8, 0.8, 0);
   pdf_circle ($pdf, (PAGE_WIDTH/2),
   → (PAGE_HEIGHT/2), ( (PAGE_WIDTH -
   → INCH - INCH)/2) );
   pdf_stroke ($pdf);
   pdf_circle ($pdf, (round
   → (PAGE_WIDTH/3) * 1), (PAGE_HEIGHT
   → - (PAGE_HEIGHT/3)), 18);
   pdf_stroke ($pdf);
   pdf_circle ($pdf, (round
   → (PAGE_WIDTH/3) * 2), (PAGE_HEIGHT
   → - (PAGE_HEIGHT/3)), 18);
   pdf_stroke ($pdf);
   pdf_arc ($pdf, (PAGE_WIDTH/2),
   → (PAGE_HEIGHT/2), 144, 210, 330);
   pdf_stroke ($pdf);
   pdf_setlinewidth ($pdf,1);
   ```

   This section of code is to act as a watermark, which means two things: First, I
   want to print it before anything else so it
   will appear behind the rest of the information. Second, I'm using a light gray for
   the color, which will not overwhelm the
   rest of the page.

   As for the content of the watermark itself,
   it's a smiley face derived from one large
   circle, two small circles, and an arc. You
   can play with the numbers yourself to
   change the size and shape of the face.

   I stroke each path immediately after it is
   created and I reset the line width before
   continuing with the page because I made it
   three times wider at the beginning of this
   section which will throw off the fonts later.

DRAWING SHAPES

3. After all of the PDF has been created, but
   before the page has been closed, add a
   border around the page.

   ```
   pdf_setlinewidth ($pdf, 6);
   pdf_setlinejoin ($pdf, 1);
   pdf_rect ($pdf, (INCH/2), (INCH/2),
   → (PAGE_WIDTH - INCH), (PAGE_HEIGHT
   → - INCH));
   pdf_stroke ($pdf);
   ```

   These four lines make a rectangle that
   will be 6 points wide, use rounded corners (`pdf_setlinejoin()`), and be consistently one-half inch inside the edges of
   the page.

4. Add a nice line underneath the subtitle.

   ```
   pdf_setcolor ($pdf, 'both', 'rgb',
   → 1.0, 0.6, 0.2, 0);
   pdf_setlinewidth ($pdf, 12);
   pdf_setlinecap ($pdf, 1);
   pdf_setdash ($pdf, 20, 15);
   pdf_moveto ($pdf, INCH, (PAGE_HEIGHT
   → - INCH - 36 - 36));
   pdf_lineto ($pdf, (PAGE_WIDTH -
   → INCH), (PAGE_HEIGHT - INCH - 36
   → - 36));
   pdf_stroke ($pdf);
   ```

   The line here, which admittedly doesn't fit in
   terms of design, will be orange in color, use a
   thick line width (12 points), have rounded
   ends (`pdf_setlinecap()`), and be dashed.
   Once I've set all the line appearance values,
   I move to the starting point and then create
   the line to the ending point.

5. Alter the form line so the form is submitted back to this page.

   ```
   <form action="create_pdf_
   → invoice2.php" method="POST">
   ```

   Since I'm going to change the name of the
   file, I have to remember to change the
   `ACTION`, too.

continues on page 411

Script 11.3 Script 11.2 has been slightly modified by adding graphics so that the final invoice is more decorative.

```
1    <?php
2    // This page creates an invoice based on user-submitted information.
3
4    if (isset($HTTP_POST_VARS['submit'])) { // Handle the form.
5
6        if ( (isset($HTTP_POST_VARS['client'])) AND (isset($HTTP_POST_VARS['amount']))  AND
         (isset($HTTP_POST_VARS['invoice_number'])) ) {
7
8            // Set the constants and variables.
9            define ("PAGE_WIDTH", 612); // 8.5 inches.
10           define ("PAGE_HEIGHT", 792); // 11 inches.
11           define ("FONT_SIZE", 18); // Large 0.5-inch type.
12           define ("INCH", 72);
13
14           // Make the invoice.
15           $pdf = pdf_new();
16           pdf_open_file ($pdf, "");
17
18           // Set the different PDF values.
19           pdf_set_info ($pdf, "Author", "Larry E. Ullman");
20           pdf_set_info ($pdf, "Title", "Invoice for " . $HTTP_POST_VARS['client']);
21           pdf_set_info ($pdf, "Creator", "See Author");
22
23           // Create the page.
24           pdf_begin_page ($pdf, PAGE_WIDTH, PAGE_HEIGHT);
25
26           // Make a smiley face watermark.
27           pdf_setlinewidth ($pdf, 3);
28           pdf_setcolor ($pdf, 'both', 'rgb', 0.8, 0.8, 0.8, 0);
29           pdf_circle ($pdf, (PAGE_WIDTH/2), (PAGE_HEIGHT/2), ( (PAGE_WIDTH - INCH - INCH)/2) );
30           pdf_stroke ($pdf);
31           pdf_circle ($pdf, (round (PAGE_WIDTH/3) * 1), (PAGE_HEIGHT - (PAGE_HEIGHT/3)), 18);
32           pdf_stroke ($pdf);
33           pdf_circle ($pdf,  (round (PAGE_WIDTH/3) * 2), (PAGE_HEIGHT - (PAGE_HEIGHT/3)), 18);
34           pdf_stroke ($pdf);
35           pdf_arc ($pdf, (PAGE_WIDTH/2), (PAGE_HEIGHT/2), 144, 210, 330);
36           pdf_stroke ($pdf);
37           pdf_setlinewidth ($pdf,1);
38
39           // Print a title.
40           $helvetica_bold = pdf_findfont ($pdf, "Helvetica-Bold", "winansi");
41           pdf_setfont ($pdf, $helvetica_bold, 36);
42           pdf_set_value ($pdf, "textrendering", 2);
43           pdf_setcolor ($pdf, 'both', 'rgb', 0.2, 0.2, 1.0, 0);
44           $width = pdf_stringwidth ($pdf, 'DMC Insights, Inc.');
45           $x = round ((PAGE_WIDTH - $width) / 2);
46           pdf_show_xy ($pdf, 'DMC Insights, Inc.', $x, (PAGE_HEIGHT - INCH));
47           pdf_setcolor ($pdf, 'both', 'rgb', 0, 0, 0, 0);
48
49           // Print the subtitle.
50           $helvetica_obl = pdf_findfont ($pdf, "Helvetica-Oblique", "winansi");
```

(script continues on next page)

Script 11.3 *continued*

```
         ┌──────────────────────── script ────────────────────────┐
51              pdf_setfont ($pdf, $helvetica_obl, 24);
52              pdf_set_value ($pdf, "textrendering", 0);
53              $width = pdf_stringwidth ($pdf, 'Invoice For Services Completed');
54              $x = round ((PAGE_WIDTH - $width) / 2);
55              pdf_show_xy ($pdf, 'Invoice For Services Completed', $x, (PAGE_HEIGHT - INCH - 36 - 18));
56
57              // Set the default font from here on out.
58              $times = pdf_findfont ($pdf, "Times-Roman", "winansi");
59              pdf_setfont ($pdf, $times, FONT_SIZE);
60
61              // Print the remaining lines.
62              pdf_set_parameter ($pdf, "underline", "true");
63              pdf_show_xy ($pdf, 'Invoice Date:', INCH, (PAGE_HEIGHT - (INCH * 3)) );
64              pdf_set_parameter ($pdf, "underline", "false");
65              pdf_show ($pdf, ' ' . date("F j, Y"));
66              $used_height = (INCH * 3) + FONT_SIZE;
67
68              pdf_set_value ($pdf, "leading", (FONT_SIZE * 2) );
69              pdf_set_parameter ($pdf, "underline", "true");
70              pdf_continue_text ($pdf, 'Invoice Number:');
71              pdf_set_parameter ($pdf, "underline", "false");
72              pdf_show ($pdf, ' ' . $HTTP_POST_VARS['invoice_number']);
73              $used_height += (FONT_SIZE * 3);
74
75              pdf_set_value ($pdf, "leading", (FONT_SIZE * 2) );
76              pdf_set_parameter ($pdf, "underline", "true");
77              pdf_continue_text ($pdf, 'Client:');
78              pdf_set_parameter ($pdf, "underline", "false");
79              pdf_show ($pdf, ' ' . $HTTP_POST_VARS['client']);
80              $used_height += (FONT_SIZE * 3);
81
82              pdf_set_value ($pdf, "leading", (FONT_SIZE * 2) );
83              pdf_set_parameter ($pdf, "underline", "true");
84              pdf_continue_text ($pdf, 'Amount Due:');
85              pdf_set_parameter ($pdf, "underline", "false");
86              pdf_show ($pdf, ' $' . $HTTP_POST_VARS['amount']);
87              $used_height += (FONT_SIZE * 3);
88
89              pdf_set_value ($pdf, "leading", (FONT_SIZE * 2) );
90              pdf_set_parameter ($pdf, "underline", "true");
91              pdf_continue_text ($pdf, "Description of Work:");
92              pdf_set_parameter ($pdf, "underline", "false");
93
94              // Determine the description of work box size.
95              $box_height = FONT_SIZE;
96              while ((pdf_show_boxed ($pdf, $HTTP_POST_VARS['description'], INCH, (PAGE_HEIGHT -
                $used_height - $box_height), (PAGE_WIDTH - (INCH * 2)), $box_height, "justify", "blind"))
                > 0 ) {
97                  $box_height += FONT_SIZE;
98              }
99
```

(script continues on next page)

Script 11.3 *continued*

```
100        // Make sure there's enough room.
101        $remaining_space = PAGE_HEIGHT - ($used_height + INCH);
102
103        $font_size = FONT_SIZE;
104        while ( $box_height > $remaining_space ) {
105            $font_size = $font_size - 2;
106            pdf_setfont ($pdf, $times, $font_size);
107
108            $box_height = $font_size;
109            while ((pdf_show_boxed  ($pdf, $HTTP_POST_VARS['description'], INCH, (PAGE_HEIGHT -
                   $used_height - $box_height), (PAGE_WIDTH - (INCH * 2)), $box_height, "justify",
                   "blind")) > 0 ) {
110                $box_height += $font_size;
111            }
112        }
113        pdf_show_boxed ($pdf, $HTTP_POST_VARS['description'], INCH, (PAGE_HEIGHT - $used_height
           - $box_height), (PAGE_WIDTH - (INCH * 2)), $box_height, 'justify');
114
115        // Outline the page.
116        pdf_setlinewidth ($pdf, 6);
117        pdf_setlinejoin ($pdf, 1);
118        pdf_rect ($pdf, (INCH/2), (INCH/2), (PAGE_WIDTH - INCH), (PAGE_HEIGHT - INCH));
119        pdf_stroke ($pdf);
120
121        // Underline the subtitle.
122        pdf_setcolor ($pdf, 'both', 'rgb', 1.0, 0.6, 0.2, 0);
123        pdf_setlinewidth ($pdf, 12);
124        pdf_setlinecap ($pdf, 1);
125        pdf_setdash ($pdf, 20, 15);
126        pdf_moveto ($pdf, INCH, (PAGE_HEIGHT - INCH - 36 - 36));
127        pdf_lineto ($pdf, (PAGE_WIDTH - INCH), (PAGE_HEIGHT - INCH - 36 - 36));
128        pdf_stroke ($pdf);
129
130        // Finish the page.
131        pdf_end_page($pdf);
132
133        // Close the PDF.
134        pdf_close($pdf);
135
136        // Send the PDF to the browser.
137        $buffer = pdf_get_buffer ($pdf);
138        header ("Content-type: application/pdf");
139        header ("Content-Length: " . strlen($buffer));
140        header ("Content-Disposition: inline; filename=" . $HTTP_POST_VARS['invoice_number'] .
               ".pdf");
141        echo $buffer;
142
143        // Free the resources.
144        pdf_delete ($pdf);
145
146    } else {
```

(script continues on next page)

Script 11.3 *continued*

```
                                                       script

147          echo "You either forgot to enter the client's name, the invoice number, or the amount
             due. Please go back and try again.\n";
148      }
149
150  } else {
151      // Display the form.
152  ?>
153  <!DOCTYPE html PUBLIC "-//W3C//DTD XHTML 1.0 Transitional//EN"
154          "http://www.w3.org/TR/2000/REC-xhtml1-20000126/DTD/xhtml1-transitional.dtd">
155  <html xmlns="http://www.w3.org/1999/xhtml">
156  <head>
157      <title>Create An Invoice</title>
158  </head>
159  <body>
160  <form action="create_pdf_invoice2.php" method="POST">
161  <table border="0" width="80%" cellspacing="2" cellpadding="2" align="center">
162      <tr align="center" valign="top">
163          <td align="center" valign="top" colspan="2">Fill out the form to have your invoice
             created!</td>
164      </tr>
165      <tr align="center" valign="top">
166          <td align="right" valign="top">Enter the client's name:</td>
167          <td align="left" valign="top"><input type="text" name="client" size="40"
             maxlength="80"></td>
168      </tr>
169      <tr align="center" valign="top">
170          <td align="right" valign="top">Enter the invoice number:</td>
171          <td align="left" valign="top"><input type="text" name="invoice_number" size="10"
             maxlength="20"></td>
172      </tr>
173      <tr align="center" valign="top">
174          <td align="right" valign="top">Enter the amount due (without the dollar sign):</td>
175          <td align="left" valign="top"><input type="text" name="amount" size="10"
             maxlength="10"></td>
176      </tr>
177      <tr align="center" valign="top">
178          <td align="right" valign="top">Enter a description of the work:</td>
179          <td align="left" valign="top"><textarea name="description" rows="5"
             cols="40"></textarea></td>
180      </tr>
181      <tr align="center" valign="top">
182          <td align="center" valign="top" colspan="2"><input type="submit" name="submit"
             value="Make The Invoice!"></td>
183      </tr>
184  </table>
185  </form>
186  </body>
187  </html>
188  <?php
189  } // Close the SUBMIT conditional.
190  ?>
```

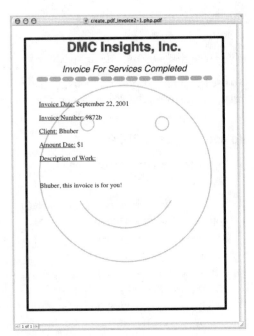

Figure 11.11 It's the invoice with a heart! The graphics, albeit silly, do help to improve the look of the invoice.

6. Save the file as `create_pdf_invoice2.php`, upload it to your server, and test in your Web browser (**Figure 11.11**).

✔ Tips

- The companion to `pdf_arc()` is `pdf_arcn()`, which draws an arc clockwise, rather than the former, which goes in a counterclockwise direction. It is new to PHP 4.0.5.

- Every function used in this section is the same in earlier versions of PHP as it is in the most recent (4.0.6).

- If you are having difficulty using the `pdf_show_boxed()` function for placing text, use `pdf_rect()` to make a rectangle that defines the bounding box of the text. If you use the same coordinates for both, the rectangle will be printed around the text box and you may be able to see what problems are there.

DRAWING SHAPES

Using Images

While it is nice to be able to add lines and other shapes to your PDFs, to really add pizzazz, you can incorporate existing images. Using images in PDFs is essentially a three-step process:

1. Open the image file.

2. Place the image in the PDF.

3. Close the image.

In actuality it can be a little more complicated than that once you take into account variable image size and such, but I've got a work-around for that issue, too.

For the most recent versions of PHP, open the image with `pdf_open_image_file()`.

```
$image_pointer = pdf_open_image_file
→ ($pdf, $format, $image_file);
```

Exactly like creating a PDF, you assign a pointer to the open image file. The `$format` should refer to the format of the image itself: JPEG, GIF, PNG, or TIFF (which is why the PDFlib requires the extra libraries). The `$image_file` should refer to the file on the server.

```
pdf_place_image($pdf, $image_pointer,
→ $x, $y, $scale);
```

Placing an image is almost as simple as specifying the x- and y-coordinates except for two things. Naturally the x-, y-coordinate refers to the lower-left corner of the image (you may be getting used to this pattern by now). Secondly, the image can be scaled (i.e., its size adjusted on the fly). The PDFlib manual goes into great details of different scaling options, but in the following script I'll demonstrate one simple method.

Finally, close the image, referring back to its pointer.

```
pdf_close_image($pdf, $image_pointer);
```

To use this information, I'll add my company's image to the top of the PDF page and alter the existing graphics and text accordingly.

To use images in PDFs:

1. Open `create_pdf_invoice2.php` (Script 11.3) in your text editor.

2. Immediately after the `pdf_begin_page()` call, open the image file (**Script 11.4**).

   ```
   $image = pdf_open_image_file ($pdf,
   → 'jpeg', 'dmci_title.jpg');
   ```

   In theory, JPEG, GIF, PNG, and TIFF are all supported image types, but you may find better success with one over another. On my system, JPEGs turned out fine but gifs were all muddled.

3. Retrieve the image's dimensions.

   ```
   $image_width = pdf_get_value ($pdf,
   → 'imagewidth', $image);
   $image_height = pdf_get_value ($pdf,
   → 'imageheight', $image);
   ```

   Users of older versions should replace these lines with `get_image_height()` and `get_image_width()`.

4. Scale the image, if necessary.

   ```
   if ( ($image_width + INCH) >
   → PAGE_WIDTH + INCH) {
   $scale = PAGE_WIDTH / ($image_width +
   → INCH);
   $x = round ((PAGE_WIDTH -
   → ($image_width * $scale) )/2);
   } else {
   $scale = 1;
   $x = round((PAGE_WIDTH -
   → $image_width)/2);
   }
   ```

continues on page 417

Script 11.4 This script builds on its predecessors by placing images within the PDF.

```php
1   <?php
2   // This page creates an invoice based on user-submitted information.
3
4   if (isset($HTTP_POST_VARS['submit'])) { // Handle the form.
5
6       if ( (isset($HTTP_POST_VARS['client'])) AND (isset($HTTP_POST_VARS['amount']))  AND
        (isset($HTTP_POST_VARS['invoice_number'])) ) {
7
8           // Set the constants and variables.
9           define ("PAGE_WIDTH", 612); // 8.5 inches.
10          define ("PAGE_HEIGHT", 792); // 11 inches.
11          define ("FONT_SIZE", 18); // Large 0.5-inch type.
12          define ("INCH", 72);
13
14          // Make the invoice.
15          $pdf = pdf_new();
16          pdf_open_file ($pdf, "");
17
18          // Set the different PDF values.
19          pdf_set_info ($pdf, "Author", "Larry E. Ullman");
20          pdf_set_info ($pdf, "Title", "Invoice for " . $HTTP_POST_VARS['client']);
21          pdf_set_info ($pdf, "Creator", "See Author");
22
23
24          // Create the page.
25          pdf_begin_page ($pdf, PAGE_WIDTH, PAGE_HEIGHT);
26
27          // Open and place the image.
28          $image = pdf_open_image_file ($pdf, 'jpeg', 'dmci_title.jpg');
29          $image_width = pdf_get_value ($pdf, 'imagewidth', $image);
30          $image_height = pdf_get_value ($pdf, 'imageheight', $image);
31          if (($image_width + INCH) > PAGE_WIDTH) {
32              $scale = PAGE_WIDTH / ($image_width + INCH);
33              $x = round ((PAGE_WIDTH - ($image_width * $scale) )/2);
34          } else {
35              $scale = 1;
36              $x = round((PAGE_WIDTH - $image_width)/2);
37          }
38          pdf_place_image($pdf, $image, $x, (PAGE_HEIGHT - $image_height), $scale);
39          pdf_close_image ($pdf, $image);
40
41          // Print a title.
42          $helvetica_bold = pdf_findfont ($pdf, "Helvetica-Bold", "winansi");
43          pdf_setfont ($pdf, $helvetica_bold, 36);
44          pdf_set_value ($pdf, "textrendering", 2);
45          pdf_setcolor ($pdf, 'both', 'rgb', 0.2, 0.2, 1.0, 0);
46          $width = pdf_stringwidth ($pdf, 'DMC Insights, Inc.');
47          $x = round ((PAGE_WIDTH - $width) / 2);
48          pdf_show_xy ($pdf, 'DMC Insights, Inc.', ($x + 10), (PAGE_HEIGHT - (INCH/2) -
            $image_height));
49          pdf_setcolor ($pdf, 'both', 'rgb', 0, 0, 0, 0);
```

(script continues on next page)

Script 11.4 *continued*

```
        script
50
51          // Print the subtitle.
52          $helvetica_obl = pdf_findfont ($pdf, "Helvetica-Oblique", "winansi");
53          pdf_setfont ($pdf, $helvetica_obl, 24);
54          pdf_set_value ($pdf, "textrendering", 0);
55          $width = pdf_stringwidth ($pdf, 'Invoice For Services Completed');
56          $x = round ((PAGE_WIDTH - $width) / 2);
57          pdf_show_xy ($pdf, 'Invoice For Services Completed', $x, (PAGE_HEIGHT - (INCH/2) - 36 -
            18 - $image_height));
58
59          // Set the default font from here on out.
60          $times = pdf_findfont ($pdf, "Times-Roman", "winansi");
61          pdf_setfont ($pdf, $times, FONT_SIZE);
62
63          // Print the remaining lines.
64          pdf_set_parameter ($pdf, "underline", "true");
65          pdf_show_xy ($pdf, 'Invoice Date:', INCH, (PAGE_HEIGHT - (INCH * 3)) );
66          pdf_set_parameter ($pdf, "underline", "false");
67          pdf_show ($pdf, ' ' . date("F j, Y"));
68          $used_height = (INCH * 3) + FONT_SIZE;
69
70          pdf_set_value ($pdf, "leading", (FONT_SIZE * 2) );
71          pdf_set_parameter ($pdf, "underline", "true");
72          pdf_continue_text ($pdf, 'Invoice Number:');
73          pdf_set_parameter ($pdf, "underline", "false");
74          pdf_show ($pdf, ' ' . $HTTP_POST_VARS['invoice_number']);
75          $used_height += (FONT_SIZE * 3);
76
77          pdf_set_value ($pdf, "leading", (FONT_SIZE * 2) );
78          pdf_set_parameter ($pdf, "underline", "true");
79          pdf_continue_text ($pdf, 'Client:');
80          pdf_set_parameter ($pdf, "underline", "false");
81          pdf_show ($pdf, ' ' . $HTTP_POST_VARS['client']);
82          $used_height += (FONT_SIZE * 3);
83
84          pdf_set_value ($pdf, "leading", (FONT_SIZE * 2) );
85          pdf_set_parameter ($pdf, "underline", "true");
86          pdf_continue_text ($pdf, 'Amount Due:');
87          pdf_set_parameter ($pdf, "underline", "false");
88          pdf_show ($pdf, ' $' . $HTTP_POST_VARS['amount']);
89          $used_height += (FONT_SIZE * 3);
90
91          pdf_set_value ($pdf, "leading", (FONT_SIZE * 2) );
92          pdf_set_parameter ($pdf, "underline", "true");
93          pdf_continue_text ($pdf, "Description of Work:");
94          pdf_set_parameter ($pdf, "underline", "false");
95
96          // Determine the description of work box size.
97          $box_height = FONT_SIZE;
98          while ((pdf_show_boxed ($pdf, $HTTP_POST_VARS['description'], INCH, (PAGE_HEIGHT - $used_
            height - $box_height), (PAGE_WIDTH - (INCH * 2)), $box_height, "justify", "blind")) > 0 ) {
```

(script continues on next page)

```
                 script
99              $box_height += FONT_SIZE;
100         }
101
102         // Make sure there's enough room.
103         $remaining_space = PAGE_HEIGHT - ($used_height + INCH);
104
105         $font_size = FONT_SIZE;
106         while ( $box_height > $remaining_space ) {
107             $font_size = $font_size - 2;
108             pdf_setfont ($pdf, $times, $font_size);
109
110             $box_height = $font_size;
111             while ((pdf_show_boxed  ($pdf, $HTTP_POST_VARS['description'], INCH, (PAGE_HEIGHT -
                $used_height - $box_height), (PAGE_WIDTH - (INCH * 2)), $box_height, "justify",
                "blind")) > 0 ) {
112                 $box_height += $font_size;
113             }
114         }
115         pdf_show_boxed ($pdf, $HTTP_POST_VARS['description'], INCH, (PAGE_HEIGHT - $used_height
            - $box_height), (PAGE_WIDTH - (INCH * 2)), $box_height, 'justify');
116
117         // Outline the page.
118         pdf_setlinewidth ($pdf, 6);
119         pdf_setlinejoin ($pdf, 1);
120         pdf_rect ($pdf, (INCH/2), (INCH/2), (PAGE_WIDTH - INCH), (PAGE_HEIGHT - INCH -
            $image_height - INCH));
121         pdf_stroke ($pdf);
122
123         // Finish the page.
124         pdf_end_page($pdf);
125
126         // Close the PDF.
127         pdf_close($pdf);
128
129         // Send the PDF to the browser.
130         $buffer = pdf_get_buffer ($pdf);
131         header ("Content-type: application/pdf");
132         header ("Content-Length: " . strlen($buffer));
133         header ("Content-Disposition: inline; filename=" . $HTTP_POST_VARS['invoice_number'] .
            ".pdf");
134         echo $buffer;
135
136         // Free the resources.
137         pdf_delete ($pdf);
138
139     } else {
140         echo "You either forgot to enter the client's name, the invoice number, or the amount
            due. Please go back and try again.\n";
141     }
142
143 } else {
```

(script continues on next page)

USING IMAGES

Script 11.4 *continued*

```
                                        script

144        // Display the form.
145    ?>
146    <!DOCTYPE html PUBLIC "-//W3C//DTD XHTML 1.0 Transitional//EN"
147            "http://www.w3.org/TR/2000/REC-xhtml1-20000126/DTD/xhtml1-transitional.dtd">
148    <html xmlns="http://www.w3.org/1999/xhtml">
149    <head>
150        <title>Create An Invoice</title>
151    </head>
152    <body>
153    <form action="create_pdf_invoice3.php" method="POST">
154    <table border="0" width="80%" cellspacing="2" cellpadding="2" align="center">
155        <tr align="center" valign="top">
156            <td align="center" valign="top" colspan="2">Fill out the form to have your invoice
               created!</td>
157        </tr>
158        <tr align="center" valign="top">
159            <td align="right" valign="top">Enter the client's name:</td>
160            <td align="left" valign="top"><input type="text" name="client" size="40"
               maxlength="80"></td>
161        </tr>
162        <tr align="center" valign="top">
163            <td align="right" valign="top">Enter the invoice number:</td>
164            <td align="left" valign="top"><input type="text" name="invoice_number" size="10"
               maxlength="20"></td>
165        </tr>
166        <tr align="center" valign="top">
167            <td align="right" valign="top">Enter the amount due (without the dollar sign):</td>
168            <td align="left" valign="top"><input type="text" name="amount" size="10"
               maxlength="10"></td>
169        </tr>
170        <tr align="center" valign="top">
171            <td align="right" valign="top">Enter a description of the work:</td>
172            <td align="left" valign="top"><textarea name="description" rows="5"
               cols="40"></textarea></td>
173        </tr>
174        <tr align="center" valign="top">
175            <td align="center" valign="top" colspan="2"><input type="submit" name="submit"
               value="Make The Invoice!"></td>
176        </tr>
177    </table>
178    </form>
179    </body>
180    </html>
181    <?php
182    } // Close the SUBMIT conditional.
183    ?>
```

I want the image to fit nicely across the top of the page (and I know that the image is far more wide than it is tall). The first thing I want to check is to see if the current image width is too large for the page. If it isn't, then the current scaling is fine (1) and the x-coordinate should be based on centering the image.

If the image is too large, I first calculate how I need to scale it by dividing the page width by my image width (plus an inch of spacing). Then I calculate the x-coordinate of the image by multiplying the image width by the scale and proceeding as I normally would (subtract from the page width, divide by two, and round).

5. Place the image in the PDF and close it.

```
pdf_place_image($pdf, $image, $x,
→ (PAGE_HEIGHT - $image_height),
→ $scale);
pdf_close_image ($pdf, $image);
```

6. Delete the orange line underneath the subtitle.

7. Alter the title, subtitle, and border placing.

```
pdf_show_xy ($pdf, 'DMC Insights,
→ Inc.', ($x + 10), (PAGE_HEIGHT -
→ (INCH/2) - $image_height));
pdf_show_xy ($pdf, 'Invoice For
→ Services Completed', $x,
→ (PAGE_HEIGHT - (INCH/2) - 36 -
→ 18 - $image_height));
pdf_rect ($pdf, (INCH/2), (INCH/2),
→ (PAGE_WIDTH - INCH), (PAGE_HEIGHT
→ - INCH - $image_height - INCH));
```

Now that the top of the page is a banner image, I need to move each of these down to make room for the image without overlap.

continues on next page

8. Once again, change the form's ACTION attribute.

```
<form action="create_pdf_
→ invoice3.php" method="POST">
```

9. Save the file as `create_pdf_invoice3.php`, upload it to your server, and test in your Web browser (**Figure 11.12**).

✔ Tips

■ The PDFlib manual recommends opening the image after the PDF object has been created but before a page has begun for improved performance. You still need to place the image after the page has been started, though.

■ On older versions of PHP, you'll need to use the specific `pdf_open_jpeg()`, `pdf_open_gif()`, etc., and not the general `pdf_open_image()`.

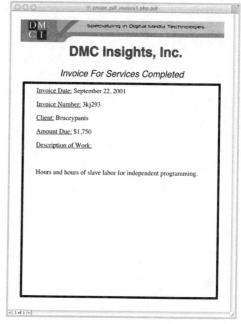

Figure 11.12 Even better than using graphics to add design to your PDFs is the ability to add images, too. This invoice uses both techniques.

USING IMAGES

Creating Multiple-Page PDFs

Two last aspects of PDF creation I would like to discuss are creating multiple page documents and saving the created PDF to the server.

Creating multiple pages is far easier than one might think. All it requires is that the one page is concluded with `pdf_end_page()` and that another is immediately begun with `pdf_begin_page()`. You will need to re-establish some settings, like the font to use, with each new page, though.

To save a file to the server, give the `pdf_open_file()` function a filename.

```
pdf_open_file ($pdf, 'my_file.pdf');
```

This will make PHP try to create (or open, if it exists) a PDF called `my_file.pdf` within the current directory. This does require open read-write permissions (*666*) on the directory to work. Unlike image generation, you can create a PDF in memory or on the server, but not both.

I'll quickly add these two new capabilities to the existing invoice-generation script, resulting in a more polished final product.

To create multiple-page PDFs:

1. Open `create_pdf_invoice3.php` (Script 11.4) in your text editor.

2. Change the `pdf_open_file()` line accordingly (**Script 11.5**).
   ```
   pdf_open_file ($pdf, $HTTP_POST_VARS
   → ['invoice_number'] . ".pdf");
   ```
   Even though the PDF will no longer be created in memory, I am still using the submitted invoice number as the name of the file.

3. Change the references to the image's x-coordinate.
   ```
   $image_x = round ((PAGE_WIDTH -
   → ($image_width * $scale) )/2);
   $image_x = round ((PAGE_WIDTH -
   → $image_width)/2);
   ```
   I'm going to give each page the same image banner and rectangle border. To ensure that the proper x-coordinate for the image does not get overridden by another $x variable used later in the script, I'll give it a more appropriate name now.

4. Remove the line that deletes the image. Again, since I will make use of the image one more time, there is no need to free up its resources prematurely.

5. After the first page is ended, create a second one.
   ```
   pdf_begin_page ($pdf, PAGE_WIDTH,
   → PAGE_HEIGHT);
   ```

6. Place the image at the top of this page, then delete it.
   ```
   PDF_place_image($pdf, $image,
   → $image_x, (PAGE_HEIGHT -
   → $image_height), $scale);
   pdf_close_image ($pdf, $image);
   ```

7. Set the font and leading information.
   ```
   $times = pdf_findfont ($pdf,
   → "Times-Roman", "winansi");
   pdf_setfont ($pdf, $times,
   → FONT_SIZE);
   pdf_set_value ($pdf, "leading",
   → (FONT_SIZE * 2) );
   ```
   Remember that the fonts are set on a page-by-page basis and must therefore be re-established before use.

continues on page 424

Script 11.5 A variation on the invoice scripts, this code creates a multipage document in PDF form.

```
1    <?php
2    // This page creates an invoice based on user-submitted information.
3
4    if (isset($HTTP_POST_VARS['submit'])) { // Handle the form.
5
6        if ( (isset($HTTP_POST_VARS['client'])) AND (isset($HTTP_POST_VARS['amount']))  AND
             (isset($HTTP_POST_VARS['invoice_number'])) ) {
7
8            // Set the constants and variables.
9            define ("PAGE_WIDTH", 612); // 8.5 inches.
10           define ("PAGE_HEIGHT", 792); // 11 inches.
11           define ("FONT_SIZE", 18); // Large 0.5-inch type.
12           define ("INCH", 72);
13
14           // Make the invoice.
15           $pdf = pdf_new();
16           pdf_open_file ($pdf, $HTTP_POST_VARS['invoice_number'] . ".pdf");
17
18           // Set the different PDF values.
19           pdf_set_info ($pdf, "Author", "Larry E. Ullman");
20           pdf_set_info ($pdf, "Title", "Invoice for " . $HTTP_POST_VARS['client']);
21           pdf_set_info ($pdf, "Creator", "See Author");
22
23           // Create the page.
24           pdf_begin_page ($pdf, PAGE_WIDTH, PAGE_HEIGHT);
25
26           // Open and place the image.
27           $image = pdf_open_image_file ($pdf, 'jpeg', 'dmci_title.jpg');
28           $image_width = pdf_get_value ($pdf, 'imagewidth', $image);
29           $image_height = pdf_get_value ($pdf, 'imageheight', $image);
30           if ($image_width > (PAGE_WIDTH + INCH)) {
31               $scale = PAGE_WIDTH / ($image_width + INCH);
32               $image_x = round ((PAGE_WIDTH - ($image_width * $scale) )/2);
33           } else {
34               $scale = 1;
35               $image_x = round((PAGE_WIDTH - $image_width)/2);
36           }
37           PDF_place_image($pdf, $image, $x, (PAGE_HEIGHT - $image_height), $scale);
38
39           // Print a title.
40           $helvetica_bold = pdf_findfont ($pdf, "Helvetica-Bold", "winansi");
41           pdf_setfont ($pdf, $helvetica_bold, 36);
42           pdf_set_value ($pdf, "textrendering", 2);
43           pdf_setcolor ($pdf, 'both', 'rgb', 0.2, 0.2, 1.0, 0);
44           $width = pdf_stringwidth ($pdf, 'DMC Insights, Inc.');
45           $x = round ((PAGE_WIDTH - $width) / 2);
46           pdf_show_xy ($pdf, 'DMC Insights, Inc.', ($x + 10), (PAGE_HEIGHT - (INCH/2) -
                 $image_height));
47           pdf_setcolor ($pdf, 'both', 'rgb', 0, 0, 0, 0);
48
49           // Print the subtitle.
50           $helvetica_obl = pdf_findfont ($pdf, "Helvetica-Oblique", "winansi");
51           pdf_setfont ($pdf, $helvetica_obl, 24);
52           pdf_set_value ($pdf, "textrendering", 0);
53           $width = pdf_stringwidth ($pdf, 'Invoice For Services Completed');
54           $x = round ((PAGE_WIDTH - $width) / 2);
```

(script continues on next page)

Script 11.5 *continued*

```
┌────────────────────────────────────────── script ──────────────────────────────────────────┐
55      pdf_show_xy ($pdf, 'Invoice For Services Completed', $x, (PAGE_HEIGHT - (INCH/2) - 36 -
        18 - $image_height));
56
57      // Set the default font from here on out.
58      $times = pdf_findfont ($pdf, "Times-Roman", "winansi");
59      pdf_setfont ($pdf, $times, FONT_SIZE);
60
61      // Print the remaining lines.
62      pdf_set_parameter ($pdf, "underline", "true");
63      pdf_show_xy ($pdf, 'Invoice Date:', INCH, (PAGE_HEIGHT - (INCH * 3)) );
64      pdf_set_parameter ($pdf, "underline", "false");
65      pdf_show ($pdf, ' ' . date("F j, Y"));
66      $used_height = (INCH * 3) + FONT_SIZE;
67
68      pdf_set_value ($pdf, "leading", (FONT_SIZE * 2) );
69      pdf_set_parameter ($pdf, "underline", "true");
70      pdf_continue_text ($pdf, 'Invoice Number:');
71      pdf_set_parameter ($pdf, "underline", "false");
72      pdf_show ($pdf, ' ' . $HTTP_POST_VARS['invoice_number']);
73      $used_height += (FONT_SIZE * 3);
74
75      pdf_set_value ($pdf, "leading", (FONT_SIZE * 2) );
76      pdf_set_parameter ($pdf, "underline", "true");
77      pdf_continue_text ($pdf, 'Client:');
78      pdf_set_parameter ($pdf, "underline", "false");
79      pdf_show ($pdf, ' ' . $HTTP_POST_VARS['client']);
80      $used_height += (FONT_SIZE * 3);
81
82      pdf_set_value ($pdf, "leading", (FONT_SIZE * 2) );
83      pdf_set_parameter ($pdf, "underline", "true");
84      pdf_continue_text ($pdf, 'Amount Due:');
85      pdf_set_parameter ($pdf, "underline", "false");
86      pdf_show ($pdf, ' $' . $HTTP_POST_VARS['amount']);
87      $used_height += (FONT_SIZE * 3);
88
89      pdf_set_value ($pdf, "leading", (FONT_SIZE * 2) );
90      pdf_set_parameter ($pdf, "underline", "true");
91      pdf_continue_text ($pdf, "Description of Work:");
92      pdf_set_parameter ($pdf, "underline", "false");
93
94      // Determine the description of work box size.
95      $box_height = FONT_SIZE;
96      while ((pdf_show_boxed ($pdf, $HTTP_POST_VARS['description'], INCH, (PAGE_HEIGHT - $used_
        height - $box_height), (PAGE_WIDTH - (INCH * 2)), $box_height, "justify", "blind")) > 0 ) {
97          $box_height += FONT_SIZE;
98      }
99
100     // Make sure there's enough room.
101     $remaining_space = PAGE_HEIGHT - ($used_height + INCH);
102
103     $font_size = FONT_SIZE;
104     while ( $box_height > $remaining_space ) {
105         $font_size = $font_size - 2;
106         pdf_setfont ($pdf, $times, $font_size);
107
108         $box_height = $font_size;
└──────────────────────────────────────────────────────────────────────────────────────────┘
```

(script continues on next page)

CREATING MULTIPLE-PAGE PDFs

Script 11.5 *continued*

```
109              while ((pdf_show_boxed  ($pdf, $HTTP_POST_VARS['description'], INCH, (PAGE_HEIGHT -
                 $used_height - $box_height), (PAGE_WIDTH - (INCH * 2))), $box_height, "justify",
                 "blind")) > 0 ) {
110                  $box_height += $font_size;
111              }
112          }
113          pdf_show_boxed ($pdf, $HTTP_POST_VARS['description'], INCH, (PAGE_HEIGHT - $used_height
             - $box_height), (PAGE_WIDTH - (INCH * 2))), $box_height, 'justify');
114
115          // Outline the page.
116          pdf_setlinewidth ($pdf, 6);
117          pdf_setlinejoin ($pdf, 1);
118          pdf_rect ($pdf, (INCH/2), (INCH/2), (PAGE_WIDTH - INCH), (PAGE_HEIGHT - INCH -
             $image_height - INCH));
119          pdf_stroke ($pdf);
120
121          // Finish the page.
122          pdf_end_page($pdf);
123
124
125          // Make the second page.
126          pdf_begin_page ($pdf, PAGE_WIDTH, PAGE_HEIGHT);
127
128          // Open and place the image.
129          PDF_place_image($pdf, $image, $image_x, (PAGE_HEIGHT - $image_height), $scale);
130          pdf_close_image ($pdf, $image);
131
132          $times = pdf_findfont ($pdf, "Times-Roman", "winansi");
133          pdf_setfont ($pdf, $times, FONT_SIZE);
134
135          pdf_set_value ($pdf, "leading", (FONT_SIZE * 2) );
136          // Determine the description of work box size.
137          $box_height = FONT_SIZE;
138          while ((pdf_show_boxed  ($pdf, "Please remit payment to:\nDMC Insights,
             Inc.\nAddress\nCity, ST ZIP", INCH, (PAGE_HEIGHT/2), (PAGE_WIDTH - (INCH * 2)),
             $box_height, "center", "blind")) > 0 ) {
139              $box_height += FONT_SIZE;
140          }
141          pdf_show_boxed ($pdf, "Please remit payment to:\nDMC Insights, Inc.\nAddress\nCity, ST
             Zip", INCH, (PAGE_HEIGHT/2), (PAGE_WIDTH - (INCH * 2)), $box_height, 'center');
142
143          // Outline the page.
144          pdf_setlinewidth ($pdf, 6);
145          pdf_setlinejoin ($pdf, 1);
146          pdf_rect ($pdf, (INCH/2), (INCH/2), (PAGE_WIDTH - INCH), (PAGE_HEIGHT - INCH -
             $image_height - INCH));
147          pdf_stroke ($pdf);
148
149          pdf_end_page($pdf);
150
151          // Close the PDF.
152          pdf_close($pdf);
153
154          // Free the resources.
155          pdf_delete ($pdf);
```

(script continues on next page)

Script 11.5 *continued*

```
                                                              script

156
157          echo "Finished! Check in the appropriate folder for the invoice.";
158
159      } else {
160          echo "You either forgot to enter the client's name, the invoice number, or the amount
             due. Please go back and try again.\n";
161      }
162
163  } else {
164      // Display the form.
165  ?>
166  <!DOCTYPE html PUBLIC "-//W3C//DTD XHTML 1.0 Transitional//EN"
167  "http://www.w3.org/TR/2000/REC-xhtml1-20000126/DTD/xhtml1-transitional.dtd">
168  <html xmlns="http://www.w3.org/1999/xhtml">
169  <head>
170      <title>Create An Invoice</title>
171  </head>
172  <body>
173  <form action="create_pdf_invoice4.php" method="POST">
174  <table border="0" width="80%" cellspacing="2" cellpadding="2" align="center">
175      <tr align="center" valign="top">
176          <td align="center" valign="top" colspan="2">Fill out the form to have your invoice
             created!</td>
177      </tr>
178      <tr align="center" valign="top">
179          <td align="right" valign="top">Enter the client's name:</td>
180          <td align="left" valign="top"><input type="text" name="client" size="40"
             maxlength="80"></td>
181      </tr>
182      <tr align="center" valign="top">
183          <td align="right" valign="top">Enter the invoice number:</td>
184          <td align="left" valign="top"><input type="text" name="invoice_number" size="10"
             maxlength="20"></td>
185      </tr>
186      <tr align="center" valign="top">
187          <td align="right" valign="top">Enter the amount due (without the dollar sign):</td>
188          <td align="left" valign="top"><input type="text" name="amount" size="10"
             maxlength="10"></td>
189      </tr>
190      <tr align="center" valign="top">
191          <td align="right" valign="top">Enter a description of the work:</td>
192          <td align="left" valign="top"><textarea name="description" rows="5"
             cols="40"></textarea></td>
193      </tr>
194      <tr align="center" valign="top">
195          <td align="center" valign="top" colspan="2"><input type="submit" name="submit"
             value="Make The Invoice!"></td>
196      </tr>
197  </table>
198  </form>
199  </body>
200  </html>
201  <?php
202  } // Close the SUBMIT conditional.
203  ?>
```

CREATING MULTIPLE-PAGE PDFs

8. Determine the appropriate text box size.

```
$box_height = FONT_SIZE;

while ((pdf_show_boxed ($pdf,
→ "Please remit payment to:\nDMC
→ Insights, Inc.\nAddress\nCity, ST
→ ZIP", INCH, (PAGE_HEIGHT/2),
→ (PAGE_WIDTH - (INCH * 2)),
→ $box_height, "center", "blind")) >
→ 0 ) {
$box_height += FONT_SIZE;
}

pdf_show_boxed ($pdf, "Please remit
→ payment to:\nDMC Insights, Inc.\n
→ Address\nCity, ST Zip", INCH,
→ (PAGE_HEIGHT/2), (PAGE_WIDTH -
→ (INCH * 2)), $box_height,
→ 'center');
```

The string I'm printing on the second page is a psuedo-mailing address for the company. Notice that I can use the escaped *n* to create new lines in the PDF document, just as I'm used to doing in text files.

Because this is the only text on the page, I'm not worried about the box being too large, so I am not making use of the second series of loops that adjust the font size.

9. Add the rectangle border.

```
pdf_setlinewidth ($pdf, 6);

pdf_setlinejoin ($pdf, 1);

pdf_rect ($pdf, (INCH/2), (INCH/2),
→ (PAGE_WIDTH - INCH), (PAGE_HEIGHT
→ - INCH - $image_height - INCH));

pdf_stroke ($pdf);
```

10. End the second page.

```
pdf_end_page($pdf);
```

If you are doing more complicated PDFs, make use of the $used_height variable to know when it's time to create a new page. Logically you could create a function that ends the current page, begins the new page, prints the appropriate

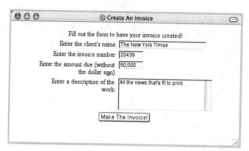

Figure 11.13 Throughout all of these examples, the form itself has remained the same, but the end result (Figure 11.16 and 11.17) has drastically improved.

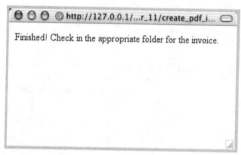

Figure 11.14 Since this script would not have otherwise sent anything to the browser, a message is relayed indicating that the PDF is available on the server.

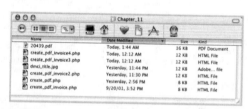

Figure 11.15 The same directory that contains the create_pdf_invoice4.php script now has the freshly made 20439.pdf file.

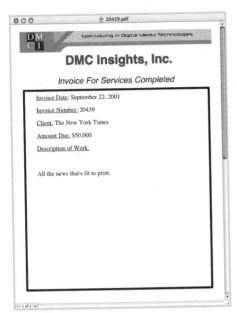

Figure 11.16 The first page of the generated PDF contains no new elements, but the second page (Figure 11.17) is a nice addition.

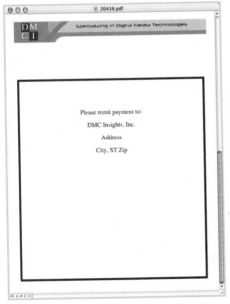

Figure 11.17 To demonstrate a two-page PDF, I've added payment information to the invoice while retaining some of the page's formatting.

image or border that every page should have, and then resets the `$used_height` variable.

11. Print a message to the user so the browser displays something.

```
echo "Finished! Check in the
→ appropriate folder for the
→ invoice.";
```

12. Delete all of the `header()` and buffer lines.

13. Change the form `ACTION` attribute one last time.

```
<form action="create_pdf_
→ invoice4.php" method="POST">
```

14. Save the file as `create_pdf_invoice4.php`, upload it to your server, and test in your Web browser (**Figures 11.13, 11.14, 11.15, 11.16,** and **11.17**).

✔ Tips

- Acrobat Reader 4 allows for longer PDF documents than earlier versions do. You can now create PDFs containing literally thousands and thousands of pages.

- The information presented in this chapter is just an overview to get you started with PDFs. The sky's the limit with what you can do from here—attach files to PDFs, insert Web links, and much, much more. See Appendix C, General Resources, for more places providing PDF information.

EXTENDING PHP

For a couple of years now, PHP has been one of the pre-eminent methods for creating dynamic Web applications. Its popularity, which expanded greatly after PHP 3, has solidified with PHP 4. With legions of smart, able programmers using PHP, it was not surprising to see the language extended beyond its original purpose of creating Web sites.

Unlike ASP (Active Server Pages, controlled by Microsoft), PHP is an *open source* technology, meaning that it can be expanded upon by anyone with the inclination. Such modifications, frequently released to the general public, even further promote the idea of learning and using PHP. This chapter, Extending PHP, discusses four ways in which PHP has been, or can be, modified for different uses. All PHP developers should familiarize themselves with two of these developments—PEAR and the Zend Optimizer. The other topics—PHP-GTK and hacking the PHP code—are not for the faint of heart but might be something you would be interested in doing. Finally, if PHP does not have a feature or a capability you think it should, there's nothing stopping you from implementing it yourself. Then you can pass your addition on to the greater PHP community.

PEAR

PEAR, the PHP Extension and Application Repository, grew out of a desire to mimic Perl's counterpart, Comprehensive Perl Archive Network, or CPAN. The purpose of PEAR (and CPAN and Tex's CTAN) is to establish a methodology for programmers to develop and share code as part of the architecture of PHP itself. Because so many programmers will frequently perform the same tasks in their applications, standardizing certain processes makes a lot of sense. PEAR is essentially an officially sanctioned set of classes that have been incorporated into PHP (as of PHP 4). Accordingly, PEAR also sets rules regulating how a class is to be structured and documented so that there is some quality control as to what code is added to the mix.

Because PEAR is relatively new, the documentation for its capabilities and, to be frank, PEAR as a whole, is still slight in build. The official Web site, http://pear.php.net (**Figure 12.1**), contains marginally more documentation than the PEAR section of the PHP manual, but your best bet in learning PEAR may be in reading the documentation written into the classes themselves (another reason why documenting your work is essential).

The first question you probably have is "Where can I find PEAR?" PEAR is included with the PHP 4 source code, in a directory appropriately named *PEAR*. Depending on your server and PHP installation, PHP may or may not already acknowledge the existence of the classes. If not, then you can do one of two things:

- Add the path to the PEAR scripts to your php.ini file as an *include_path*.

- Place the PEAR files on your server where your other scripts can include them.

PEAR offers a couple of dozen categories of classes, covering caching PHP pages, XML, encryption, HTML generation, HTTP tricks, email, and more. To demonstrate how to use PEAR, I'll use the *database abstraction* and the *script timing* classes. The former gives you the option of writing database-independent code so that you can switch your database application without making major modifications to your application. The latter allows you to establish benchmarks and track how long parts of your scripts take. The example itself will be a page that allows you to query a database via the Web browser.

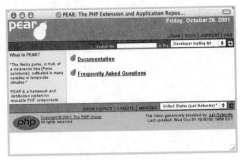

Figure 12.1 The PEAR Web site is currently lacking in content, but as PEAR is more developed and used, that will certainly change.

To use PEAR:

1. Create a new HTML document in your text editor (**Script 12.1**).

```
<!DOCTYPE html PUBLIC "-//W3C//DTD
→ XHTML 1.0 Transitional//EN"
"http://www.w3.org/TR/2000/
→ REC-xhtml1-20000126/DTD/
→ xhtml1-transitional.dtd">
<html xmlns="http://www.w3.org/
→ 1999/xhtml">
<head>
<title>Database Query Script</title>
</head>
<body>
```

continues on page 431

Script 12.1 The db_query.php file uses two of PEAR's classes to accomplish database abstraction and to time script execution.

```
1   <!DOCTYPE html PUBLIC "-//W3C//DTD XHTML 1.0 Transitional//EN"
2       "http://www.w3.org/TR/2000/REC-xhtml1-20000126/DTD/xhtml1-transitional.dtd">
3   <html xmlns="http://www.w3.org/1999/xhtml">
4   <head>
5       <title>Database Query Script</title>
6   </head>
7   <body>
8   <?php
9   // This page displays and HTML form and handles it. The purpose is to directly query a database
    via the Web browser.
10
11  if (isset($HTTP_POST_VARS['submit'])) { // If the form has been submitted, process it.
12
13      // Set the database parameters.
14      $db_password = 'password';
15      $db_username = 'username';
16      $db_database = 'database;
17      $db_host = 'localhost';
18      $db_type = 'mysql';
19
20      // Require the PEAR database and timing classes.
21      require_once ('DB.php');
22      require_once ('Benchmark/Timer.php');
23
24      // Start the timer.
```

(script continues on next page)

429

Script 12.1 *continued*

```
                                          script
25        $timer = new Benchmark_Timer;
26        $timer->start();
27
28        // Establish a connection.
29        $db = DB::connect ("$db_type://$db_username:$db_password@$db_host/$db_database");
30
31        // If the connection worked, continue.
32        if (DB::isError($db)) {
33
34            die (DB::errorMessage($db));
35
36        } else { // OK to query the database.
37
38            $result = $db->query($query);
39            if (DB::isError($result)) {
40                die(DB::errorMessage($result));
41            } else {
42                echo '<table align="center" cellpadding="2" cellspacing="2" border="0">';
43                while ($row = $result->fetchRow()) {
44                    echo '<tr>';
45                    foreach ($row as $key => $value) {
46                        echo "<td>$value</td>";
47                    }
48                    echo '</tr>';
49                }
50                echo '</table><br /><hr />';
51            }
52
53            // Close the connection.
54            $db->disconnect();
55
56        }
57
58        // Stop the timer and print the result.
59        $timer->stop();
60        $timer_result = $timer->getProfiling();
61        echo "The PHP execution took {$timer_result[1]['total']} seconds.<br />";
62
63    } // Close the submit conditional.
64
65    // Display the form.
66    ?>
67    This page allows you to query a database. Enter your query--in proper SQL form--in the text box
      below, then click Submit.<br />
68    <form action="db_query.php" method="post">
69    <textarea name="query" rows="5" cols="40"></textarea><br />
70    <input type="submit" name="submit" value="Submit" />
71    </form>
72    </body>
73    </html>
```

PEAR

2. Begin a section of PHP and check to see if the form has been submitted.

```
<?php
if (isset($HTTP_POST_VARS['submit']))
{
```

This will be yet another example in which the page will both display and handle the form. Since I'm assuming that the intended user of this page will be me (or some other administrative-level person), I'm not going to be too concerned about security or user carelessness.

3. Establish all of the database particulars.

```
$db_password = 'password';
$db_username = 'username';
$db_database = 'database';
$db_host = 'localhost';
$db_type = 'mysql';
```

As I'm sure you are aware, this information could also be more securely stored in a separate configuration file. Because I'll be using a database abstraction layer, I add a fifth variable identifying what Database Management System I will be using. The entire script will function the same for any DBMS I choose to use (that is supported by PEAR, technically) and I'll need to change only this one variable from application to application. Some other options you have for $db_type are odbc, msql, pgsql (PostgreSQL), and oci (Oracle).

4. Include the two necessary PEAR classes.

```
require_once ('DB.php');
require_once ('Benchmark/Timer.php');
```

The DB.php file contains the *DB* class, the first requisite class for database abstraction. The other PEAR classes for database access are stored within the *DB* folder and will be called from within DB.php.

The Timer.php script, located in the *Benchmark* folder, includes all of the necessary timing code.

5. Start a timer.

```
$timer = new Benchmark_Timer;
$timer->start();
```

Most PEAR classes require the use of an object. Here I am creating an object called $timer that is an instance of the *Benchmark_Timer* class. The start() method will turn the timer on.

6. Connect to the database.

```
$db = DB::connect ("$db_type://
→ $db_username:$db_password@$db_
→ host/$db_database");
```

The syntax for the *database abstraction* class is slightly different from what you might be used to when working with object-oriented programming. You do not have to create a new instance of a class but can begin by immediately connecting to the database. The connect() method takes an argument in the form of *database type://database username:database password@database host/database name*. Each one of these elements corresponds to the variables set a few lines above. The connect() method will use the proper database connection function based on the value of $db_type (or database type), be it ocilogon() for Oracle, mysql_connect() for MySQL, or odbc_connect() for Microsoft Access and other databases that do not have direct support in PHP (for the last instance, you would use *odbc* as your database type, not *access*).

7. Confirm that the connection worked.

```
if (DB::isError($db)) {
die (DB::errorMessage($db));
```

The *DB* class includes error-handling capabilities via the isError() function. If isError() returns TRUE, then a problem occurred that can be related by the errorMessage() function.

continues on next page

PEAR

8. Query the database.

```
} else {
$result = $db->query($query);
```

The method for querying the database—regardless of which DBMS you are using—is query(), which takes an argument that is the SQL query itself. The purpose of this page will be to handle queries entered into an HTML form, which is where the $query variable will be derived from. Because this script is intended for my (or another secure user's) purposes, I'm not going to worry about what the query itself is and any possible maliciousness. If you intend to use this script on a live site, you will want to password-protect or otherwise limit access to this file.

9. Print the query result.

```
if (DB::isError($result)) {
die(DB::errorMessage($result));
} else {
echo '<table align="center"
→ cellpadding="2" cellspacing="2"
→ border="0">';
while ($row = $result->fetchRow()) {
echo '<tr>';
foreach ($row as $key => $value) {
echo "<td>$value</td>";
}
echo '</tr>';
}
echo '</table><br /><hr />';
}
```

Again, I'm going to check to see if there is an error and, if there isn't, I'll print all returned rows. The fetchRow() method will do just that. Then I can break each row, which is retrieved as an array, into its individual parts and display this as a table.

10. Close the database connection.

```
$db->disconnect();
}
```

The disconnect() function will close the connection to the database. Since $db is not formally an object, I'm not concerned with unsetting it.

11. Turn off the timer and show how much time elapsed.

```
$timer->stop();
$timer_result = $timer->
→ getProfiling();
echo "The PHP execution took
→ {$timer_result[1]['total']}
→ seconds.<br />";
```

In its simplest use, the *Benchmark_Timer* class creates an array listing the start time of a certain marker, the time elapsed since the previous marker, and the total time elapsed from the start time to this marker. Since I have not formally declared any markers, the getProfiling() function will return this information from the time I started the timer until the time I stopped it. Accessing the value at $timer_result[1]['total'] will give me the total number of seconds elapsed.

12. Close the submit conditional and the PHP section, then make the HTML form.

```
}
?>
This page allows you to query a
→ database. Enter your query--in
→ proper SQL form--in the text box
→ below, then click Submit.<br />
<form action="db_query.php"
→ method="post">
<textarea name="query" rows="5"
→ cols="40"></textarea><br />
<input type="submit" name="submit"
→ value="Submit" />
```

```
</form>
</body>
</html>
```

The form just shows a text area into which I can enter a database query. I could spruce it up by allowing the user to specify the database, or I could list the databases and tables up front.

13. Save the file as db_query.php, upload it to your server, and test in your Web browser (**Figures 12.2**, **12.3**, **12.4**, **12.5**, and **12.6**).

continues on next page

Figure 12.2 The script as it is requires that I have some knowledge of the database to query it properly.

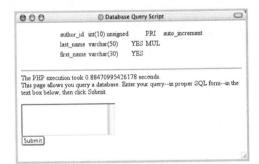

Figure 12.3 The result of my query (Figure 12.2) is displayed in the Web browser, along with how long the script took to execute.

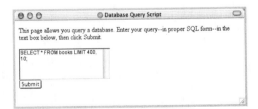

Figure 12.4 This page allows me to directly query the database without need of a command-line interface or phpMyAdmin.

Figure 12.5 Because the *larrys_books* database (which I'm querying here) is relational in design, some of the returned information will seem cryptic.

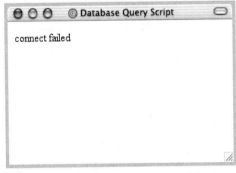

Figure 12.6 The error-handling capability of the *DB* class will tell me problems such as if the script could not connect to the database.

PEAR

✔ Tips

- You will probably want to experiment with how errors are managed because some reports are less useful than others (**Figure 12.7**). If the site is for your own use, or in debugging mode, printing out the exact query is a good way to help solve the problem.

- The PEAR class—the parent for every other class—includes extensive error-handling capabilities. You can set how errors are to be handled using

  `$db->setErrorHandling`
  `→ (PEAR_ERROR_DIE);`

  Two other options (besides `PEAR_ERROR_DIE`) are `PEAR_ERROR_RETURN` and `PEAR_ERROR_PRINT`.

- The *Benchmark_Timer* class also includes the ability to time specific parts of a script using the *setMarker()* method. Check the class' documentation for an example.

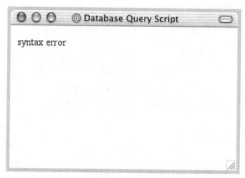

Figure 12.7 While the class includes error reporting, it does lack a level of detail you would otherwise desire.

Zend

Zend Technologies Ltd. is responsible for creating the Zend Engine at the heart of what makes the new version of PHP so powerful. But Zend (**Figure 12.8**) has much more to offer the PHP programmer.

At Zend's Web site (www.zend.com) you'll find resources such as articles and tutorials on programming with PHP, scripts that other programmers have uploaded, tips, the PHP manual, and more. Further, Zend offers both free and commercial products that can help you in your PHP development and usage. (I should make it clear that I don't work for Zend but am just endorsing the company as the second-best resource for PHP programmers after www.PHP.net.)

Figure 12.8 Zend.com is your second-best resource for PHP information after the official PHP home page (www.php.net).

One product Zend offers is the Zend IDE, an integrated development environment for writing, developing, and debugging PHP scripts (**Figure 12.9**). The IDE includes many features that text editors also have, including syntax highlighting, automatic indentation, and automatic code completion. Besides being tied into PHP for testing purposes, it also links to the PHP manual online (**Figure 12.10**).

A free application that Zend created is the Zend Optimizer. This program runs on the Web server and is intended to improve the run-time performance of the scripts you write in PHP. Zend claims that use of the Zend Optimizer will improve performance by 40 to 100 percent. I'll go over its installation (for the FreeBSD platform, which mimics other Unix installations) here.

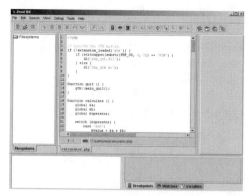

Figure 12.9 The Zend IDE is a solid text editor and development tool for programming with PHP.

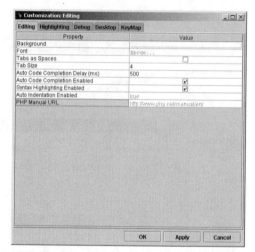

Figure 12.10 Among the numerous features built into the Zend IDE is a link to the PHP manual and other help files.

ZEND

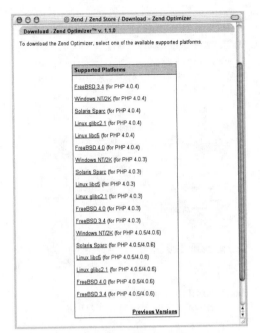

Figure 12.11 Because the Optimizer's code is not released, Zend may not have compiled versions for your operating system (the one drawback with the product).

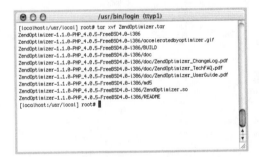

Figure 12.12 The downloaded file contains not only the Optimizer itself but also documents describing how it works.

Figure 12.13 Adding these three lines to your php.ini file will tell PHP to use the Zend Optimizer.

To install the Zend Optimizer:

1. Download the version of the Zend Optimizer that corresponds to your operating system and the version of PHP you are running (**Figure 12.11**).

   The code for the Zend Optimizer is not open source, meaning that you have to use a precompiled version and cannot compile your own, as you might do with PHP. Zend releases the Optimizer according to the operating system being used and the version of PHP running. You must match up both.

2. Unpack the downloaded file on your server (**Figure 12.12**).

   Zend recommends that you create a directory (as a Unix example, /usr/local/Zend/lib) for storing the Optimizer file.

3. Edit your php.ini file by adding the following information (**Figure 12.13**):

   `zend_optimizer.optimization_level=15`

   `zend_extension="/usr/local/Zend/`
   `→ ZendOptimizer.so"`

   If you are not also using the Zend Encoder (another application that Zend offers), add `zend_optimizer.enable_loader = 0`.

   I place this information at the very end of my php.ini file, although it does not really matter where you put it. I also add a comment so that I know who added this information and when. The most important consideration is that the second line refers to exactly where the ZendOptimizer.so file is on your server.

   continues on next page

ZEND

4. Stop and restart your Web server (**Figure 12.14**).

For Apache, I use `apachectl stop` and `apachectl start`, not `apachectl restart` or `apachectl graceful`.

5. Load a `phpinfo()` script in your Web browser to see if PHP recognizes the Optimizer (**Figure 12.15**).

✔ Tips

■ To use the Zend Optimizer, your PHP installation must be compiled with `--disable-debug`, which is the default.

■ If you want to test the power of the Optimizer yourself, use the *Benchmark_ Timer* class to see how long a script takes to execute with and without the Optimizer. The longer and more complex the script, the more its performance should be improved with the Optimizer.

■ The Zend Encoder, as mentioned above, can work with the Optimizer. The Encoder is designed to encode and decode your PHP scripts to further protect them from hackers.

Figure 12.14 The last step in the installation process is to stop then restart your Web server (here I have just stopped Apache).

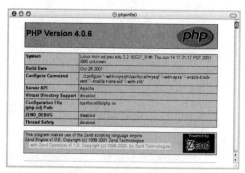

Figure 12.15 If the installation worked, your `phpinfo()` script will now indicate that the Zend Optimizer is running.

ZEND

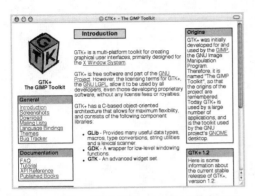

Figure 12.16 The official GTK home page will give you a history of the application, along with a detailed reference of all the available widgets.

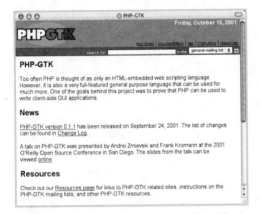

Figure 12.17 PHP-GTK's Web site is currently lacking in depth, but that will change as the system is better supported and used.

PHP-GTK

Before the advent of PHP-GTK, PHP could only be used to develop Web applications. In other words, PHP required a Web server such as Apache or IIS to function and it could not run on its own. This meant that everything PHP did was server-side and the closest you could come to writing stand-alone applications would be to run a server on your computer.

GTK+, which stands for GIMP Tool Kit (GIMP being the GNU Image Manipulation Program), is an open source application that works on multiple platforms. The GTK home page, www.gtk.org (**Figure 12.16**), describes the system's origins and usage but from a C programming perspective (it, like PHP, is written in C).

The PHP-GTK Web site, http://gtk.php.net (**Figure 12.17**), discusses how GTK can be accessed specifically from a PHP script. To use PHP with GTK you need a binary version of PHP, GTK+, and the php_gtk module. You can download and configure all of these for a Unix (Linux, etc.) system or retrieve preconfigured binaries for Windows (which, in my case, uses a development version of PHP 4.0.8). I'll go over the basics of how GTK works, then demonstrate a PHP application of it.

GTK uses widgets to make applications. A widget is anything that helps create an interface to the code, including buttons, windows, and more. To build an application, you create new instances of widgets (PHP uses an OOP interface to GTK), then apply different properties by calling that widget's methods.

As I said, a widget is the generic term for any element an application may have, but there are special widgets called containers that are used as a parent for other widgets. The primary container will be a window.

A widget listens for signals—user events—and then enacts a callback—the function that gets called upon for that event. You assign a function to an event using the `connect()` method.

```
$widget->connect('event', 'function
→ (callback)');
```

This is somewhat similar to JavaScript in that you can have objects do things if an event occurs (such as an image rollover if the mouse moves above an image), but it is more like how Macromedia Director behaves, if you are familiar with that application. The primary event I'll demonstrate is *clicked*, indicating that the mouse button was clicked on the widget.

You can pass a value to the callback function by adding it as a parameter to the `connect()` call.

```
$widget->connect ('clicked', 'function',
→ 'value');
```

This is just the basics of how you'll use GTK with PHP. Every widget has its own methods and attributes, and GTK includes dozens upon dozens of widgets. I'll explain in more detail in this example, a simple graphical calculator.

To use PHP-GTK:

1. Create a new PHP document in your text editor (**Script 12.2**).

`<?php`

Since this page will not be accessed via a Web browser, there is no need to include any HTML.

continues on page 445

Script 12.2 This file takes advantage of PHP-GTK to write a client-side calculator application.

```
1   <?php
2
3   // This script uses GTK to create a calculator.
4
5   // Include the GTK module.
6   if (!extension_loaded('gtk')) {
7       if (strtoupper(substr(PHP_OS, 0, 3)) == 'WIN') {
8           dl('php_gtk.dll');
9       } else {
10          dl('php_gtk.so');
11      }
12  }
13
14  // This function is for when the window is closed.
15  function quit () {
16      gtk::main_quit();
17  }
18
19  // The calculate() function does the actual math.
20  function calculate () {
21      global $a;
22      global $b;
23      global $operator;
24
25      switch ($operator) {
26          case 'add':
27              $value = $a + $b;
28              break;
29          case 'subtract':
30              $value = $a - $b;
31              break;
32          case 'multiply':
33              $value = $a * $b;
34              break;
35          case 'divide':
36              $value = $a / $b;
37              break;
38      }
39      set_window ($value); // Display the calculated value.
```

(script continues on next page)

Script 12.2 *continued*

```
             script
40    }
41
42    // Function for assigning the operator being used.
43    function operator ($thing, $which) {
44        global $operator;
45        $operator = $which;
46    }
47
48    // Function for resetting the calculator.
49    function clear () {
50        global $a;
51        global $b;
52        global $operator;
53
54        $a = FALSE;
55        $b = FALSE;
56        $operator = 'na';
57
58        set_window (0);
59    }
60
61    // Function for assigning values.
62    function assign ($thing, $number) {
63        global $a;
64        global $b;
65        global $operator;
66
67        if ($operator == 'na') {
68            $a .= $number;
69            set_window($a); // Display the value.
70        } else {
71            $b .= $number;
72            set_window($b); // Display the value.
73        }
74    }
75
76    // Function for displaying value in the calculator 'window'.
77    function set_window ($value) {
78        global $display;
79        $display->set_text ($value);
80    }
81
82
83    // ******************
84    // ****************** End of Functions
85    // ******************
86
87    // Create a new window.
88    $window = &new GtkWindow();
89    $window->set_title ('Calculator');
90    $window->set_default_size (320, 320);
91
92    // Create another container.
```

(script continues on next page)

PHP-GTK

442

Script 12.2 *continued*

```
93      $box = &new GtkVBox();
94      $window->add($box);
95
96
97      // Make a table.
98      $table = &new GtkTable(5, 6);
99      $table->set_row_spacings(2);
100     $table->set_col_spacings(2);
101     $table->set_border_width(5);
102     $box->pack_start($table);
103
104
105     // Make the 0-9 buttons.
106     for ($i = 0; $i <= 9; $i++) {
107
108         switch ($i) {
109             case "0":
110                 $x = 1;
111                 $y = 5;
112                 break;
113             case "1":
114                 $x = 1;
115                 $y = 4;
116                 break;
117             case "2":
118                 $x = 2;
119                 $y = 4;
120                 break;
121             case "3":
122                 $x = 3;
123                 $y = 4;
124                 break;
125             case "4":
126                 $x = 1;
127                 $y = 3;
128                 break;
129             case "5":
130                 $x = 2;
131                 $y = 3;
132                 break;
133             case "6":
134                 $x = 3;
135                 $y = 3;
136                 break;
137             case "7":
138                 $x = 1;
139                 $y = 2;
140                 break;
141             case "8":
142                 $x = 2;
143                 $y = 2;
144                 break;
```

(script continues on next page)

Script 12.2 *continued*

```
                                                    script
145              case "9":
146                  $x = 3;
147                  $y = 2;
148                  break;
149          }
150      $button = &new gtkbutton($i);
151      $button->connect ('clicked', 'assign', $i);
152      $table->attach($button, $x, ($x+1), $y, ($y+1));
153  }
154
155  // Place the remaining buttons.
156  $decimal = &new gtkbutton('.');
157  $decimal->connect ('clicked', 'assign', '.');
158  $table->attach($decimal, 2, 3, 5, 6);
159
160  $equals = &new gtkbutton('=');
161  $equals->connect ('clicked', 'calculate', $i);
162  $table->attach($equals, 3, 4, 5, 6);
163
164  $clear = &new gtkbutton('C');
165  $clear->connect ('clicked', 'clear');
166  $table->attach($clear, 4, 5, 1, 2);
167
168  $add = &new gtkbutton('+');
169  $add->connect ('clicked', 'operator', 'add');
170  $table->attach($add, 4, 5, 2, 3);
171
172  $subtract = &new gtkbutton('-');
173  $subtract->connect ('clicked', 'operator', 'subtract');
174  $table->attach($subtract, 4, 5, 3, 4);
175
176  $multiply = &new gtkbutton('*');
177  $multiply->connect ('clicked', 'operator', 'multiply');
178  $table->attach($multiply, 4, 5, 4, 5);
179
180  $divide = &new gtkbutton('/');
181  $divide->connect ('clicked', 'operator', 'divide');
182  $table->attach($divide, 4, 5, 5, 6);
183
184  $display = &new gtklabel('display');
185  $display->set_text ('0');
186  $table->attach($display, 1, 4, 1, 2);
187
188  // Reset the calculator.
189  clear();
190
191  // Connect the quit function and finish the script.
192  $window->connect('delete_event', 'quit');
193  $window->show_all();
194
195  gtk::main();
196  ?>
```

PHP-GTK

2. Include the proper GTK module.

```
if (!extension_loaded('gtk')) {
if (strtoupper(substr(PHP_OS, 0, 3))
→ == 'WIN') {
dl('php_gtk.dll');
} else {
dl('php_gtk.so');
}
}
```

These lines of code are the best way to incorporate GTK. It will first check to see if GTK is already loaded. If not, it will load either php_gtk.dll for Windows operating systems or php_gtk.so for Unix. Using this system, your code should be as portable as PHP.

3. Create a quit() function.

```
function quit () {
gtk::main_quit();
}
```

One of the events you will want to watch for is when the user quits or closes the application. At that time, the quit() function will be called, which in turn makes use of GTK's main_quit() method.

4. Write the calculate() function.

```
function calculate () {
global $a;
global $b;
global $operator;
switch ($operator) {
case 'add':
$value = $a + $b;
break;
case 'subtract':
$value = $a - $b;
break;
case 'multiply':
$value = $a * $b;
break;
```

```
case 'divide':
$value = $a / $b;
break;
}
set_window ($value);
}
```

The calculate() function will do the actual math. It uses three global variables—the $a number, the $b number, and the $operator. After doing the math, the determined value will be shown in the calculator display via the set_window() function. This calculator will be very simple, doing only four basic operations on two numbers.

5. Write a function for assigning the operator.

```
function operator ($thing, $which) {
global $operator;
$operator = $which;
}
```

Most of this beginning code consists of functions written in basic PHP. This function takes two arguments—a $thing and a $which. You'll see what the former is later on (although it is not used in this case), and the $which will be what operator (add, subtract, multiply, divide) was clicked.

6. Create a function for clearing the calculator.

```
function clear () {
global $a;
global $b;
global $operator;
$a = FALSE;
$b = FALSE;
$operator = 'na';
set_window (0);
}
```

This function will reset the three main global variables and make the calculator's display window 0.

continues on next page

PHP-GTK

7. Make a function for building up numbers.

```
function assign ($thing, $number) {
global $a;
global $b;
global $operator;
if ($operator == 'na') {
$a .= $number;
set_window($a);
} else {
$b .= $number;
set_window($b);
}
}
```

When any of the number buttons are clicked, along with the decimal point, the calculator will need to keep track of the $a and $b values (which will be used for the calculations). If, for example, the user clicks 1 then 2, I want that to turn into a 12. So, the function works like so: It receives the $thing (more later) and the $number. If the $operator variable is equal to *na*, which means that it has been reset or has no value, then the user is building up the $a number and the new value should be concatenated to the old. If $operator has a value such as *add* or *subtract*, then the user has stopped entering the $a number and is working on entering the $b number. The number that the user is making will be displayed in the calculator window. This all makes sense if you think of the process: To add 5 and 10, you click 5, then +, then 1, then 0, then =.

8. Write the function that will set the value of the display window.

```
function set_window ($value) {
global $display;
$display->set_text ($value);
}
```

The global $display variable refers to the widget that is the calculator's display window. The widget itself is a label, which is merely a display of text. The set_text() method will reveal a string (or, in this case, a number) on that label. Anytime a number is entered or a calculation is made, this function will be called so that the resulting number is shown.

9. Make the window widget.

```
$window = &new GtkWindow();
$window->set_title ('Calculator');
$window->set_default_size (320, 320);
```

The $window variable is the first and most important of all the widgets. It acts as a container for everything. When making widgets you make instances based upon classes, and you should always reference the object (using &). The GtkWindow() widget has multiple methods, including set_title() and set_default_size().

10. Make a secondary container.

```
$box = &new GtkVBox();
$window->add($box);
```

The box is a second container widget into which I'll place the calculator. I could have multiple boxes within my window, should I choose (perhaps another box would contain a *Close* button). I use the window's add() method to physically place the box into it.

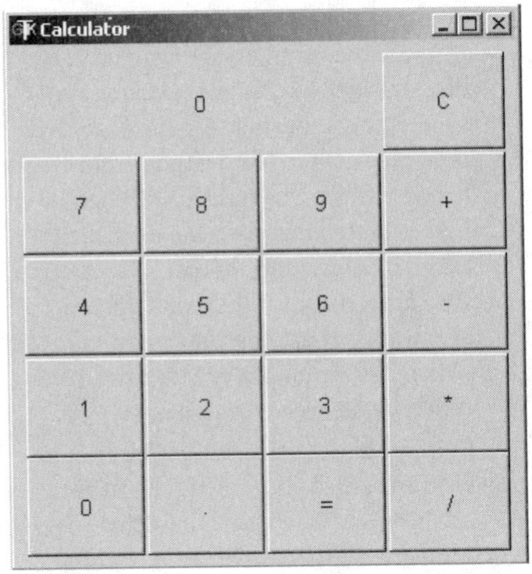

Figure 12.18 This is the calculator that will be created by the script.

11. Create a table.

```
$table = &new GtkTable(5, 6);
$table->set_row_spacings(2);
$table->set_col_spacings(2);
$table->set_border_width(5);
$box->pack_start($table);
```

Making tables with GTK is slightly trickier than it is with HTML. I first make a new table object, setting the number of rows and columns I intend to use. The tricky part is that since I want my table to have four rows and five columns (**Figure 12.18**), I need to add one extra of each. This is because elements are placed from, say, row 1 to row 2 and column 1 to column 2. Thus, an element in the fourth row will go from row 4 to row 5.

The final line in this section of code, `$box->pack_start($table);`, says to place the table just created onto the box made earlier.

12. Place all of the number buttons.

```
for ($i = 0; $i <= 9; $i++) {
switch ($i) {
case "0":
$x = 1;
$y = 5;
break;
case "1":
$x = 1;
$y = 4;
break;
case "2":
$x = 2;
$y = 4;
break;
case "3":
$x = 3;
```

continues on next page

```php
$y = 4;
break;
case "4":
$x = 1;
$y = 3;
break;
case "5":
$x = 2;
$y = 3;
break;
case "6":
$x = 3;
$y = 3;
break;
case "7":
$x = 1;
$y = 2;
break;
case "8":
$x = 2;
$y = 2;
break;
case "9":
$x = 3;
$y = 2;
break;
}
$button = &new gtkbutton($i);
$button->connect ('clicked',
→ 'assign', $i);
$table->attach($button, $x, ($x+1),
→ $y, ($y+1));
}
```

To make these ten buttons, I loop through the numbers 0 through 9. I then determine the x- and y-coordinates of each on my table (use Figure 12.18 as a reference). Once I know that, I can create a new button. The button will then be told to watch for when the user clicks on it, by attaching the assign() function to the *clicked* event. When that occurs, I also want to pass the value of the button, which is the number or $i, to the function as well.

Looking back at the assign() function written earlier, you will see that it receives a $thing and a $number. The $thing is the widget itself (i.e., the button), and the $number is this $i value here.

The final step is to place this button on the table, using the predetermined x- and y-coordinates. The attach() function takes the following arguments: the widget being attached, the x starting point ($x), the x stopping point ($x+1), the y starting point ($y), and the y stopping point ($y+1).

13. Create the rest of the calculator's buttons.

```php
$decimal = &new gtkbutton('.');
$decimal->connect ('clicked',
→ 'assign', '.');
$table->attach($decimal, 2, 3,
→ 5, 6);
$equals = &new gtkbutton('=');
$equals->connect ('clicked',
→ 'calculate', $i);
$table->attach($equals, 3, 4, 5, 6);
$clear = &new gtkbutton('C');
$clear->connect ('clicked',
→ 'clear');
```

```
$table->attach($clear, 4, 5, 1, 2);
$add = &new gtkbutton('+');
$add->connect ('clicked',
→ 'operator', 'add');
$table->attach($add, 4, 5, 2, 3);
$subtract = &new gtkbutton('-');
$subtract->connect ('clicked',
→ 'operator', 'subtract');
$table->attach($subtract,
→ 4, 5, 3, 4);
$multiply = &new gtkbutton('*');
$multiply->connect ('clicked',
→ 'operator', 'multiply');
$table->attach($multiply, 4, 5,
→ 4, 5);
$divide = &new gtkbutton('/');
$divide->connect ('clicked',
→ 'operator', 'divide');
$table->attach($divide, 4, 5, 5, 6);
```

Each of these other buttons (for the different operators and so forth) is established in exactly the same way as the number buttons. Each is connected to a function that will be called when that button is clicked.

14. Make the display window.

```
$display = &new gtklabel('display');
$table->attach($display, 1, 4, 1, 2);
```

The display window of the calculator is not going to be a button, since it won't ever be clicked, but will instead be a label—a simple noneditable text field. The text of the label is set using set_text() as you see in the set_window() function.

15. Call the clear() function to reset the calculator.

```
clear();
```

If you look at the code above, you will see that this function voids out any value for $a and $b and resets the $operator. It also sets the value of the display window to 0.

16. Finish the script.

```
$window->connect('delete_event',
→ 'quit');
$window->show_all();
gtk::main();
?>
```

The window needs to have a *delete_event* assigned to it, should the user quit the application. Here I am linking it to the quit() function written earlier. Next, I call the show_all() method, which reveals every element—the box, the table, the buttons, and the label—within the window. The opposite of show_all() (or show() for a specific widget) is hide(), which makes a widget invisible without destroying it. Finally, I call the main() method, the most important line of all. This function starts a loop in which the application will watch for user events. Unlike a standard PHP script, which does nothing else once it has completed running, this script will continue to be active until the user quits the application. It's the main() method that gives it this dimension.

17. Save the file as calculator.php and load it on your computer or server that supports PHP-GTK.

continues on next page

PHP-GTK

18. Access the command-line interface on your server/computer (**Figure 12.19**).

Because this script will not be run through a Web browser you need to start it through a direct command.

19. Type in the location of your PHP binary followed by the location of the script (**Figure 12.20**).

```
C:\php\php.exe C:\samples\
→ calculator.php
```

The is the standard command-line method for running a file with an application.

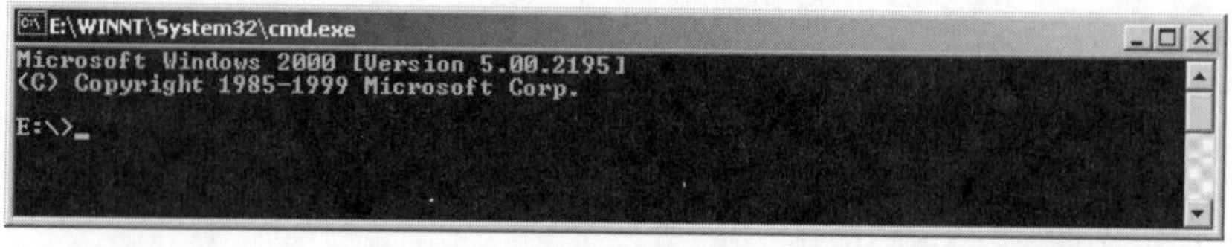

Figure 12.19 I use Run > cmd from Window's Start menu to get to the command line.

Figure 12.20 To run my script with PHP, I specify the location of the application followed by the location of the file.

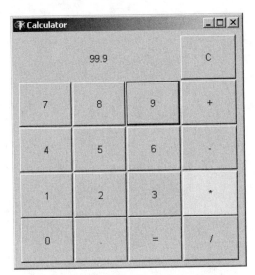

Figure 12.21 The calculator allows me to enter multiple-digit numbers for addition, subtraction, multiplication, and division.

Figure 12.22 The calculation is made after I click on equals and is displayed in the top window.

20. Test the calculator that appears (**Figures 12.21** and **12.22**). Note that as the calculator is written, it only allows for simple (one operator) calculations, and you must click clear in between each calculation. Hopefully this script has given you the know-how to make your own improvements to it, should you desire.

✔ Tips

- You can use the print() or echo() functions to send text to the command-line window. This will give you a way to debug your scripts.

- You can connect multiple callback functions to a single widget using multiple $widget->connect() lines. The callback functions will be called in order when the event signal is sent.

- Until the PHP-GTK manual fills out, you'll need to make use of the GTK reference manual to see all of the possible widgets and methods.

- Depending on your operating system, another way to run PHP-GTK scripts would be to double-click on the file and have it open automatically with the PHP binary.

PHP-GTK

PHP Source Code

PHP is an open source technology. Most programmers understand this to mean that it is free. While this is true, it is only half of the story. Just as important to PHP use as the cost is the fact that the PHP code itself is freely available for you to peruse or modify. In fact, unless you are using a precompiled binary version of PHP (on Windows), you already have all of the source code on your computer.

PHP is written in the C programming language, which is also where PHP gets a fair amount of its syntactical structure. If you know C, then hacking PHP will come fairly natural to you. If not, it will be more of a stretch but not impossible.

Playing around with the PHP source code itself is not something that the large majority of programmers will ever do and thus I'll not demonstrate it here (frankly, it's not something I tend to do myself).

✔ Tips

- The Zend API gives PHP coders an avenue for modifying how PHP behaves.

- Open source add-ons to your PHP module, such as the GD library, can also be modified, should you desire to do so.

- There is a difference between open source and free. The Zend Optimizer or Microsoft's Internet Explorer are both free, but you are not given access to the source code to make your own improvements.

INSTALLATION

While the beginning PHP programmer may not have occasion to install PHP, it won't be too long before that situation does arise. Fortunately, installing PHP and the common Web servers, such as Apache and IIS (Internet Information Server), is relatively straightforward and can normally be done without a hitch. The two main considerations for your installation are the operating system and the Web server application you want to use. These two factors will normally dictate whether you install a precompiled version (e.g., a Windows binary) or configure your own (Linux). If you are running Apache, you'll probably want to use PHP in its module form, but this won't necessarily be an option otherwise.

Installation gets more complicated when you try to bring in extra libraries such as Mcrypt and the PDFlib. If you want to be able to use the Zend Optimizer or other advanced features, such as PHP-GTK, that too will determine how you should go about setting up PHP. Fortunately, PHP is fairly easy to reconfigure, and added functionality can be achieved via the dl() function, which incorporates external modules into a script.

In this appendix, I'll cover the basics of installing PHP with a Web server on the three major platforms: Linux, Windows, and Macintosh. The basics I cover here, along with the added tips and references, should be sufficient to help you understand the installation process. If not, the online version of the PHP manual is especially helpful with its numerous user-submitted tips regarding specific installations on different platforms.

Installing PHP with Apache on Linux

Linux, being another open source product like PHP and Apache, is a natural operating system for Web servers. The difficulties that can occur in setting up a Linux server are insignificant once you factor in the long-run ease of use and stability that the platform offers: Unix Web servers have been known to run for months without ever crashing or needing to be rebooted. On top of this, most software you'll want to install on a Linux computer will be free or open source (meaning you can access the application code, too). This isn't always the case, though, because the PDFlib and other libraries require fees, so be sure to check the applicable licenses for any application you might use.

Most Linux servers come with Apache and PHP preinstalled, but not necessarily the latest versions with all of the features you require. If you want to upgrade the software on your Linux box, rest assured that installing PHP, MySQL, Apache, and so forth on a Linux server can be daunting at first but becomes old hat once you've done it a couple of times (and faced all the problems that you are bound to face).

Most particularly when installing PHP on a Linux server, be sure to make a list of all libraries you'll want PHP to support before beginning. This system works best when configured and left alone, rather than attempting to make continued upgrades. Frequently a third-party library you are building support for will be the cause of a problem. Some common software to use with PHP are:

- Zlib (www.gzip.org/zlib), a compression library

- GD (www.boutell.com/gd), for image support

- JPEG (www.ijg.org), for image support

- MySQL (www.mysql.com) or PostGreSQL (www.postgresql.org) or another database application

- Mcrypt (mcrypt.hellug.gr), for security

- OpenSSL (www.openssl.org), for secure http transactions

- Mod_SSL (www.modssl.org), also for secure HTTP transactions

To install the following software you will need root access and use of the gunzip (or gzip), gcc (a compiler), make, and tar applications.

Figure A.1 All of the Linux installation will be done via the command-line interface, either remotely via telnet (or SSH) or directly on the server in a terminal window.

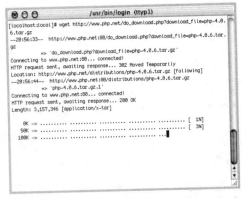

Figure A.2 The wget application allows you to download the various pieces of software directly to the server.

Figure A.3 Unpacking the files using tar will create the folder with all of the required items decompressed.

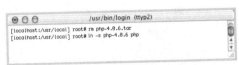

Figure A.4 After running gunzip and tar on each downloaded file, I remove the .tar file and then make a link to the folder, using an easier name in place of the longer, more formal one.

To install PHP with Apache and MySQL on Linux:

1. Connect to your server as root via the command-line interface (**Figure A.1**).

2. Get Apache, PHP, and MySQL and place them in the /usr/local directory.

    If you are working on the server from a remote location you can either download each to your computer and then upload them to your server or use wget, an FTP-like application. Here is an example of using wget (**Figure A.2**).

    wget http://www.php.net/do_download.
    → php?download_file=php-4.0.6.tar.gz.

    Be sure to download the most current, stable version of each. Shy away from beta releases unless you are prepared to help debug the application (which there's nothing wrong with doing if you are up to the task). You'll want to grab versions described as source code that come with an extension like *name.tar.gz*.

3. Unzip and unpack each item (**Figure A.3**).

    gunzip php-4.0.6.tar.gz

    tar xvf php-4.0.6.tar

    I'm just demonstrating with the PHP file here, but you will have to do the same for every piece of software you download, including Apache, MySQL, Mcrypt, etc.

4. If you want, delete the .tar file and create symbolic links for your newly created folders (**Figure A.4**).

    rm php-4.0.6.tar

    ln -s php-4.0.6 php

continues on next page

INSTALLING PHP WITH APACHE ON LINUX

The first line removes the .tar file, which is not automatically deleted after unpacking the file (as the .gz file is removed upon unzipping it). The second line creates a link so that *php* can be used in place of *php-4.0.6* when referring to the location of the PHP files. Doing the same for your libraries and database can simplify configuration and operation of the server later (although I would not do this for your Web server because /usr/local/apache will be used for the server binaries).

5. Preconfigure Apache. (**Figure A.5**).

cd apache_1.3.22

./configure --prefix=/usr/local/apache

The prefix option tells Apache where to create all the binary files that will be the actual Apache application.

6. Configure, make, and install MySQL (**Figures A.6** and **A.7**).

ln -s mysql-3.23.43-pc-linux-gnu-
→ i686 mysql

cd mysql

./configure

make

make install

MySQL, with its very long directory name, is a good candidate for a link, which is what I make in the first line. Then I move into the directory, run the configuration script, make the binary, and install it. The final result is shown in Figure A.7.

7. Install the databases and start MySQL.

scripts/mysql_install_db

bin/safe_mysqld &

bin/mysqladmin -u root password
→ 'SetYourPassword'

MySQL requires a default database called *mysql* which will be installed, along with a test database, when you run the mysql_install_db script. Then you can start MySQL with safe_mysqld, which starts a

Figure A.5 Once you are in the Apache directory, run the configuration script on it once before you configure and install PHP.

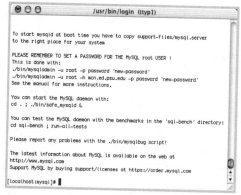

Figure A.6 Here I've made a symbolic link so that the term mysql refers to the longer-name, actual MySQL directory.

Figure A.7 Once you complete the configuration, make, and installation of the MySQL application, it is ready to be started.

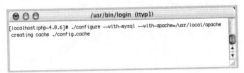

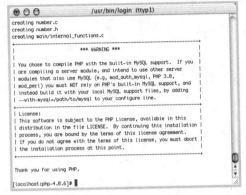

Figure A.8 Here I'm running a very basic configuration for my PHP, adding only support for Apache and MySQL.

Figure A.9 Once PHP has been successfully configured, you'll see this message. The next step is to make and install the binaries.

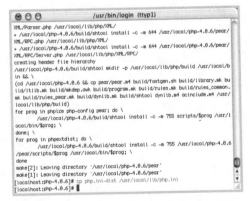

Figure A.10 The server needs access to the php.ini file so I copy the distributed version over to /usr/local/lib.

daemon that keeps MySQL up. In this last step, I use the `mysqladmin` utility to set the password for the root user.

8. **Configure, make, and install every extra library.**

   Each library you download and install will have its own `README` or `INSTALL` file that gives you a sense of how to configure and make it. The key, as far as PHP and Apache are concerned, is to make and install all of your third-party software before configuring PHP. Normally the process will just entail running `./configure`, then `make`, then `make install`.

9. **Configure, make, and install PHP** (**Figures A.8** and **A.9**).

   ```
   ./configure --with-mysql --with-
   → apache=/usr/local/apache
   → --enable-track-vars
   make
   make install
   ```

   This is the most important part of the installation process. If there's a problem, this is a primary place for that to be discovered. Be sure to reference every library that you want to be supported by PHP in your configuration directive.

10. **Copy the `php.ini` file (Figure A.10).**

    ```
    cp php.ini-dist /usr/local/
    → lib/php.ini
    ```

    The `php.ini` file, which will be stored in the /usr/local/lib directory, contains all of the configuration settings for how PHP will run. It can also be manually edited.

11. **Go back to Apache, configure, make, and install.**

    ```
    cd ../apache_1.3.22
    ./configure --activate-module=src/
    → modules/php4/libphp4.a
    make
    make install
    ```

continues on next page

INSTALLING PHP WITH APACHE ON LINUX

After PHP has been configured, you can formally configure Apache. Then you make and install the binary.

12. Copy the Apache configuration file to the new directory.

```
cp conf/httpd.conf /usr/local/
→ apache/httpd.conf
```

The `httpd.conf` file is the equivalent of the `php.ini` file in that it dictates how the server functions. Here I'm copying the distributed version over to its proper location.

13. Check the `httpd.conf` file for PHP support.

```
vi /usr/local/apache/conf/httpd.conf
```

One of the most common problems with installing PHP is not getting the Web server to acknowledge PHP files properly. Double-check that Apache is configured correctly by using a text editor such as `vi` to read the configuration file. The following two lines should be present and not commented (no pound symbol [#] before them).

```
AddType application/x-httpd-php
→ .php .phtml .php3 .php4
AddType application/x-httpd-php-
→ source .phps
```

Within `vi`, use the *x* key to delete a character. To insert new text, first hit *i*, then type your new text. When you are finished, press Escape. You might also want to add PHP files as a recognizable index by finding and altering the following line:

```
DirectoryIndex index.html index.php
→ index.phtml
```

Once the file is as you want it, type :wq then press Return.

INSTALLING PHP WITH APACHE ON LINUX

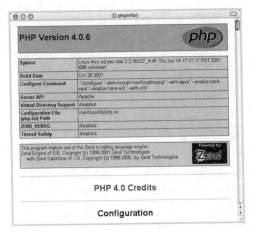

Figure A.11 You've probably seen the phpinfo() page before, which tells you if PHP and your Web server are running properly and much, much more.

14. Start Apache.

```
bin/apachectl configtest
bin/apachectl start
```

The apachectl script is used to start, stop, and restart Apache. You can use configtest to see in advance if Apache will have any problems. If not, then start the Web server.

15. Test your server in your Web browser (**Figure A.11**).

Use a script containing just

```
<?php
phpinfo();
?>
```

Load this file to your server and run it in your Web browser. If it displays a slew of information, you are good to go. If it displays the PHP code or asks you what to do with the file, then Apache does not know how to handle PHP scripts and you should recheck your httpd.conf file.

✔ Tips

■ If there is a previous installation of PHP on the server, you'll want to go into that version's directory and either delete the config.cache file or run make clean and make distclean to remove the previous installation from memory.

■ This explanation tells how to run PHP as an Apache module. You can also use it as a CGI binary. There are different security and programming issues if you run PHP as a binary so check the PHP manual for more information.

■ If you want to slow down the display when you configure PHP, use ./configure –with-options | more. This displays the resulting lines of text one page at a time, allowing you to catch any problems.

Installing PHP on Windows with Xitami

The second-most popular platform on which to run PHP is probably Windows. I'll be demonstrating how to set up PHP on Windows 2000, but you can also load PHP on Windows 98, Me, or XP. Especially if you are running an NT version of Windows you'll most likely use IIS as your Web server application. If so, just install IIS per its own instructions (it will install from your OS CD-ROM), then follow the instructions that come with the binary version of PHP for making it compatible with IIS (I'll be going through that aspect of the installation here, too).

You can also run Apache on Windows (depending on the version of Apache and Windows you are using) but, for the sake of variety, I'll use Xitami, another open source Web application. In this example I will not be installing a database application because there are many different logical options, including SQL Server, Microsoft Access, and MySQL, but making PHP support any database is not difficult, just modify your php.ini file.

To install PHP on Windows:

1. Download the latest version of PHP from www.php.net/downloads.php.

   With Windows installations, you'll want to use the binary version of PHP.

2. Download the latest version of Xitami from www.xitami.com/download.htm.

3. Unzip the PHP file to a logical directory, such as C:\php (**Figure A.12**).

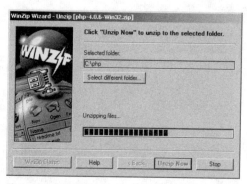

Figure A.12 WinZip is the application of choice for all of your unzipping needs on the Windows operating system. I prefer to create a new directory specifically for my PHP application.

INSTALLING PHP ON WINDOWS WITH XITAMI

4. Copy `php.ini-dist` to the Windows directory.

   If you are running Windows, this means you'll want to copy `php.ini-dist` to `C:\WINDOWS`; if you are running NT, it will be either `C:\WINDOWS` or `C:\WINNT`. In any case, rename the file after you've copied it to `php.ini`.

5. Copy the two DLL files that come with PHP to your SYSTEM or SYSTEM32 folder (**Figure A.13**).

The two required DLLs are `msvcert.dll` and `php4ts.dll`. If the former file is already present in your SYSTEM directory, there is no need to copy it over.

6. Double-click on the Xitami `.exe` file you downloaded and run through the Xitami installation (**Figures A.14**, **A.15**, and **A.16**).

   Enter a secure administrative name and password when prompted.

continues on next page

Figure A.13 After you've unzipped the PHP package, you'll need to copy the two DLL files and the `php.ini-dist` file to your operating system's folders.

Figure A.15 Once Xitami has completed the installation process, it is ready to start serving pages.

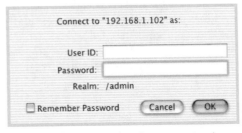

Figure A.16 You'll need to use the username and password you selected when installing Xitami to use the administration page.

Figure A.14 The Xitami installer will lead you through setting up the Web server.

INSTALLING PHP ON WINDOWS WITH XITAMI

7. Start Xitami.

Depending on how you answered the installation questions, you should be able to start Xitami through a desktop icon, a menu bar item, or the Start menu.

8. In your Web browser, go to `http://localhost/admin` or `http://127.0.0.1/admin` (**Figure A.17**), entering the administrative username and password when requested.

9. Click Configuration on the left side (see Figure A.17).

10. Click Filters in upper-left corner (**Figure A.18**).

11. Enter `.php` as the file extension and `c:\php\php.exe` as the Filter command or script (**Figure A.19**).

This is how you tell Xitami to use the PHP executable to process files with the `.php` extension. If you place PHP in a different directory, fill in the proper path for your server here.

12. Click Save in upper-left corner (Figure A.19) and then click Restart in the upper-right corner (Figure A.18) on the next page that appears.

13. Place a `phpinfo()` script in your Web root (by default `\Xitami\webpages`) and run it in your Web browser.

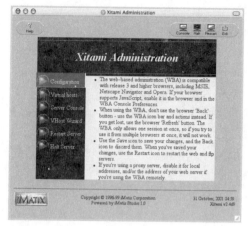

Figure A.17 This is the main administration page for managing the Xitami Web server.

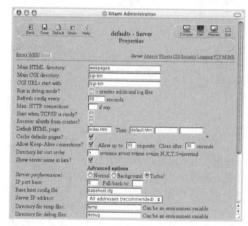

Figure A.18 The Configuration link from the main page (Figure A.17) leads you here where you can set many different variables for how Xitami operates.

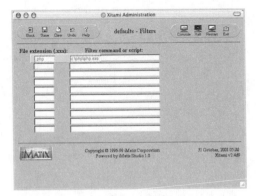

Figure A.19 Use the Filters page to add different file extensions, referring to the PHP binary that will process them.

✔ Tips

■ If you are running an NT version of Windows (NT, 2000, XP), you have the option of running Xitami, Apache, MySQL, and so forth either as an application or as a service, depending on your needs. Running any of these as a service means it will automatically start up when the server is turned on.

■ It is best to install and use only one Web server on a Windows machine. IIS, for example, will interfere with the operation of another Web server if present.

INSTALLING PHP ON WINDOWS WITH XITAMI

Installing PHP on Mac OS X with Apache

Mac OS X, which I cannot be more fond of, is an ideal operating system for today's Web developer. It merges the simplicity and beauty of the Macintosh interface with the stability and power of a Unix foundation. For the Mac users looking for a hassle-free operating system, OS X still fills the bill. For more advanced users who want a computer that can hold its own for development, OS X is now a viable alternative. But enough glorification of the operating system. I'll get down to the nitty-gritty.

First I should point out that OS X comes with Apache as the default Web server. The Web sharing option in the Sharing control panel (**Figure A.20**) actually starts and stops Apache. Unless you really feel the need to have the most current version of Apache, you can run your Web server as it comes installed. I should mention that, because of the way Apache is integrated into the overall OS, it's highly recommended that you do not attempt to upgrade or alter the actual Apache configuration.

With respect to PHP, you have (just offhand) three options. The first is to enable the PHP that's already present. To do this, just open Apache's configuration file, located at /etc/httpd/httpd.conf in a text editor. Then uncomment or add these two lines (see the Linux installation instructions earlier in this appendix for more information about doing this):

```
AddType application/x-httpd-php .php
```

```
AddType application/x-httpd-php-source
→ .phps
```

Figure A.20 The Sharing control panel in Mac OS X turns Apache on and off, among other duties.

Figure A.21 You'll need to use cURL to download the file from Marc's Web site.

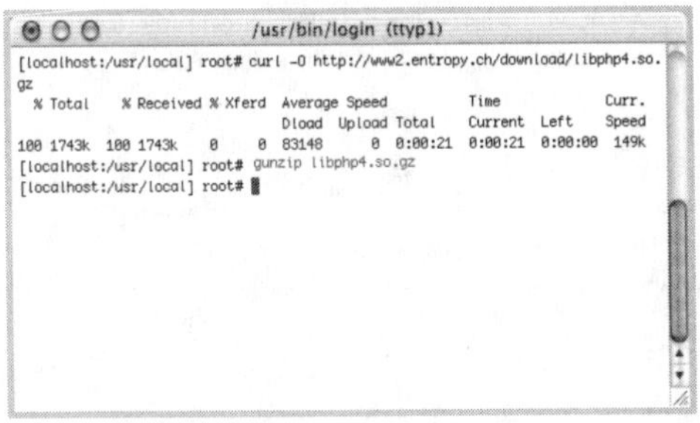

Figure A.22 Once the file is on your computer, unzip it with gunzip.

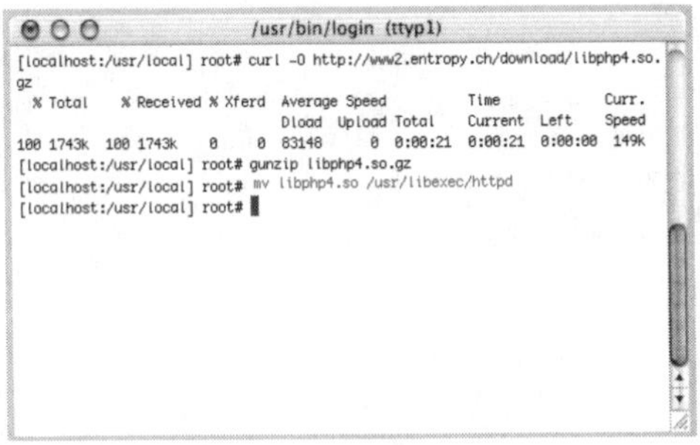

Figure A.23 Move the compiled PHP module to the /usr/libexec/httpd directory so that Apache will be able to use it.

After you've done this, stop and start Apache from the Sharing control panel.

The second option for installing and configuring PHP is to follow the steps as you would for Linux (again, see the Linux instructions). This time, configure PHP as a DSO module (i.e., use --with-apxs instead of --with-apache) to work with Apache. Then edit Apache's httpd.conf file and proceed.

The third, and perhaps the best option, is to use a precompiled library that Marc Liyanage provides through his Web site. He has taken the time and energy to make a PHP configuration that will be more than sufficient for most PHP programmers. It includes support for MySQL, PostgreSQL, PDFlib, cURL, GD, and more. My instructions below are based on those found at his Web site (www.entropy.ch/software/macosx/php/).

To install PHP on OS X:

1. Open the terminal application and direct yourself to /usr/local.

   cd /usr/local

2. Retrieve the PHP library (**Figure A.21**).

   curl -0 http://www2.entropy.ch/
   → download/libphp4.so.gz

   This is the file that Marc has created and plans to keep updated. It is based on version 4.0.6 of PHP.

3. Unzip the file once it has completely downloaded (**Figure A.22**).

   gunzip libphp4.so.gz

4. Move the file to the /usr/libexec/httpd/ directory (**Figure A.23**).

   mv libphp4.so /usr/libexec/httpd/

   continues on next page

5. Activate the PHP module (**Figure A.24**).

`cd /etc/httpd`

`sudo apxs –e –a –n php4`
`→ libexec/httpd/libphp4.so`

Without getting into too much detail, this is the first step in telling Apache (apxs) to use the PHP4 module that was just installed.

6. Edit the `httpd.conf` file.

`vi httpd.conf`

`AddType application/x-httpd-php .php`

`AddType application/x-httpd-php-`
`→ source .phps`

These two lines in the all-important `httpd.conf` file need to be either added or uncommented (probably the latter). You can separate different allowable file extensions to handle as PHP (including `.html`, `.phtml`, etc.) with this first line.

7. Restart Apache (**Figure A.25**).

You can either use `apachectl restart`, `apachectl graceful`, or `apachectl stop` and `apachectl start` at the command prompt, or you can turn Web sharing on and off via the Sharing control panel.

8. Test PHP in your Web browser with a `phpinfo()` script.

There are two options here. First, you could place the test script in the `/Library/WebServer/Documents` folder and go to `http://localhost/test.php` in your Web browser. Second, you could place the script in `~/Sites`, where ~ is your home directory, then go to `http://localhost/~username/test.php` in your Web browser. You can also use the dummy IP addresses *127.0.0.1* or *192.168.1.1* in place of *localhost*.

Figure A.24 After the module has been moved to Apache's directory, you need to activate it.

Figure A.25 The final step (after editing your `httpd.conf` file) is to restart Apache.

Becoming the Root User

Mac OS X, being a FreeBSD Unix derivative, has the concept of a root user, although Apple does not make this common knowledge for security purposes. The root user has the ultimate permissions and can do anything to the operating system, including destroy it. While you can do certain things as an administrative user, other commands require root access. There are two methods for entering commands as root:

◆ Use sudo. The sudo command allows you to do one thing at a time as another user.

◆ Establish the root user and log in under that name.

Just to be clear, establishing a root user and working under that name is a dangerous and less-secure way of operating. However, if you are like me and used to having root access to a Unix-type operating system, then knowing how to be root is important. First, bring up the Terminal application. Run sudo passwd root (**Figure A.26**). You will then be prompted for the existing password, for which you just hit Return. Then you enter the new password twice (**Figure A.27**). Finally to log in, type su root, then enter the password at the prompt (**Figure A.28**).

Figure A.26 To create a root user with Mac OS X, first invoke the passwd command.

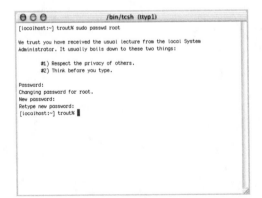

Figure A.27 You'll need to enter a new password twice to confirm it.

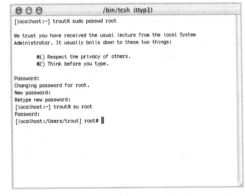

Figure A.28 Now that root is established, you can log in using su root.

✔ Tips

- If you are running an earlier version of the Mac OS (prior to X), you have three options for running PHP on your computer. Your first is to install Connectix's Virtual PC application, which gives you the ability to run Windows or Linux on your Mac. The second option is to install LinuxPPC. The third option, and the only way to truly run PHP under a Mac OS 8 or 9 interface, is to use Tenon Intersystems' WebTen application.

- Installing some more advanced software on OS X may require some of the tools from the Developer's Disk that comes with the operating system. If you think you'll be installing PHP, MySQL, and the like, you might want to consider installing the software on this CD.

- Some libraries will try to configure themselves with the gcc compiler, which does not come with OS X. If you run into this problem, edit the makefile document, changing references to gcc to cc.

- Some libraries are unable to identify the operating system when doing installation on OS X. If you run into an error compiling or configuring some software, try copying the config.sub and config.guess files from the /etc directory to the software's directory. These two documents should give the library the data it needs to compile.

- If you really get into what can be done with Mac OS X, check out Fink (http://fink.sourceforge.net), a project for porting Unix applications to the Darwin (OS X's FreeBSD) platform.

Databases

As you develop more complex Web applications, your need for databases will increase. Lucky for you, PHP's support for most popular database applications is one of the language's strongest suits. In this book I've used a MySQL database on a number of occasions, attempting to indicate the basics and then some for how it can be used. Similarly, I've created a flat text file database to store some information as well. This is a viable option on smaller-scale sites without a tremendous amount of traffic or complexity.

Since this is a book on PHP, I did not include extensive coverage of databases. This appendix will remedy that to some degree. I'll list a number of resources, and give you a sense of where to go for more information. The book's companion Web site, `www.DMCinsights.com/phpadv`, lists database-related books and has a more extensive and up-to-date collection of URLs. This appendix will provide you with a good reference for most of your database questions.

Database Applications

PHP supports practically every database you might attempt to use with it. The most common databases are:

- MySQL, www.mysql.com (**Figure B.1**)

- mSQL, www.hughes.com.au

- PostgreSQL, www.postgresql.org

- Oracle, www.oracle.com

- DB2, www.ibm.com/db2

- Interbase, www.interbase.com

- SQLServer, www.microsoft.com/sql/default.asp

- Microsoft Access, www.microsoft.com/office/access/default.htm

- dBase, www.dbase.com

- filePro, www.fptech.com

- Sybase, www.sybace.com

Figure B.1 The home page of the very popular MySQL database.

SQL Terminology	
TERM	USAGE
ALTER	Change the format of a table
CREATE	Create a table or database
DELETE	Delete rows from a table
DROP	Delete table columns, entire tables, or databases
INSERT	Add a row to a table
SELECT	Retrieve information from a database
SHOW	Retrieve information about the structure of a database or table
UPDATE	Modify a database entry

SQL

SQL, or Structured Query Language, defines the syntax for how questions should be asked of a database. SQL, like HTML and XML, is a regulated standard, which means that it should work the same way from one RDBMS to another. However, just as Web browsers support HTML differently, some database applications will support SQL that others might have problems with. Ultimately, your best bet is to check with the manual of the particular application you are using.

Now for a list (**Table B.1**) and a brief discussion about the standard SQL commands and operators.

```
ALTER TABLE table_name ADD COLUMN
→ column_name column_definition;
```

Adds a new column to the table.

```
ALTER TABLE table_name DROP COLUMN
→ column_name;
```

Deletes the column from the table, along with all of that column's data.

```
ALTER TABLE table_name ADD INDEX
→ index_name (column_name);
```

Adds an index to the table on column *column_name*.

```
ALTER TABLE table_name CHANGE COLUMN
→ column_name new_column_name new_
→ column_definition;
```

Changes the definition of column *column_name* from what it was to *new_column_definition*. This is useful if you want to change the type of data stored.

```
CREATE DATABASE database_name;
```

Creates a new database.

continues on next page

SQL

Appendix B

CREATE TABLE table_name (column_name
→ column_definition);

Creates a new table, structured according to the column definitions.

DELETE FROM table_name WHERE
→ column_name = 'x';

Removes every row from the table where *column_name* is equal to *x*.

DROP TABLE table_name;

Deletes the table and all of its columns, rows, and data.

DROP DATABASE database_name;

Deletes the database and all of its tables, columns, rows, and data.

INSERT INTO table_name VALUES
→ ('x', 'x', 'x');

Inserts the value *x* into the three columns of a new row in *table_name*. This syntax will work only if the number of values specified exactly matches the number of columns.

INSERT INTO table_name (column1_name,
→ column3_name) VALUES ('x', 'x');

Inserts the value *x* into the first and third columns of a new row. This syntax will work as long as the specified columns exist.

INSERT INTO table_name VALUES
→ ('x', 'x', 'x'), ('x', 'x', 'x');

Inserts two rows into the table.

SELECT * FROM tablename;

Returns every column of every row.

SELECT column1_name, column2_name FROM
→ table_name;

Returns the two columns for every row.

UPDATE table_name SET column_name = 'x';

Sets the value of *column_name* to *x* for every row in the table.

Clauses

On your queries, primarily when using SELECT, UPDATE, or DELETE, normally you will want to use clauses to limit the information returned. The four common clauses are WHERE, GROUP BY, ORDER BY, and LIMIT. They can be applied just to a column name or they can be used in conjunction with parentheses and operators to create more elaborate conditionals. You can also, and frequently will, use multiple clauses in the same query.

SELECT column_name FROM table_name WHERE
→ column_name LIKE 'Elvis%'

Retrieves the *column_name* values from the table where the values begin with Elvis, allowing for Elvis, Elvis Costello, Elvis Presley, etc.

SQL

Table B.2 Here are the main operators you might use to create expressions for your queries. You can also use parentheses to group clauses, too.

SQL Operators

OPERATOR	USAGE OR MEANING
+	Addition
−	Subtraction
*	Multiplication
/	Division
%	Wildcard (multiple character)
_	Wildcard (single character)
=	Equal to
!=	Not equal to
>	Greater than
<	Less than
=>	Greater than or equal to
<=	Less than or equal to
AND	Create multiple conditions
BETWEEN	Determine a range
LIKE	Use with a wildcard for finding similarities
NOT	Condition must be FALSE
OR	One condition or the other must be TRUE

```
SELECT * FROM table_name WHERE
→ column_name = 3;
```

Retrieves every column of information but only on the rows where *column_name* is equal to 3.

```
SELECT * FROM table_name GROUP BY
→ column_name;
```

Retrieves everything from the table but the data will be organized by *column_name*.

```
SELECT * FROM table_name ORDER BY
→ column_name ASC;
```

Retrieves everything from the table in an ascending order of column *column_name*.

```
SELECT * FROM table_name ORDER BY
→ column1_name ASC, column2_name DESC;
```

Retrieves everything from the table first order by *column1_name* ascending, then ordered by *column2_name* descending within the primary order. For example, everything is first order by *column1_name*. If some rows have the same values for that column, those will then be further ordered by *column2_name*.

```
SELECT * FROM table_name LIMIT 50;
```

Retrieves the first 50 rows of data from the table.

```
SELECT * FROM table_name WHERE (column_
→ name/2) >= '10' LIMIT 99, 50;
```

Retrieves 50 rows of data from the table beginning with the 100th row.

Table B.2 lists the SQL operators.

SQL

MySQL Resources

This book had a pretty strong leaning towards using MySQL databases, partly because it is one of the most common applications used with PHP today. Accordingly, here are three tables of MySQL-specific information you might want to have at your fingertips (**Tables B.3**, **B.4**, and **B.5**).

Table B.3 The DATE_FORMAT() function, like the PHP date() function, takes parameters that dictate how the returned string looks.

DATE_FORMAT() Parameters	
TERM	RESULT
%a	Weekday as three-letter abbreviation (Sun, Mon...)
%e	Day of the month (1-31)
%h	Hour as two-digits (01, 02...)
%i	Minute as two-digits (01, 02...)
%l	House as one or two-digits (1, 2...)
%M	Month (January, February...)
%p	A.M. or P.M.
%r	Time as HH:MM:SS AM(PM)
%T	Time as HH:MM:SS
%W	Weekday (Sunday, Monday...)
%y	Year as two digits
%Y	Year as four digits

Table B.4 These are the most basic column types you can use in your MySQL databases, along with the size each takes up.

SQL MySQL Field Types

Name	Refers To	Example	Length
INT	Integer	8	4 bytes
DECIMAL (Max, Decimal)	A floating-point number of Max length with up to Decimal numbers to the right of the decimal.	10.29	Max + 2 bytes
VARCHAR	A string of variable length.	Underworld	Length plus 1 bytes
TEXT	A text string.	Text is normally used form much longer strings...	Length + 2 bytes
ENUM Left	A list of options, of which one may be selected. 1 or 2 bytes		
SET	A list of options, of which many may be selected.	Jessica, Karen, Liz, Rebecca	1-4 or 8 bytes
DATE	Date in the format YY-MM-DD	96-04-20	3 bytes
TIME	Time in the format HH:MM:SS	10:23:01	3 bytes
DATETIME	Date and time in the format YY-MM-DD HH:MM:SS	96-04-20 10:23:01	8 bytes

Table B.5 This is only a sampling of the functions MySQL has that can be used in queries. MySQL even allows you to define your own functions.

MySQL Functions

Function	Meaning
ABS(number)	Absolute Value
AVG(column_name)	Average
CONCAT(column1_name, column2_name)	Concatenation
CEILING(number)	Returns the next integer
COUNT(column_name)	Counts how many items are in the result
CURRENT_DATE(date)	Returns the current date
DATE_FORMAT(date, formatting)	Returns a date formatted accordingly
DAYNAME(date)	Name of the day for a particular date
DAYOFMONTH(date)	Name of the month for that particular date
FLOOR(number)	Returns the integer value of a decimal
FORMAT(number, decimal)	Formats a number to *decimal* places
LOWER(string)	Converts a string to lower case
MAX(column_name)	Finds the maximum value in a column
MIN(column_name)	Finds the minimum value in a column
MONTH	Returns the numerical value of the month
NOW()	Returns the current timestamp
ROUND(number, decimal)	Rounds a number to *decimal* places
SUM(column_name)	Totals the values of a column
TRIM()	Removes all of the white space from the front and back of a column
UPPER(string)	Turns a string into upper case

Other Resources

There are not as many database-related links on the Web as there seem to be specifically for PHP, but they do tend to be more focused. The common general Web development sites such as Webmonkey (www.webmonkey.com) and DevShed (www.devshed.com) do discuss database issues as well. For database-specific information, check out these four sites:

◆ SQL Course, www.sqlcourse.com, an excellent tutorial on SQL and databases for beginners

◆ SQL Course 2, www.sqlcourse2.com, picks up where SQL Course leaves off

◆ SearchDatabase.com, www.searchdatabase.com, a database content provider (**Figure B.2**)

◆ SQL.org, www.sql.org, a portal for most everything involved with databases

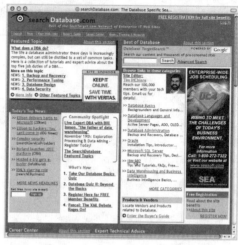

Figure B.2 The SearchDatabase.com site is a great provider of database information and links.

Command Database Mistakes

It won't take too long before you encounter most of the database mistakes listed here, as the combination of PHP and a database gives you twice as many opportunities for problems. The most common database error is caused by an incorrect query syntax. Either an extraneous quotation mark exists or a clause is left dangling or a table name is misspelled. Beyond that, watch out for:

◆ The database application itself is not running.

◆ The submitted username and password does not equate into permission to access a particular database.

◆ No database was selected to run queries on.

◆ An improper (or no) table or column name was used in a query. This can happen if you use a variable for either and the variable is not set properly.

GENERAL RESOURCES

I hope the 12 chapters of this book have covered the PHP issues of greatest interest to you. However, no one book can cover everything today's PHP Web developer might want to know about. If you want more information on any one topic, or if you are looking to learn about something I did not discuss, the resources listed in this appendix will be of use to you (all of the resources listed here will be Web links). Other forms of information, including books, can be found at the companion Web site (`www.DMCinsights.com/phpadv`). As I've designed it, this site is the perfect complement to *PHP Advanced for the World Wide Web: Visual QuickPro Guide*. The site will be kept current and will be flexible in its content, according to the demands of the reader. There you will find all of the scripts from this book as well as:

- ◆ More Web links (about 150 as of this writing)
- ◆ Sample scripts not used in this book
- ◆ Extra tutorials, as I create them
- ◆ A support forum for questions and issues arising from this book
- ◆ Reviews and listings of other resources such as books and software

PHP-Specific Sites

The first place every PHP programmer should be familiar with is PHP's official home page, found at www.php.net (**Figure C.1**). The most important pages there display the PHP Manual (www.php.net/manual/en) with user-submitted feedback on specific topics.

A close second in utility to www.php.net is Zend's Web page, www.zend.com (**Figure C.2**). The PHP Manual can also be found there along with a code repository, tutorials, articles, PHP-specific software (see Chapter 12, Extending PHP, for two examples), and many other resources.

Next up is PHPBuilder, www.phpbuilder.com. PHPBuilder contains dozens upon dozens of articles on how to do certain things with PHP (**Figure C.3**), lists PHP programmers available for hire, and has a code repository. There is also a very frequented forums to help you solve any problems.

For your software needs, you might consider turning to Keith Edmunds' list of PHP Editors, www.itworks.demon.co.uk/phpeditors.htm. He has compiled practically every possible text editor you could use for PHP development. Readers can also submit reviews of a particular application and see what platforms are supported and at what cost.

In Chapter 1, Advanced PHP Programming, I reference the PHP Coding Standard, housed at http://utvikler.start.no/code/php_coding_standard.html (I've created a link to the page from www.DMCinsights.com/phpadv/coding_standard.php to be updated should the original be moved). The PHP Coding Standard covers, in great detail, how your code should be structured and written, with examples and justification. Also in Chapter 1, I pointed you toward PHPDoc (www.phpdoc.de), an application that will automatically document your PHP scripts.

Figure C.1 By now you are most certainly familiar with the PHP home page, the first stop for all of your PHP needs.

Figure C.2 Zend.com, besides creating the software at the core of PHP 4, is a fantastic resource for any PHP programmer.

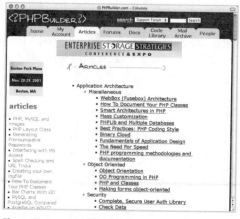

Figure C.3 The established and popular PHPBuilder.com includes dozens of tutorials on every popular topic.

Figure C.4 phpWizard.net, among other things, is the home of some very popular software, including phpMyAdmin.

One of the frequent questions I am asked involves finding a PHP Web host. As the language's popularity increases, PHP support from a Web host or ISP is becoming more and more popular. Two sites you can use to simplify the hunt are `http://hosts.php.net` and `www.od-site.com/php`.

If you have access to a newsgroup server (through your ISP or through a subscription service), you'll find quick and intelligent answers to your PHP questions at one of the many PHP-related newsgroups. The most popular English-language newsgroup is probably alt.php, but there are others and many in different languages, including French, German, and Russian. For that matter, there are newsgroups specific to relevant technologies such as Apache, MySQL, PostgreSQL, etc. You'll get better responses, though, if you are sure to check the manuals before posting questions.

The list of PHP-specific Web sites could go on for pages, so I'll conclude with three more that I find to be useful. The first, phpWizard. net, `www.phpwizard.net` (**Figure C.4**), not only provides tutorials but is also the home of phpMyAdmin and other fantastic PHP-driven software.

The PHP Resource Index, `http://php.resourceindex.com`, is a catchall of PHP information. There you'll find a code library, links to online articles, listings of books, and more.

Finally, PHPDevelper.org, `www.phpdeveloper.org`, is a professional-caliber site with great content. Its strongest point may be its tutorials—about 100 in number, covering just about every topic imaginable.

The above listings are just a sampling of what is currently available. Your best bet is to use the links page made available at `www.dmcinsights.com/phpadv` to find the resources that work best for you.

PHP SPECIFIC

Additional Libraries

When installing PHP you have to consider what other features you would like to be able to use, such as image creation, XML, or encryption. Downloading and installing the appropriate libraries so they can be included in your PHP configuration can save you needless recompiling at a later date. With that in mind, a list of common libraries to use with PHP:

◆ GD, www.boutell.com/gd, for creating images (**Figure C.5**)

◆ The JPEG library for making JPEG-formatted images, available from the Independent JPEG Group, www.ijg.org

◆ LibPNG, www.libpng.org/pub/png, another image library that gives you the ability to make PNGs

◆ FreeType fonts, http://freetype.sourceforge.net, software for using TrueType fonts when generating images

◆ Zlib, www.gzip.org/zlib, for compression and decompression of files

◆ cURL, http://curl.haxx.se, a networking-utilities library

◆ PDFlib, www.pdflib.com, for generating PDF documents (**Figure C.6**)

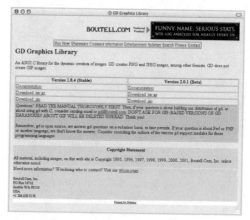

Figure C.5 The GD Graphics Library is a common add-on to most PHP installations, allowing for the generation of images on the fly.

Figure C.6 The PDFlib is the more popular of the two PDF-creation libraries supported by PHP (the other being ClibPDF).

ADDITIONAL LIBRARIES

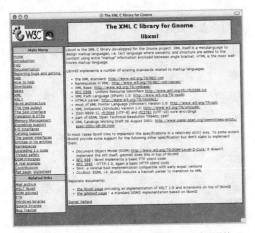

Figure C.7 If you want to use a DOM parser for XML with PHP, you'll need the libxml software, available from www.xmlsoft.org.

◆ OpenLDAP, `http://openldap.org`, software that allows you to run the Lightweight Directory Access Protocol on your server

◆ IMAP, `www.washington.edu/imap/`, the Internet Message Access Protocol, a different type of email server

◆ Mcrypt, `http://mcrypt.hellug.gr`, for increased security

◆ Mod_SSL, `www.modssl.org`, and OpenSSL, `www.openssl.org`, for secure server transactions

◆ Libxml, `www.xmlsoft.org`, an open source, DOM-based XML parser (**Figure C.7**)

◆ Pspell, `http://pspell.sourceforge.net`, and Aspell, `http://aspell.sourceforge.net`—two libraries that give PHP the capability to perform spell checking on documents

Security

Web server, operating system, and PHP security are all topics that could merit their own books. Unfortunately, outdated information is very detrimental when it comes to security. Thus, the best way to stay in touch with the relevant security issues of the day is to track the following Web sites:

CERT, www.cert.org (**Figure C.8**), is an institution associated with Carnegie Mellon University that tracks and reports on relevant Internet security issues.

SecurityFocus, www.securityfocus.com, lists security-related issues primarily for the Windows and Unix operating systems. It also tracks bugs and viruses of which Webmasters should be cognizant.

Insecure.org, www.insecure.org, was developed from a hacker's perspective. It provides different security tools and information with a Unix focus.

The W3C's Security Resources, www.w3.org/security/, is the World Wide Web Consortium's compendium of pertinent Web security information (**Figure C.9**).

Tripwire, www.tripwire.org/, is an open source security application that runs on your server (or computer) and monitors key files. It is currently available for the Unix family of operating systems.

OpenSSH, www.openssh.org, is a free application that provides for secure telnet and FTP.

A Study in Scarlet, www.securereality.com.au/studyinscarlet.txt, is a paper presented by Shaun Clowes that discusses a number of PHP-specific security issues.

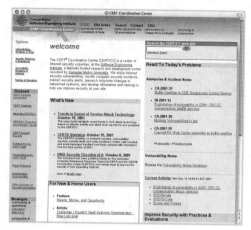

Figure C.8 Carnegie Mellon's CERT Coordination Center is one of the very best sites for staying aware of important Internet security issues.

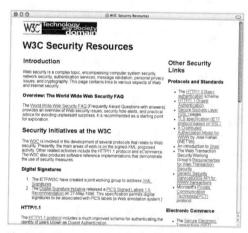

Figure C.9 The World Wide Web Consortium also keeps a listing of relevant security issues and frequently asked questions at its site.

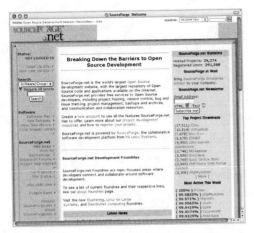

Figure C.10 SourceForge.net houses many open source projects, including several discussed in this book.

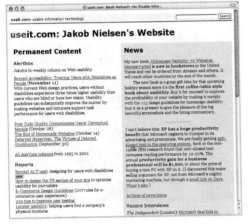

Figure C.11 You can hone your Web development thinking by reading some of the essays that Jakob Nielsen has posted at his site, www.useit.com.

Other Resources

There are a number of Web links worth knowing that do not fit conveniently into one of the other categories in this appendix (or otherwise do not merit their own category). Some of these links are general Web development and a number are specifically related to the technologies discussed in this book. Again, check the companion Web site for more current, descriptive, and complete listings.

General

E-gineer, `www.e-gineer.com`, is an Internet information site. Although it does not specialize in PHP, it has excellent information on installing and using the language.

SourceForge.net, `www.sourceforge.net`, which I've referenced numerous times throughout this book, claims to be the world's largest repository of open source applications (and there's good cause to believe that). Thousands of different technologies are developed through and hosted by SourceForge.net. (**Figure C.10**).

HotScripts, `www.hotscripts.com`, is a portal containing hundreds of scripts for every imaginable programming language.

Web development

Developer Shed, `www.devshed.com`, is a general Web development site that includes articles discussing the various programming languages and technologies you are likely to use.

WebMonkey, `www.webmonkey.com`, is very similar to Developer Shed, although it is broader in scope.

Useit.com, `www.useit.com`, is Jakob Nielsen's Web site for discussing Web usability. Nielsen, who has written books on the subject, presents numerous do's and don'ts for Web development (**Figure C.11**).

OTHER RESOURCES

HTML validation

There are several HTML validation applications freely available online. These will tell you—even with PHP-generated pages—if the resulting HTML has any problems. This concept is more and more important as XHTML and XML are more widely embraced. The two best free validators are the W3C's (http://validator.w3.org) and Bobby (www.cast.org/bobby).

XML

The XML FAQ, http://www.ucc.ie/xml, is a great beginner's introduction to XML (**Figure C.12**).

O'Reilly's XML Web site, www.xml.com, is one of the better online resources for your XML needs.

The official home page of XML, as much as there is one, can be found through the W3C (www.w3.org/XML).

Open source

If you are intrigued by what other open source projects exist besides PHP, see www.opensource.org and the GNU Project at www.gnu.org.

Apache Web server

Since the Apache Web server is the most popular server in use, especially on non-Windows operating systems, it's no surprise that there are several Web sites dedicated to the software. After you've read everything at Apache's home page (http://httpd.apache.org), go to Apache Week (www.apacheweek.com, **Figure C.13**) and Apache Today (www.apachetoday.com).

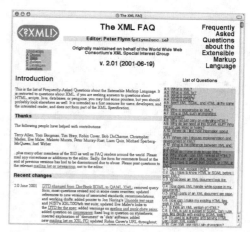

Figure C.12 The XML FAQ, which grew out of the W3C, is a perfect minimalist introduction to XML.

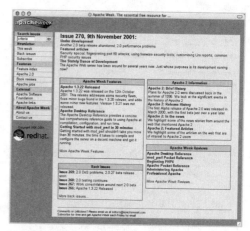

Figure C.13 The Apache Week site is a good resource for information pertaining to the Apache Web server.

Figure C.14 Everything you could ever want to know about PDF technology can be found by going to PDFzone.com.

E-commerce

E-commerce on the Internet has as many variables to it as just about anything you might develop. There are two things you know for certain: You'll need to provide secure transactions, and you'll need to be able to take payments. To do the former requires SSL installed (see the Additional Libraries section above) and a certificate. You can get a certificate—which is meant to demonstrate the safety of shopping on your site—from either VeriSign (`www.verisign.com`) or Thawte (`http://thawte.com`). One of the many payment options is CyberCash (`www.cybercash.com`), which is well-supported by PHP.

PDF creation

If you really get involved with making PDFs from PHP, you will probably want to investigate PDF technology in greater detail. Besides the obvious (`www.pdflib.com`), also check out PDFzone (`www.pdfzone.com`, **Figure C.14**), Planet PDF (`www.planetpdf.com`), and naturally Adobe (`www.adobe.com`).

JavaScript

In my opinion, JavaScript resources on the Web tend to be inconsistent. You'll frequently need to peruse several just to find the information you are looking for. When the need arises, I recommend starting with:

◆ www.javascript.com

◆ http://javascript.internet.com

◆ www.jsworld.com

INDEX

INDEX

X

PEACHPIT PRESS

Quality How-to Computer Books

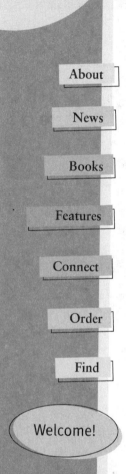

About

News

Books

Features

Connect

Order

Find

Welcome!

Visit Peachpit Press on the Web at www.peachpit.com

- Check out new feature articles each Monday: excerpts, interviews, tips, and plenty of how-tos

- Find any Peachpit book by title, series, author, or topic on the Books page

- See what our authors are up to on the News page: signings, chats, appearances, and more

- Meet the Peachpit staff and authors in the About section: bios, profiles, and candid shots

- Use Connect to reach our academic, sales, customer service, and tech support areas and find out how to become a Peachpit author or join the staff

- Click Order to enter the online store; order books or find out how to find Peachpit books anywhere in the world

Peachpit.com is also the place to:

- Chat with our authors online
- Take advantage of special Web-only offers
- Get the latest info on new books